P9-BHY-741

ALSO BY ROBERTO CALASSO

I. The Ruin of Kasch

II. The Marriage of Cadmus and Harmony

III. Ka

IV. K.

V. Tiepolo Pink

VI. La Folie Baudelaire

The Forty-nine Steps

Literature and the Gods

Ardor

Ardor

ROBERTO CALASSO

TRANSLATED FROM THE ITALIAN

BY RICHARD DIXON

FARRAR, STRAUS AND GIROUX

NEW YORK

Farrar, Straus and Giroux
18 West 18th Street, New York 10011

Printed in China
Originally published in Italian in 2010 by Adelphi Edizioni, Italy, as *L'ardore*
English translation published in the United States by Farrar, Straus and Giroux
First American edition, 2014

Library of Congress Cataloging-in-Publication Data
Calasso, Roberto, author.
[Ardore. English]
Ardor / Roberto Calasso ; translated from the Italian by Richard Dixon.
pages cm
Includes index.
ISBN 978-0-374-18231-1 (hardback) — ISBN 978-1-4299-5580-5 (ebook)
1. Vedas—Criticism, interpretation, etc. I. Dixon, Richard, translator.
II. Title.

BL1112.26 .C3513 2014
294.5'921046—dc23

2013044345

Designed by Jonathan D. Lippincott

www.fsgbooks.com
www.twitter.com/fsgbooks • www.facebook.com/fsgbooks

1 3 5 7 9 10 8 6 4 2

TO CLAUDIO RUGAFIORI

How many fires are there, how many suns, how many dawns, how many waters? I say this, O you Fathers, not as a challenge. I ask it to know, O you poets.

—*Ṛgveda*, 10, 88, 18

CONTENTS

I

REMOTE BEINGS

They were remote beings. Remote not only from modern man but from their ancient contemporaries. Distant not just as another culture, but as another celestial body. So distant that the point from which they are viewed becomes almost irrelevant. Nothing much changes whether that point is today or a hundred years ago. For those born in India, certain words, certain forms, certain objects may seem familiar, like an invincible atavism. But they are scattered fragments of a dream whose story has been blotted out.

We cannot be sure when or where they lived. When: more than three thousand years ago, though dates vary considerably between one scholar and another. Area: the north of the Indian subcontinent, but with no exact boundaries. They left no objects or images. They left only words. Verses and formulas that marked out rituals. Meticulous commentaries that described and explained those same rituals. At the center of which appeared the *soma*, an intoxicating plant that has not been identified with any certainty, even today. Even then they spoke of it as a thing of the past. They could, it seems, no longer find it.

Vedic India had neither a Semiramis nor a Nefertiti. And not even a Hammurabi or a Ramses II. No Cecil B. DeMille has managed to film it. It was the civilization in which the invisible prevailed over the visible. Like few others, it was liable to be misunderstood. There is no point looking for help from historical events, since there is no trace of them. Only texts remain: the Veda, the Knowledge. Consisting of hymns, invocations, incantations in verse. Of ritual formulas and prescriptions in prose. The verses form part of highly complex ritual actions. They range from the double libation, *agnihotra*, which the head of the family has to carry out alone, each day, for almost his entire life, to the most impressive sacrifice—the "horse sacrifice," *aśvamedha*—involving hundreds and hundreds of men and animals.

The Āryas ("the nobles," as Vedic men called themselves) ignored history with a disdain unequaled in the annals of any other great civilization. We know the names of their kings only through mention in the *Ṛgveda* and anecdotes in the Brāhmaṇas and the Upaniṣads. They had no concern for leaving a record of their conquests. And those events about which we do have information deal not so much with exploits—military or administrative—but with knowledge.

When they spoke of "acts," they were thinking mostly about ritual acts. It is no surprise that they never founded—nor ever attempted to found—an empire. They preferred to think about the essence of sovereignty. They identified it in its duality, in its division between brahmins and *kṣatriyas*, between priests and warriors, *auctoritas* and *potestas.* These are the two keys, without which no door is opened, no kingdom governed. The whole of history can be considered in the light of these relations, which are constantly changed, adjusted, concealed—in the double-headed eagles, in the keys of St. Peter. There is always a tension that wavers between harmony and deadly conflict. On this diarchy, and its endless implications, the Vedic civilization focused its attention with supreme and subtle clear-sightedness.

Worship was entrusted to the brahmins. Government to the *kṣatriyas.* The rest was built on this foundation. But, like everything else that happened on earth, even this relationship had its model in heaven. A king and a priest were there as well: Indra was the king, Bṛhaspati the brahmin of the Devas, the chaplain to the gods. And only the alliance between Indra and Bṛhaspati could guarantee life on earth. But from the very beginning, between the two, there was a third figure: Soma, the object of desire. Another king, as well as an intoxicating juice. One who would behave ungraciously and elusively toward the two representatives of sovereignty. Indra, who fought to gain the soma, would in the end be banished by the very gods to whom he had presented it. And what of Bṛhaspati, the inapproachable brahmin with a voice of thunder, "born in the cloud"? King Soma, "arrogant with the supreme sovereignty he had acquired," abducted Bṛhaspati's wife Tārā and had intercourse with her. From his seed she gave birth to Budha. When the child was born, she laid him on a bed of *muñja* grass. Brahmā then asked

Tārā (and it was the height of shame): "Tell me, my daughter, is this the son of Bṛhaspati or of Soma?" Tārā then had to tell the truth, that he was the son of King Soma, that she had betrayed her husband. And she, the model for all wives, had to admit it, for otherwise no woman would have been believed again (though repercussions of the event continued to be felt, from eon to eon). And a bitter war had to be fought between the Devas and the Asuras, the anti-gods, before Soma was finally persuaded to return Tārā to Bṛhaspati. The *Ṛgveda* says: "Terrible is the wife of the brahmin, if she is abducted; such a thing creates disorder in the highest heaven." That should have been enough for shortsighted humans, who sometimes asked why, and over what, the Devas and Asuras fought each other in the heavens, in those constant battles of theirs. Now they knew: over a woman. Over the most dangerous woman: over the wife of the most important of brahmins.

There were no temples, no sanctuaries, no walls. There were kings, but they had no safe and clearly defined kingdoms. From time to time they moved around on chariots with spoked wheels. Those wheels were their great innovation: before them, the kingdoms of Harappa and Mohenjo-daro had known only hard, solid, slow wheels. Whenever they stopped, their first concern was to build fires and to kindle them. Three fires: one circular, one square, and one the shape of a half moon. They knew how to bake bricks, but used them only for building the altar that was central to one of their rites. It was the shape of a bird—a hawk or an eagle—with outstretched wings. They called it the "fire altar." They spent most of their time in an empty, gently sloping clearing where they busied themselves around the fires murmuring words and singing fragments of hymns. It was an unfathomable way of life, requiring long training. Their minds teemed with images. Perhaps this was also why they had no interest in fashioning and sculpting figures of the gods. As if, already surrounded by them, they felt no need to add others.

When the people of the Veda descended into the Saptasindhu, the Land of the Seven Rivers, and then onto the Ganges plain, much of the area was covered by forest. They opened the way with fire, which was a god: Agni. They let him draw a web of burnt scars. They lived in temporary villages, in huts built on pillars, with cane walls and straw roofs. They followed the herds, moving continually eastward. Stopping sometimes before vast expanses of water. It was the golden age of the ritualists.

Groups of men could then be seen some distance away from the villages, each group—of around twenty—some distance from the other, moving over bare spaces, around fires permanently lit, with a hut close by. A murmuring of voices could be heard from afar, scored with chants. Every detail of life and death was at stake, in that coming-and-going of men absorbed in their activity. But all this would not have been obvious to an outsider.

There are very few tangible remains of the Vedic period—no buildings survive, no ruins or traces of buildings. At most, a few meager fragments on show in various museums. Instead, they built a Parthenon of words: the Sanskrit language, since *saṃskṛta* means "perfect." So said René Daumal.

What was the underlying reason for not wanting to leave any traces? The Westerner, with his usual euhemeristic presumption, would immediately suggest the materials have perished in the tropical climate. But the reason is another—and it is mentioned by the ritualists. If the only event of any importance is the sacrifice, then what should be done with Agni, the altar of fire, once the sacrifice is finished? They replied: "After the completion of the sacrifice, it rises up and enters that bright [sun]. Therefore do not worry if Agni is destroyed, since he is then in that yonder orb." Every construction is temporary, including the fire altar. It is not a fixed object, but a vehicle. Once the voyage is complete, the vehicle can be destroyed. Thus the Vedic ritualists did not develop the idea of the temple. If such care was given to constructing a bird, it was to make it fly. What remained on earth was an inert shell of dust, dry mud, and bricks. It could be left behind, like a carcass. It would soon be covered once more with vegetation. In the meantime, Agni was in the sun.

The world was divided into two parts, village and forest. Each followed different rules. What applied to one was not true of the other—and vice versa. All villages would one day be abandoned by their communities, as their seminomadic existence slowly moved on. No sacred places were fixed, umbilical, created once and for all, like temples. The sacred place was the scene for the sacrifice. It had to be chosen each time following set criteria: "As well as being on high ground, that place shall be flat; and as well as being flat, it shall be firm; and as well as being firm, it shall slope eastward, since east is the direction of the gods; or otherwise it should face northward, as north is the direction of men. It shall be raised slightly to the south, because that is the direction of the ancestors. If it had been lower to the south, the sacrificer would have soon passed into the underworld; in this way the sacrificer will live long: that is why it is slightly raised to the south."

High, flat, firm: these are the first requirements for the place of sacrifice. As if the intention was to define a neutral surface, a backdrop that brings perfect clarity to the action. This is the origin of the *stage* as a place ready to accommodate all possible meanings. How modern—indeed, the very stage of modernity. The place must, first, be *high*. Why? Because the gods leave the earth from high ground. And men must imitate them. Then *firm*. Why? So that it has *pratiṣṭhā*, "foundation." Then the place must *slope eastward*: once again, because east is the direction of the gods. But most important: *slightly raised to the south*, as if turning away from the direction of the ancestors. The dead lie there and the officiants would quickly slide toward death if the ground were to slope southward. In just a few words, by marking out an ordinary space in the mind's eye, among brushwood and stones, the blank setting has been described for every action. It is the first *locus*—and here, at one and the same time, we are told how the world is made, where the gods have gone, and where death lies. What else do we have to know, before any gesture starts? The ritualists were obsessive in their instructions, but never bigoted.

On the sacrificial ground there is little to see. It is bare, monotonous. But most of what happens cannot be seen: it is a journey into the invisible, fraught with danger, anguish, risk of ambush—a hazardous voyage, like that so loved by Conrad, with a ship ill-matched to face the demands of the forces of nature. And it was one of Conrad's characters who explained the difference between the carefree manner of people living on land and the precision of anyone living at sea. Only the latter understand that one wrong step, one badly tied knot, could mean disaster. But an error on land can always be put right. The sea alone denies us that "sense of security" which leads to miscalculation.

Though they must have had no great experience of oceans, but rather of majestic rivers, the Vedic people loved referring to an "ocean," *samudrá*, *salilá*, whenever they spoke of anything to do with heaven. For the sky itself was the real ocean, the Milky Way, which continued right onto the earth. And there they found the first image of that continuum from which all ceremonial gestures and words sprang. Like prudent and wary seamen, they thought of that boat, that voyage, during various times of the rituals—for example, at the beginning of a certain chant: "The *bahiṣpavamāna* chant is in truth a boat heading toward heaven: the priests are its mast, and its oars are the means they use to reach the heavenly world. If one of them is unworthy, he alone will make [the boat] sink: he will make it sink in the same way that someone boarding a boat already full will make it sink. And in fact every sacrifice is a boat sailing heavenward: and so an unworthy priest must be kept away from any sacrifice."

Though the sacrificial stage, to an outsider, seems like any other place, a tremendous concentration of forces dwells there—and focuses on few objects: they are fragments of the "thunderbolt," *vajra*, that supreme and mysterious weapon with which Indra defeated Vṛtra, the enormous monster who kept the waters captive within himself. One object is the wooden sword that the officiants hold. Another is an element of terrifying simplicity: the post. But the cart that transports the rice is also a sacrificial force. And the arrow used by the warriors recalls the breaking of the *vajra* as it struck Vṛtra. The separation of these objects between brahmins and *kṣatriyas*, between priests and warriors, is also a shrewd division of powers between the two forms of sovereignty whose balance is always at risk: the brahmins are responsible for the wooden sword and the post; and the *kṣatriyas* for the cart and the arrow. Two against two: the *kṣatriyas* closer to everyday life (the cart and the arrow are required by the tribe on the move and in battle); the brahmins more abstract, but none the milder for this (the wooden sword, the solitary post). The most incongruous object, much like a toy—the *sphya*, the "wooden sword"—is given to the brahmin. But it is also the only one of the four objects that represents the thunderbolt in its totality, as it was once brandished by Indra. Only a brahmin can hold the wooden sword, since it "is the thunderbolt and no man can hold it: so he holds it with the help of the gods." When one reaches closest proximity to the gods, only a brahmin can act. The story of Indra's thunderbolt, however, explains why, from the beginning, power is never whole, but is split into two irreducible parts.

The fabric of relationships between *auctoritas* and *potestas*, between spiritual and temporal power, between brahmins and *kṣatriyas*, between the priest and the king: a perpetual and boundless theme in India from the *Ṛgveda* to the *Mahābhārata* (which is all a story of plots and variants within these relationships) and to the Purāṇas ("Antiquities"). Complementary and sometimes hostile relationships: but such conflict was never expressed in the crude terms of a struggle between spirit and force. The brahmins' ancestors were "seers," the *ṛṣis*—and first among them, the Seven Seers, the Saptarṣis, who dwelt in the seven stars of the Great Bear and held terrible destructive power. They were capable of swallowing up, parching, hurling thunderbolts at whole portions of the cosmos. The armies of a king were never as devastating as the *tapas*, the ardor of a *ṛṣi*.

The *kṣatriyas*, on the other hand, were eager not just for power. On many occasions, especially in the Upaniṣads (but also in the Brāhmaṇas), we meet *kṣatriyas* who enlighten illustrious brahmins on certain extreme doctrines, on points that the brahmins themselves could not fathom.

There is an enormous variance between the rudimentary physical remains of the Vedic civilization and the complexity, difficulty, and boldness of its texts. In the cities of the Indus, bricks were used for construction; storehouses and vast water tanks were created. The Vedic people knew about bricks and used them, but only for piling up on the fire altar. A whole theology was developed around "bricks," *iṣṭakā*, which were associated with "oblation," *iṣṭi*. And building itself was first and foremost a ritual. The elements of daily life could not have been simpler, but their meanings appeared overwhelming. Though reduced to the minimum, everything was always too much. Even a cautious and laconic scholar like Louis Renou recognized that "the Veda moves in a state of panic." In contrast to all priestly rigor, the hymns seemed to him to be not just "poems composed in 'cold blood,'" but "frenetic works, produced in an atmosphere of oratorical jousting, where victory is gained by best formulating (or: most rapidly guessing) the mystical-ritual-based enigmas." And where defeat could mean a sentence of death. Heads burst into pieces, with no need of an executioner. There is no lack of documented cases.

Among all those who belonged to the Indus civilization, we know one name alone: Su-ilisu, an interpreter. He appears as a dwarf, or a child, on an Akkadian seal. He is sitting on the lap of a person wearing rich, heavy ornaments. The words carved over the image read: "Su-ilisu, translator of Meluhha." Other seals speak of merchandise from Meluhha, from that Indus civilization whose territory was bigger than that of Mesopotamia, Egypt, and Persia, and which lasted at least a thousand years, finally dying out, for reasons entirely unknown, around 1600 B.C.E. The names are lost. The only one that remains is that of Su-ilisu, interpreter of a language that still resists all attempts to decipher it—assuming that it is a language, a point over which there is still dispute.

For several years there have been feverish attempts to unearth horse bones in the Punjab. Brandished as blunt weapons, they were supposed to have been used to defeat and disperse the odious Indo-Europeans who were said to have come *from outside*, from beyond the Khyber Pass. Thus it would be proved that their innovation—the horse—was already to be found in those regions. For—according to some—all that is most ancient and memorable must necessarily grow on Indian soil. And the undeciphered script of Harappa should already contain quite enough to make it clear that Sanskrit and the *Ṛgveda* descend from there. None of this has been supported by the archaeological evidence, and it goes against what is said in the Vedic texts. The *soma*, whatever it might have been, grew in the mountains, which aren't part of the landscape of Harappa and Mohenjo-daro. As for warriors riding on chariots with horses, there is no trace of them in the seals of the Indus civilization. If one compares it with the *Ṛgveda*, it is difficult to avoid the impression that they are two parallel worlds. And yet they must have come into contact in some manner. But in some manner that still remains unclear.

In Vedic India, history was not something worthy of note. Historiography makes its appearance much later, not just many centuries after Herodotus and Thucydides, but at the time when the medieval chronicles were being written in the West. The chronology to which the ritualists refer is generally a time of the gods and of what took place before the gods. Only in rare cases is reference made to something "antiquated," so as to indicate a passage to the time of mankind. And invariably it relates to changes within a ritual. For example, in the most complicated and impressive ritual, the *aśvamedha*, the "horse sacrifice": "That *aśvamedha* is, so to speak, an antiquated sacrifice, for what part of it is celebrated and what part not?" After having followed the meticulous, bewildering instructions on the hundreds of animals to be sacrificed during the *aśvamedha* and on the various ways they had to be treated, on the beads to be threaded into the mane of the horse and on the "ways of the knife" that had to be followed when cutting into the flesh of the horse, making a sudden change of course it is said that the "*aśvamedha* is an antiquated sacrifice" (or "abandoned," *utsannayajña).* Perhaps the speculations of the liturgists already related to a glorious lost past, when there was still a perfect link between the chants, the numbers, and the animals killed. Perhaps they already felt like seventeenth-century scholars waging a war of quotations over some long-gone event. But the fewer the references to the pure, corrosive sequence of time, the more devastating are their effects. And any attempt to establish an immediate, simple, and unambiguous relationship between the texts of the Vedic ritualists and any factual reality will appear all the more futile. Unlike the Egyptians, the Sumerians, or the Chinese of the Zhou dynasty, they avoided linking events to the years. *Verum ipsum factum* did not apply. Liturgical acts were the only *factum* connected to a *verum.* All that was carried out before and outside the ritual belonged to the vast frayed realm of untruth.

Vedic India is founded on a rigorous exclusivity (only those who take part in the sacrifice can be saved) and at the same time on a need for total redemption (extending not only to all humans, but to all living beings). This twofold claim, which will sound unreasonable to the other great religions (which are more closely bound to secular good sense) reappears in the picture of an ancient, endless feast: "But those creatures that are not admitted to the sacrifice are lost; he therefore admits to the sacrifice those creatures here on earth who are not lost; behind mankind are the beasts; and behind the gods are the birds, the plants and the trees; and so whatever exists here on earth is admitted to the sacrifice. And verily, both gods and men and their forebears drink together, and this is their feast; in ancient times they drank together visibly, but now they do so in the invisible."

Nothing else was as serious, for gods just as much as for men, as being excluded from the sacrifice. Nothing was so certain to bring loss of salvation. Life, alone, was not enough to save life. There had to be a form, a sequence of gestures, a constant endeavor to avoid perdition. And for salvation to happen, it had to extend to everything, it had to carry everything with it. There was no salvation of the individual—being or species. Behind mankind could be glimpsed the incalculable multitudes of beasts, united with man by their being *paśu*, potential sacrificial victims. Whereas behind the gods rustled all the trees and shrubs, with their inhabitants, the birds, which had easier access to the sky.

This overwhelming vision is offered in few words—and has no equivalent in any of the other great ancient civilizations. There is no trace of it in any Greek (not to mention Roman) texts, it is certainly not a biblical view (where man, since the very beginning in the Garden of Eden, is branded as the dominator), nor in any Chinese texts. Only the cruel Vedic people, as they relentlessly devoted themselves to bloody sacrifices, thought about how to save the trees, the plants, and all other living beings, together with themselves. And they thought it could be done in only one way: to admit all those creatures to the sacrifice. They also thought it was the only way of overcoming the toughest challenge—the perpetuation of that invisible feast which had once been visible to all, and in which all took part.

As we become more familiar with the Vedic world, we soon have the impression of finding ourselves in a self-sufficient, self-segregated world. Its neighbors? What was there before? How was it formed? There is room for doubt on everything. This explains a certain perverse pleasure among the great Vedists about the object of their studies: they know that once they have entered, they will never leave. A master like Louis Renou made an implicit reference to this in 1951, on one of the rare occasions when he allowed himself to speak in general terms: "Another reason for this decline in interest [for Vedic studies] is the isolation of the Veda. Nowadays our attention is centered on cultural influences and points of contact between civilizations. The Veda provides little of this sort of material, for it developed in isolation. Yet perhaps it is really more important to begin by studying certain individual manifestations in and for themselves, and to examine their own internal structure." But this is exactly what Abel Bergaigne, founder of the glorious dynasty of French Vedists, was doing back in the nineteenth century: studying the *Ṛgveda* as a complete world in itself, which found justification in itself alone. An inexhaustible study, as Renou himself well knew: he was to publish seventeen volumes of his *Études védiques et paninéennes*, in which he gradually translated and interpreted the hymns of the *Ṛgveda*, considering them each time from varying angles, but without ever completing the task. Neither Egypt, nor Mesopotamia, nor China, nor least of all Greece (with its provocative lack of liturgical texts) can offer anything even remotely comparable to the Vedic corpus in terms of the rigor of its formal structure, its exclusion of all reference to time—whether as history or chronicle—the intrusiveness of its liturgy, and, finally, in terms of the refinement, profusion, and meticulousness of the internal links between the various parts of the corpus.

There have always been, and continue to be, plenty of strongly held theories about the origins of those who described themselves as Āryas and composed the Vedic corpus. But the enormity and uniqueness of their *textual* undertaking is all the more remarkable if the description of their historical existence is reduced to the few certain elements, as Frits Staal once formulated them: "More than three thousand years ago, small groups of semi-nomadic peoples crossed the mountain regions that separate Central Asia from Iran and the subcontinent of India. They spoke an Indo-European language, which developed into Vedic, and imported the rudiments of a social and ritual system. Like other speakers of Indo-European languages, they celebrated fire, called Agni, and like their Iranian relatives, they adopted the cult of *Soma*—a plant, probably hallucinogenic, that grew in the high mountains. The interaction between these Central-Asian adventurers and earlier inhabitants of the Indian subcontinent gave birth to the Vedic civilization, named after the four Vedas, oral compositions that have been transmitted by word of mouth up to the present day." These words of Staal, in their spareness of tone, as though written to meet the requirements of a popular encyclopedia, transmit something of that wonder that anyone should feel before the unprecedented and unparalleled undertaking of these (few) "Central-Asian adventurers." From the very beginning, it was an undertaking concerned not so much with territorial conquest (unclearly definable, unimpressive, not supported by any strong political structure, lacking even the invention of the "city," *nagara*, a word that is more or less absent from the oldest texts—and in any event does not correspond to any documentable evidence: there is no trace of any Vedic city). Instead, it involved a *cult*, closely bound up with texts of extreme complexity, and an *intoxicating plant*. A *state of awareness* became the pivot around which turned thousands and thousands of meticulously codified ritual acts. A mythology, as well as the boldest speculation, arose out of the fateful and dramatic encounter between a liturgy and rapture.

Ya evaṃ veda, "he who knows thus," is an oft-recurring formula in the Veda. Knowing—and knowing *thus*, in a certain way that was distinct from all other knowing—was evidently something most important for Vedic men. Power, conquest, pleasure appeared as secondary factors, which were part of knowledge, but certainly couldn't supplant it. The Vedic vocabulary is extremely subtle and highly distinctive in defining everything to do with thought, inspiration, exaltation. They practiced the discernment of spirits—as certain Western mystics would say many centuries later—with an astonishing assurance and perspicacity that make any attempt at translation look clumsy. What is *dhī*? Intense thought, vision, inspiration, meditation, prayer, contemplation? From time to time, all of these. And in any event the assumption was the same: the supremacy of knowledge over every other path to salvation.

Why were Vedic men so obsessed by ritual? Why do all of their texts speak, directly or indirectly, about liturgy? They wanted to think, they wanted to live only in certain states of awareness. Having rejected all else, this remains the only plausible reason. They wanted to think—and above all: they wanted to be aware of thinking. This happens, for example, in performing a gesture. There is the gesture—and there is the attention that is concentrated on the gesture. Attention gives the gesture its meaning.

Ancient Rome was also a highly ritualistic society, but ritual never became so radical. In Rome, over and above ritual was practice, the ability to deal with situations as they arose. Ritual was thus channeled into law, *fas* was absorbed—or at least attempts were made to absorb it—into *ius*. But for the Vedic people, the highest concentration of thought was into gesture—and for no ulterior purpose. To think *brahman*, which is the *extreme* of everything, means to be *brahman*. This is the underlying doctrine.

The more arguments rage over secularization, the easier it is to forget that the West, if that is what we want to call something which was born in Greece, has been secular from the very beginning. Without a priestly class, exposed to the continual risk of being excluded from the light, with no prospects of reward or redemption in other worlds, the Greeks were the first wholly idiosyncratic beings. This resonates through every verse of Sappho or Archilochus. And that which is idiosyncratic acts as the very backbone of secularity. How then do we explain the unbridgeable distance between modernity and the ancient Greeks? The Greeks knew who and what their gods were. More than believing in their gods, they met with them. For the Greeks, an *átheos* was, above all, someone who is abandoned by the gods, not someone who refuses to believe in them, as the moderns proudly claim—though they cannot avoid fashioning their secular institutions using theological categories. But the sacred, if surreptitiously injected into secularity, becomes a poisonous substance.

Vedic India and ancient Greece mirror each other. In India: all texts are sacred, liturgical, of nonhuman origin, kept and transmitted by a priestly class (the brahmins). In Greece: all texts are secular, often attributed to authors, transmitted outside a priestly class, which does not exist as such. The Eumolpidae, the family who supervised the Eleusinian Mysteries, were not expected to compose texts. When certain figures converge—as in the case of Helen and the Dioscuri, which bears a remarkable similarity to the stories of Saraṇyū and the Aśvins—that affinity indicates that we are approaching something inextricably ingrained in the experience of every mind. They are all stories focusing on the *simulacrum* (*ágalma*, *eídōlon*), the *reflection* (*chāyā*), and the *copy* (twin resemblance). Stories around stories, since the stories are woven with simulacra and reflections. It is the mythical material that reflects on itself, in the same way that the *ṛṣis* often spoke, in the hymns of the *Ṛgveda*, about the verses they were composing. They are moments in which the many whirling rivers of history seem to flow into the same ocean, the ocean that provided the title for a collection of stories that is India's counterpart to the *Thousand and One Nights*: the *Kathāsaritsāgara*, the Ocean of the Rivers of Stories.

Quite a number of scholars have recently toned down their descriptions of the Vedic people so far as they could, for fear of being accused of presenting them as blond Aryan predators. They are no longer conquerors who burst forth from the mountains, laying waste to the kingdom of the indigenous tribes and cruelly subjugating them. They are now a group of migrants who filter down to new lands, a few at a time, meeting hardly any resistance, since the previous Indus civilization was already extinct, for reasons that have still to be discovered. A proper correction, supported by the scant archaeological evidence, but one that sometimes arouses a suspicion of excessive zeal. And, to remove any inappropriate scruple, it is enough to recall, in the words of Michael Witzel, that "the Nazis persecuted and murdered hundreds of thousands of the only true Aryans in Europe, the (Rom, Sinti) gypsies. It is well known that they speak an ancient neo-Indian language that has close links with the modern Dardic, Punjabi and Hindi languages."

The Āryas may not have thrown themselves into crushing conquests, but the realm of imagery, at least, is captivated by the thunder of their horses and their war chariots, unknown before then in the lands of the Indus. As in a cloud of luminous dust, they were preceded by the ranks of the Maruts, the "storming sons of Rudra." This is how the hymns of the *Ṛgveda* describe them: "Come, O Maruts, with your chariots made of thunderbolts, laden with songs, laden with spears, with horses like wings! Fly to us like birds with the noblest drink, you of beauteous magic!"; "The earth shakes in fear before their surge: like an over-laden ship, quivering"; "Even the vast mountain has taken fright, even the ridge of the sky shakes at your fury. When you Maruts sway armed with lances, you flow like water in the same direction." It is difficult to think of those who sang of the Marut exploits as mild seminomadic shepherds, worried only about their herds and transhumance. Splendor and terror were with them when they were accompanied by the Maruts, with their flashing lances on their shoulders, studded with colorful decorations, with gold coins fixed to their breasts, united, compact, as if they were all simultaneously yielded up from the sky.

When Louis Renou published his first translations of the *Ṛgveda* in 1938, he quoted the words of Paul-Louis Couchoud as an epigraph to the Introduction: "Poetry was on the wrong track, [Mallarmé] said with a smile, 'starting from the great Homeric deviation.' And if anyone asked him what there was before Homer, he answered: 'Orphism.' The Vedic hymns . . . have something to do with Mallarmé's Orphism." Renou didn't return to this theme in the Introduction, nor did he mention Mallarmé again. But epigraphs are the *locus electionis* of latent thoughts. That was the right place to suggest that the history of poetry did not end with Mallarmé, but had been Mallarméan at birth. "The Orphic explanation of the Earth," the ultimate definition of poetry according to Mallarmé, does not apply so much to the late Orphic hymns, but above all to the Vedic hymns from which, a few streets away from rue de Rome, Abel Bergaigne was already unraveling the endless tangle of images. In order to feel the Mallarméan resonance it is enough to open the hymns at random, for example at the beginning of 4.58, the hymn to *ghṛtá*, ghee, the clarified butter used in rituals. This is how Renou translated it in 1938: "From the ocean the wave of honey has surged: with the stalk of the *soma* it has assumed the form of ambrosia. This is the secret name of the ghee: tongue of the gods, navel of the immortal."

For a Westerner trained in philology, it is hard to think of anything more frustrating than Indian history. Quicksand in every direction. Dates and figures never certain. Here the centuries move back and forth as months do elsewhere. No passage is entirely convincing. What brought about the passage from the *Ṛgveda* to the Brāhmaṇas? And why from the Brāhmaṇas to the Upaniṣads? And from the Upaniṣads to the Sūtras? Every literary genre is already sketched out in what came before. Or else it stands in contrast with what came before. Alternatively—and this is the most disconcerting case—the two genres coexist. How can we unravel this knot? Or how, at least, can we fathom its densest part? The path that takes us farthest is still the self-referential one. The *Ṛgveda* has to be understood through the *Ṛgveda*—and nothing else (as in Bergaigne and in Renou). The Brāhmaṇas are understood through the Brāhmaṇas—and nothing else (as in Lévi and in Minard). Meanwhile the passage from the *Ṛgveda* to the Brāhmaṇas is still uncharted, or barely explored terrain. As if understanding Homer made it impossible to understand Plato—and the other way around. Whereas the whole of Greece must inevitably be seen as stretching between Homer and Plato.

Viewed from the standpoint of the Enlightenment, the Veda is as dark as night, dense, with no apparent inclination toward clarity. It is a world that is self-sufficient, highly tensioned, even convulsive, wrapped up in itself, with no curiosity about any other manner of existence. Streaked by all kinds of violent desires, it has no thirst for objects, vassals, pomp. If we are looking for an emblem of something utterly alien to modernity (however it might be defined), something that might look upon it with complete indifference, we find it in the Vedic people.

In the preface to the first edition of *The World as Will and Representation* (1818), Schopenhauer wrote that access to the Vedas by means of the Upaniṣads "is in my view the greatest advantage which this still young century has to show over previous centuries." Momentous words: in comparison with the century that had just ended, the new period, according to Schopenhauer, offered a wonderful bonus, as the result of a single book, the daring edition of several Upaniṣads, translated into Latin from a Persian version, published by Anquetil-Duperron in 1801–1802 under the title *Oupnek'hat*, and later read by Schopenhauer in the 1808 edition. That text alone was enough to tip the balance of knowledge in favor of the nineteenth century.

Certain details help us understand the strangeness, the intractable Vedic singularity. The first complete commentary that we have of the Veda is that of Sāyaṇa, which dates from the fourteenth century. As if the first commentary we had on Homer had been written 2,100 years after the *Iliad.*

The world of the Veda is made of this: its elements: fire, water; among the animals: the cow, the horse, the goat; an "ocean," *samudrá,* which can be heavenly, earthly, in the mind, each having incalculable limits; the word, *eros*, the liturgy; rocks, mountains; ornaments in clothing or on the body; bands of warriors, stockades torn down, the clash of arms.

Certain key words crop up time and again. With seemingly persistent monotony. And yet each of those words has a profusion of meanings, for the most part coded. If we follow Grassmann's Vedic dictionary, *padá*, the cow's hoof print, also means, in order of importance: "step," "footprint," "track," "sojourn," "region," "(metrical) foot." But you can also add: "radius," "(single) word," or "speech." If we are talking about the "hidden *padá*," Renou says it is "the mystery par excellence, which the poet tries to reveal." Already we are a long way from the cow's hoof print, which itself is mysterious and venerable, since a special "libation on the hoof print," *padāhuti*, is dedicated to it.

In the beginning there was a mute king, Māthava of Videha, who kept in his mouth the fire called Agni Vaiśvānara, Agni-of-all-men, that form of Agni which all living beings keep inside themselves. Next to him, a perennial shadow, a brahmin, Gotama, who provoked him, first with his questions that remained unanswered, then with his ritual invocations, to which the king, according to the liturgy, should have answered. And the king still remained silent, for fear of losing the fire he had in his mouth. But in the end the brahmin's invocations succeeded in driving out the fire, making it erupt into the world: "He [the king] was unable to hold him back. That [Agni] erupted from his mouth and fell down to this earth." And, from the moment Agni fell down to earth, he began to burn it. King Māthava found himself at that moment by the Sarasvatī River. Agni then began to burn the land eastward. It marked out a path—and the king and the brahmin followed it. A question remained in the mind of the brahmin, so he asked the king why Agni had fallen from his mouth when he had heard a certain invocation and not before. The king answered: "Because ghee is mentioned in that invocation—and Agni loves it." That, for the brahmin, was the founding ruse. The first act of history is therefore not that of the ruler, of the *kṣatriya*, of the warrior. It is an act of the brahmin, of he who kindles every event, who compels the fire to leave its refuge. What immediately follows is a brief outline of what would always happen thereafter: man follows the path left by the fire, which goes before him, scorching the land. This is civilization, before all else: a trail marked by flames. And in the euphoria of conquest there is no need to think that desire or human greed take over. Men always follow: it is Agni who conquers.

The brahmin Gotama's shrewdness had worked. With his words of enticement—but above all the mere mention of ghee, Agni's favorite food—he had managed to start the ritual, which in turn had set history in motion. But that story had a precedent, dating back to the period of the relentless conflicts between the Devas and the Asuras. At one time the arrogant Asuras "continued to offer sacrifices in their own mouths," whereas the Devas preferred to offer them to each other. At that point their father, Prajāpati, chose the Devas and gave them the task of offering sacrifices. He preferred them because, even before being entirely sure to whom they had to make their offering, they had agreed that the offering should be *external*, that it *passed* from one being to another, rupturing the membrane of self-sufficiency, reminiscent of the formless body of Vṛtra, the primordial monster.

If Vedic men had been asked why they did not build cities, or kingdoms, or empires (even if they had a concept of cities, kingdoms, empires), they could have replied: we did not seek power, but *rapture*—if rapture is the word that best describes the effect of *soma.* They described it like this, in the most direct way: "We have now drunk *soma*, we have become immortal, we have attained the light, we have found the gods. What can the hatred and malice of a mortal do to us now?" Vedic men wanted nothing more, but also nothing less. They built a huge edifice of rites and formulas to enable them to utter those few words. They were the beginning and the end. Palaces, kingdoms, and vast administrative systems are more a hindrance than a gain for anyone who has attained this. All human glory, all conquerors' pride, all thirst for pleasure: they were only an obstacle. And the intoxication wrought by *soma* was not an exultant but uncontrollable state. For they said of *soma*: "You are the guardian of our body, O *soma*; you have settled into every limb as a keeper." Intoxication was a protective shell, which could be broken at any time, but only through the weakness of the individual. He then turned to that substance which was also a king, beseeching favor, as if to a benevolent sovereign: "If we break the holy vow, pardon us like good friends, O god, for our own good." This physiological familiarity with the divine was such that *soma*, in invigorating the body from within, sustained it. Not even the Greeks, who were experts in rapture, would have dared to have merged possession and supreme control together into one state, granted by those "glorious" and "salvific drinks," of which it is said: "Like the harness of the chariot, so you hold together my limbs." And what will be the ultimate desire, now that it seems almost within grasp? Infinite life: "O King Soma, prolong our days like the sun prolongs the days of spring." Subtlety, lucidity: the infinite is presented as a gradual, imperceptible expansion of the dominion of light.

II

YĀJÑAVALKYA

Sometime before the days of the Buddha—no one can be quite sure when—there appeared the figure of Yājñavalkya. Sacrifice (*yajña*) is in his name, but the meaning of *-valkya* is not so clear. He had received his learning from the Sun, Āditya. To *know*, one must *burn*. Otherwise all knowledge is ineffective. One must therefore practice *tapas*. *Tapas* means "ardor"—it means the heat within the mind but also cosmic heat. And the Sun is the being that produces heat more than any other. To gain learning, it is natural to turn to him. In the oldest texts, wherever Yājñavalkya appears, he speaks little and speaks last. His speech is cutting, decisive. To clash with him is a fearful prospect. Even the "shrewd" Śākalya, whom Staal described as "the first great linguist in human history," since he established the Padapatha version of the *Ṛgveda*—the one we still read today, with its text divided into separate words—had to suffer its consequences. He was unable to answer a question posed by Yājñavalkya and his head burst into pieces. His bones were gathered by scavengers who did not know to whom they had belonged.

In dangerous situations Yājñavalkya goes on regardless. He seems to enjoy provocation and challenge. One day it was King Janaka of Videha who wanted to put Yājñavalkya in difficulty. But he did not manage to get the better of him:

"Janaka of Videha once asked him: 'Do you know the *agnihotra*, Yājñavalkya?' 'I know it, O king,' he said. 'What is it?' 'It is milk.'

" 'If there were no milk, with what would you sacrifice?' 'With rice and barley.' 'If there were no rice and barley, with what would you sacrifice?' 'With other grasses that were about.' 'If there were no other grasses about, with what would you sacrifice?' 'With the plants that I found in the forest.' 'And if there were no forest plants, with what would you sacrifice?' 'With the fruits of the trees.' 'And if there were no fruits of the trees, with what would you sacrifice?' 'With water.' 'If there were no water, with what would you sacrifice?'

"He said: 'Then there would be nothing else here, and yet there would be the offering of truth (*satya*) into faith (*śraddhā*).' 'You know the *agnihotra*, Yājñavalkya: I give you a hundred cows,' said Janaka."

That day, King Janaka had pushed Yājñavalkya to the limit. To do so, he had used the idea of the simplest ritual, the *agnihotra:* the mere act of pouring milk into the fire. He wanted to find out what would be left if even the most basic things disappeared. It was a device for uncovering the relentless process that operates in every offering. Yājñavalkya immediately separated out the two essential points in every sacrificial act: substitution and the transposition from the visible to the realm of the mind. This in turn was reduced to its ultimate terms, beyond which the substance to be offered and the agent that consumes that substance (the milk and the fire of the *agnihotra*) no longer exist as such. The two ultimate terms were: *satya*, "truth," something that was not part of people's lives from the very beginning ("men are the untruth"), but which they had to attain so as to be in a position to offer something; and *śraddhā*, "faith," in particular faith in the effectiveness of the ritual, a feeling without which the entire edifice of thought collapses. Only *śraddhā* can replace fire, since *śraddhā is* fire. *Śraddhā* is the Vedic axiom: the firm belief, which cannot be demonstrated but is implied in every act, that the visible acts on the invisible and, above all, that the invisible acts on the visible—that the realm of the mind and the realm of the tangible are in continual communication. They had no need for *faith*, except in this sense. Everything else followed from that. It required Yājñavalkya to say it with such incisiveness.

Janaka, a king famous for his magnanimity and learning, was pleased with Yājñavalkya's answers on the *agnihotra.* To such an extent that, according to the version in the *Jaiminīya Brāhmaṇa*, "he became his disciple." Humbly, he said to Yājñavalkya: "Teach me." The situation was reversed. Now it would be Yājñavalkya who asked the questions, who wanted to work, like a surgeon, precisely on the weak joints in Janaka's knowledge. Yet that knowledge was impressive. With great benevolence, Yājñavalkya described Janaka as someone who, before setting off on a long journey, "finds for himself a chariot or a boat." These, for him, were the *upaniṣads*, the "secret connections" that he had gathered together to enable him to pursue the long journey of knowledge. Yājñavalkya, it seems, paid no similar homage to anyone else. But though so laden with power and knowledge, Janaka had reached a point where the "secret connections" no longer helped him. Yājñavalkya sought to question him on that very point. Abruptly—as was his style—he asked: "When you are freed from this world, where will you go?" With equal frankness, Janaka answered: "I don't know where I will go, my lord."

It is an exchange that disposes once and for all of every bigoted vision of Vedic India. Here the wise king, Janaka, acknowledges being lost and ignorant, like everyone, at the moment when one leaves the world, from which it is possible to *release* oneself (an Indian obsession, like "salvation" will be for Christians), but without necessarily knowing *where one is going.* At this point Yājñavalkya, in an Upaniṣad, offers an insight that goes *beyond* the *upaniṣads* (in the sense of "secret connections").

In order to explain *where we go* after death, Yājñavalkya mentions neither life nor death. He has the temerity to say, as if his words were a detailed reply: "Indha [the Flaming One] is the name of that person (*puruṣa*) in the right eye; in truth he is *indha*, but he is called Indra to hide his real name. The gods love what is secret and abhor what is obvious." The last sentence appears countless times in the Brāhmaṇas, as a warning that we are crossing into esoteric territory. And the esoteric is such, above all, because the gods love it, whereas they don't like what is clear at first sight. This is the Indian response—many centuries ahead—to that "hatred of what is secret" on which, according to Guénon, the West would be based. Here Yājñavalkya gives us a lightning demonstration of what might be the secret. In declaring what happens after death, he does not describe an earth or a heaven of everlasting life. But he speaks of physiology. He speaks of that minuscule figure we see reflected in the pupil of another's eye. And he calls it a "person," *puruṣa*, a being about which the *Bṛhadāraṇyaka Upaniṣad* itself said: "The *ātman*, the Self, existed alone in the beginning in the form of Puruṣa." In this case the king of the gods, Indra, is a cover for another figure, the mysterious Indha, the Flaming One, who has a female companion, Virāj (the name of a meter but also the consort of Puruṣa). But why should these two minuscule reflected figures reveal to us what happens after death? Because they are linked together in an extremely long and continually renewed coitus in the space inside the heart: a protective cavern. And what do they live on? "Their food is the red mass inside the heart." Here, like a cusp, metaphysics penetrates physiology. The coitus between Indra and Virāj is wakefulness—and the state that reigns at the end of coitus is sleep: "For, as here, when human coitus comes to an end the man becomes, as it were, insensible, so then he becomes insensible; because this is a divine union, and this is the supreme happiness." The two figures reflected in the two eyes enabled Yājñavalkya to enter the cavity of the Self and surprise it in its constant and double erotic activity, which is the mind itself. And from here Yājñavalkya rises straightaway to the peak of negative theology: "As for the *ātman*, the Self, it can only be expressed in the negative: ungraspable, because it cannot be grasped; indestructible, because it cannot be destroyed; detached, because it doesn't become attached; without ties, nothing stirs it, nothing wounds it. In truth, Janaka, you have attained non-fear (*abhaya*)." And here is an echo of the speech that will denote the *mudrā* of the hand raised to shoulder height: the most typical gesture of the Buddha.

The boldness of Yājñavalkya's reply should be stressed. He is speaking to someone who already knows much, but whose knowledge lacks one final step. He does not think it appropriate to use words of reassurance, nor to make any promises. Yājñavalkya needs only to refer to one physiological fact—the figure reflected in the pupil—in order to produce the revelation of something that encapsulates everything: the Self as an unshakable power that acts unremittingly in every living being, even if it is not perceived. Nothing else is needed to attain "non-fear," which is the only form of peace. As soon as he had heard him, Janaka said to Yājñavalkya: "May *abhaya*, non-fear, peace, be with you, Yājñavalkya."

In two boundless Indian works, the presumed author is also a character in the work itself. As Vyāsa is for the *Mahābhārata*, so Yājñavalkya is for the *Śatapatha Brāhmaṇa*. In the case of Vyāsa it is impossible to give any historical identity to him; in the case of Yājñavalkya it is almost impossible. But their appearance as characters is equally necessary. The author is an actor who appears on the scene and then disappears, like so many others. And at the same time he is the eye behind which there is none other, the eye that allows everything to unfold before the eye of that nameless being who listens, who reads.

How did Janaka react when Yājñavalkya showed him, in just a few words, what happens after death—and with reference only to the figure we see reflected in the pupil? The *Bṛhadāraṇyaka Upaniṣad* tells us immediately after: "At that time Yājñavalkya went to Janaka of Videha, with the intention not to speak." A magnificent *incipit*, once again in keeping with the stern character of Yājñavalkya. But Janaka remembered that on another occasion, when he had argued on the *agnihotra*, Yājñavalkya had granted him a *vara*, a "boon": the chance to make a wish that he had to fulfill (Indian stories—above all the *Mahābhārata*—tend to be stories that interweave boons and curses, as in Wagner's *Ring*). Now was the moment to make that wish—which was to continue questioning Yājñavalkya.

Then something surprising happened: the *ṛṣi* who hadn't wanted to say anything, the *ṛṣi* who regularly spoke with sharp, cutting jibes, before immediately passing on, withdrawing into silence, this time spoke at length, with brilliant eloquence, as if yielding to an uncontrollable impulse. And finally he explained in detail the doctrine of the *ātman*, in the most intense and beguiling terms. Never again in Indian literature, not even in Kṛṣṇa's teaching of Arjuna in the *Bhagavad Gītā*, would doctrine find such luminous words. There was also a moment when Yājñavalkya had the impression he had gone too far. He thought then: "The king is clever, he has taken all my highest doctrines from me."

If Yājñavalkya wanted to grant a "boon" to Janaka of Videha after his disputation on the *agnihotra*, he had good reason. For on that occasion Janaka had shown himself to be finer than three brahmins, one of whom was Yājñavalkya himself. After having questioned them he had left on his chariot: proud, scornful, dissatisfied. The three brahmins knew they hadn't been up to the task. "They said: 'This king has beaten us: come, let us challenge him in a disputation.'" Then Yājñavalkya had come forward and stopped them, with well-picked words. If they had in fact won, he said, the incident would have left no impression. It is normal for brahmins to defeat a king in a theological argument. It is almost their raison d'être. But if Janaka happened to win? Better not to think about it . . . The world would have been turned upside down. So Yājñavalkya preferred to go to Janaka alone and humbly asked him what he knew about the *agnihotra.* He discovered that Janaka knew much. It was then that he granted him a "boon"—and Janaka asked to question him further. "Janaka, from then on, was a brahmin."

If ancient Indian history as a whole is one of rivalry, bullying, and deceit between brahmins and *kṣatriyas*, the story of Yājñavalkya and Janaka can be seen as the opposite, as an example of a harmonious relationship. Janaka remains drawn to Yājñavalkya, he knows that the brahmin possesses a superior knowledge—and is ready to yield everything to him. But at the same time Janaka is the warrior who can compete with the brahmins not just on equal terms, but sometimes surpassing them in learning, as happens in the case of the *agnihotra.* Only then will Yājñavalkya acknowledge that the balance has shifted, and grant him a boon. And only when he has to fulfill that boon will he agree to set out the doctrine with a magnanimity that he has never shown before, proceeding in a state of lucid rapture, passing from prose to verse and from verse to prose, adding more and more detail and lavish imagery. That teaching will turn Janaka into a brahmin. The only convincing picture of a happy, and therefore effective, relationship between a philosopher and a man of power is not that between Plato and Dionysius—which was tense and ill-fated from the very beginning—but the relationship between Yājñavalkya and Janaka.

The rituals gave constant cause for disputation—and thus it happened that Yājñavalkya's guidance was sought. Some disputations could be at the same time metaphysical, psychological, and sexual. For example: where to place the ghee used for the offering to the wives of the gods? If the ghee was placed on the altar, the wives of the gods found themselves being separated from the gods themselves, who were squatting, absorbed in thought, *around* the altar. The prudent sacrificer, who did not wish to create ill-feeling between the divine couples, took pains therefore to place the ghee a little to the north of the altar, on a line traced with a wooden sword, so that the gods' wives remained beside their husbands. But some ritualists were less timorous, more cursory, concerned more about metaphysics than the marital harmony of the gods. Most notable among them was Yājñavalkya. Each time, his words were aimed straight at their target. He was rather like certain Zen masters in Chinese painting who seemed to emanate a barely contained physical power and looked upon the world as if it were a dry leaf.

Several ritualists had long plagued Yājñavalkya, asking him where the ghee should be placed, so as not to create friction between the gods and their wives. Yājñavalkya was well aware that the sacrificers were concerned not so much about the gods but about their own wives, who would have also felt *excluded*, in obvious imitation of the gods' wives. A wife who feels excluded is always dangerous. She begins to feel dissatisfied with her husband. And then, who knows, she may take advantage of that estrangement to go looking for other men. Yājñavalkya knew all this. And his answer was intentionally insolent, touching on the sore point: "What does it matter if his [the sacrificer's] wife goes off with other men?" Why so curt? As always happened with Yājñavalkya, his bluntness served to get straight to the metaphysical point, his only real interest. The ghee must be placed on the altar because the sacrifice must be edified by the sacrifice itself. If it were placed outside, the sacrifice would have to apply to something external, whereas it is essential for the sacrifice to be self-sufficient and self-generating, with all the paradoxes and contradictions that this implies. This was the supreme precept. And it certainly couldn't be compromised by any concern for the marital harmony of a sacrificer. On that matter there was no turning back. Yājñavalkya spoke in this tone.

One day Yājñavalkya said he had to choose a place of worship for Vārṣṇya, who wished to celebrate a sacrifice. So Sātyayajña (about whom we know nothing, except that his name means "Descendant of True Sacrifice") said: "In truth the whole earth is divine: a place of sacrifice is anywhere where a sacrifice can be made after having marked out the place with the appropriate formula." Once again Yājñavalkya stepped in where there was a point of theology to be resolved. His interlocutor's statement was enough to end any excessive geomantic concern. And it touched on a crucial question: all is decided when a sacrificial formula is imprinted on a place, like a seal, and so transforms it. But the text of the *Śatapatha Brāhmaṇa* goes further and says—without it being clear whether it is still a doctrine of Sātyayajña or has been added by Yājñavalkya—"the officiants are the place of sacrifice: the brahmins who perform the sacrifice are stability, being experts in doctrine, able to recite it, men of wisdom: we consider that to be the greatest proximity [to the gods], so to speak." Wherever we find a perfect brahmin, that is the place of sacrifice. These words have a distant resonance in Thomas Mann when he said that, wherever he was, there too was the German language.

Janaka wanted to celebrate a sacrifice with large ritual fees. Large ritual fees meant many officiants. He assembled a thousand cows. On the horns of every cow he strung pieces of gold. Janaka wanted to understand which of the brahmins had attained the greatest knowledge; who was the *brahmiṣṭha*, "the wisest in *brahman*" (the whole of India has been a question of *brahman*). The cows would be presented to him. Yājñavalkya then told his disciple Sāmaśravas: "Lead them away." The brahmins were shocked: "How can he say who has gone further in *brahman*?" The king's priest, Aśvala, then stepped forward and asked Yājñavalkya: "Are you the one who went further than anybody else in *brahman*?" Yājñavalkya replied: "Let us pay homage to the *brahmiṣṭha*, but I wish to have the cows." At this point Aśvala dared to question him.

It was a long exchange. Yājñavalkya answered the questions of seven brahmins and a woman. The brahmins were Aśvala, Jāratkārava Ārtabhāga, Bhujyu Lāhyāyani, Uṣasta Cākrāyaṇa, Kahola Kauṣītakeya, Uddālaka Āruṇi, and Vidagdha Śākalya. The woman was Gārgī Vācaknavī, the weaver.

What did they want to know? First was Aśvala, a priest in the king's household, a *hotṛ*, who was accustomed to reciting hymns and formulas as well as pouring oblations. He wanted to begin with what is most certain, with what forms the basis of everything: the ritual. He had to find out if that arrogant Yājñavalkya really knew the basics of the ceremonies.

But he also wanted to find out whether Yājñavalkya was able to connect ritual with what was the first and final question: death. *Ritual* and *death*: anyone able to give an explanation about these two words can say that he is knowledgeable in *brahman*, that he is intimately versed in it. He began with death: "Everything here is in the hold of death, everything is subject to death: in what way can a sacrificer escape from the grip of death?"

Talking about the "sacrificer" was the same as talking about what, from Descartes onward, is the "subject": the generic, sentient being who observes the world and encounters death. Implicit in the question was this: even before trying to say what it is, thought must serve as an escape from death, which is a "grip." Man is the animal who attempts to escape from the predator. But how? Through ritual, which involves—very often—the killing of animals. This is what Aśvala thought, this is what he did every day. But was it right? Was it enough? And how would Yājñavalkya now respond? He would have known that behind his question was another: "What do I, an officiant, a *hotṛ*, do to escape death?"

Yājñavalkya understood—and replied with supreme subtlety: "By way of the *hotṛ*, of fire, of speech. For the *hotṛ* of the sacrifice is speech. What this speech is, is fire. It is the *hotṛ*, it is liberation, it is total liberation." Words which meant: "Aśvala, you will escape death by doing what you do every day." After this reply, every further question would seem superfluous.

Deeply thrilled, Aśvala did not show it, but sought to continue with equal delicacy. Yājñavalkya's reply had solved the problem that had always worried Aśvala in his work as officiant. But Yājñavalkya was an officiant too. Not a *hotṛ* but an *adhvaryu*, one of those concerned with gestures, who busied themselves in the ritual operations, murmuring the formulas in a sort of continual hum. If he did not have full speech, which enabled the *hotṛs* to save themselves, how could he escape death? This is what Aśvala now sought to ask, with a respectful show of interest: "'Yājñavalkya, all of this is reached by night and day, is subject to night and day; by what means can a sacrificer free himself from this grip?' 'Through the *adhvaryu*, through sight, through the sun: in fact sight is the *adhvaryu* of the sacrifice, this sight is the sun yonder, it is the *adhvaryu*, it is release, it is total release.'"

Like two accomplices in a recursive exchange, both Aśvala and Yājñavalkya had maintained the same formulaic structure in the question and answer. And revealing themselves as allies in the same enterprise: the sacrifice. If the sacrifice could free a certain type of officiant, it would have acted in just the same way for the other, indeed for all the others, including the *udgātṛs*, the "chanters"—and in the end for the brahmins, a passive and silent presence in the ceremonies, but who were the invisible chamber where everything happened instantaneously. If

Yājñavalkya's answers were correct, the very lives of those who were questioning him could be considered saved, freed: *sā muktiḥ, sātimuktiḥ. Ati*, "the other side from," "beyond." Released "beyond" everything.

Idaṃ sarvam, "this all": that is what they called the world and all that exists. And "this all" was prey to death—or rather to Death, a figure, male. This was Aśvala's first thought—and his first question for Yājñavalkya. Did the "sacrificer," *yajamāna*—therefore mankind in general, for whom the officiants operated each day (and Aśvala was one of them)—have some means of escaping death? Did the rites have the power of acting on death, against death? It was not a question of overcoming or eliminating death. That would have been a foolish demand. It was a matter of indicating a way by which someone "is totally released (*atimucyate*)" from the grip of death. It wasn't enough to be released, you had to be released "beyond." To be released from "this all," from the whole world.

No question was more elementary and primordial. And Yājñavalkya also gave the most elementary answer: all Aśvala had to do was what he did every day. All he had to do was act as a *hotṛ*, as an officiant at the sacrifice who utters the right formulas, it was enough for him to use speech and fire. The unity of the *hotṛ*'s gestures, of his voice and the fire on which the oblation was burned, were enough, according to Yājñavalkya, for death to come no more, for Death to strike no more.

Question and answer were formulated in just a few words. Before theorems, the axioms had to be set out. And Yājñavalkya had immediately stated the axiom on which life around him was based. From there, if they wished, they could go further into *brahman*, as King Janaka had asked.

The questions that followed Aśvala's incisive first question were *not* superfluous, even though it might seem they were asked out of a desire for completeness (to establish that the other officiants—the *udgātṛ*, the *adhvaryu,* and the brahmin—could free themselves, just like the *hotṛ*). Aśvala asked Yājñavalkya how it was possible not to be subject to day and night, to the first fifteen days and the second fifteen days (the waxing and waning of the moon). He meant: how can we not be subject to the fading away of all things, how can we not be subject to time? Death was just the sting of time. One had to begin from that torment. But behind death was the actual fact of disappearing. So sacrifice, first and foremost, brought death, with the killing of the victims, but also brought about actual disappearance, with the pouring or burning of oblations in the fire. Release from bondage (to death, to time) came about through a series of acts (the sacrifice) that emphasized that bondage. It was a conundrum that Aśvala wished to leave to other questioners. For now, through Yājñavalkya, he had learned that if you wanted "total release" you had to continue doing exactly what you had always done.

Aśvala's question on the *udgātṛ* and the *adhvaryu* followed the same lines as the first, substituting death with time. But, in moving on to the role of the brahmin officiant, Aśvala changed register. This reflected the peculiarity of the brahmin's role. If officiants were like a string quartet, the brahmin would be like an instrumentalist who never plays and intervenes only when the others go wrong. The passive supervision of the brahmin is unlike the role of the other officiants, who are restricted to gesture, action, speech. So Aśvala's question took a different form. He said: "The atmosphere offers no point of support. What path will the sacrificer take to get to the celestial world?" Yājñavalkya's answer was: "By way of the brahmin officiant, by way of the mind, of the moon. The brahmin is the mind of the sacrifice." So release could also be attained by way of the brahmin, thanks to a sudden change of level in the argument, which coincided with the reference to the mind. And it might seem disturbing that something as changeable as the mind (compared for this reason with the moon) could provide a "point of support"—and thus release from mutability itself, from which the gradual disappearance of everything follows. It was another conundrum. But here again, Aśvala, a meticulous officiant, did not wish to linger any further. He was more anxious to find out whether Yājñavalkya was able to give a clear description of the *sampads*, the "equivalences" that punctuate every stage of the sacrifice. And Yājñavalkya, once again, gave immediate and satisfactory answers. His knowledge was not only metaphysical but also technical.

Any mention of the "mind," *manas*, always means taking a step up (or down—it's just the same). The mind is never on the same level as everything else. It can be present everywhere or nowhere. In any case, nothing will change in the description and operation of whatever happens.

With the same scant persuasiveness, everything can be regarded as inconceivable without the mind, or conceivable only if there is no mind. The prime characteristic of the mind is that of not allowing any expressible certainty as to either its presence or its absence.

This was perfectly in line with the role of the brahmin officiant. It was possible to describe the proper performance of a sacrifice ignoring the presence of the brahmin officiant. But it could also be described as the operation of successive states of mind in the brahmin himself, of the algorithm taking place within him. And Yājñavalkya therefore said that the brahmin officiant "is the mind of the sacrifice."

Vedic sacrifice wasn't just a ceremony during which a prescribed sequence of gestures was carried out, but a speculative tournament where life was put at risk. The *brahmodya* (the disputation on *brahman*), an integral part of the rite, could always end up with the head of one of the disputants *bursting out.* And it could happen for two reasons: either because the disputant couldn't answer a question or because he had asked one question too many. An unsatisfactory answer, one question too many: these were the two cases that brought the risk of death. "If you do not explain this to me, your head will burst out" is Yājñavalkya's threatening response to Śākalya's insinuations. And it certainly wasn't a momentary excess: it was part of the rite, it was implicit in the rite. If those contemplating *brahman* do not risk their head, it means they are not speaking of *brahman.* On that occasion, when Śākalya could not answer, his head flew into pieces. Yājñavalkya even threatened Gārgī, the woman theologian, this time because Gārgī was in danger of *asking too much* when she had put the question "With what weft are the worlds of *brahman* woven?" Gārgī then kept silent and survived.

Was the prohibition on putting certain questions an attempt to protect a particular sphere of knowledge, without being under any obligation to explain it? If that were so, it would have been no more than a trite priestly strategy of a kind that all future Voltaires would have readily mocked. But that wasn't the case. As can be seen in another clash between Gārgī and Yājñavalkya.

Gārgī, in addition to being a theologian, was also a weaver. She felt that metaphysics should be perceivable in her art as in everything else. This was why she preferred to put questions connected with her trade: it was what she knew best. So, on two occasions, she asked Yājñavalkya for explanations about the "weft" used to weave a certain thing. Since she had once been spurned for her question—and threatened with a horrible death—one might have expected Gārgī to choose a different route. Instead she spoke once again about "weft." But changing the *way* in which she put it (and perhaps this was the point: the prohibition was not on a certain question, but on a certain way of putting it). It shouldn't be thought, however, that Gārgī's manner this time was any milder or more obsequious. On the contrary—Gārgī announced straightaway that she would speak "like a warrior from the land of the Kāśi or the Videha, who comes forth holding two arrows ready to shoot the adversary." But the formulation of her question had changed. This time it was Kantian. Gārgī asked first with what weft *time* ("that which is called past, present, future") was woven. Yājñavalkya answered: "with the weft of space (*ākāśa*)." But Gārgī still had her second and *last* question in reserve: "With what weft is space woven?" At this point Gārgī might have been expecting a blunt refusal to answer, as on the previous occasion, together with the threat of death. This didn't happen. Indeed, Yājñavalkya's answer was immediate and expansive. He said that the weft of space was woven on the "indestructible" (*akṣara*). And he embarked on a lofty, intense, poetic explanation about *akṣara.* Anyone, he said, who doesn't know it, whatever merits he has gained from good works—from sacrifices or abstinence—will remain "miserable." Many centuries—almost thirty—were to go by before that "indestructible" would again be described with similar authority, in the aphorisms that Kafka wrote at Zürau between September 1917 and April 1918. Kafka was shorter, more succinct than Yājñavalkya, perhaps because he too feared his head might burst at any moment. But the purpose of their words was exactly the same.

Questioned by Gārgī, Yājñavalkya defined the "indestructible" through what it was not, as the whole succession of great mystics would later do. And he added a detail to be found nowhere else: the indestructible "eats nothing and no one eats it." Here spoke the voice of the *adhvaryu*, that officiant who constantly carries out the necessary acts during the sacrifice. And that is exactly what Yājñavalkya was. For the expert on sacrifice, the chain of Agni and Soma, of the devourer and the devoured, is essential in defining what belongs to this world and what does not. Only what is not a part of that chain can be said to be *beyond*—and beyond that we cannot go.

Yājñavalkya's discourse went a little further, continually interspersed with Gārgī's name, as if the brahmin wanted to keep a tight hold on the weaver's attention. He was, indeed, about to reach the crucial point: people are proud of seeing, of hearing, of perceiving, of knowing. They firmly believe they are made of all this. And now Yājñavalkya spoke of "this indestructible, O Gārgī, that is not seen and sees, not heard and hears, not thought and thinks, not known and knows." And at the same time "it is the only one that sees, the only one that hears, the only one that thinks, the only one that knows." People, whatever they do, are therefore passive, acted upon by an entity they may not even recognize. And, if they ever become aware of it and turn toward what is acting in them, they are obliged to realize that they cannot know it. And yet only "he who does not leave this world without having known this indestructible" can be considered a brahmin. But how can we know something that doesn't let itself be known? In only one way: by becoming to some extent that thing itself.

The weft of that which is, of that space with which even ungraspable time is woven, is made of this, said Yājñavalkya. And that weft is indestructible. That weft is *the* indestructible, *akṣara.* Gārgī then turned to the other brahmins who were listening and told them, with ill-concealed insolence, that they ought to feel satisfied. She then added that no one would ever beat Yājñavalkya in a *brahmodya.*

The *Śatapatha Brāhmaṇa* is impressive in its length, venerable for its antiquity, and has been assiduously studied and plundered by scholars, who should have been persuaded to give it the prime consideration that every work deserves: to be viewed as one work—above all in its form. This hasn't happened. There is, even now, no complete edition of the *Śatapatha Brāhmaṇa*, since it ought to include the *Bṛhadāraṇyaka Upaniṣad* as its final part. In December 1899, having reached the end of his magnificent enterprise of translating the *Śatapatha Brāhmaṇa*, which had taken him twenty years, Julius Eggeling calmly noted: "The present volume completes the theoretic exposition of the sacrificial ceremonial, and thus brings us to the end of our task. The remaining six chapters of the last book of the Brāhmaṇa form the so-called *Bṛhadāraṇyaka*, or great forest treatise, which, as one of the ten primitive Upaniṣads, is included in Professor F. Max Müller's translation of those old theosophical treatises, published in the present series." It was a candid way of announcing that one part of the *Śatapatha Brāhmaṇa* had been lopped off. And on various occasions thereafter, this missing part—one of the most famous texts of Indian thought—would be translated and annotated either alone or with other Upaniṣads.

The philological choice was very odd, as if Plato's *Republic* had continued to circulate without its tenth book, which contains the story of Er the Pamphylian, who, twelve days after his death, "was already lying on the funeral pyre, when he came to life again and told the story of what he had seen in the other world" with descriptions that, from then on, became embedded in Western thought. Or as if, remaining on Indian soil, the *Mahābhārata* had been published without the *Bhagavad Gītā*.

The *Śatapatha Brāhmaṇa*, in the Eggeling edition, does not therefore contain the "hundred paths"—the hundred "lessons," *adhyāyas*, to which the title refers—but only ninety-four of them. To read the last six we have to continue on with the *Bṛhadāraṇyaka Upaniṣad*. And there is a further twist: not only has the amputation of the text become accepted, but an entirely baseless theory has developed over many years about the existence of a radical contradiction between the early Upaniṣads and the Brāhmaṇas, coinciding with a revolt by the "princes" (the *kṣatriyas*, according to Renou's translation) against the mean brahmins, who were superstitiously devoted to ritual. And it has therefore been decided, with supreme scholarly arrogance, to ignore the declaration in the *Śatapatha Brāhmaṇa* itself, at the end of its final part, that this is the work of one of those brahmins: Yājñavalkya. To be unequivocally recognized as the author of *and* character in both the Brāhmaṇa and the subsequent Upaniṣad, Yājñavalkya had to wait for the brilliant article by Louis Renou: "Les Relations du Śatapathabrāhmaṇa avec la Bṛhadāraṇyakopaniṣad et la personnalité de Yājñavalkya." Published in 1948 in *Indian Culture*, a journal with a limited circulation and dotted with numerous Vedic acronyms and abbreviations as well as copious philological discussions, that study can be found today, all by itself, in the second volume of Renou's *Choix d'études indiennes*. A crucial issue—the recomposition of the first clearly recognizable *author* to appear in Vedic India—continues thus to remain in philology's protective shadow. And yet no one could be as worthy as Yājñavalkya to stand as a Vedic counterpoint and counterpart to the Buddha.

The brahmin is recognized by a certain light, by a brightness called *brahmavarcasa*, "brahmin radiance." That light is given out by *brahman* and it is the brahmin's only purpose, observed Yājñavalkya: "The brahmin should seek this: to be illuminated by *brahman*." But the kindling of that light takes place at the same time as that of the fire, of the meters, and of the seasons. The brahmin who recites the "kindling verses (*sāmidhenī*)" is himself one of those whom the verses must kindle. And, in the same way that the fire accompanied by the verses has a more intense light, "invulnerable, untouchable," so too will the brahmin have a light that is different from every other man. This is the perceptible origin of his authority. If it is ever said, often with some resentment, that the brahmin appears "invulnerable, untouchable," it will be because there is still one last, perhaps even distorted, glimmer of the firelight transmitted in him that another brahmin had once kindled when pronouncing the "kindling verses."

All the divine forms are present in the fire: when it is first lit and gives off only smoke, it is Rudra; when it burns, it is Varuṇa; when it blazes, it is Indra; when it dies down, it is Mitra. But the only form in which the fire emits an intense light, without any need for flame, is *brahman*: "When the embers glow intensely, that is *brahman*. And if anyone wishes to attain brahminic splendor, let him make his offering then." The mysterious quality of the brahmins is above all a moment in the life of the fire, recognizable every day. The mystery appears as something that can be seen by all—a "manifest mystery," as Goethe would one day say. It is no longer hidden, no longer inaccessible. The sacrificer who wishes to come close to it has only to choose *that moment* to present his offering. All that is required is constancy: the sacrificer shall always make his offering to the same type of fire for a year. Every time he must wait for the moment of the embers. He cannot make his offering one day to the blazing fire, one day to smoke, one day to the dying fire. It would be like searching for water by digging shallow holes with a spade, always in different places. Nothing will ever be found.

During Baudelaire's last years, cartoonists ridiculed him for writing "Une charogne." That poem was the most scandalous of all, more even than his erotic poetry. No poet, it was said, had ever dared to liken the body of his beloved to the abandoned carcass of an animal.

And yet someone prior to Baudelaire had, with no less daring, spoken of a carcass. It was Yājñavalkya, if certain words found in the fourth *kāṇḍa* of the *Śatapatha Brāhmaṇa* can be attributed to him. "The gods dispersed part of that smell and deposited it in domestic animals. This is the stench of carrion of domestic animals: no one must therefore hold their nose at the smell of carrion, this is the smell of King Soma."

Two figures—the beloved and King Soma—appear in the foul smell of the carcass. For Baudelaire, there is a shudder of revulsion and secret gratification. For the moderns, it is the horror that is supposed to lurk behind the appearance. That is why they are so frantic. They rush away, they don't stop, they fear that appearance will transform itself before their eyes. For Yājñavalkya, however, acceptance was complete. Indeed, it was connected to a precept imposed on a very primitive sense: the sense of smell, reluctant to obey.

Something remote and powerful had to be implicit in that prohibition. It had to go back to the most dreadful moment for the gods, when Indra had hurled a thunderbolt at the formless Vṛtra, but wasn't at all sure he had killed him. So he hid. Crouched behind him were the gods, equally doubtful and terror-stricken. They said to Vāyu, Wind: "Vāyu, go and find out if Vṛtra is dead or alive; you are the fastest among us: if he is alive, come back straightaway." Vāyu agreed, after having asked for a reward. When he returned, he said: "Vṛtra is slain, do with the slain what you wish." The gods rushed off. They knew that Vṛtra's body was swollen with *soma*, since Vṛtra was born from *soma*. Each wanted to plunder the corpse, to take the largest portion of it. They realized that the *soma* stank: "Its pungent stench wafted toward them: it was not fit for offering nor was it fit for being drunk." So once again they asked for Vāyu's help: "Vāyu, blow over him, make him palatable for us." Vāyu asked for another reward. Then he began blowing. The foul smell began to disperse. The gods deposited it in the smell of carrion that is in domestic animals. Then Vāyu blew again. Finally the *soma* could be drunk. The gods continued to squabble over its portions. Round about, the world was strewn with rotting carcasses. But the *soma* was also in them. People would be expected to remember this. If they came across them, they should not hold their noses.

The ritualists were extremely demanding: the *soma*, the intoxicating plant that grows on Mount Mūjavant, might have become less easy to find, it might have disappeared, but the rites that celebrated it would have continued in just the same way. A substitute would have been given for something that was unique. A fatal step. The rite would have been celebrated with another plant that lacked the powers of the *soma.* But the hymns remained. And if one day, roaming about, any humans were to come across the carcass of an animal, they were forbidden to hold their nose. Even in that rotting body, as in all bodies, the *soma* had once been deposited. Indeed, that repulsive smell was the "distinctive sign of King Soma." The *soma* is Good in its raw state. Already intolerable in itself, it becomes all the more intolerable when it is mixed with the "evil of Death," *pāpmā mṛtyuḥ*. In that precise moment it has to be accepted, inhaled, left to penetrate into us. Good is something against which nature rebels. But nature has to be tamed. This is what rites are for. And not even this was enough for the ritualists. Thought must be extended even to chance. Even to a sudden encounter with the carcass of an animal while wandering off the beaten track.

That Self, *ātman*, which "in the beginning existed alone," had the form of a "person," *puruṣa*, but was not simply a man. And it saw nothing outside. It sought pleasure, but "pleasure is not for someone who is alone." It therefore decided to split itself in two: a female and a male being. "For Yājñavalkya has said: 'We are each one half.'" Shorter and more abrupt here, in keeping with Yājñavalkya's style—but the doctrine was the same as that which Aristophanes would one day put forward during the symposium recounted by Plato.

Yājñavalkya's observation has enormous implications. First, it explains why "the emptiness created is filled by the woman." It was like this even in the beginning, because the Self, as soon as it split in two, coupled with that woman who had come out of him. "Thus men were born." The first reference is made at this point to woman's thought: "Then she reflected: 'How can he have intercourse with me, after having produced me from himself? Come, I need to hide myself.' She became a cow, he a bull. He joined with her: cows were born. She became a mare, he a stallion." The gesture of the woman in flight (out of hostility? to seduce better? for both reasons?) and the zoological sequence are evoked with supreme rapidity. Strindberg's war of the sexes and Zeus's animal metamorphoses. They continue without respite: "Thus everything is produced that goes in couples, down to the ants." And even though such stories of multiple and metamorphic coitus could be Greek, the detail of the ants is the hallmark of the Vedic author.

There is something about sexual pleasure that makes it different from everything else, and supreme. "*Érōs aníkate máchan*," "Eros invincible in battle," wrote Sophocles—and he was never proved wrong. But why is this so? Once again, the most immediate and convincing answer was given by Yājñavalkya: "In the same way that a man in the arms of the woman he loves knows nothing else outside, nothing else inside, so too this person (*puruṣa*), embraced by the *ātman* of knowledge, knows nothing else outside, nothing else inside." No other pleasure is so akin to *ātman*, because no other leads so closely back to the beginning, when *ātman* had the "form of Puruṣa"—and that Person, alone and previous to the world, "was the size of a man and a woman in tight embrace."

According to Renou, the *brahmodya*, with its high element of risk, was the formal unit that linked the Brāhmaṇas to the Upaniṣads. As additional proof, in *kāṇḍas* 10 and 11 of the *Śatapatha Brāhmaṇa* and in the part dominated by Yājñavalkya in the *Bṛhadāraṇyaka Upaniṣad*, we meet "the same speakers, the same type of scenes, often the same particular phrasing." So that it can be said not only that the Upaniṣads do not conflict, but also that "they are no other . . . than the faithful continuation of the Brāhmaṇas."

Renou went even further: "It should be noted, looking deeper, that the very notion of *brahman*, as elaborated in the thought of the Upaniṣads, is also itself a product of the *brahmodya*: in the sense that it is under this form of dialectic and in this climate of dispute that the speculation on *brahman*, the nucleus of the Upaniṣads, is constituted."

In the *Bṛhadāraṇyaka Upaniṣad* we find not only supreme examples of *brahmodya*, but also a first attempt by this form to slip away from itself, to leave its own shell and set off in a new direction, which—in the absence of any other term and even before the notion existed—might be described as that of the *novel*. The protagonist is still Yājñavalkya. But the tone suddenly changes. The great *brahmodya* with Janaka has ended and we reach the final section of the fourth "lesson" with these words: "At that time Yājñavalkya had two wives, Maitreyī and Kātyāyanī. Maitreyī knew how to speak of *brahman*, Kātyāyanī possessed the knowledge of women. When Yājñavalkya decided to start another kind of life, he said: 'Maitreyī, I want to leave these places to lead the life of a wandering monk: so I want an agreement to be made between Kātyāyanī and you.'"

Here, for the first time, we are far removed from the climate of disputation and ritual. We are part of an intimate, sober, informal discussion between an elderly couple. The essence of the prose, of the prose that tells a story without any meter and without any ritual obligations, seems to be inviting us to eavesdrop on a private matter, the unique story of three people. The great brahmin Yājñavalkya takes leave of his readers through his two wives, Maitreyī and Kātyāyanī, about whom we know nothing except that one is versed in *brahman* while the other possesses the knowledge typical of women (whatever that might mean). It is a moment of great intensity, not only because it is the prelude to a discourse by Yājñavalkya that can be considered his final word on the *ātman*—and in particular on that "love for the Self" without which even *brahman* "abandons" us—but also because it is repeated twice in the *Bṛhadāraṇyaka Upaniṣad*, in similar terms (2.4.1–14; and 4.5.1–15). And it is at the end of his instruction to Maitreyī that Yājñavalkya repeats his negative definition of *ātman*, in exactly the same terms as those he had already used with King Janaka. This time Yājñavalkya does not leave the scene to move on to other disputations and other sacrificial gatherings. This time we read: "Having spoken thus, Yājñavalkya left." The text continues for another two *adhyāyas*, without involving him further. That scene with Maitreyī, those words on *ātman* are his last appearance before he goes off into the forest. And the detail confirming that we have entered the world of the novel is that Yājñavalkya's final concern was to establish an "agreement" between the two wives whom he was about to leave.

III

ANIMALS

Consumed by the arrogance of knowledge, the young Bhṛgu, son of the supreme god Varuṇa, was sent off by his father into the world (into this world, according to the *Śatapatha Brāhmaṇa*, into the other world according to the version in the *Jaiminīya Brāhmaṇa*) to *see* what knowledge alone could not reveal, to find out how the world itself is made. Without this, all knowledge is pointless.

In the east, Bhṛgu came across men who were slaughtering other men. Bhṛgu asked: "Why?" They answered: "Because these men did the same to us in the other world." He saw the same strange scene in the south. In the west there were men eating other men and sitting about, calmly. In the north as well, amid piercing cries, there were men eating other men.

When he returned to his father, Bhṛgu seemed speechless. Varuṇa looked at him with satisfaction, thinking: "Then he has seen." The moment had come to explain to his son what he had seen. The men in the east, he said, are trees; those in the south are flocks of animals; those in the west are wild plants. Last, those in the north, who cried out while they ate other men, were the waters.

What had Bhṛgu seen? That the world is made up of Agni and Soma, of these two brothers. Brought up as two Asuras in Vṛtra's belly, they abandoned him to follow the call of another brother, Indra, and to pass over to the side of the Devas. Then "one of the two became the devourer and the other became food. Agni became the devourer and Soma the food. Down here there is nothing else than devourer and devoured." And there are these two poles in everything that happens, without exception and at every level. But Bhṛgu discovered something else: the two poles were reversible. At a certain moment the positions will switch, indeed they *will have to* switch, because this is the order of the world. This explains why all that is said about Agni can also, at a certain moment, be said about Soma. And vice versa. A phenomenon that had already baffled Abel Bergaigne.

The revelations that Bhṛgu came across were set one within the other. First of all: the final act from which all others followed was the act of eating—or at least the act of severing, of uprooting. Every act that consumes a part of the world, every act that destroys. There is no neutral state, no state in which this doesn't happen. The act of eating is a violence that causes what is living, in its many forms, to disappear. Whether grass, plants, trees, animals, or human beings, the process is the same. There is always a fire that devours and a substance that is devoured. This violence, bringing misery and torment, will one day be carried out by those who suffer it on those who inflict it. Such a chain of events cannot change. But the serious damage, the paralysis that this causes in those who become aware of it, can—we are told—be treated, remedied. This is Varuṇa's knowledge, which Bhṛgu could not have learned without the impact of what he saw when he traveled the world—or the other world. And what was the remedy? The very act of perceiving that which is—and of manifesting it, not just with words, but with gestures: in this particular case, with a series of gestures to be carried out in the *agnihotra*, the most basic of all rites. Pouring milk into the fire—every morning, every evening—meant accepting that what appears disappears and that what has disappeared *serves* to give sustenance to something else, in the invisible. This was the lesson that Varuṇa sought to give his son.

It is easy to imagine from the story of Bhṛgu how the Vedic seers were skilled in detecting evil with supreme ease. Evil for them was already apparent at the moment when an axe first struck a tree or a hand uprooted a plant. It was metaphysical evil, inherent in everything that is forced to destroy a part of the world in order to survive, therefore above all in mankind. Compared with the moderns, who tend to limit evil to intentional acts, the Vedic seers had a conception of evil that covered a far wider area. And it included certain involuntary acts, as well as acts that just cannot be avoided if mankind wants to survive—for example, the act of eating. Evil is therefore everywhere and in everything. This explains why sacrifice is also everywhere and in everything. Sacrifice is the act by which evil is brought to consciousness, using an art learned from "he who knows thus." That process in which evil is repeated and is directed, in its entirety, toward consciousness, through gestures and formulas, is the supreme remedy we can use in combating evil. Otherwise, all that remains is the mechanism revealed during Bhṛgu's journey. Those who eat will be eaten. Those who slaughter will be slaughtered. Those who eat food will themselves become food.

The widespread atrocities, the endless and unrestrainable alternation between devourer and devoured, that Bhṛgu had encountered during his wanderings to the four corners of the world—and which his father, Varuṇa, taught him to overcome through the practice of sacrifice—never disappear, but indeed become threateningly apparent during the performance of the sacrifice itself. The sacrificial flames are like eyes, "they fix their attention on the sacrificer and focus on him." What they would most desire is not the oblation, but the sacrificer himself. In front of the fire, the sacrificer feels he is being observed, stared at. The eye that is studying him is the eye of the fire. Before he himself formulates a desire, he feels it is the fire that desires him, his flesh. Here occurs the substitution, the redemption of Self: a last, swift operation to which the sacrificer resorts so as to offer the fire something instead of himself. The sacrificer offers food to avoid becoming food himself.

Bhṛgu encountered during his terrifying journey a world in which animals devoured people. But this wasn't just a reversal of the order. It was also a lightning glimpse of the history of humanity, as if someone had at last taught Bhṛgu about some of his forebears. The period during which men, rather than devouring, were devoured is none other than the first, very long chapter of their history. Varuṇa wanted his son's education to include this vision of the past, in the same way that a young boy might be sent to a good college to learn his country's history. The Vedics were also this: they ignored history, more than any other people—but they remained in contact, more so than any other people, with remote prehistory, which showed through in their rites and in their myths.

In the Vedic landscape there is one object that evokes terror and veneration: the sacrificial post. Of all the emblems of that time, it is the only one still visible. In certain Indian villages, even today, a piece of wood can be seen sticking out of the ground, for no apparent reason. Madeleine

Biardeau has found many of these in various parts of India, noting that they are that "post," *yūpa*, the "thunderbolt" of which the Vedic ritualists spoke. But why a "thunderbolt"? To understand this, we have to go back to a distant story:

"There are an animal and a sacrificial post, for they never immolate an animal without a post. This is why: animals did not originally submit to the fact of becoming food, in the way that they have now become food. In the same way as man walks upright on two legs, they also walked upright on two legs.

"Then the gods noticed that thunderbolt, i.e., that sacrificial post; they put it in the ground and, for fear of it, the animals became crooked and four-legged, and so they became food, as today they are food, because they gave in: this is why they immolate the animal at the post, and never without a post.

"After having brought the victim forward and lit the fire, he ties the animal. This is why it is so: the animals did not originally submit to the fact of becoming sacrificial food, in the way that they have now become sacrificial food and are offered in the fire. The gods cage them: even caged in this way, they did not give in.

"They spoke: 'In truth, these animals do not know how this happens, that sacrificial food is offered in the fire, and they do not know that safe place [the fire]: let us offer fire in fire after having fastened the animals and lit the fire, and they will know that this is how the sacrificial food is prepared, that this is its place; that it is in the fire itself that the sacrificial food is offered: and they will then yield and be favorably disposed to being immolated.'

"After having first fastened the animals and lit the fire, they offered fire in fire; and then they [the animals] knew that this is truly how the sacrificial food is prepared, that this is the place; that it is in the fire itself that the sacrificial food is offered. And as a result they yielded and were favorably disposed to being immolated."

It would be very hard to find another text that describes with such great precision, with such great pathos, the decisive step that formalized the slaughter of domestic animals: the establishment of the meat diet. It was a necessity, but above all a guilty act, an act of enormous guilt. To justify its necessity, form was given to the theological edifice of the sacrifice, a temple-labyrinth, full of passages and tunnels, with countless junctures. And the sacrifice was needed to incorporate the guilt within it, indeed it would intensify and preserve it, as if in a casket. That guilt alluded to another, more deep-seated guilt, a consequence of which would be the sacrifice: the *guilt of imitation*, of that distant decision that had led a species of beings who had been prey to assume the behavior typical of their predator enemies. The first act against nature that would one day be seen as human nature itself—no other species would be so bold.

More than a "sick animal," according to Hegel's definition, man is an animal who essentially imitates (and imitation can also be seen as a human sickness). Man is the only being in the animal kingdom who has relinquished his nature, if by nature we mean that repertory of behavior with which every species appears to be equipped from birth. Strong, but not so strong that he didn't have to recognize his own defenselessness in the face of other creatures—predators—man decided at a certain moment (which may also have lasted a hundred thousand years) not to fight against his adversaries but to *imitate* them. It was then that the being who had been prey taught himself to become a predator. He had teeth, not fangs—and his fingernails were not enough to rip into flesh. Nor did his body produce a poison, like snakes, who were formidable predators. He therefore had to resort to something no other predator had: the weapon, the instrument, the tool. This is how the flint and the arrow were created. At this point, through imitation and the production of tools, two important steps were taken—mimesis and technology—which the remainder of history would try to develop, up until today. Looking back, the upheaval produced by that first step—of mimesis, by which humans, of all creatures, decided to imitate precisely those who had so often killed them—is incomparably more radical and devastating than any subsequent step. A response to this upheaval was the sacrifice, in its many forms. Nothing else can explain why such uncharacteristic behavior, in comparison with anything else in the animal kingdom, occurred more or less everywhere, in a wide variety of forms but invariably sharing certain essential features. The sacrifice, before it assumed any other meaning, was a response to that immense upheaval within the species—and an attempt to redress a balance that had been upset and violated forever.

Only in this way can sacrifice be understood: not just a way of covering up guilt, a *pia fraus* that enables the world to continue thanks to priestly stratagem. But a daring speculation that above all exalts guilt. It exalts it to the point of persuading the victim to become favorably disposed to being immolated. This, obviously, is not what happens. No one imagines that the goat or the horse let themselves be persuaded to be killed and butchered. None of the ritualists could have believed that. But to carry out a gesture in that direction, to express words with that intention: this is the supreme effort granted to thought, granted to action, where we come face to face with the irreconcilable. An illusory, transitory attempt. And yet that conscious illusion is the only force that makes it possible to establish a distance, albeit minimal, from the plain act of killing.

Nowhere else in antiquity (later the question would no longer be raised, since man was so convinced of his moral superiority) did anyone ever dare to suggest that animals originally walked upright and *became* four-legged only because they were terrified of something: of a solitary octagonal post, crowned with a bundle of grass to cover its bareness. The discovery of the post was not attributed to man, but to the gods, as if the post were indeed the *axis mundi*—and as if life were inconceivable without it. And yet the post is not enough: it forces animals to walk on four legs, in terror, but it does not persuade them to allow themselves to be slaughtered. The gods now had to propose a theological nicety: they explained to the animals that the sacrifice was an offer of "fire in fire." Mysterious words: but the whole of the *Śatapatha Brāhmaṇa*, and in particular the sections on the fire altar, is devoted to describing it. That "thunderbolt" which is the sacrificial post was therefore not enough. The terror was overcome, but the animals still did not yield. Theory, lofty liturgical speculation, then took over. Only then did the animals give in. Or at least it was said that the animals gave in.

The terror is not only in the animals. It is in man. As soon as he saw the appearance of the "post," the *yūpa*, man understood that he would have to kill those creatures who, until a moment before, were walking with him and by his side. He would have to take hold of the rope that is invariably tied to the post. It is a moment of paralysis. The liturgy then says: "Be bold, O man!" The man then continues, tries to be brave. Once again, he clings to theology: the knot his hands are already inadvertently preparing is none other than "the noose of world order." As for the rope, it is "Varuṇa's rope." It is as if the gods themselves were acting. And with this the guilt is offloaded onto the gods. At the critical moment—the moment when the officiant ties the animal to the post—every part of his body is taken over by a god, limb for limb. Even the impulse that makes him act is attributed to Savitṛ, who is the Impeller. So he says: "At the impulse of the divine Savitṛ, I tie you with the arms of the Aśvins, with the hands of Pūṣan, you who are liked by Agni and Soma." The one who acts is like a sleepwalker. How can he be guilty?

But nothing—not even the gods—is ever sufficient to offload the guilt. So a few moments later, the sacrificer will feel the need to ask the victim's mother and father for permission to kill: "And may your mother consent, and your father . . ." But not even this is enough. Then the sacrificer adds: "And your brother, your companion in the herd." And by this he means: "Any creature related to you by blood, with their consent I kill you." Nothing less than unanimity is required when it comes to killing.

According to the *Śatapatha Brāhmaṇa*, it was not true that human beings, over the course of millennia, *achieved* the upright position, freeing themselves from their life as four-legged primates. On the contrary: humans were the only ones to have remained standing upright, while all the other animals became crooked and had to *learn* to walk on four legs. What decided their fate? Sacrifice, then killing. Animals cannot remain upright *for fear of being killed*: they have seen the post, they know they are destined to be tied to it, they know they will then be killed. Humans remain standing because they know they are the sacrificers. This is the dividing line that guides the course of human history.

At this point a chorus of voices will say that the Darwinian view has supplanted the thinking of the *Śatapatha Brāhmaṇa* once and for all, as if the latter were a childish and disturbing prelude to the discovery of what really happened. But would it not be an irreparable loss for us to eliminate the Vedic vision? Does it not offer something to human knowledge that would otherwise remain unspoken and ignored? This is where the shared bond between man and the animal world finds its unshakable foundation, which goes well beyond any feeling of empathy. It is no longer man who is emancipated from his animal companions. But it is the animals who are seen as fallen beings, having had to submit to the condition of victim. An enlightened humanity could accept both Darwin's vision and that of the Brāhmaṇas at one and the same time, with an impartial farsightedness—an improbable humanity.

"He then puts on a garment, for completeness: in fact in this way he puts on his own skin. That same skin that belongs to the cow was originally on man.

"The gods said: 'The cow endures everything down here; come, let us put that skin onto the cow which is now on man: in that way it will be able to endure rain and cold and heat.'

"Having flayed the man, they therefore put his skin onto the cow, so that it could now endure the rain and the cold and the heat.

"In this way the man was flayed; so when even a blade of grass or something else cuts him, blood gushes forth. They then put that skin, the robe, on him; and for this reason man alone wears a robe, because it was put onto him like a skin. Care must therefore be taken in dressing well, so that one's skin is completely covered. This is why people love seeing even an ugly person dressed well, since he is clothed with his own skin.

"He shall therefore not appear naked before a cow. Because the cow knows it is wearing his skin and runs away for fear that he wants to take it back from it. Even cows are therefore trusting when they approach those who are well dressed."

If we want an example of an unfathomable story in the Brāhmaṇas, then this could be it. Only Kafka, in his stories about animals and men, reached a similar pitch. Here the basis of history is the whole of prehistory: man's long dark period of laborious differentiation from other beings, which culminated in all these creatures being successfully grouped together under a single word: *animals*. In that period we see man's astonishing, gradual transformation from prey to predator. The discovery of the meat diet: the primordial guilt and overwhelming stimulus for the development and spread of power. A story too distant and too secret to have left any verbal trace. But a story that has embedded itself in the least accessible level of human sensibility.

Man feels an irredeemable guilt toward the cow, as well as toward the antelope—an animal that cannot be sacrificed (because it is wild) though it will become the heraldic animal of sacrifice. It is true that "the cow supports everything down here," but in return man flays it. To feed himself, man kills a being that up until then is feeding him. So extreme is the guilt that, to speak of it, he will have to invent a story that turns the situation upside down. Man will then find a justification: in his trepidation, in his uncertainty, in remembrance of his defenselessness.

Man is the only flayed animal. And not just by nature—at one time he too had a skin—but because the gods, at a certain point, decided to flay him and give his skin to the cow. This is the true story of primordial times—the story to which men were forced to go back when they began to eat the flesh of the cow and also to flay it. To justify himself, man had to keep alive the memory of a time when he was an animal like so many others, protected like all of them by a skin. Then he became a single sore: "Having been flayed, man is a sore; and, by anointing himself, he is healed of his soreness: because the skin of the man is on the cow, and even fresh butter comes from the cow. He [the officiant] supplies him with his own skin, and for this reason [the sacrificer] has himself anointed." In his state of dereliction, this being who no longer has any defense from the world regains his own skin through the butter that anoints him: with that beneficial anointment the cow gives back to man something of what it has received from him. It follows, among other things, that man is a sort of outcast of nature. A blade of grass is enough to make him bleed. His only possibility of survival, and of saving himself from that excess of suffering which is his lot, is through artifice: the anointment that covers his body, the clothes that form a new skin. At that point, thanks to the powerful catapult of practices ignored by every other being, man can return to mingle with nature. But he must not appear naked in front of the cow: the animal would remember the cruel story of what had happened and would run off, fearful of losing its beloved hide. The cow flees from man not just for fear of being flayed, but because man—a flayed being—might try to take back his skin, which now adorns the cow. There is an unaccountable embarrassment when a naked human body finds itself among animals: a feeling that is difficult to deny, but on which no attention ever appears to have been focused. For the Vedic ritualists, however, it was the mark of distant and painful events that had left a mark in the rite. And above all, it was the recollection of the only possible way to justify relations with these mild animals that were close to human life through rain, heat, and ice. At the same time it should be added that, in the long history that separates the Vedic ritualists from Beau Brummell, never has such a clear-sighted explanation been given for the importance of dress. And never has a more convincing justification been offered for the peculiar embarrassment people feel about nudity.

Vedic India is the only place, throughout world history, where the following question has been asked: why is it true that "man should not be naked in the presence of a cow"? People seem to have had no concern about the question, either in ancient times or today. But the Vedic ritualists did. They also knew the answer: because "the cow knows it is wearing his [man's] skin and runs away for fear that he might want to take it back." And they then add a note of charming frivolity, based on another disconcerting observation: "Cows are therefore trusting when they approach those who are well dressed." Perhaps only Oscar Wilde, had he known it, would have been able to comment with authority on this reason for *dressing well.*

As for the Vedic ritualists, they gave it credence through a story that others would one day have called a myth, but which in their words sounded like a dry, anonymous account of how things began. Everything started when the gods, watching events on earth, realized that the whole of life was supported by the cow. Men were its parasites. One of the gods—we don't know which—urged humans to allow their skin to be used to cover the cows. So the gods flayed man. If we try to go back to the very beginning, this is therefore the natural human state: the Flayed Man, as in sixteenth-century anatomical drawings. Unlike the naïve positivists, who presented primordial man in natural history museum display cabinets with a monkey-like covering of hair, the Vedic ritualists saw him not as the mighty lord of creation, but as the being who was most exposed, most easily vulnerable from the world outside. For them, man didn't just conceal a wound, but was a single wound. They wanted to add an eloquent detail: man is a hemophiliac by vocation, as even a blade of grass can make his blood gush forth.

Among the many characteristics that distinguish man (depending on the point of view: he is the only one who speaks, the only one who laughs, the only one who cries, the only one who celebrates sacrifices), the fact that he is the only creature who feels the need to dress is generally seen as the clearest sign of his inextricable link with artificiality. But, here again, the Vedic ritualists thought differently—and refuted in advance all those who came later. According to them, when at the beginning of the rite of "consecration," *dīkṣā* (which is also an initiation), the sacrificer wears a linen robe, at that moment "he wears his own skin." Only then does man regain his "completeness." Only then does he return to that which was his original state.

This is a complete reversal of the current view: here artifice indicates the reconquering of nature as something whole. But it is still a temporary reconquest since, at the end of the liturgy, man will have to free himself of all the objects (and garments) he has used during the rite, thus returning to his condition of being impure and flayed. *Naturalness* is a temporary state, linked to a garment and a certain sequence of gestures (the rite).

Anointing was one of the most frequent gestures in rituals, in places far and wide, right up to the ceremony that consecrated Western kings. But none of the explanations given for it is as wild as the one offered by the Vedic ritualists. It presumes that man starts off, not from nothing, but from less than nothing. His original condition is not just that of an impure being, immersed in untruth. In the beginning, man doesn't even have his whole body. Before he begins to act, someone has acted on him, flaying him. Man, in the beginning, is therefore a single sore. The wound, for him, is not one injured part of his body, but the totality of his body. The anointment covers this edgeless wound with a soft, wet, invisible film that makes movement and life possible. To understand the immensity of the ritual work, and its meticulous obsessiveness, it has to be placed in the context of this human condition at the very beginning, which is one of complete helplessness and pure pain. And only this can justify it.

If people at the very beginning (in other words, people who had not yet instituted sacrificial rites) were flayed and suffering beings, lacking in "completeness," the decision to kill oxen and cows could only seem like a blasphemy. They looked upon those tame and mighty animals who grazed everywhere, protected by their magnificent hide, as a living provocation, rather like certain rich people who flaunt jewelry bought at auction from families that have fallen on hard times. Wrapped in improvised clothing, so as not to raise suspicion, men approached the animals and killed them. They had decided to put an end to the lives of those beings who until then had been a support for life itself. Sacrifice, the theory and practice of sacrifice, was a long, exasperated, captious, daring reworking of that gesture into actions, into formulas, into chants. People now went about in linen robes: it is said that the warp and weft of the cloth belonged to Agni and Vāyu and that "all the divinities had a part" in producing them. The same gods who had flayed them in the first place now took pains to protect them.

The most widespread objection to modern vegetarianism goes like this: you avoid eating beef, but the hides are used to make your shoes, your belts, your clothes. How can you be consistent in claiming to condemn the killing of these animals, which is also being done to clothe you? There is no convincing solution to this question—and the answer given by those who declare they wear only cord or plastic shoes or cloth or metal belts is simply pathetic. The industrial production cycle is much more sophisticated—and there is no way of totally avoiding contact with the secondary products of meat slaughter.

The Vedic ritualists did not find themselves in this dilemma, but knew perfectly well that the act of eating animal flesh was a *crux metaphysica* that might not even have a solution. And it is precisely here that Yājñavalkya stepped in.

We are in the third *kāṇḍa* of the *Śatapatha Brāhmaṇa*, in a part of the work that, according to tradition, was written by Yājñavalkya himself. But, exactly as would happen in the *Mahābhārata*, where Vyāsa was the author and occasionally appeared as a character, so too in that Brāhmaṇa, composed in the form of a treatise, Yājñavalkya manages several times to find his way into various scenes, always in crucial passages. Always with sharp, abrupt comments, like Marpa with his cane, ready to use it to wake up the pupil who would one day become Milarepa.

What happens after the passage where people had been flayed and their skins now clothe cattle? This is by decree of the gods. It follows that if people are not allowed even to show themselves naked in front of cows so as not to frighten them, they certainly won't be allowed to kill them, let alone eat them. Here we find ourselves close to the origin of the prohibition on meat-eating in India. From here an uninterrupted line leads us to the cows wandering in the city traffic or lying pensively on temple steps. And yet didn't the same Vedic ritualists spend their time meticulously describing animal sacrifices in which a part was then offered to the gods and a part was eaten by the officiants?

The point was very delicate—and had to be resolved by Yājñavalkya. First, according to the text, an officiant takes the consecrated person—who now wears a linen robe and so once again has a skin—into the hut built in the sacrificial area. And immediately after, it adds the requirement "that he [the consecrated person] shall not eat cow or ox; for the cow and the ox certainly support everything here on earth." Once again, a decision from the gods had to be sought. They said: "Certainly the cow and the ox support everything here; come, let us bestow on the cow and the ox whatever strength belongs to the other species!" It wasn't therefore just the human hide that had been transferred to cattle. But strength in general, dispersed throughout nature. So cows became a concentration of everything. To kill them would have meant killing everything. "If someone were to eat an ox or a cow, it would be as if, so to speak, he were to eat everything or, so to speak, as if he were to destroy everything." Already the insistence—twice in two lines—on the particle *iva*, "so to speak," warns us that we are in a highly fraught and dangerous area. The tone is serious—and immediately afterward there is a resounding threat, one of the earliest formulations of the doctrine of reincarnation: "One [who acts] thus could be reborn as a strange being, as one of evil repute, as one of whom it is said: 'He has caused a woman to abort' or 'He has committed a sin.' So he must not eat (the meat of) an ox or cow."

The words are short, abrupt, they do not seem to allow for any reply. But they are turned on their head in the next sentence: "Nonetheless Yājñavalkya said: 'I, for my part, eat it, provided it is tender.'" The text then moves on, without any comment. Yājñavalkya's metaphysical probe had touched a point that is usually avoided: there is a *pleasure* in eating the flesh of dead animals that is deeply physiological, just like sexual pleasure. In that case too, pleasure and guilt come together—and remain inseparable. When we go back beyond a certain threshold in phylogenesis, there is no escaping these simultaneous conflicting drives, which are not yet feelings but dark and highly powerful imperatives: allusions to our most distant memories, from which, however, we are separated by an insuperable barrier, like dreams that have been blotted out.

What conclusions can be drawn from all this? The doubt cannot be solved. The teaching set out in the *Śatapatha Brāhmaṇa* seems to require abstinence from meat, with various arguments and a severe tone. Yet the supposed author of the text breaks in impetuously and insolently to say the opposite. What would be the right doctrine?

Guilt connected to sacrifice—guilt about killing and destruction in general: more fundamentally, *guilt about what disappears*—extends not just to animals, but to the plant world, so as plants and trees can be saved by sacrifice. *Everything* is killed, starting from the sacrificer, who has just—temporarily—avoided it, when "Agni and Soma have taken he who sacrifices between their jaws," and starting from Soma himself, who will be killed by the pestle in the mortar. Others will eventually be tied to the "post" before being killed. And for each victim the event is described through euphemism: the sacrificial killing is called "appeasement." During the sacrifice, the officiant speaks to the sacrificial horse using words of high, visionary, tender lyricism, promising that no harm will come to it and that it will follow the path of the gods, in the same way as Siberian hunters speak with gentleness and devotion to the bear they are about to kill. Something similar happens with the tree. The officiant is even required to reassure it: "This sharp-edged axe has led you toward great bliss." The reference to "bliss" is meant to mitigate the impact of a "thunderbolt": "for the axe is a thunderbolt." *Thunderbolt* is everything that has an absolute power. But the ritualists were too subtle to define only certain potentially lethal arms in this way: "the razor is a thunderbolt," but it is also true that "water is a thunderbolt," and "ghee is a thunderbolt," in the same way that "the tree they cut down to make the sacrificial post is a thunderbolt" and "the year is a thunderbolt." And one day it happened that "the gods perceived that thunderbolt: the horse." In the case of the tree, of that "lord of the forest" which is chosen for the sacrifice of *soma*, the mitigation of guilt will be achieved above all by placing a blade of *darbha* grass on the trunk. It would be foolish to mock the meagerness of such means. A tuft of *darbha* grass alone can purify the face of a "consecrated one," a *dīkṣita*, one who can therefore perform a sacrifice: "For impure, indeed, is man; he is foul within, in that he speaks untruth; and *darbha* grass is pure."

Choosing the tree to cut down, from which to make the *yūpa*, the sacrificial "post," which in itself epitomizes the totality of the sacrifice, is like choosing any other victim: it is the act in which the mystery of election is revealed. The ritualist therefore considers it with great care, so that the sacrificer must bring all his keenness into play. What tree will he choose? Not the closest one in the forest. That would be too crude and too simple. It would be as if all you had to do was take one step forward to be chosen—and one step back not to be. But nor will the sacrificer choose the tree farthest away. The last would then be the most likely—and all, if they wanted to avoid being chosen, would rush to the most conspicuous positions. Here again the choice would lose its mystery. No, the sacrificer will choose "on the nearer side of the farther" and "on the farther side of the nearer." And where in the forest does *the farther* begin? Where does *the nearer* reach its limit? No one can know this. Not even the sacrificer, until that inscrutable moment when he will say to the tree, in that grim, unctuous tone that all victims recognize: "We favor you, O divine lord of the forest."

This way of dealing with the mystery of election brings us face-to-face with an implacable difference and peculiarity, from the brahminic point of view. An average Westerner today (but most probably, also, an ancient), in front of a whole forest where he has to choose one tree among many, all equally suitable, would say: the first, or the last, or one at random. All three criteria are rejected by the Vedic ritualist. We might, with some surprise but no difficulty, accept the reasoning that leads to rejecting the choice of the first and the last. But the more delicate and difficult point is the exclusion of the third (and more obvious) possibility: the random choice. Here we are dealing with choice—and not only that, but the choice of something that makes the sacrifice possible. And eliminating, or at least circumventing, arbitrary discretion in this choice means abrogating the sovereignty of chance where it hurts most. But will the sacrificer succeed in his intent? Not exactly. Chance will be circumscribed, but not removed altogether. Above all, it will be *covered*. The choice is presented as motivated—but the motivation has to coexist with discretion. Searching for the chosen object "on the nearer side of the farther" and "on the farther side of the nearer" may sound like gibberish, but indicates an act that is not casual and yet can only remain impenetrable, even if carried out by an ordinary officiant and not by an inaccessible divinity. This guarantees that what happens—and above all what happens at the crucial moment, that of the choice—is not totally arbitrary, but nor can it be reconstructed through a finite series of steps. This is what will one day, with Gödel, be called "undecidable." It is as if radical indeterminacy had taken over thought here, detaching itself from chance as well as from any *ratio.* While not being casual, the choice remains impenetrable, above all for he who has performed it.

How long must the sacrificial post be? Five cubits, it is stated, with a wealth of explanations: "For fivefold is the sacrifice and fivefold is the animal sacrificed and there are five seasons in the year." That should be enough.

But following immediately after are the reasons—no less convincing—why it ought to be six cubits or eight or nine or eleven, twelve, thirteen, fifteen. An example of the brahminic luxuriance of correspondences, which immediately brings to mind something that cancels them out. And their incorrigible arbitrariness. A frequent mistake, which ignores the fact that certain sizes are ruled out: the post cannot be seven, ten, or fourteen cubits. *Not* everything is therefore equivalent. But the crucial passage is at the end, where there is a discussion about the possibility of the post *not* even being measured. The "immeasurable," like the continuum, the implicit or the indistinct, is to be considered and respected, above all when it is a thunderbolt, if we remember that the first thunderbolt, that of Indra, was itself "immeasurable"—and thanks to its power the gods conquered everything. Here we see two fundamental impulses in brahminic thought brought together: the exasperating mania for exhaustive classification on the one hand; and the underlying willingness to recognize an immensity that overwhelms everything and can be felt everywhere.

We read at school and in science books that men were first hunters and gatherers, then herdsmen and tillers of the soil. Two stages that divide the history of humanity over hundreds of thousands of years, agriculture occupying by far the smaller part. But it would be enough to say that people lived in an initial phase *with* animals (killing them and being killed by them) and in a later phase *on* animals (through their domestication). They nevertheless had to kill animals, whether hunting them or butchering them. What changed was the relationship with the creatures they killed: consanguineous and kindred in the first phase, useful and submissive in the second.

Moreover, the description "hunting and gathering" conflates two distinct phases. Before being gatherers and hunters, people had to be gatherers and *hunted*. Certain kinds of predator were far better at hunting than humans were. The fangs of tigers or wolves were far more powerful than human hands. But this gray area of prehistory is lost in the description "hunting and gathering." That was when, over a period of tens of thousands of years, the irreversible transition to hunting took place.

The *Odyssey* announces it from the sixth verse of the first book: Odysseus is *he who remains alone.* An anomalous situation, which required a whole poem to express it—and the whole of literature afterward, up to Kafka. No one in the *Iliad* remained alone. Even Achilles, the loner par excellence, was surrounded by many. As for Odysseus, he certainly hadn't been looking for solitude—circumstances had brought it upon him. An irreparable rift causes him, one day, to become separated from his companions. It is one single episode, enough to divide his fate and his name from that of all the others forever: Odysseus is the only one who hasn't fed upon the Sun's herds of cattle.

Already in open sea, his ship was approaching the island of Thrinacia when Odysseus heard a mysterious sound: a distant and continuous rumble. He then understood: the sound came from the animals on that island which Circe and Tiresias had warned him to avoid. Guided by the two radiant daughters of Helios, Phaethusa and Lampetia, those animals—"seven herds of cattle and as many flocks of beautiful sheep / of fifty beasts each"—were the Sun's herds. Each of them the substance of a parcel of time, one of the three hundred and fifty days of the lunar year. They were beings that "do not give birth / and never die." They were everlasting life. Odysseus knew he should not have sailed so close to that animal sound. None of the many intelligent stratagems for which he would become famous went as far, none penetrated the ambulacra of divinity as much as his steadfast obedience to that mysterious prohibition. It is useless being clever unless you're a theologian. And Odysseus, that day, was an outstanding theologian.

Not so his companions. Wracked by hunger, blinded by necessity ("all forms of death are abominable for wretched mortals / but the most miserable is death by hunger and through hunger to suffer fate," said Eurylochus then to Odysseus's companions), they surrounded and slaughtered the Sun's herds. What then took place was a primordial wound that could never be healed. Life killed life. It was the first guilty act, from which all others followed. But men are never straightforward. They wanted to disguise their greed by staging a sacrifice, even without the right ingredients (libation wine, barley) for performing the ceremony. Food was no longer a secondary consequence of the sacrifice. On the contrary, the sacrifice was the pretext for devouring the food. And Odysseus's companions, in fact, feasted for six days on the flesh of the slaughtered animals, "the finest of the Sun's cows." They had chosen them carefully—and far exceeded the extent of their hunger. They ate for the pleasure and sense of supremacy felt by those who eat dead flesh.

Yet it was not dead flesh. When they laid the skewers on the fire, they realized those pieces of flesh were moving, as if they were breathing. And above all, they gave out a deep, endless sound. No one else witnessed that scene of supreme horror. There was only one outside observer, the only one who watched and did not eat: Odysseus. It was then that their destinies broke apart forever. Odysseus had suddenly become the *lone man* ("I am one against many, and you force my hand," he had said to his companions, heralds of the whole of humanity). He knew he would continue to live among those who kill life. But he would no longer have any fellow travelers. They would soon all be drowned. Odysseus's only company then was the gleaming-eyed goddess, Athena.

Men today, who recoil from sacrifice, bow their heads when faced with the self-sacrifice of a god who creates the world (Prajāpati) or who saves it (Christ). Self-sacrifice is the very essence of the sublime, heroic gesture. Abnegation marks nobility of spirit.

But, apart from the gods, self-sacrifice is also practiced by the animals. There is much evidence, above all in central and eastern Asia, of animals who *yield* to the hunter to be killed. They are moved to pity by his hunger and offer themselves to his arrows. The supreme gesture belongs to gods and animals. Men can only imitate them.

IV

THE PROGENITOR

The god at the origin of everything didn't have a name but a title: Prajāpati, Lord of the Creatures. He discovered this when one of his sons, Indra, told him: "I want to be what you are." Prajāpati asked him: "But who (*ka*) am I?" And Indra answered: "'Exactly what you just said.' So Prajāpati became Ka."

Indra wanted his father's "greatness" or, according to others, his "splendor." And Prajāpati had no difficulty in divesting himself of it. So Indra became king of the gods, even though Prajāpati had been "the sole lord of creation." But it was neither "greatness" nor "splendor" that made Prajāpati the "god alone above the gods," a formula that smacks of incompatibility only for latter-day readers in the West. What Prajāpati could not renounce was something else: the unknown, the irreducible unknown. At the moment in which he knew he was Ka, Prajāpati became guarantor of the uncertainty involved in questioning. He guaranteed that it would always remain. If Ka didn't exist, the world would be a sequence of questions and answers, at the end of which everything would be fixed once and for all—and the unknown could be erased from life. But since Prajāpati "is everything"—and Prajāpati is Ka—there is a question in every part of everything that finds an answer in the name of everything. And this in turn takes us back to the question, which opens onto the unknown. But this is not an unknown that is due to the inadequacy of the human intellect. It is unknown even for the god who includes it in his name. Divine omniscience does not extend to itself.

No wonder the gods, sons of Prajāpati, increasingly ignored their father, to the point of forgetting him. For a power to be exercised, it has to be based on certainty. And Prajāpati, though he was the one "whose commandments all the gods acknowledge," had delegated the exercise of his sovereignty without raising any resistance. He had kept back for himself only the unknown, which was encapsulated in his name. An unknown that surrounded every certainty like an undrainable ocean lapping an island. For the administration of ordinary life, the preeminence of the unknown was a danger—and had to be obliterated. For the fathomless life of the mind—at the point where the mind reconnected with its origin, Prajāpati—it was the very breath of life. In the same way that Ka had been "the sole breath of the gods."

Prajāpati: the creator god who is not entirely sure he exists. Prajāpati is the god who has no identity, who is the origin of all insoluble paradoxes. All identities arise from him, who himself has none. And so he takes a step back, or to one side, allowing the rush of mortal beings, ready to forget him, to carry on. But they will then return to him, to ask him the wherefore. And the wherefore can only be similar to what made them first emerge: a rite, a composition of elements, of forms, a temporary—the only—guarantee of existence. Compared with every monotheistic god, and with all other plural deities, Prajāpati is more intimate and more remote, more elusive and more familiar. Any reasoning person continually encounters him wherever speech and thought arise, wherever they dissolve away. That is Prajāpati.

The *Śatapatha Brāhmaṇa* returns on innumerable occasions to the scene that takes place "at the beginning," when Prajāpati "desired." And on most occasions we read that Prajāpati wanted to reproduce himself, wanted to know other beings apart from himself. But there is a passage where it says that Prajāpati had another desire: "May I exist, may I be generated." The very first being to be unsure of his own existence was thus the Progenitor. And he had good reason, since Prajāpati was an amalgam of seven *ṛṣis*, those "seers" who, in turn, had been seven "vital breaths," though incapable of existing *alone.* Prior to the drama of things generated there was the drama of that which feared it could not exist. This was what forever marked Prajāpati's character and made him the most phantom-like, the most anxious, the most fragile of all creator gods. He never resembled a sovereign who elatedly surveys his dominions. He left that feeling to one of his sons, Indra—and he pitied him for it. He knew that, along with euphoria, and bound up with it, Indra would face mockery and retribution.

To gather the difference between Prajāpati and the gods, it is enough to murmur a ritual formula. The low voice is indistinct—and that indistinctness already brings us in contact with the nature of Prajāpati, which is precisely this: indistinct. By playing with meter, with names, with formulas, with murmurs, with silence, the sacrificer manages to move about among the various forms of the divine. But, even in the case of the most elementary gesture, he will have to reach that vast, mysterious level, that indistinctness where he encounters only Prajāpati—and himself.

Unlike Elohim, Prajāpati does not have a hand in creation as a working craftsman, but is the process of creation itself: in it he is made and he is unmade. The further Prajāpati goes in creation, the more he is dismembered and exhausted. His view of what he does is never from the outside. He cannot look upon his work and say: "It is good." As soon as he looks outward, he evokes another being, Vāc, the "second," a column of water, which was a female, pouring between sky and earth. And immediately the two copulate. Prajāpati was so little external to his creation that, according to some texts, it was he himself who became impregnated: "With his mind he united with Vāc, Speech: he became pregnant with eight drops." They became eight deities, the Vasus. Then he set them upon the earth. Copulation continued. Prajāpati was once again impregnated, by eleven drops. They became other deities, the Rudras. He then set them in the atmosphere. There was also a third copulation. And Prajāpati was impregnated by twelve drops. This time they were the Ādityas, the great gods of light: "He placed them in the sky." Eight, eleven, twelve: thirty-one. Prajāpati was impregnated by another drop: the Viśvedevāḥ, All-the-gods. They had reached thirty-two. Only one was missing to complete the pantheon: Vāc herself, the thirty-third.

Prajāpati now began to uncouple himself from her. He was exhausted, he could feel his joints disconnecting. The vital breaths, the Saptarṣis, left him. And with them went the thirty-three deities, trooping off together. Prajāpati was alone once again, as at the beginning, when everything around him was void. He was no longer the only one, but the thirty-fourth, whom they would soon forget to include among the list of gods. And one day, far in the future, certain scholars would say that he was a late and bloodless abstraction, no more than a lucubration of the ritualists.

"In truth, here at the beginning was *asat.* To this they say: 'What was this *asat*?' The *ṛṣis*: they were, at the beginning, the *asat.* And to this they say: 'Who were these *ṛṣis*?' Now, the *ṛṣis* are the vital breaths. For before all this they, desiring this, wore themselves out (*riṣ-*) in toil and ardor, so they are called *ṛṣis.*"

If *asat* is an inhabited place, it must certainly also *exist*, but in special ways. At the beginning it contains only vital breaths, which Indra manages to kindle (*indh-*). The name *ṛṣi* is derived from that ardor which is *tapas*; the name Indra comes from the kindling of the vital breaths. *Asat* is therefore a place where at the beginning energy is burning. And so from the vital breaths were born "seven persons (*puruṣas*)." The first beings with bodily features were therefore the *ṛṣis*: the Saptarṣis, the original Seven Ṛṣis. But the Saptarṣis were immediately aware of their limited power. Generated by the vital breaths, they themselves could not procreate. Their first desire was therefore to act in concert, transforming themselves into a single person. This had to be their task: to compress themselves, condense themselves into one single body, occupying its various parts: "Two above the navel and two below the navel; one on the right side, one on the left side, one at the base." There was now a body, but it had no head. Still they worked away. From each of them was extracted essence, sap, taste, *rasa.* And they concentrated it all into the same place, as if into a jar: that was the head. The person made up from the Seven Seers was now complete. And "that same person became Prajāpati." This was how the Progenitor was created, he who generated everything, including the vital breaths, Indra, and the Saptarṣis who had laboriously created him.

Leaving aside the complications of mutual procreation, by which the Saptarṣis give form to Prajāpati, who in turn would generate them (a regular process in Vedic thought) and leaving aside any consideration of the sequence of time, it seems clear that *asat* is a place for something that seeks to manifest itself, that burns to manifest itself, but which is prevented from doing so. At the same time, all that forms part of "that which is," *sat*, and above all Prajāpati, will owe its origin to *asat*, which goes back to that obscure period in which the Seven Seers wore themselves out developing an ardor, dedicating themselves to the first of all acts of asceticism, if the word is used once again to mean "exercise," *áskēsis*. As for *asat*, more than *nonbeing* (in the sense of the *mḕ ón* in Parmenides), it appears to be closer to something one might call the "unmanifest."

Prajāpati is not only "he who finds that which is lost," but he himself is also the first to be lost. His supernumerary essence is such that at any moment Prajāpati risks being *too much*. Creatures appear thanks to the superabundance that exists in Prajāpati, but—once their worlds are established—they soon tend to look only after themselves, forgetting their origin. Indeed, they no longer recognize him. It seems they have made Prajāpati suffer even this harsh humiliation. When Prajāpati had finished emanating beings, "he became emaciated. They didn't recognize him then, since he was emaciated. He anointed his eyes and his limbs." The last act of the now abandoned Progenitor. Prajāpati went back to being alone, as at the beginning, but now because he was unrecognizable. As he was anointing his eyes and limbs, gaunt and defenseless, Prajāpati was inventing makeup. He was doing these things because he wanted to be recognized again. Men and women would one day try to do the same: "When their eyes and limbs are anointed, they become beautiful: and others notice them." This is the first *éloge du maquillage*, whose pathos and frivolity Baudelaire would appreciate.

What is the horse? It is one of Prajāpati's eyes that had swollen up and then fallen out. The *Śatapatha Brāhmaṇa* doesn't hesitate for a moment over this statement (nothing is strange for the Vedic ritualist), indeed it moves on immediately to describe the enormous implications: "Prajāpati's eye became swollen; it fell out: from it was produced the horse; and inasmuch as it swelled up (*aśvayat*), that is the origin of the horse (*aśva*). Through the sacrifice of the horse the gods restored it [the eye] to its place; and verily he who performs the horse sacrifice makes Prajāpati complete, and becomes complete himself: and this indeed is atonement for everything, the remedy for everything. With it the gods overcame all evil, they even overcame the killing of a brahmin with it; and he who performs the horse sacrifice overcomes all evil, overcomes the killing of a brahmin."

The eye swells up because it *wants* to fall out. And it wants to fall out because it wants to meet another eye—and reflect itself in it. There is no sense producing the world unless there is first of all an eye that looks at it and, in so doing, absorbs Prajāpati in itself, in the same way that Prajāpati absorbs the world in his gaze. At this point Prajāpati and his eye-become-horse are equal and opposite powers, that contain in them (in their own pupil) the image of the other. Paradoxically, however, the horse-born-from-the-eye is whole, complete, but that is not so for Prajāpati, the Progenitor. The wounded orbit of the eye that has fallen out remains open. Prajāpati now wanted to create an eye that would watch him, but he wanted it *within himself.* It was the first time that any being wanted to make himself a duality of Self and I. For this to happen, the horse-eye had to be reinstated to its original place. The gods would take care of that with the horse sacrifice. The reinstatement of a fragment (the eye) had to be done through the killing of a whole being (the horse).

There is an immense variety of Vedic rites, but all—without a single exception—converge in one action: offering something in the fire. Whether it is milk or sap from a plant or an animal (according to certain texts, also from a human being), the final action is the same. For the Vedic ritualists, killing has not just to do with blood. For them—and they have persistently repeated it, time and again—*every* offering is a killing. Even the most basic of rites, the *agnihotra*, the libation of milk in the fire, renews the gesture of Prajāpati, who originally, when nature did not yet exist, offered his own eye to satisfy the hunger of his son Agni: "Prajāpati found nothing that he could sacrifice [to Agni]. He took his own eye and offered it in oblation saying: 'Agni is the light, the light is Agni, *svāhā*.' " The eye is the most painful *pars pro toto* to be chosen by a suicidal god: Prajāpati. The procedures take on a whole variety of forms, the unshakable unity is to be found only in the act of offering in fire.

Prajāpati not only had the privilege of being abandoned by his children, the beings whom he had just "emanated (*asṛjata*)." But he also managed to have himself canceled from history for centuries. When his name resurfaced in the pages of late nineteenth-century Western Indologists, their tone was often disparaging. And what appeared most irksome of all were the stories of Prajāpati's *self-emptying* after the creation (it is strange that none of these scholars—often devoted Christians—recalled Paul's description of Christ's *kénōsis*: and yet the same word was used). Deussen found these stories "bizarre." But A. B. Keith went further: he spoke of "stupid myths" with gruff impatience ("the details of these stupid myths are wholly irrelevant"). The idea of a creator who, worn out after his work, turns himself into a horse and hides his face underground for a year, while from his head sprouts a tree, *aśvattha* (*Ficus religiosa*), which in turn arouses speculation about the relationship between the horse, *aśva*, and the tree . . . well, all of this must have seemed too much for certain austere Western scholars. Where, then, would we draw the line between the great civilizations (such as India) and those *primitive* peoples for whom, by definition, anything is permissible?

Creation, for Prajāpati, was not a single act, but a succession of acts. Continually obstructed, often unsuccessful. His exhausting series of creative actions is like the human attempt to put together a series of *right* gestures: the ritual. In ancient Rome, a ceremony could be repeated as many as thirty times if the gestures and words were not entirely *right*. For Prajāpati, the greatest obstacle was that of creating beings of a sexual nature. His first creatures could only take care of themselves. They appeared perfect, but soon disappeared (like President Schreber's "fleeting-improvised-men"). But what was missing? Nipples. Those orifices from which food could be transmitted to other creatures—thus establishing the chain of living creatures. We know very little about the very first attempts, but from various indications they would appear to have been short-lived, as if there was a lack of substance. So the moment arrived when Prajāpati said to himself: "'I want to create a firm foundation on which the creatures I will emanate shall establish themselves solidly rather than continuing to wander foolishly from place to place without any firm foundation.' He produced this earthly world, the intermediate world, and the world yonder." It wasn't just a matter of obtaining creatures who could last, but of providing them with firm land on which to rest. The earth, the intermediate space, the celestial world were to be that setting, that background.

Prajāpati's drama took place without witnesses and continued for a long time, before even the arrival of the gods. It was an autistic drama, which saw no respite nor the consolation of an external viewpoint that could empathize or condemn—it didn't matter which—but could at least play a part in what was happening. There was no way of distinguishing prodigies or disasters from mirages. And yet they were all that Prajāpati had. This had to be the source for what one day, after long reworking, would naïvely be called *reality.*

The ritualists soberly relate that: "While he [Prajāpati] was practicing *tapas*, lights rose up from those armpits of his: and those lights are those stars: there are as many stars as the pores of those armpits; and there are as many of those pores as the *muhūrta*, the hours, in a thousand years." That was Prajāpati's heroic period. He held his arms high, in the darkness, for that is the position of those who invoke and those who make offerings. That is the measure of everything: the measure of a Person with arms held high. Globes of light rose from his armpits and lodged themselves up in the vault of the sky. They designed patterns, gradually illuminating a scene that was still desolate and silent. The first change happened after a thousand years—a breeze. It was "that wind which, blowing, cleanses everything here; and that evil which it cleansed is this body." The wind that blew after a thousand years of heat and stagnation was certainly a relief for Prajāpati. But we are not told how long it lasted nor whether it succeeded in eliminating—and not simply purifying—evil.

Prajāpati, a lonely god, the source of all things, is certainly not an omnipotent god. But every action of his is fateful, for he is the founder—and immediately also threatens to be fateful for himself. Producing his firstborn son, Agni, from his mouth, he makes him become a mouth, forced to devour food. From then on, the earth would be a place where someone devours someone else, where fire incessantly consumes something. Agni's appearance, therefore, from the very first moment, coincides with Death.

The first drama had thus begun, without an audience. Agni is born—and Prajāpati, deep in thought, has doubts about his son. He seems to have difficulty in understanding that, if Agni can do nothing but devour, the only being he'll be able to devour is his father. Thus we see the first terrifying picture: "Agni turns to him with his mouth wide open." This gaping mouth of the son, ready to devour his father, is what underlies the whole huge sacrificial construct, as if there would never be sufficient complexity and intricacy to conceal the brutality of that image. What happens afterward is a strange, mysterious process: "His greatness escaped from him [Prajāpati]." The terror had produced in the god a separation, indeed the expulsion of a power, here called "greatness." What was this greatness? It was Speech, Vāc. A female being that lived in Prajāpati and whom terror had released from within him. And Vāc now stood before him like another being, who spoke to him.

Prajāpati knew it was essential to offer something to stop his son from devouring him. *But there was no substance.* Only after much rubbing of hands did Prajāpati manage to create something substantial: a liquid much like milk that was the sweat his terror had caused to pour from his skin. Offer it? Or not? At that moment a mighty voice resounded, outside of Prajāpati, and said: "Offer it!" Prajāpati obeyed—and it was then that the world's fate was decided. As he performed the offering, he realized it was he himself who had spoken: "That voice was his own (*sva*) greatness which had spoken (*āha*) to him." Prajāpati then gave out that sound: *svāhā*, the quintessential auspicious invocation that has accompanied countless offerings, up to today.

A violent, rushing scene, containing within it the first splitting of personality: if Speech had not been expelled from inside Prajāpati and had not spoken to him, nothing could have persuaded Prajāpati to perform the offering. On the other hand—and here the delicacy of the liturgist is exceptional—so long as Prajāpati, namely the one who had produced everything in the world, including the gods, remained in doubt, "he stayed firm on the better side," inasmuch as he had caused Speech, Vāc, to come out of himself. And his unknowing saved him.

The scene lets us see the first appearance of the offering as the ultimate means for self-defense. The moment is crucial, since the world from then on will be based on the offering—on an uninterrupted chain of offerings. But another irreversible, less apparent, event had occurred in that scene. And its consequences would be of no less importance. As soon as Prajāpati formed the word *svāhā* for the first time, it brought self-reflection into existence. *"Sva āha,"* "that which is his has spoken," implies the formation of two persons, of a first and a third person within the same mind, which is Prajāpati. All of what we call thought—but also the whole immense, nebulous, frayed extension of mental activity—established then the two poles that would support every instant of awareness. As soon as one recognizes one's own voice in a separate being, one creates a Double in continual dialogue with the one called I. And the I itself turns out not to be the ultimate, but only the penultimate foundation for what happens in the mind. Alongside an I there will always be a Self—and as well as the Self there will always be an I. That was the moment when they split apart and recognized each other. It was only because Prajāpati's I was gripped by uncertainty that he could then obey his Self, which spoke to him through Vāc. The ritualist doesn't want to tell us this explicitly, but this is the nub of the doctrine. Here it appears in its remotest, rawest, most inaccessible form. As well as its decisive form. If Prajāpati had not obeyed that voice, the world would not have managed to be born. The offering was the means, the only possible means for escaping from a deadly threat. A threat for the Progenitor, long before there were people. So people must imitate him performing the *agnihotra*, pouring milk into the fire, every morning and every evening.

Prajāpati was laid out and his body was one single pain. The gods approached to relieve his suffering—and perhaps to cure him. They were holding *havis*, offerings of vegetables, rice, barley, as well as milk, ghee, and cooked foods. With these offerings they wanted to treat Prajāpati's loosened joints. Especially between day and night, since Prajāpati was made up of time. Hence dawn and dusk. That was the moment to act. So they established the *agnihotra*, the libation to be performed each day at sunrise and sunset. Then they concentrated on the phases of the moon, which also make time and its junctures visible. Finally they thought about the seasons, their beginnings, discernible and certainly painful in the body of the Progenitor.

The ritual action inevitably took place during those dangerous transitional moments when the presence of time was apparent: entering daylight and leaving it. *Agnihotra* thus became the most important rite, a cell that unleashed a vast energy, which invaded the totality of time.

"Prajāpati conceived a passion for his daughter, who was either the Sky or Uṣas, the dawn:

"'Let me couple with her!' he thought and he coupled with her.

"This was certainly wrong in the eyes of the gods. 'He who acts thus toward his own daughter, our sister, [does wrong],' they thought.

"The gods then said to the god who is lord of the animals: 'He who acts thus toward his own daughter, our sister, surely does wrong. Pierce him!' Rudra, having taken aim, pierced him. Half of his seed fell to the ground. And thus it happened.

"In relation to this, the *ṛṣi* said: 'When the Father embraced his Daughter, coupling with her, he spilled his seed on the earth.' This became the chant called *āgnimāruta*: it shows how the gods made something emerge from that seed. When the anger of the gods subsided, they cured Prajāpati and removed that arrow; for Prajāpati is certainly the sacrifice.

"They said: 'Think how all of this may not be lost and how it may be a small portion of the offering itself.'

"They said: 'Take it to Bhaga, who is seated to the south: Bhaga will eat it as a first portion, so that it will be as if it were offered.' So they carried it to Bhaga, who was sitting to the south. Bhaga looked at it: it burnt out his eyes. And so it was. That is why they say: 'Bhaga is blind.'

"They said: 'It has not yet been appeased: take it to Pūṣan.' So they took it to Pūṣan. Pūṣan tasted it: it broke his teeth. So it was. That is why they say: 'Pūṣan is toothless.' And that is why, when they prepare a lump of boiled rice for Pūṣan, they prepare it with ground rice, as is done for someone toothless.

"They said: 'It has still not been appeased here: take it to Bṛhaspati.' So they took it to Bṛhaspati. Bṛhaspati hurried to Savitṛ, for Savitṛ is the Impeller. 'Give impulse to this for me,' he said. Savitṛ, as the one who gives impulse, therefore gave impulse, and having received impulse from Savitṛ, it did not harm him; that is why since then it is appeased. And this is the first portion."

The gods already exist, insofar as they are there on the scene, indeed they incite Rudra to shoot their father with his arrow to punish him for the wrong he is doing—certainly not the incest, since further on in the same *Śatapatha Brāhmaṇa*, having reached the story of Manu and the flood, we read that Manu coupled with his daughter and "through her he generated this line [of people], which is the line of Manu; and whatever blessing he invoked through her, everything was granted to him." On the other hand, it is from the very seed spilled on the ground by the wounded father, at the moment when he separates himself from his daughter, that the gods themselves will then emerge, starting with the Ādityas, the greater gods. And they are born because it is they themselves who stir and warm their father's puddle of seed, transforming it into a burning lake. It is as if the gods had to be born *a second time*—and this time from a guilty and interrupted sexual act: as if, in a certain way, they had provoked the violent scene so that they could be born in this new way, which people would one day regard as being quite unnatural.

The gods then experience two successive feelings: anger toward their father and a concern to look after him. The anger corresponds to the violence that is always present in the sacrifice. The healing of the wound, which is the sacrifice itself, would instead be the element of salvation implicit in the sacrifice. The two elements coexist in the tiny fragment of flesh torn from Prajāpati's body where he had been pierced by the arrow. That is the very flesh of the sacrifice, since "Prajāpati surely is this sacrifice," but the metal arrowhead is hurled from another world: Prajāpati is the hunter hunted, the sacrificer sacrificed. This is unbearable even for the gods. That scrap of flesh is like an intolerable ultrasound that overwhelms them. The sacrifice is more powerful than the gods.

But this much was needed to form the *first portion* of the sacrifice, the first fruit that contained within it the devastating power and meaning of the whole thing: "Now, when [the officiant] cuts the first portion (*prāśitra*), he cuts that which is wounded in the sacrifice, that which belongs to Rudra." Sacrifice is a wound—and the attempt to heal a wound. It is a guilty act—and an attempt to amend it. "That which is wounded in the sacrifice, that belongs to Rudra": the work of the brahmins, and of everyone else, is always a vain attempt to heal a wound that is inherent in the very act when existence emerges, not only prior to mankind, but prior to the gods. The gods, then, were only spectators and instigators. Prajāpati, Rudra, and Uṣas were actors. And the scene was a world before the world, a world that will never become identical to the world.

The cosmic balance is kept by two tiny entities of huge power: the grain of barley in the heart, of which the Upaniṣads will speak, capable of spreading beyond all worlds, and the *prāśitra*, the "first portion" to which the brahmin is entitled, that scrap of Prajāpati's flesh torn by the tip of Rudra's arrow. It is also said that it has to be as big as a grain of barley or a *pippal* (*Ficus religiosa*) berry.

There is something excessive, corrosive, about that part of Rudra. And yet it was necessarily the *first offering* of the sacrifice. Without that beginning, the whole work would have been futile. But that first offering was what is intractable, uncontrollable. The gods were already in despair. They were already yielding to a pure force that was overwhelming them. At that moment the supreme astuteness of the brahmin was apparent. For some time Bṛhaspati had been performing rites for the gods. They hadn't yet realized that this gave him wisdom greater than theirs. Bṛhaspati had the help of Savitṛ, the Impeller, but then he was the first and only one to let his mouth touch that tiny scrap of flesh. He ate it, he said, "with Agni's mouth": fire with fire. But he dared not chew it. Then he rinsed his mouth with water, in silence. The gods understood at once why the brahmins are indispensable. They understood that the brahmin is "the best physician" for the sacrifice. Without him it wouldn't have been possible to take a single step. For them, every possible task was a sacrifice, but the sacrifice could not be performed without the help of the being who dared to let his mouth touch the scrap of wounded flesh. In their purity, in the whiteness of their garments, the brahmins from then on carried with them the memory of the gesture by which the blood of the wound had for the first time disappeared into one of them, who had absorbed it without it destroying him. And from then on they would sometimes display a certain arrogance toward even the gods.

The brahmin is different from all others because his physical makeup is such that he can take poison that would kill anyone else. Śiva managed to drink the poison of the world in the same way, which then turned his neck blue. Although Śiva and the brahmins would show themselves to be fierce rivals in various circumstances, it was not enough to hide their basic complicity: that of being the only ones able to absorb the poison of the world. The brahmin does not act, except when he alone can act, as in the case of the *prāśitra*, which can be eaten only by him. He does not speak, except when he alone can speak—and this occurs if errors are made in carrying out the sacrifice. The brahmin then has three possible invocations—*bhūr*, *bhuvas*, *svar*—which operate as medicines applied to the loosened joints of the ceremony. Those words cannot be confused with the other words of the liturgy. The brahmin's speech "is filled with the limitless unspoken, *anirukta*, of which silence is the emblem." As bearer of the "limitless unspoken," the brahmin is the direct representative of Prajāpati. When Prajāpati disappears from mythology, and his place is taken by Brahmā, the brahmins will remain.

Otherwise, the brahmin silently watches what is happening. He is seated to the south, for that is the dangerous area, from which an attack may come at any time. From whom? When the gods were officiating, they were frightened of being ambushed by the anti-gods, the Asuras and the Rakṣas, the wicked demons. Men, on the other hand, must watch out for the "malevolent rival": generally speaking, the enemy, the adversary, the ever-present shadow in every liturgical celebration.

The brahmin is the "guardian" of the sacrifice. In this respect he is like the Saptarṣis, who keep watch over the earth from the seven stars high up in the Great Bear. His silence likens him to Prajāpati and keeps him away from the throng of the gods. All the brahmin's tasks are reduced to one: to heal the wound that is the sacrifice. It is his main concern that the wound be inflicted in the right way, and he thus oversees the actions and words of the other priests. Finally he reassembles the tattered sacrifice by cloaking it in silence.

There are many paradoxes in the relationship between Prajāpati and Mṛtyu, Death (a male being). Prajāpati was given a lifespan of a thousand years when he was born. And since a thousand indicates totality, it might be thought that this indicates a limitless period. But when Prajāpati devoted himself to producing creatures, when he was pregnant with them, Death appeared in the background and seized them one by one. The result of the duel was obvious: "While Prajāpati was producing living beings, Mṛtyu, Death, that evil, overpowered him." Prajāpati was therefore defeated and thwarted during the very process of creation. For a thousand years he had to practice *tapas* to overcome the evil of Death. But which years are being referred to? Are they the same thousand years that marked his lifespan? Prajāpati's life in that case would have been one long, relentless struggle fighting the—already established—supremacy of Death. The life of the one to whom creatures owe their lives would therefore have been most of all an attempt to respond to Death and to avoid his power.

With what means did Prajāpati create beings and worlds, in his repeated attempts? With "ardor," *tapas*, and with the "vision" of ritual. Connected acts: ardor stirs vision, vision heightens ardor. There is no trace of a *will*, of a supreme and abstract decision imposed from outside. Or rather: all will is a "desire," *kāma*, which is developed in ardor and emerges in vision. No will can be split away from its elaborate physiology.

Death is not an intrinsic part of divinity, but is an intrinsic part of creation (since successful creation is sexual: in the same way, in the natural world, death will appear together with sexual reproduction). There is no creation without death—and death dwells not only in creatures but also in their Progenitor. So the gods, children of Prajāpati, accused him of creating Death. They were sometimes obsessed by the notion that Prajāpati was himself Death. But, as always with children, they knew little of their father's past. The fact that he was Year, therefore Time, exposed him to continual disintegration. He could not avoid coexisting with those two inveterate parasites, whom he himself had created but who lurked within him and similarly went to lurk in every other created being.

The connection between evil and Mṛtyu, Death, as well as that between death and desire finally became clear when it was realized that "Death is hunger." This revelation summed up the bond between desire and evil, through Death. Hunger is a desire, but a desire that involves killing, for it makes something disappear. The inevitability of that Evil which is Death was thus found in the first desire to prolong and perpetuate life, which is hunger.

Men complained, as the gods had already done, that their father, Prajāpati, had also created Mṛtyu, Death. They always remembered that: "Above creatures, [Prajāpati] created Death as the one who devours them." But Prajāpati was also the first to feel a terror of Death, which dwelt within him, even though wrapped in something immortal. That part of him feared Death with the same intensity and violence that would later be experienced by humans. The first to escape into hiding—before Agni, Indra, or Śiva—was Prajāpati, who, to escape Death, became water and clay. The earth was first created as a refuge from the fear of Death. And yet Death was benevolent toward Prajāpati. It reassured the gods that it would not hurt him. It knew, in fact, that Prajāpati was protected by the immortal part of him. But Death went further: it invited the gods to seek out their lost father, it invited them to put him back together. The fire altar therefore not only saved Prajāpati from agony, but it put his dismembered body back together *at the instigation of Death.* An ambiguity that would never be dispelled. After all, Death, of all of his children, had been the first to ask where their father had disappeared. Meanwhile the gods had perhaps already begun to feel the indifference they would later show toward their father. But they set to work and, layer by layer, arranged the bricks of the altar of fire one upon the other.

It was Prajāpati who defeated Mṛtyu, Death, in an interminable and inconclusive duel ("they continued for many years without succeeding for long in being triumphant"). In the end Death took refuge in the women's hut. But elsewhere, in other stories (earlier? later? contemporaneous?), Prajāpati *is* Death. As such, he terrified not just men but also the gods: "The gods were frightened of this Prajāpati, the Year, Death, the Ender, fearing that he, through day and night, might bring an end to their lives." Various rites were invented to erase—or at least alleviate—the fear: the *agnihotra*, the New Moon and the Full Moon sacrifice, the animal sacrifice, the *soma* sacrifice. But they ended in a succession of failures: "In offering these sacrifices they did not attain immortality."

It was Prajāpati himself who taught the gods and people how to go further. He had seen them busy building a brick altar, but they continually got the size and shape wrong. Like a patient father, Prajāpati told them: "You do not arrange me in all my forms, you make me either too large or not large enough: and so you do not become immortal." But what should the right form be? That which would succeed in completely filling the cavity of time, by stacking as many bricks as there are hours in the year: 10,800. That was the number of bricks *lokampṛṇā*, "that fill the space." And this time the gods succeeded in becoming immortal.

Mṛtyu was worried. He thought that men who imitated the gods would one day have been able to become immortal themselves. So "Death said to the gods: 'Surely in this way all men will become immortal and what then will be my part?' They said: 'From now on no one will be immortal in their body: only when you have taken the body as your part will they who are to become immortal, either through knowledge or through sacred works, become immortal after being separated from their body.'" Even when all the calculations are right, even when the 10,800 + 360 + 36 bricks match Prajāpati's instructions one by one, the final interlocutor is always Death. He had no intention of relinquishing his part, simply because the gods had become masters in creating forms. If men had now succeeded, through stacking bricks, in becoming immortal, Death would have lost his purpose, like an idle shepherd abandoned by his flock. The gods saw an opportunity here for establishing another obstacle for mankind. They had no intention of watching their own hard-earned privileges being eroded. So a pact was sealed, over the heads of men, between Death and the gods. Yes, men would become immortal, but without their bodies. The mortal remains were surrendered to Death forever. And this is the point that has always made every promise of immortality doubtful. Men in fact preferred their ephemeral bodies to the splendors of the spirit. They distrusted disembodied souls, vaguely tiresome and sinister entities. So the agreement between the gods and Death was seen as a trick.

The celestial immortality granted by the gods to mankind was a reduced immortality. Over the course of time, the celestial body was destined to dwindle and disintegrate. There would be a renewed attraction toward the earth, like a powerful downward suction. Life would begin again in other forms. But death would also be repeated. In this way people ended up seeing their many lives essentially as a sequence of deaths. And they thought that celestial immortality was not enough to escape from repeated death. They had to free themselves from life itself.

Already in the Brāhmaṇas—and not just in the Upaniṣads—the real enemy is not Death, Mṛtyu, but "recurring death," *punarmṛtyu.* The obsession with the chain of deaths—and therefore of births—is not Buddhist, but Vedic. The Buddha formulated a radically different way of escaping from the chain. But the doctrine that had prevailed before him was no less bold.

What happened to Death after the exhausting duel with Prajāpati, after he had taken refuge in the women's hut? No one ever saw him leave, even to this day. That doesn't mean that Death disappeared. To see him, all we have to do is look up. The sunlight dazzles us in a diffused glow.

But within it we can make out a black circle. It stays, persistently, in the eye. It is a figure, a man in the Sun: that is Death. And it will always be there, for "Death does not die," protected all around it by the immortal. This is its challenging paradox: the endlessness of the shell also guarantees the endlessness of what it conceals—in this case, Death. When one celebrates the immortal, then at the same time—without knowing it—one celebrates Death, which is "within the immortal."

"Prajāpati was burning while he was creating the living beings here. From him, exhausted and overheated, Śrī, Splendor, came forth. She lay there, resplendent, glistening and trembling. The gods, seeing her so resplendent, glistening and trembling, fixed their minds upon her.

"They said to Prajāpati: 'Let us kill her and take all this away from her.' He said: 'This Śrī is a woman and people do not kill a woman, but instead take everything from her and leave her alive.'"

Śrī, the splendor of the world, was the first to be robbed. She was a radiant young girl, who quivered in solitude, while eager eyes stared at her. Their first thought was to kill her. Straightaway they told her father. Prajāpati was dying. He was thinking of his own death. Creation had torn him from inside. And now his children had come asking his approval because they wanted to kill his last, his youngest daughter. Prajāpati knew anger and fury would have no effect on the gods. They were too greedy. They were, after all, beings without qualities, they still had to conquer charm and power. They were little different than street robbers, who were bound to turn up sooner or later, though people didn't yet exist—not even bandits. So Prajāpati said: "Killing a woman is something you don't do. But robbing her of all she has, right down to the thinnest anklet, that's all right." The gods followed the advice of their father, whom they already scorned—after all, he was the only being who knew anything. The gods knew only that they were the world's *parvenus.* They left, persuaded by their father.

There were ten of them—nine male and one female. They surrounded Śrī and overpowered her. Each of her attackers had something particular they wanted to steal. Śrī was left abandoned, trembling more than ever. But she was still resplendent, since, for every shimmer of light they stripped from her, another appeared. And yet she was unaware of it. Desperate, humiliated, she too decided to ask her father's advice.

Prajāpati was still dying. Everything had happened as he had expected. Now he had to give his daughter the best advice. Śrī could never retrieve her superb ornaments by force. They would have laughed in her face. The kinder ones would have asked for something in exchange. So Prajāpati suggested the idea of sacrifice. In a desolate clearing she had to prepare a certain number of offerings. Modest, laid out on potsherds. But what else was there around? Brushwood and sand. Like a diligent girl in her home kitchen, Śrī prepared offerings to the ten beings who had attacked her. Humbly, she asked back various parts of herself, such as her Sovereignty and her Beautiful Form. The gods listened to her invocations in silence—and they admired her precision. Then, cautiously, they approached and accepted her poor offerings. Śrī could gradually dress herself once again in her glistening wrappings. But this did not deprive the gods of them. Each would continue to preside over those splendors—at least as long as other beings (humans, for example) continued, after Śrī, to present their offerings, ideally on a more lavish scale.

"In the beginning," *agre*, the sacrifice, was a stratagem suggested by Prajāpati to his daughter as a response to the greediness of the gods. Human beings did not play a part in it until very much later—and then only as imitators of those events. The act preceding every act was one of violence, of prolonged pain, whose consequences were to be remedied, mitigated. "What appears, at the very moment it appears, is ready for robbery," thought Prajāpati, who had been the first to suffer it himself, insofar as they had robbed him of himself without a second thought. The same had happened to his daughter. But, if the world wanted to exist, if it wanted to have a history and some kind of meaning, everything that had emerged from Prajāpati and had then disappeared like stolen goods had to be rediscovered and restored. A lengthy undertaking, as long as the world itself. For all to be well, other things—perhaps some water or a rice cake—had to be consumed, destroyed. The sacrifice was a task to be carried out every day. That was the task, the only task. Every action, every gesture would be a part of it. This was what Prajāpati thought, lying there abandoned.

What happened to Prajāpati at the end of his thousand lonely and agonizing years? The *Śatapatha Brāhmaṇa* notes: "In regard to this, it is said in the *Ṛgveda*: 'The labor that the gods look upon with favor is not in vain': for in truth, for him who knows this, there is no laboring in vain and the gods look with favor on his every action." This comment comes at the end of the account of the thousand years Prajāpati spent practicing *tapas*, while weighed down by Death. And it is an answer to the first doubt that worried the ritualists: is *tapas* effective? And will it always be effective? Prajāpati's *tapas* was enough to create the world: but will the *tapas* of men in some way inherit its effectiveness? The answer is in the verse of the *Ṛgveda*: there is nothing automatic in the effectiveness of *tapas*, which is labor, an exemplary striving, but an effort that may also be pointless, insofar as nothing is effective unless the gods look on it with favor. At the same time, the gods cannot but look favorably on the efforts of "he who knows thus": knowledge in some way compels the gods, forces them to look with everlasting favor on "he who knows thus." The gods therefore fear the knowledge of men. In the face of knowledge, they know they cannot resist.

When Prajāpati was dismembered, the sequence of the scenes that took place varies between different sacred texts. With Agni, the firstborn son, who immediately wanted to devour his father, there was the irrepressible tension of the drama between father and son, reduced to its basic elements. All around, everything was empty and desolate. With the other children, the Devas, once again the scenes were fraught with drama, yet with a streak of comedy—and of macabre humor, if only in the picture of the children running away, anxious and furtive, clutching some fragment of their father's body. But with the Gandharvas and the Apsaras, we enter phantasmagoria. Here, the painter called upon to celebrate the event might easily have been Fuseli. From Prajāpati's aching limbs, the Gandharvas and the Apsaras came out in pairs, like a corps de ballet, models for all Genies and Nymphs. They held each other by the waist—they were the first couples. Nor did they worry about stealing some fragment of their father's body. First of all, they were "perfume," *gandha*, and "beauteous form." This marked the beginning of erotica: "From then on, anyone who seeks out his companion desires sweet perfume and beauteous form."

But the dying father was watching them and was already thinking how to capture them, how to reabsorb them into his own body, from which they had come. But this time there was no fight, nor even any bargaining, as had been the case with Agni, with the Devas, with the Asuras. This time everything took place as if in a Busby Berkeley routine. Prajāpati chose encirclement. And the weapon used for encircling Genies and Nymphs would be the chariot, soon to be packed, teeming, with those fickle, reckless beings. In turn, "this chariot is the yonder sun." And in its light the soft bodies of the Apsaras became moths. In this way Prajāpati reclaimed those countless demonic beings who had left him, bound together in pairs.

After creating living beings, Prajāpati had witnessed a cruel spectacle: "Varuṇa captured them [with his noose]; and, once captured by Varuṇa, they swelled up." These hydropics had to be cured with *varuṇapraghāsa* oblations, one of which involved sprinkling *karīra* berries (from the caper family) on certain dishes of curded milk: "Then follows a cake on a potsherd for Ka; for, by that cake on a potsherd for Ka, Prajāpati granted happiness (*ka*) to the creatures, and so now the sacrificer grants happiness to the creatures by that cake on a potsherd. This is the reason there is a cake on a potsherd for Ka." That cake on a potsherd served to indicate something that might otherwise have been overlooked. People had already realized that the mystery of identity didn't lie in the gods, but in their Progenitor: Prajāpati. But now, beyond that name, which was more an appellative, another name was discovered, which was an interrogative pronoun: Ka, *Who*? And beyond that? No other names were known. This was the indefinite, limitless outpouring that was the very nature of Prajāpati. A nature that made it necessary to move one step further than the gods. But in what direction? Little was known about Prajāpati, as regards his boundless immensity. And, of that little, what stood out was the suffering, the long torment of his dismembered and ulcerated body. What else? Pure desire—or desire developed in arduous, enervating *tapas*. He was thus to be approached with caution, as when someone is in pain. And here the unexpected was revealed: Ka also means *happiness*. So *karīra* berries were sprinkled on curds: to confer happiness on living creatures. This was surprising enough. He who was the image of agony became the path to happiness. But what was happiness? Prajāpati's children, for example, seemed to know only hunger or flight. Yet now they discovered that concealed in their father was something else, the syllable *ka* in the *karīra* plant. How can one reach it? Prajāpati once answered the question with the precision of a surveyor: "However much you offer, that is my happiness." Happiness appeared to be connected, firmly bound up with the offering. And the offering was first that brick construction in which Prajāpati's body was reassembled. In fact: "Inasmuch as for him there was happiness (*ka*) in what was offered (*iṣṭa*), therefore they are bricks (*iṣṭakā*)." The word describing the bricks of the fire altar thus encapsulated within itself, with the most powerful link, that of one syllable with the next, the *offering* (*iṣṭi*) and *happiness* (*ka*). Thereby meaning "happiness in the offering." The father's phrase was a surprise that became etched on the memory of his children. From then onward they busied themselves, as never before, around the fire altar; they learned to lay out a composition of *happy bricks*, for they stubbornly sought to reassemble the lost identity of their father. Only in that way would they restore happiness to him, only in that way would happiness have descended upon them, through that cake laid out on a potsherd.

But the linguistic speculation of the ritualists is relentless. A further meaning emerges in the *Chāndogya Upaniṣad.* And it comes from the highest authority, the fires that the student Upakosala had tended for twelve years while he was a novice at the house of Satyakāma Jābāla. The master had taken leave from his disciples, all except Upakosala, who pined and refused to eat. The master's wife asked him why and Upakosala replied: "In this person there are many desires. I am full of illness. I will not eat." It was then that the fires decided to intervene. They were thankful to the pupil who had carefully tended them. They wanted to explain to him, in the fewest words, something essential. They said: "*Brahman* is breath, *brahman* is happiness (*ka*), *brahman* is space (*kha*)." The pupil remained puzzled. He said: "I know that *brahman* is breath. But I do not know what are *ka* and *kha.*" The fires answered: "What is *ka* is *kha*, what is *kha* is *ka.*" The text adds: "They therefore explained to him breath and space." From linguistic commentaries (*Bṛhaddevatā* and *Nirukta*) we learn that Ka was also *kāma*, "desire," and *sukha*, "happiness." But now *kha*, "space," was also found in the same name. And what this was is explained at a crucial point in the *Bṛhadāraṇyaka Upaniṣad*: "*Brahman* is *kha*, space; space is primordial, space is windswept."

Etymologists and lexicographers help us approach certain telling details that the ritualists do not always make clear. Behind the dismembered body of Prajāpati, who "has run the whole race" and has ended up falling on his own eye, from which food flowed forth as if it were tears ("From him, thus fallen, food flowed forth: it was from his eye on which he lay that the food flowed"), behind his indistinct figure from whom his son Indra soon sought to take away greatness and splendor, one began to see a boundless extension of desire, over and above which was a happiness that came before all existence, in a space that came before everything and was able to contain everything, in a perpetual circulation of winds. And this was Ka.

Ka, *kha*: written differently, sounding almost the same, those two syllables, put together, had to heal all sadness. Why? In *ka*, Prajāpati loomed this time only in the shadows, whereas the meaning of "happiness," *sukha*, was clearly apparent. Happiness spread out into space (*kha*)—and space allowed happiness to breathe. On another occasion, another master explained to Upakosala the simple opening of space called *kha* (which also means "orifice," "wound," "zero").

But how does *brahman* appear in *kha*, in "open space"? In the form of an hourglass. Its upper part extends out into the totality of outer space. Its neck narrows to a point that is almost imperceptible, in a minuscule cavity in the heart of each person. Behind it there opens up an immensity equivalent to that of the outside world. This is the lower part of the hourglass. The grain of mustard, of which the Upaniṣads (and the Gospels) speak, passes through the neck and extends out into the invisible. One passage in the *Chāndogya Upaniṣad* states all this (a revelation that shatters all previous thinking) in the quietest, most direct way, as in a calm, persuasive conversation: "That which is called *brahman* is this space, *ākāśa*, which is outside man. This space which is outside man is the same as the one within man. And this space within man is the same as that inside the heart. It is what is full, unchangeable." The aura that surrounds people is the impression that allows us to detect the presence of the lower part of the hourglass. For the German romantics, inner exploration was a relentless search for the neck of the hourglass, without the assistance of rituals and fires.

Arka: a word belonging to a secret language, about which we know little. It was familiar to Armand Minard, the most austere priest of the

Śatapatha Brāhmaṇa, who dedicated his life's work to a word-by-word commentary on it, with the perverse satisfaction of making it even more inaccessible: "*arká-*: ray (flash of lightning, flame, fire, sun),—plant whose flamed leaves carry the offering to Rudra in his lustral century (*śatarudriya*),—laud, hymn (= *uktha*), which is perhaps the first meaning (Ren. JAs 1939 344 n. 1). This polysemy opens up endless speculations (thus X 6 2 5-10). And the word (almost: **525 a**) always, as here (and **363**), taken in two or more senses." These words are a comment on the *Śatapatha Brāhmaṇa*, 10, 3, 4, 3 ("Do you know the *arka*? So, may your Lordship deign to teach it to us") and they make us feel the rapturous shiver of Minard's philology. In contrast, Stella Kramrisch has another style: "*Arka* is anything that radiates. It is ray, splendor, and lightning. It is the song."

The passage Minard comments on is a provocative example of a series of riddles, where the human body appears behind the description of *arka* as a flower, *Calotropis gigantea* ("Do you know the flowers of the *arka*? With this he meant the eyes"—and so forth for the other organs), and behind the *arka* can be seen the profile of Agni, up to the last comparison: "He who regards Agni as *arka* and as man, in his body this Agni, the *arka*, will be built up through the knowledge that 'I here am Agni, the *arka*.'" But also to be found in *arka* were Ka as well as *ka*, "happiness." Immediately after the opening of the *Bṛhadāraṇyaka Upaniṣad*—an overwhelming procession of divinities led by the young girl called Dawn, Uṣas, who reveals herself to be "the head of the sacrificial horse"—we move on to *arka*: "In the beginning there was nothing here below. Everything was wrapped in Death [Mṛtyu], in hunger, for hunger is Death. He [Mṛtyu] had this thought: 'Let me have a Self.' So he began to pray. And, while he was praying, waters were generated. He said: 'While I was praying [*arc-*] happiness came to me [*ka*; this according to Senart, but *ka* also means 'water,' and so Olivelle translates the passage: 'While I was occupied in a liturgical recital, water poured forth from me'].' This is where the name *arka* comes from. Happiness goes to the one who knows thus why *arka* is called *arka* [Olivelle is in difficulty here, so that he has to translate as follows: 'Water pours forth from the one who knows thus']."

But the story carries on: "The froth of the waters solidified and was land. On the land he [Mṛtyu] toiled. When he was exhausted and hot, the essence of his brilliance became fire." After the waters and the land, other parts of the world were formed: the sun, the wind. It was the breath of life that broke down into pieces. Death then wished: "Let me give birth to a second Self. Death, which is hunger, coupled mentally (*manasā*) in coitus (*mithunam*) with Speech, Vāc. That which was the seed became the Year." Speech, Vāc, as a daughter with whom to have immediate intercourse, then the appearance of Time (Year): we have already come across this in the *Śatapatha Brāhmaṇa*, the long text of which the *Bṛhadāraṇyaka Upaniṣad* forms the final part. There, however, it was all about Prajāpati; here it is Mṛtyu, Death, who continues to behave like Prajāpati. He practices *tapas*, becomes exhausted, dismembered. "The breaths: splendor, energy" flee from his body. His body swells, as also happens in the stories about Prajāpati. It is a carcass, but his mind is still in it. Mṛtyu then decided to make another body for himself. He formulated the same words in his mind as he had spoken at the beginning: "Let me have a Self." He then became a horse, *aśva*, since he had "swollen," *aśvat.* And once Mṛtyu has swollen up in the horse, he can sacrifice it, since "what was swollen had become fit for sacrifice (*medhya*)." This is the origin of the "horse sacrifice," *aśvamedha.* Here we sense the action of the same coded, lightning process that operated for the word *arka.* The text, in fact, immediately points it out: "They are two, *arka* and *aśvamedha*, but there is one single divinity, which is Mṛtyu." Throughout, up to the institution of the *aśvamedha*, which is the greatest of all sacrifices, Mṛtyu and Prajāpati have each followed in the footsteps of the other, like two doubles. But only now, in the Upaniṣad of the Forest, is the piercing obsession of the Vedic ritualists given form, which in the Brāhmaṇas appears only fleetingly: "recurring death," *punarmṛtyu*, the greatest of all ills that can be suffered. And the power that makes it possible to escape it is Mṛtyu, Death, itself: "He [who knows this] avoids recurring death, death cannot reach him, Mṛtyu becomes his Self, he who knows thus becomes one of these divinities."

How was this astonishing reversal reached, through which Death became liberation from death? It was a process with various stages. In the beginning, "Prajāpati created living creatures: from upward breaths he produced the gods, from downward breaths mortals. And, over living creatures, he created Death as the one who devours them." Farther on, the same *kāṇḍa* of the *Śatapatha Brāhmaṇa* speaks of Prajāpati who, "having created living things, felt emptied and was frightened of Death." Later, it says: "Death, which is evil (*pāpmā mṛtyuḥ*)" overcame Prajāpati while he was creating. The farther we venture in the text, the closer Mṛtyu comes to Prajāpati and surrounds him: an impending presence, finally a dueling presence. When we reach the *Bṛhadāraṇyaka Upaniṣad*, the situation is reversed: there is no more mention of Prajāpati, it is now Mṛtyu—and it is Death who now submits to all the tests, to all the labors faced by Prajāpati. Does this mean the Upaniṣad radically changes viewpoint? Definitely not. Everything had already been established. Back in the tenth *kāṇḍa* of the *Śatapatha Brāhmaṇa* we read that Prajāpati is "the Year, Death, the Ender."

At the age of eight, the young brahmin came before the master and said: "I am here to become a pupil." The master then asked him: "*Ka* (Who, What) is your name?" The question included the answer: "*Ka* is your name." At that moment the pupil came under the shadow of Prajāpati, taking even his name: "Thus he makes him one belonging to Prajāpati and initiates him." Everything else was a consequence. The master took his pupil's right hand and said: "You are a disciple of Indra. Agni is your master." Powerful divinities, who cast a shadow. And in that shadow were Prajāpati and the pupil himself, who was about to undergo a long transformation. It would last twelve years.

"Prajāpati is truly that sacrifice which is performed here; and from which these creatures are born: and likewise they are born again today." These clear-cut words are found three times within a few pages. They sound like a warning, an opening chord. They remind us that Prajāpati's theology is above all a liturgy. It is not just a matter of reconstructing Prajāpati's original actions in which living beings were created. It is now a matter of carrying out corresponding actions so that living beings continue to be produced. Prajāpati's action is uninterrupted and perpetual. It is the action that is carried out in the mind, in every mind, whether it knows it or not, when forms break away from its inarticulate and borderless dominion—forms that have an outline and stand out among everything else.

For the Vedic seers, cosmogony was not the traditional tale of primordial times, but a literary genre that allowed for an indefinite number of variants. And all were compatible—*iva*, "so to speak." Or at least, all converged on one ever-present point—the sacrifice. Sacrifice was the breath of the multiple cosmogonies: stories of a specific sacrifice that at the same time were the foundation of the sacrifice. There are many different versions in one and the same work about what originally happened to Prajāpati. And each new version is meant to explain some detail about the world as it is. If the stories about Prajāpati were not so richly varied, the world would be poorer, less vital, less capable of metamorphosis. The more variegated the origin, the denser and more impenetrable is the texture of everything. It is generally described as "the three worlds": the sky, the earth, and atmospheric space. All that happens takes place between these three layers of reality. And this would be quite enough to complicate the picture, since the relationships between the three levels are extremely dense.

But the ritualist is a man of doubt. For every movement he performs, he is goaded by a question: is this *the* gesture to perform? Will this gesture cover the whole of reality? Or will there still be a further reality that this gesture cannot touch? Hence, at one point, the ritualist refers to a *fourth world.* If this world existed, it would be a disturbing revelation, since everything done up to that point had involved only three worlds. Isn't the mere existence of the fourth enough to frustrate such a vision? And won't perhaps the fourth world feel outraged about never having been taken into consideration? Yet "uncertain it is whether the fourth world exists." An irresolvable doubt as to the very existence of an entire world is therefore acknowledged. What should be done? The ritualist is used to opening up a way—perhaps a temporary one—through this maze. If the existence of the fourth world is uncertain, then "uncertain is also what is done in silence." A further movement must then be added to the movements carried out while reciting a formula, which is done in silence. That gesture will be the recognition that the fourth world *might* exist. That is enough to go further, on toward other gestures. But that silent doubt lingers behind all speculation. Until all of a sudden, from one side, and with a nonchalance typical of the esoteric, a sentence appears with the long-awaited answer: "Prajāpati is the fourth world, beside and beyond these three." The answers to riddles have a peculiar feature: they become riddles themselves, and even more far-reaching. This is the case here. If Prajāpati is the "fourth world"—and the existence of the fourth world is "uncertain"—the existence of

Prajāpati himself would be uncertain. If we trace back to the one who created living beings, we do not encounter something more sure and solid, but something whose existence we can indeed legitimately put in doubt, something we can nevertheless ignore without this upsetting in any way the workings of everything, of those "three worlds" with which we are constantly involved. The theological daring of the ritualists is dazzling: implicit in the mystery is its capacity to instill doubt as to its own existence, the ability to allow everything to exist without having to refer to the mystery itself. Nothing protects a mystery better than the denial of its very existence.

Prajāpati: the background noise of existence, the steady hum that goes before every sound graph, the silence behind which we perceive the workings of a mind that is *the* mind. It is the *id* of what happens, a fifth column that spies on and sustains every event.

V

THEY WHO SAW THE HYMNS

The hymns of the *Ṛgveda* were said to have been *seen* by the *ṛṣis*. The *ṛṣis* may therefore be described as "seers." They saw the hymns in the same way as we see a tree or a river. They were the most disconcerting, least easily explainable beings in the Vedic cosmos. Chief among them were the Saptarṣis, the Seven who lived in the stars of the Great Bear, who have some affinity with the Seven Greek Sages, with the Islamic *abdāls*, and with the Seven Akkadian Apkallus of the Apsu. But something in the very nature of the *ṛṣis* was an epistemological scandal: they alone were allowed to belong to the unmanifest and at the same time take part in the events of everyday life, which they secretly ruled.

And this itself was alarming: that a metaphysical category, the *asat*, the "unmanifest," was a category of beings that had a name. Hermann Oldenberg felt an immediate need to clear away any inappropriate comparisons: "This non-being was of quite a different kind to Parmenides' non-being—and there is very little here of his rigor in discussing with passionate seriousness the non-being of the non-existent." Oldenberg's embarrassment was justified and we can still detect the pride of someone who had been educated following the nineteenth-century idea of classicism. With the *ṛṣis*, in fact, one has to go in quite another direction. Only the starting point is the same: the *asat* which Oldenberg translates as "non-being." Now, if *asat* refers to the *ṛṣis*, the nonbeing would refer to a category of beings. These, in turn, would correspond with the "vital breaths," *prāṇas*—and here we plunge into the realm of physiology. Moreover, nonbeing acts through the practice of *tapas*, the "ardor" that overheats consciousness. Too many palpable elements are attributed to this nonbeing. And above all: too many elements that then continue to appear and operate in the existent, in whatever exists. A network of cracks thus forms in it, as if to suggest that not everything that appears in the existent belongs to the existent. These metaphysical passages were not congenial to the West. Oldenberg could barely restrain his indignation: "The non-being starts to think, to act so readily, in spite of any *Cogito ergo sum*, like an ascetic preparing to perform some magic trick." Oldenberg thought he was expressing a paradox, or even an absurdity. But his words could have been interpreted as a plain, accurate description. The *ṛṣis* watched him from high up in their stars, with that exasperating seriousness of theirs, more derisive even than sarcasm.

The Vedic seers saw the hymns of the *Ṛgveda* in much the same way that others among them *found* the rites that were later to be celebrated and studied. Knowledge was an encounter with something preexisting, sight of which the gods now and then allowed. They were not interested in educating and guiding the human race, which they looked upon with mixed feelings, sometimes benevolent sometimes hostile, so that "from time to time, following the whim of the moment, the celestial power communicates to mankind first one, then another fragment of inestimable knowledge" (Oldenberg again).

How, though, was this knowledge deposited and arranged? The metrics are too perfect, the vocabulary too varied, the overall composition too complex, so it must be presumed that the *Ṛgveda*—the concrete product of that knowledge—was developed over a long period that began before even the descent into India, in other regions toward the northwest, and in other climates. Traces of these events, enigmatic as always, can be spotted in certain hymns. The most dazzling ancient poetry is already imitating an archaic style, as if the earliest Greek statuary were that of the Master of Olympia. When it first came to us, passed down through thousands of memories, unaltered, the word of the *ṛṣis* seemed already to be a "tributary of a long, learned tradition." And the *Ṛgveda* was already a *saṃhitā*, a "collection," an anthology that "mixes together an older, less differentiated, mass that heads of clans or schools would have drawn from at different moments."

When something (or someone) is created, produced, emanated, composed—especially at the beginning of the world—the Vedic texts repeat countless times that this happened through *tapas*, "ardor." But what is *tapas*? Many Indologists have avoided the question, having been led astray by the Christianizing translations ("asceticism," "penance," "mortification") that began with the first nineteenth-century editions (and can still be found today). After all, it is well-known that ascetics, penitents, and disciples practicing self-mortification are to be found in India more than anywhere else. They, it is said, are the latest practitioners of *tapas*. And the question would seem to be resolved with a general reference to spirituality.

Now *tapas* is certainly a form of asceticism in the original sense of "exercise," but it is a very particular exercise that implies the developing of heat. *Tapas* is akin to the Latin word *tepor*—and indicates fervor, ardor. Those who practice *tapas* could be described as "ardent." They generate a heat that can become a devastating blaze. This is what happened with various *ṛṣis* who every so often shook the world.

The *ṛṣis* are not gods, they are not demons, they are not men. But they often appear earlier than the gods, indeed earlier than the being from which the gods had emanated; they often display demonic powers; they often move about like people among people. The Vedic texts feign indifference toward these incompatibilities, as if they didn't recognize them, perhaps because the hymns of the *Ṛgveda* appear to be composed by the *ṛṣis* themselves. Elsewhere, in other places and periods, we search in vain for figures that combine their characteristics, all converging into one: incandescence of mind. With this the *ṛṣis* were capable of attacking all other beings, whether gods, men, or animals.

The *ṛṣis* reached an unattainable level of knowledge not just because they thought certain thoughts but because they *burned*. Ardor comes before thought. Thoughts are given off like steam from a boiling liquid. While the *ṛṣis* were sitting, motionless, and contemplating what was happening in the world, whirling inside them was a scorching spiral that would one day break off to become the hymns of the *Ṛgveda* or the "great sayings," *mahāvākya*, of the Upaniṣads.

There is nothing more misleading than to imagine the *ṛṣis*, and above all the Seven Seers, as calm and affable beings, detached from the world's vicissitudes. On the contrary, if the world continues on its course, it is primarily due to the immense reserves of *tapas* that the Seven Seers channel, moment by moment, into the veins of the universe. But this *tapas* can occasionally be directed against the world itself—and wreak havoc. Nor can it be said that the incandescent mass of ardor lets itself be steered by the *ṛṣis*. When Vasiṣṭha, one of the Seven Seers, wishes to kill himself in despair over the death of his children, his *tapas* prevents him from doing so. He threw himself off a very high cliff, only to land on a vast lotus, as if on a soft bed. His *tapas* was too powerful to allow its bearer to kill himself.

The story of the relationship between the Seven Seers and their consorts, the Pleiades, dates back to the earliest times, and is never properly explained. The Saptarṣis, in their celestial residences, signaled the north with the Pole Star. If they had once also been called "bears," *ṛkṣa*, there was presumably something in their appearance that resembled those animals, in the same way that we see the Seven Apkallus of Sumer, the "Holy Carps," covered in fish scales. The Saptarṣis were three pairs of twins, plus a "seventh single-born." They were loved and respected by their consorts but separated from them by a vast expanse of sky, since the Pleiades lie to the east. So Agni, their first lover, crept in. He was the first to seduce the lonely women neglected by their husbands. With his flames he began licking the toes of the wives of the *ṛṣis*, while they were gathered around the fire. In the end he became the lover of each of them. Only the stern Arundhatī refused him. Thus one day, when the Pleiades went down to the waters of a reed bed to meet the runaway Agni, it was an old lover in difficulty they found.

When it came to deciding on setting up the fires, the ritualists pondered: should the protection of the Pleiades be refused, since they were adulterers, or sought for the same reason, since they betrayed the *ṛṣis* with Agni? The alternative was this: either to place the fires under the Pleiades, seeking in some way to attract their complicit gaze, or keep away from them, as they were an example of adultery—or at least, of the couple's distance (and at this point the worried ritualist noted "it is a misfortune not to have intercourse [with one's wife]"). The dilemma raised once again a delicate, recurring question. The *ṛṣis* are sages with immense power, formidable anger, often contemptuous and stern even toward the gods. But they are unable to ensure the fidelity of their wives. The Pleiades, who were ravishing and also severe, couldn't resist the enticements of a god. This was what happened with Agni, their long-term lover. But the most scandalous event was Śiva's visit to the Cedar Forest, when they followed him dancing, in rapture. The story itself took place against a background of cruel revenge. The *ṛṣis* were above all the husbands chosen by Dakṣa for his daughters. And Śiva was he who had taken Satī, Dakṣa's favorite daughter, against his will. This was the beginning of the conflict that ended with the burning of Satī's body. And Śiva, through the *ṛṣis*, now mocked those in the world who would continue to represent Dakṣa's authority, his priestly power.

Tracing these stories back to their origins within the divine, they were a new expression, in erotic terms, of the conflict between Brahmā and Śiva, as a result of which Śiva had cut off Brahmā's fifth head and had then spent a long time wandering about dressed as a beggar, with the god's skull fastened to his hand as a bowl. But what had caused the conflict between Brahmā and Śiva? That is highly unclear, little can be gleaned about it. While Brahmā is the source of order and priestly authority, Śiva is the perpetual certainty that this order will eventually break down, that it will not withstand the impact of a force that exists beyond ritual. Order thus falls apart over the course of history. And this is why the Saptarṣis's wives were powerless to resist Agni's persistent, passionate courtship.

The Vedic seers regarded the passage of the mind from one thought to the next, and its ever deeper immersion into the same thought, as the model for every journey. To speak about oceans, mountains, and skies they had no need for daring explorations. They could remain motionless beside their belongings, during a pause in their migrations. The result would be the same. Traveling, they thought, was an essentially invisible activity. And, if anything, it takes its form in a series of liturgical actions. So in the kindling rituals they were above all concerned with kindling the mind, the only steed capable of carrying them to the gods. And they murmured: "Yes, that which carries to the gods is the mind."

The activity that the whole of creation depends on takes place in mind alone. But it is of a kind that immediately demonstrates the effectiveness of the mind over what lies outside it. And, for the mind, the effects of what lies outside it are within the body itself. An invisible combustion is thus produced, a gradual heat, up to the ardor achieved through the operation of the mind. It is *tapas*, well known to Siberian shamans, ignored or banished in Western thought. Ubiquitous and supreme, rarely are its powers defined, because they are too obvious. But the ritualist sometimes consents to explain them: "In truth, with *tapas* they conquer the world." What affects the world, what assails it is *tapas*, the inner ardor of the mind. Without it, all gestures, all words are useless. *Tapas* is the flame that passes covertly or overtly through everything. Sacrifice is the occasion for which those two conditions of ardor—visible in fire, invisible in the officiant—meet and combine.

This is the greatest approximation allowed, if we want to describe the most elusive yet inevitable of facts: the feeling of being alive. Reduced to its proprioceptive as well as its thermodynamic essence, it is a sensation of something alight, something that burns on a slow and continual flame. All other characteristics are added and superimposed on this, which is their assumption and support. The word *extinction*, *nirvāṇa*, taught by the Buddha, had to appear as the negation par excellence of what was presented as life itself. Sacrifice, as an act of burning something, therefore had to appear as the most exact visible equivalent of the state which is the basis of life itself.

The *ṛṣis* had the task of keeping and controlling world order. But they also had another function, which threatened to disrupt world order at any moment. Stories were based around the *ṛṣis.* In the interminable tangle of dealings between men and gods, at every turn there was a *ṛṣi*'s curse, or his "boon," *vara.* Great epic stories such as the *Mahābhārata* or the *Rāmāyaṇa*, which resemble immense luxuriant trees, would one day be presented as the work of a *ṛṣi*, Vyāsa or Vālmīki. But, much earlier, the framework of the stories they retold had been based on the acts of other *ṛṣis*, among whom there may have been the person who would one day become author of the poem that told these stories. This is what happened with Vyāsa and the *Mahābhārata*—as if Homer had been one of the Greek heroes who fought under the walls of Troy.

There are no archaeological remains of Vedic kingdoms, but the *Ṛgveda* describes various conflicts and battles. They culminated in the "Battle of the Ten Kings," where the Bharatas, under their chieftain Sudās and armed with axes, managed to defeat a coalition of ten warlords—Āryas and non-Āryas—who were surrounding them. So the Bharatas won, and it is the name by which India is still known today. Or this, at least, is what we may infer, since the hymns never recount a sequence of events, but allude to them, addressing gods and men who already knew what had happened. What were the salient features of the war? In describing the enemies of the Bharatas, the text declares only that they were "without sacrifices (*áyajyavaḥ*)." That was quite enough. It was taken for granted that every war is a war of religion. As for the Bharatas themselves, they were supported by both Indra and Varuṇa, not always friendly divinities. How had this miracle been possible? Thanks to the work of a seer, the *ṛṣi* Vasiṣṭha, who had arranged that alliance and had taken over as chaplain to the Bharatas, ousting another seer, Viśvāmitra, who had immediately crossed over to the enemy line. After that, they had been in perpetual conflict. They argued sitting on opposite banks of the Sarasvatī—and their voices traveled across the roaring flow of the waters. Even when Vasiṣṭha transformed Viśvāmitra into a heron—and Viśvāmitra in turn transformed Vasiṣṭha into a crane—they continued fighting in the air, pecking furiously with their beaks. They detested each other for deep religious reasons, "totally committed to attachment or aversion, always full of desire and hatred."

Viśvāmitra had once threatened to destroy the three worlds, but Vasiṣṭha relied on his secret: he was the only *ṛṣi* to have seen Indra "face to face." And when the hymns mention the battles, they do not pause to describe the kings, the warriors, and their exploits, but rather the gods and *ṛṣis*, as if the decisive conflicts could take place only between them. If Sudās turned out to be a great ruler in the end, it was not so much because he had defeated the Ten Kings, but because Vasiṣṭha had once taught him how to perform a particular type of *soma* sacrifice. Sudās was grateful. He gave Vasiṣṭha two hundred cows and two chariots, as well as women, jewels, and four horses.

VI

THE ADVENTURES OF MIND AND SPEECH

Manas, "mind" (later *mens* in Latin), "thought." But above all the pure fact of being conscious, awake. For the Vedic people, everything came from consciousness, in the sense of pure awareness devoid of any other attribute. They invoked it delicately, as "the divine one that comes forward from afar when we awake and falls back when we slumber." Likewise "she through whom the seers, able creators, operate in the sacrifice and in the rites." They said it was an "unprecedented wonder, dwelling in living beings." They recognized in it "what envelops all that was, is and shall be." They called it "stable in the heart and yet moveable, infinitely fast." The unattainable speed of the mind: here it was named, evoked, adored perhaps for the first time. Finally the much-repeated wish: "May that which it [the mind] conceives be propitious for me." The mind is an external power, equal to the gods and superior to the gods, which conceives in solitude and can, through its grace, reverberate in the mind of every living being. And the first, the highest wish, is that this might take place "propitiously." *Manas* would then act like "a good charioteer," it would become the one "who powerfully guides his men like steeds, by the reins."

Absolutism of the mind, a prerequisite of Vedic thought, certainly doesn't mean omnipotence of the mind, as if supremely magical powers were attributed to it. If that were the case, the result would have in the end been a crude construction, equivalent—in reverse—to one where such sovereign powers were attributed to an entity called "matter."

To appreciate the power peculiar to the mind, one has to go back to a most mysterious state, that in which "there was no unmanifest (*asat*) and there was no manifest (*sat*)." The same words are found in a passage of the *Śatapatha Brāhmaṇa* with the addition of an *iva*, "so to speak," which increases the uncertainty and mystery. And with a clarification from which everything else follows: "At that time there was only this mind (*manas*)." What then is mind? Of all that exists, it is the only element that already existed before there were the manifest and the unmanifest. A sort of shell in which everything else *is*, or *is not.* Mind is the only element *from which there is no way out.* Whatever happens or has happened, mind was already there. Mind is the air in which consciousness breathes. So consciousness was there before the existence of something that could have consciousness. The guardians come before what they must guard. The *ṛṣis* were there before the world.

The fact that *manas* was there before everything became separated between manifest and unmanifest gives the mind an ontological privilege over every other element. The world may even be infinite, but it will not succeed in canceling out the entity that has always watched over it. There again, the picture of a cosmos totally devoid of consciousness is something that many assume but no one has ever succeeded in portraying. And yet that would be the most radical positivist view: wasn't the mind supposed to be an *epiphenomenon*? If consciousness has to be something that belongs only to the *higher functions* (as they used to be called), what happened before those functions were formed? A sort of unsullied naturalness must have existed. But natural in relation to what? And what if consciousness is something that *emerges* at some point, like birds and insects, as evolutionism—that sturdy branch sprouting from the tree of positivism—would have it? What then would earlier history have been? A long story of massacres between automatons, assuming we can be sure that automatons have no consciousness.

There again, the fact of mind being present even before the separation between manifest and unmanifest instills a peculiar weakness in it. And the same would be true for the other hypothesis, that the mind is indeed born from the unmanifest: "That unmanifest, which was alone, then became mind, saying: I want to be." It is true that others would never have given it such preeminence, since *manas* is nevertheless the first being to be emitted from nonexistence, but at the same time its proximity to the beginning still makes the mind doubt its own existence. On the one hand, *manas* fears its own insubstantiality, its return into *asat*; on the other, the mind is tempted to see everything as an hallucination, since everything actually sprang forth from mind. This insuperable uncertainty, the anxiety peculiar to mind, was transmitted to Prajāpati, the god closest to the mind, the only one of whom it is said that he *is* the mind: "Prajāpati is, so to speak, mind"; "mind is Prajāpati."

The world can function without any reference to mind, in the same way that the gods will carry on with their tangled exploits without needing to refer to Prajāpati. It once happened that Prajāpati himself missed his turn while he was dividing up the portions of the sacrifice among the gods. He was the first to behave as if he himself didn't count. The mind, in fact, can easily convince itself that it doesn't exist. Born before existence, it is continually tempted to consider itself nonexistent. And in a way its existence is never complete, as it is always mixed up with *something that was there before anything else.* That is enough to place it in doubt.

Manasā, "mentally," "with the mind," is a word that appears 116 times in the *Ṛgveda.* There is nothing similar in the founding text of any other ancient civilization. It is as though the Vedic people had developed a peculiar lucidity and an obsession toward that phenomenon they called *manas*, "mind," which imposed itself on them as something evident, with a force unknown elsewhere.

The first couple, from which all other couples are descended, could only have been formed by Mind and Speech, Vāc (the Latin *vox*). Mind is Prajāpati—and the first oblation goes in fact to him; Speech is the gods. So the second oblation goes to Indra, king of the gods. These two powers belong to two different levels of being, but to demonstrate their effectiveness they have to unite, *to be yoked together*, with appropriate devices. By themselves, Mind and Speech are powerless—or at least insufficient to transport the offering to the gods. The horse of the mind must allow itself to be harnessed with speech, with meter: otherwise it will be lost.

But how will the action of the two powers be perceived, moment by moment, in the ritual? "When this is performed in a murmur, mind transports the sacrifice to the gods and, when this is performed aloud, speech transports the sacrifice to the gods." It will therefore be in the ceaseless alternation between murmuring (or silence) and clear, distinct speech that we may perceive the combined action of Mind and Speech, like a perpetual oscillation between two levels, both present if what we do is to be effective.

Yet it is not enough to establish what are the two powers that can alone bear the oblation to the gods. The ritualists loved detail and lists of equivalents. They were not content to establish a polarity, as Western metaphysicians would one day do. So where do we begin? With ladles and spoons. *Manas*, the male element (a slight strain on linguistic interpretation is needed in this speculation, since *manas* is neutral), is equivalent to the "ladle," *sruva* (masculine noun), and with it carries out "the libation that is the root of the sacrifice"; whereas *vāc*, the female element, is equivalent to the spoon with a spout, *sruc* (a feminine noun), and with it offers "the libation that is the head of the sacrifice." Silence also belongs to mind, since "undefined is the mind and undefined is that which takes place in silence." Mind is equivalent to the sitting position, speech to the standing position.

The most difficult point is the search for a balance between Mind and Speech. These two beings are not of equal power. Mind is "far more unlimited." When, together, they become the yoke for the horse of the oblation, the imbalance is apparent. The yoke leans to the heavier part, that of the mind. So it will not be effective, and will skew the movement. So a supplementary plank must be inserted on the side of speech, to balance the weight. This supplementary plank is a sublime metaphysical device—and the oblation succeeds in reaching the gods only thanks to it. The reason for it helps us to understand why speech is never complete, but always flawed or made up of other factors, compromised by its flimsiness—or, in any case, its lack of weight.

Relations between Mind and Speech were always difficult and fraught. They sometimes clashed like two warriors—or two lovers. Each wished to do better than the other. "Mind said: 'I am surely better than you, for you say nothing that I don't understand; and since you imitate what I have done and follow in my wake, I am surely better than you.'

"Speech said: 'I am surely better than you, for I communicate what you know, I make it understood.'

"They appealed to Prajāpati for him to decide. He decided in favor of Mind and said [to Speech]: 'Mind is indeed better than you, for you imitate what Mind has done and you follow in his wake'; and in truth he who imitates what his better has done and follows in his wake is inferior.

"Then Speech, having been contradicted, was upset and miscarried. She, Speech, then said to Prajāpati: 'May I never be your oblation-bearer, I who have been rejected by you.' So whatever thing is celebrated in the sacrifice for Prajāpati, is celebrated quietly; for Speech was no longer the oblation-bearer for Prajāpati."

The dispute between Mind and Speech over supremacy is reminiscent of what would happen in Greece between the spoken and written word. And perhaps in this sliding of levels lies an insuperable difference between Greece and India: in Greece, Speech, Logos, takes the place held in India by Mind, Manas. Otherwise, the points of dispute are the same. What in India is accused of being secondary, imitative, and derivative (Speech) in Greece becomes the force that directs the same accusations against the written word. In Greece, all that happens takes place within speech. In India, it originates in something that *precedes* speech: Mind. In the same way that the Devas gradually forgot Prajāpati, though only after a long period when they sought his help, particularly when they had to fight their elder brothers, the Asuras, so too the Olympians regarded themselves from the very beginning as the ultimate reality, relegating the exploits of Cronos and his "twisted mind" to the dark and cruel history of their beginnings, even though he had given his measures and order to the cosmos.

The wars between the Devas and the Asuras were fought in many different ways and ended in many different ways, though the outcome was always the same—with the Devas victorious. But before that happened, there was a constant series of setbacks and reversals. The decisive moment came when the gods took refuge in Mind and the Asuras in Speech.

Mind meant sacrifice. The nature of Mind was such as to make it correspond with sacrifice and the sky. This is told in the story explaining why the sacrificer should tie the horn of a black antelope to his garment: "He then ties a black antelope horn to the edge of his garment. Now the Devas and the Asuras, each created by Prajāpati, received their father's inheritance: the Devas took Mind and the Asuras Speech. So the Devas took the sacrifice and the Asuras speech. The Devas took the yonder sky and the Asuras this earth."

And so it happened that the war between the Devas and the Asuras was transformed into the story of the relations between a male being, Yajña, Sacrifice, and a female being, Vāc, Speech, herald of the Asuras. Here the enemy lines and the clash of arms fade away. The stage was cleared—ready for playing out the first comedy of love. The Devas peered out from the wings. They were no longer warriors but prompters, whispering from the sides. As soon as they saw Vāc's radiance, they thought all they had to do to defeat the Asuras was to abduct her. So imperious must have been the power emanating from Speech. It is true not only, as Herodotus wrote, that the abduction of a woman lies at the origin of every war, but also that the final conquest of a certain woman marks the end of war. So the Devas began to whisper to Yajña, telling him how to seduce Vāc. What resulted would establish the traditional rules of courtship between men and women, like a code of manners that would remain basically unchanged for centuries:

"The Devas said to Yajña, Sacrifice: 'This Vāc, Speech, is a woman: make a sign to her and she will surely invite you to come to her.' Or perhaps he himself thought: 'This Vāc is a woman: I'll make a sign to her and she will surely invite me to come to her.' So he made a sign to her. But she at first rejected him, from a distance: for a woman, when a man makes a sign to her, at first rejects him, from a distance. He said: 'She has rejected me, from a distance.'

"They said: 'Just make a sign to her, sir, and she will surely invite you to come to her.' He made a sign to her; but she answered him, so to speak, only by shaking her head: for a woman, when a man makes a sign to her, answers, so to speak, only by shaking her head. He said: 'She has answered me only by shaking her head.'

"They said: 'Just make a sign to her, sir, and she will invite you to come to her.' He made a sign to her, she invited him to come to her. For a woman in the end invites the man to come to her. He said: 'She has in fact invited me.'

"The Devas reflected: 'This Vāc, being a woman, we had better be careful she doesn't seduce him. Say to her: "Come here to where I am" and then tell us whether she has come to you.' Then she went to where he was. For a woman goes to a man who lives in a fine house. He told of how she had come to him, saying: 'She has in fact come.'"

The story couldn't be more perfect than it is and is heavily spiced with Vedic irony—an irony that has largely gone unnoticed over the centuries, in India as well as the West—for example, where it says: "For a woman goes to a man who lives in a fine house." With their taste for both basic and systematic detail, the Vedic ritualists managed to recount the comedy of seduction in all its classic phases, as if it were a rite—the kind of comedy that, from the Greek poets up to the story of Don Giovanni, has been represented only in sharp, hot morsels, without worrying about reconstructing the sequence in all its stages, as happens here. This amorous approach is a crucial step in a cosmic game—and at the same time is the model for what will take place over and over again in narrow lanes, public squares, drawing rooms, bars, and cafés throughout the world.

In the story of Yajña and Vāc, it is taken for granted that the Devas will win their war, as they have chosen the side of the Mind and of Sacrifice. At the same time, though, they badly need Vāc, the adversary's prime force. Mind must first of all assert its supremacy over Speech, since the operation of Mind involves language, yet also goes beyond it. Thinking is *not* a linguistic act: this was a basic idea of the *ṛṣis*. But thinking *can* also be a linguistic act, once the Devas, through Yajña, succeed in bringing Vāc across to their side. And that passage brings an enhancement in the implicit power of the Devas, as well as the defeat of the Asuras. At this point the gap between the Devas and Asuras opens up once and for all: the Asuras are now beings who have *lost* speech. They become "barbarians (*mlecchas*)" as soon as Vāc abandons them. This is the first expression of scorn for the barbarian as a babbler. And the brahmin's work, preeminently work of the mind, would follow the greatest rigor in the use of speech, so as not to descend into the "language of the Asuras." The Devas thus gained the highest and most unassailable power. But inherent in this supreme power was a supreme danger. Indra, king of the Devas, discovered it for himself. And so it happened that Indra "thought to himself: 'A monstrous being will surely spring from this union of Yajña and Vāc: let it not take advantage of me.' Indra became an embryo and entered into that coupling." A few months later, as his birth was approaching, Indra thought once again: "The womb that has contained me certainly has great vigor: no monstrous being must be born from it after me, lest it should take advantage of me." So Indra ripped out Vāc's womb, into which he had introduced himself, so that it was impossible for it to give birth to another being. That torn and tattered womb is now on the head of the Sacrifice like a pleated turban: "Having seized it and held it tightly, he ripped out the womb and put it on the head of Yajña, Sacrifice, for the black antelope is sacrifice: the skin of the black antelope is the same as the sacrifice, the horn of the black antelope is the same as that womb. And since Indra ripped out the womb holding it tightly, for that reason the horn is tied tightly to the edge of the garment; and since Indra, having become an embryo, was born from that union, for that reason the sacrificer, after having become an embryo, is born from that union."

Speech and Mind must both remain on the side of the Devas, but they must not be *united*: intercourse between Mind and Speech would end up creating a being of such power that it would overwhelm the power of the Devas. And the Devas have lived, from the beginning, in terror of such a moment. With pain and effort they have conquered the sky and immortality. Now they are chasing humans away, removing all traces of the sacrifice while, on the other hand, they are keeping watch to make sure no power is unleashed by rites that might overwhelm them. If relations between Speech and Mind were from then on unstable, clouded, and marked at times with ill-concealed hostility, it is due to Indra's ruthless intervention: one of those vile and mysterious exploits of his that trigger enormous consequences.

The relationship between Mind and Speech thus established what was to happen in the world: not simply a pair of lovers, but a scene of horror that recalled a brutal attack. A male being, Sacrifice, bears on his head the torn uterus of his lover Speech, where he will never be able to pour his semen. The Devas wanted it this way so that the balance of power would never again be upset—in this case, against them. This is the condition in which the world must live. This is where one should go back in order to understand sexual attraction, but also the insuperable imbalance and disunity that has reigned between Mind and Speech from then on. In the West, it is a theme that finds echoes in the nostalgia and perpetual, helpless evocation of the language of Adam.

Another layer of implications in the story of Yajña and Vāc and their fateful coitus is that of the conflict, of the latent and deadly hostility between myth and ritual. While the stories of the Olympians in

Greece manage to free themselves from their ritual associations, to proliferate and eventually be lost in the vast estuary of Alexandrian literature, in Vedic India the process is the reverse: the progressive subjection of the mythical stories to ritual action, as if their purpose was simply that of illustrating it—and not to exist in their own right, as a primary manifestation of the divine. Perhaps this is why the Devas always retained a certain cowardly and ineffectual streak. A sequence of ritual acts had once made them into what they then were. Another sequence, breaking free from their control, would one day be able to bring them down.

Although they were opposites in everything else, Athens and Jerusalem ended up establishing a strategic alliance and basing it on one word: *lógos*. An alliance sealed with the opening verse of John's Gospel. From the time of the Greek sages, *lógos* had been a power connected to speech, to discourse, even though it did not let itself be wholly absorbed into it. *Noûs*, on the other hand, had always been a force independent from speech. With John's Gospel, *lógos*, in becoming the Word and the divine incarnation, reestablished its sovereignty. Any further power was inconceivable. And so thought and mind were indissolubly linked to speech. From then on, nondiscursive thought was to be pushed aside, or even underground. It was the Egypt of thought, its *facies hieroglyphica*, that was swallowed up, driven away by the formidable forces of *lógos* as Reason and of *lógos* as the Word.

Vedic India remained extraneous and hostile to this drama without ever giving way. The Brāhmaṇas already abandon the mythical stories and liturgical sequences devoted to the irreversible imbalance between Mind and Speech, to the greater weight of the first over the other. Then in the *Chāndogya Upaniṣad* the relationship is described more bluntly: "The mind indeed is more than speech." The watershed between East and West, over which so much thought has been given, can be traced to this point. All the rest follows from that radical divergence, which India would never abandon, following it from the Veda to the Vedānta.

In saying this, the *Chāndogya Upaniṣad* uses a language that is neither philosophical nor oracular, but serenely apodictic: "The mind indeed is more than speech. As a fist holds two *āmalaka* or *kola* or *akṣa* fruits, in the same way the mind holds speech and name. If the mind thinks: I want to study the hymns, then they are studied; I want to celebrate sacrifices, then they are celebrated; I want to obtain children and cattle, then they are obtained; I want to devote myself to this and the other world, then they are devoted to. For the Self, *ātman*, is mind, the world is mind, *brahman* is mind. Venerate the mind."

Sacrifice is not only the offering of a specific substance, such as the prodigious *soma.* Sacrifice is also a concerted action that produces a substance: " 'It is honey,' they say; for honey means the sacrifice." But if we watch a sacrifice, we don't see this honey. We see gestures accompanied by words. And the essence of the word is in its being a substitute: but for what? For the thing named, say the Western theorists. The Vedic ritualists thought differently: the word substitutes the honey produced by the sacrifice, honey that the gods sucked and drained away to prevent men finding the path to heaven through the sacrifice: "The sacrifice is speech: for with it he provides that part of the sacrifice which has been sucked and drained away." For the word to substitute the honey, it has to have a sacrificial nature already. Let us recall how Yajña, Sacrifice, as soon as he saw Vāc, Speech, thought: "Let me couple with her," as if nothing for him were quite like it. And nothing attracted him more. This is why speech comes into action.

For the Vedic ritualists, everything involved composition, work. Even the splendor of Indra (who is also the sun) was not so in the beginning: "In the same manner that everything else is now dark, so was he then." It was only when the gods composed their "favorite forms and desirable powers" that Indra began to shine. Never had composition been recognized as having so much power: in its forms, gestures, words. This is the secret inheritance that ritual—through devious paths and deep oblivion—has consigned to art.

VII

ĀTMAN

***Brahman* or the knowledge of it are no different among very powerful beings such as Vāmadeva or in the much less powerful men of today. But one may suspect that in men of today the fruit of the knowledge of *brahman* is uncertain.**

—Śaṅkara, *Bṛhadāraṇyakopaniṣadbhāṣya*, 1.4.10

From the *Ṛgveda* to the *Bhagavad Gītā* a way of reasoning is developed that never acknowledges a single subject, but rather presupposes a dual subject. This is because the constitution of the mind is dual: consisting of a gaze that perceives (eats) the world and of a gaze that contemplates the gaze directed at the world. The first expression of this idea appears with the two birds in hymn 1.164 of the *Ṛgveda*: "Two birds, a couple of friends, are perched on the same tree. One of them eats the sweet berry of the *pippal*; the other, without eating, watches." There is no more basic revelation than this. And the *Ṛgveda* presents it with the clarity of its enigmatic language. The dual constitution of the mind implies that two birds dwell perpetually within each of us: the Self, *ātman*, and the I, *aham*. Friends, alike, sitting on the tree at the same level, one might seem the double of the other. And so it is in the life of many, who never manage to distinguish between them. But, once their difference has been recognized, everything changes. Every moment becomes the superimposition of two perceptions that can add together, cancel each other out, multiply each other. When they multiply each other, according to the mysterious formula 1×1, thought springs forth. Even if, seen from outside, all remains the same. The answer seems still to be 1.

Ātman, the Self, is a discovery. How to attain it was the ultimate doctrine for the disciples who had studied and assimilated all the Vedas. No one attained it unless he was capable of considering what was going on in his own mind as an uninterrupted exchange between the I, *aham*, and the Self: similar and opposing powers, the one—*aham*—intrusive yet insubstantial, the other—*ātman*—supreme and untarnishable, yet difficult to coax out from its habitual hiding place. To reach it required constant work, and yet it was only a small part of the way the Self took to reveal itself. And then there was everything that appeared before the eyes: the world. And here another endless round of exchanges began that ended up entirely transforming the appearance of the outside world, to the point of making it become external by convention only. Meanwhile, in parallel, the inner world expanded and accommodated the essential parts of everything: worlds, gods, Vedas, the vital breaths. "Let him know this: 'All the worlds I have placed within my Self, and my Self I have placed in all the worlds; all the gods I have placed within my Self, and my Self I have placed within all the gods; all the Vedas I have placed within my Self, and my Self I have placed within all the Vedas; all the vital breaths I have placed within my Self, and myself I have placed within all the vital breaths.' For imperishable, in fact, are the worlds, imperishable the gods, imperishable the Vedas, imperishable the breaths, imperishable is all this: and in truth anyone who knows this passes from imperishable to imperishable, conquers recurring death and reaches the full measure of life."

Relations between the Self, *ātman*, and the I, *aham*, are tortuous, fragile, ambiguous. And it couldn't be otherwise. Everything goes back to the beginning, when there was only the Self, in the form of a "person," *puruṣa*: "Looking around, he saw nothing other than his Self. And the first thing he said was: 'I am.' And so was born the name 'I.'" It is the primal scene of consciousness, which reveals the precedence of a reflexive pronoun—*ātman*, one's Self. Thinking about one's self precedes thought. And thinking about one's Self takes the form of a person, *puruṣa*: it has a physiognomy, an outline. This is immediately indicated with another pronoun: I, *aham.* In that moment a new entity appears, which has the name I and is superimposed point by point on the Self, from which it is born. From then on—until knowledge, *veda*, flashes forth—the I will be indistinguishable from the Self. They look like identical twins. They have the same outline, the same sense of omnipotence and centrality. After all, at the moment when the I appeared, there was still nothing else in the world. And so the first to fall into the delusion of the I was the Self. After the creatures were created, the Self, as a result of its many erotic metamorphoses, looked at the world and realized that it had created it. And it said: "Indeed I (*aham*) am creation," already forgetting that this I was only the first of his creatures.

The doctrine of I and Self, *aham* and *ātman*, like all Vedic doctrines, can neither be proved nor disproved. It can only be experienced: by each person, on himself. This doctrine may sound odd to those who think of their minds as clear-cut, solid objects, which at most are turned on and off, almost like switches, when sleep takes over or when they wake up. If, however, the mind operating in each person is not one single block, but is at least crossed by a fissure, varying in depth from moment to moment, between the one who is looking and another being, who gazes back at the one who is looking, then we begin to glimpse what lies behind the division between *aham* and *ātman*. But it is only a beginning. The words that form in the mind—and tend to create a self-contained fortress—must also realize they are facing another (nonlinguistic, perpetually active) part with which at any moment they may clash or amalgamate or become entwined (but these ways of relating are far more numerous and subtle).

The consequences of this realization are incalculable. And they do not necessarily lead along the Vedic path, with all its impressive apparatus of correspondences and connections. But they certainly lead to a realization that the unknown is much greater than had first been acknowledged. An unknown that is not just outside the mind, but inside it and perhaps vaster even than the unknown that lies outside. This realization could therefore be the basis on which thought begins to develop.

How do we explain why the figure that appears in the pupil of the eye has assumed such an importance? Because it is the only point on the surface of the human body that has a *reflection*, therefore the capacity not only to see, but to reflect what the eye sees in another form. And that form will be impalpable and minuscule, but will *correspond*, point for point, to the figure that the eye perceives in the outside world, so that even the being who dwells in the pupil will have a head, a body, legs and arms, just like the person who appears in the world in front of the eye. And that person will also have another eye, into which the eye of the onlooker will be reflected. This ensures a potentially perpetual and interminable *communication of reflections*. If that tiny figure were not there in the pupil, the human body would be a compact surface and would offer no glimpse of the other life that carries on in the sealed chamber of the mind.

Self-referentiality, this movement of thought that was enough for Gödel to break up the whole edifice of formal systems, beginning with arithmetic, appeared on the linguistic scene for the first time when the reflexive pronoun *ātman*, valid for all people, singular and plural, appeared as an entity, a noun, usually translated as "Self." This happened in the Veda: first at the end of certain hymns—not the most ancient—from the *Atharvaveda*, then more frequently in the Brāhmaṇas, to the point where *ātman* became the ubiquitous hallmark of the Upaniṣads. Indian thought from then on revolved around this word, treating it in a whole variety of ways, from Buddha to Śaṅkara. Never allowing it, though, to lose its centrality. India begins and ends with something that was to become central in the West only at the beginning of the twentieth century, with the discovery of the paradoxes in set theory.

The Vedic ritualists certainly didn't react like those Western thinkers who were appalled when they discovered those paradoxes, because they saw every claim to a coherent and consequential speculative structure fall to pieces. The Vedic ritualists, instead, seemed perversely attracted by paradoxes in general. In them they saw the very substance of enigmas. And enigmas formed the bedrock of what they expressed, in their hymns and in their commentaries on ritual. They were different ways of describing, formulating, illustrating, applying the same unknown quantity, which they called *brahman.*

There was a teacher, Sanatkumāra, and his pupil, Nārada. The teacher was a *kṣatriya*, a warrior, and his pupil a brahmin. Nārada was one day to become an ever-present *ṛṣi,* the one who most enjoyed involving himself in the affairs of others. A tireless talker. But before that he had been one of the many pupils who used to appear before his teacher with a burning ember. The teacher anticipated him, saying: "You come to me with that which you know." Sanatkumāra evidently knew that Nārada was no ordinary pupil, but was already overburdened with learning. And this had to be corrected. "Tell me what you know," asked the teacher, "I will tell you what goes beyond this." Impudent irony, since "know" in Sanskrit is *veda.* And the pupil proudly and diligently displayed his knowledge: "The *Ṛgveda*, the *Yajurveda*, the *Sāmaveda*, fourthly the *Atharvaveda*, fifthly the ancient stories." Everything so far followed the prescribed order. But the pupil wanted to excel, so he continued to list other knowledge he had acquired: "The Veda of the Vedas, the ritual for the ancestors, the computation of numbers, divination, the art of finding treasures [according to Olivelle, but Senart translates it as "knowledge of time"], dialogues, monologues, the science of the gods, the science of ritual, the science of the spirits, the science of government, the science of the celestial bodies, the science of snakes." Worn out by his list, Nārada concluded: "Here, sir, is what I know."

Then, straight after, Nārada showed himself in a new aspect: no longer the faultless pupil, proud of his knowledge, but an anxious and bewildered young man, a prototype of the hapless student. He said: "I know nothing, sir, apart from liturgical formulas (*mantras*), I do not know the Self (*ātman*). But I have heard of it, sir, from others like you: 'He who knows the Self goes beyond suffering.' I, sir, am suffering. Sir, ferry me to the other bank of suffering."

The immense Vedic expanse, brimful of gods and powers, was suddenly reduced to one narrow gap. The same that would attract the Buddha—and, one far-off day, Schopenhauer. The teacher came straight to the point and answered: "All you have listed are nothing more than nouns." And this marked the beginning of a breathtaking passage. Using a recursive procedure, Sanatkumāra began a succession of interlinked thoughts that spanned worlds before returning right back to the beginning. For each power, he explained which power was even greater. "Speech indeed is more than nouns." Puzzlement, at first. For that which speech knows (the Vedas and all the learning listed by Nārada) seems to be exactly the same as that which nouns make it possible to know. But here he was referring to the god Speech, Vāc, celebrated in the *Ṛgveda* as she who penetrates everything and to whom nothing can be denied: "The sky, earth, air, atmosphere, waters, incandescent energy, gods, men, animals, birds, plants and trees, all the beasts down to worms, insects and ants, the just and the unjust, true and false, good and bad, pleasant and unpleasant." Speech is more powerful than nouns to exactly this extent.

Here a comparison is made with "mind," *manas*, which is the next power. Now it will be Speech that gives way. *Manas*, in its turn, is not the last word, but if anything the first. For *manas* is a generic, all-embracing word. More powerful than *manas* will be some of its modalities.

How to dismantle and reassemble the mind has never been taught with such precision as in the Upaniṣads. *Manas* therefore yields to a further power, which is *saṃkalpa*, "intention," "plan." It is the word used by the sacrificer when he declares that he has decided (has planned) to celebrate a sacrifice. *Saṃkalpa* is more than mind since it is what sets mind in action. *Saṃkalpa* is the first impulse that leads to the deployment of that which is. And here Sanatkumāra, with supreme subtlety, drew this category out of its narrow psychological context, making it fill the cosmos. Once the mind is set in motion, not only are words spoken, not only are words fixed in writing, but "sky and earth are founded on intention"—and, following them, the rest of the world, right down to food and life. A sudden, acrobatic, overwhelming passage. An exemplary Vedic gesture.

The *saṃkalpa*, however, is just a first sign of the sharpening of the mind. Something else still has to be revealed. "Awareness (*citta*) is more than intention." Another important threshold, which certain translations fail to notice. Senart translates *citta* as "*raison*" (reason), Olivelle as "thought." And yet *citta* is neither reason, which is misleading, nor thought, which is too broad. *Citta* is the word used for the act of *becoming aware.* And bringing to consciousness. In the end, it is the pure fact of being conscious. The primacy of awareness over everything is the cornerstone of Vedic thought. If *citta* meant reason or general thought, Sanatkumāra's line of argument would lose its meaning at the point where he says: "So, however much someone may know, if he is without awareness they will say of him: 'He is not there.' If he knew, if he were a sage, he would not be so lacking in awareness." The *ṛṣis*, the first sages, are the masters of consciousness. Their function, more than any other, before any other, is to be watchful. And so they watch over the world and its *dharma* so that it comes to no harm. But they may only do so if, like the gods, they have perpetual wakefulness.

With each threshold it might be thought the last has been reached. If *citta*, awareness, is indeed fundamental, what power could be greater? The speculative machine now proceeds with ever more subtle distinctions. "Meditation (*dhyāna*) indeed is more than awareness." The words already point to certain Buddhist harmonics: in Pali teachings, the word *citta* will become synonymous with "mind"; and *dhyāna* is a word of key significance for the Buddha. But here the grandiose Vedic perspective—cosmic rather than psychological—opens up once more: "The earth, in a certain way (*iva*), meditates; the atmosphere, in a certain way, meditates; the waters, in a certain way, meditate; gods and men, in a certain way, meditate; therefore those among men who reach greatness are, in a certain way, partaking of meditation." The word *iva*, which marks entry into the indefinite and the casting off of the literal, is used for the earth as for gods and for men. All and everything meditates, *in a certain way*. And beyond meditation? "Discernment (*vijñāna*) is more than meditation." *Vijñāna*: once again a term that will have an important role in Buddhism. To understand its particularity, we have to think of the discernment of spirits that would be practiced by Evagrius and the Desert Fathers—and, one day, by Ignatius of Loyola.

One might think that *vijñāna* is the last link in Sanatkumāra's chain. But it is not. With a sudden change of tack it continues: "Strength (*bala*) is more than discernment. One man alone, with his strength, can make a hundred sages tremble." The words here catch us by surprise and turn the game upside down. Just when we thought we were following an *itinerarium mentis*, we find the reappearance of simple strength. Strength as a simple physical quality. But it is enough. And straightaway, here opens up another series of powers that go further. There is no more mention of mind. Now it is "food," *anna*; waters; "incandescent energy," *tejas*; space. Having reached space, we might begin to lose track. What would there be beyond space? Another surprise: memory. With another unexpected move, he goes back into the mind. And beyond? Hope. And, stronger than hope, *prāṇa*, the "breath," which here means life itself. Having reached life, finally there is a pause. And the teacher says to his pupil: "He who sees this, he who knows this, that person is an *ativādin*." An *ativādin* is someone far beyond (*ati*), who cannot be reached with words.

Have we arrived at the end of the chain? No. Another more intricately linked chain begins. As if to strip the pupil of the illusion of having found an answer. The teacher continues: "The only one who wins with the word is he who wins with truth." What follows is a further recursive procedure. Truth this time is surpassed by the discernment of thought (*manas*, which finally reappears). Thought surpassed by faith in the effectiveness of the rites, *śraddhā*. Faith by perfect practice. This is surpassed by sacrifice. Sacrifice by joy. Here once again, a surprise:

"Only when you feel joy do you sacrifice. You must not sacrifice when you are prey to suffering. Sacrifice only when you feel joy. But you have to know joy." By the time we have become accustomed to the succession of powers and there is still no end in sight, we suddenly find ourselves taken back to the starting point: the moment when the student Nārada appeared before the teacher and said: "I, sir, am suffering." Now the opposite power finally appears: "joy," *sukha.* A word very close in sound to *śoka*, "suffering." The path has to be found from one to the other. The teacher continues, unflinchingly: "Joy is fullness. There is no joy in what is limited." But where is that fullness, the pupil wants to know. "It is below, it is above, it is to the west, it is to the east, it is to the south, it is to the north, it is all of this." Here once again we feel close to a final word. And it is exactly here that the sharpest psychological arrow strikes. The teacher continues. "But the same can be said of egoity [*ahaṃkāra*, the word that from now on will be used to describe what Western psychology calls "ego"]: the I is below, it is above, it is to the west, it is to the east, it is to the south, it is to the north, the I is all of this." Once again, an irony: the imaginary supremacy of the I is the strongest obstacle to perception, simply because it is what most resembles the true final word: *ātman*, Self, which other masters had pointed out to Nārada, as if it were the way out of suffering. And the teacher, first of all, describes *ātman* in the same terms used for the I, placing it in all directions of space. But, as had already happened once with *vāc*, "speech," in relation to nouns, something more can also be said about *ātman.* And it will be the decisive phrase: "He who sees like this, who thinks like this, who knows like this, who loves *ātman*, who plays with *ātman*, who copulates with *ātman*, whose happiness is in *ātman*, that man is supreme, he can have all he desires in all worlds." Now the moment has come in which the chain could be followed in reverse. From life, power by power, down to the nouns, since "all of this follows from *ātman.*"

Two verses follow. The first seems to be a response to the Buddha in advance, since it names the three evils that appeared to him immediately before leaving his father's house (substituting all-encompassing "pain," *duḥkha*—another key Buddhist word—for old age): "He who sees, does not see death, nor illness, nor pain. He who sees, sees all, he attains everything everywhere." The second verse is a numerical riddle, like those often found in the *Ṛgveda.* Finally it says that, with this chain of arguments, the master Sanatkumāra taught Nārada to "cross the darkness." And the word *mokṣa*, "release," rings out. There is no mention of any response from Nārada: he was at last practicing silence.

Sanatkumāra's teachings to Nārada on *ātman*, in the *Chāndogya Upaniṣad*, is a recursive progression toward an indefinite point, *ātman*, which, once discovered, is found to encapsulate all preceding powers. The progression moves constantly forward, but there are crucial transitions: above all the transition from discursiveness to nondiscursiveness, at the point where "speech," *vāc*, becomes subordinate to "mind," *manas.* Then the beginning of a hierarchical separation of the mind (*manas*, *citta*, *dhyāna*, *vijñāna*), which seems to trace a preliminary outline of what will for centuries be the teachings of Buddhism. Finally the rejection of a linear progression, which instead turns out to be circular. *Ātman* is not reached from the peak of the mind (*vijñāna*), but from there we drop down into the undifferentiated outside world, into simple "strength," *bala*, then returning into the mind with another sudden leap: the passage from "space," *ākāśa*, to "memory," *smara.* But the most delicate and risky transition comes toward the end, the penultimate step, when Sanatkumāra ventures to infer "fullness," *bhūman*, from "joy," *sukha*: "Joy is fullness." *Bhūman* is above all a cosmic power. It is limitless. And from this limitlessness, which is both mental and cosmic, Sanatkumāra could hazard the final step and thrust the arrow of his thought into *ātman.* But here the final obstacle emerges: the I, *aham.* Because all the characteristics of limitless expansion which belong to "fullness" also belong to the I. Which is central to every world, a self-appointed sovereign, an unlimitable domain. And, above all, it is the most insidious imitation of Self. The I superimposes itself so perfectly on Self that it can conceal it. This, in fact, is what happened during the course of Western philosophy: it never worried about giving a name to the Self, but always chose the I as the point of observation, even if it was only called that much later on, with Kant. Before him, it was the unquestionable subject, the first person of Descartes's *Cogito.* But for Sanatkumāra, the I is the most daunting obstacle, that which can forever deny access to the Self. If the search had not continued, it might have been supposed that it had reached its completion with the I. But how is the final step taken? Here, once again, we see Sanatkumāra's subtlety. It is not a question of driving away, rejecting the I. That would be pointless—and contrary to the physiology of the psyche. It is a matter of following its movements and then adding others to it, which the I could not pretend to. Only if a new entity appears, which is the Self, *ātman*, can we speak of "he who loves the Self," "whose happiness is in the Self." This new being will no longer be the I, with its illusory supremacy, because its supremacy has been transferred to the Self, with which each individual plays and interacts. The point of arrival is a dual subject who is irreducible, unbalanced (the Self is infinite, the individual is any being whatsoever in this world), intermittent (the perception of the dual subject is not something there right from the start, but something to achieve, the hardest yet most efficacious achievement). This is why the master's teaching is sought, this is why Sanatkumāra offered to tell Nārada "what goes beyond this."

At the age of twenty-four, after twelve years of study, Śvetaketu went back to his father, the teacher Uddālaka Āruṇi. He had studied all the Vedas, was "conceited, proud of his knowledge, arrogant." Much like Nārada. Now he had to go *beyond*, guided by his father. The path is different each time. The introduction chosen by Uddālaka Āruṇi was extremely fast. It was just to let his son know that all he had learned was probably not of greatest importance. Then suddenly Uddālaka Āruṇi began to tell how the world was made, almost as if his son had never heard anything about it: "In the beginning, my child, there was nothing but being, one without a second. Some say: In the beginning, there was nothing but nonbeing, one without a second." Similar words would be heard in Ionian Greece or at Elea. He continues by saying that this being "thought." The being who thinks here is the one whom the Brāhmaṇas called Prajāpati. For Uddālaka Āruṇi it was enough to call him *sat*, the existent one. And those which were generated from him, from it, did not have the names of gods, but of elements: it was *tejas*, incandescent energy, and not Agni, who was a son; it was *āpas*, the waters, and not Vāc, who was a daughter; lastly *anna*, food. Compared with the Brāhmaṇas, everything became one step more abstract, though the doctrine remained identical.

Uddālaka Āruṇi, like Sanatkumāra, would also resort to recursive progressions. But with impatience. And at the end he would refer sarcastically to the "grand lords and grand theologians" who gain pleasure from these teachings. His thinking pointed elsewhere, to three words—to introducing the Self, *ātman*, and saying immediately: "*Tat tvam asi*," "This you are." In its hastiness, Uddālaka Āruṇi's reasoning is not particularly efficacious. On the other hand, the effect of the three final words is wonderful. *Cogito ergo sum* seems a meager, dry fruit in comparison.

The cosmogony that Uddālaka Āruṇi concisely described to his son revealed, in its pre-Parmenidean physiognomy, a new, modern conception, quite opposite to the doctrine that Śvetaketu had learned while studying the *Ṛgveda*. For it is said there: "In the primordial era of the gods, being was born from nonbeing." This doctrine is found again in the *Taittirīya Upaniṣad*: "In the beginning this [the world] was nonbeing and from it was born being." And in another passage of the *Chāndogya Upaniṣad* we read: "In the beginning all was nonbeing, this was being. Then it developed, it became an egg."

This presupposes that *sat* and *asat* are to be translated as "being" or "nonbeing" (as does Renou). And nothing fundamentally changes if they are translated as "existent" and "nonexistent" (as does Olivelle). But to what extent do *sat* and *asat* correspond to "being" and "nonbeing," words that carry the weight of the whole history of Western philosophy? *Asat*, more than a place for that which is not, might be the place for that which *is not manifest*. Deeply rooted in Indian thought is the certainty that most (three quarters) of what exists is hidden, unmanifest—and thus it is destined to remain. This is incompatible with the view of nonbeing intended by both Plato and the Sophists in their arguments. The specific difference, the unbridgeable gap between Greece and Vedic thought, could already be found in this word, the first word: *sat*.

The suspicion is confirmed and strengthened by a dark, vertiginous cosmogonic hymn in the *Ṛgveda* (10.129). This is how it starts, in Renou's last translation: "Neither nonbeing existed then, nor being. / The space of the air did not exist, nor the firmament beyond. / What moved powerfully? Where? Under whose gaze? / Was it the water, unfathomably deep?" *Sat* and *asat* are not there, because "this universe was only an indistinct wave (*apraketáṃ salilám*)." But we cannot say that *asat* is not.

Asat awaits only the "distinctive sign (*praketa*)" that separates it from *sat.* In all this, where "darkness was hidden by darkness," we could say that something existed called the "One" (as in Plotinus, but here it is something neuter, which becomes masculine in other passages). Who or what is this One coming before the gods? Another hymn describes it: "To the navel of the unborn, the One is fixed, / he on whom rest all creatures." But the One must also emerge from the indistinct, where "it breathed by its own impetus, without there being breath." What power can move it? *Tapas*, "ardor." "Then, by the power of Ardor, the One was born / empty and clad in emptiness." These verses are enough to show the inadequacy of the long-used Christianized translations of *tapas* (*penance*, as favored by Eggeling, *austerities*, *Kasteiung*, *ascèse*). Ardor is the only power that can dissolve the dark fixity of the beginning—and let the first distinction emerge: the One. Which appears immediately to have a disconcerting nature: it is "empty," *ābhu*, and "clad in emptiness." Puzzled, Renou notes: " 'empty' (*ābhu*) or conversely 'potential' (*ābhū*)." Karl Geldner suggests more casually that the word refers to the "great void" of "original chaos." But there is no trace in the *Ṛgveda* of a concept of chaos as something that "gapes open," as implied by the Greek *chaíno.* And *ābhu*, "empty," appears in only one other instance in the 1028 hymns, to mean "empty-handed." Renou's perplexity is therefore justified. At the beginning of the Veda, however much we look, we find never a "void" but something "full," *pūrṇa*, or a "superabundance," *bhūman*: something that overflows and, by overflowing, makes the world exist, since every life implies a boundless source of surplus. That One "clad in emptiness" must therefore be considered one of the more obscure points of the hymn.

The power that appears immediately after ardor—and almost as its immediate consequence—is *kāma*, "desire." An unparalleled definition is given for it: "Desire, which was the first seed of the mind." And here Renou translates *manas* as "consciousness," bending the text in a direction that is implicit in it, because the original form of the mind—or at least that most dear to the Vedic seers—was the pure act of being conscious. And this is the point in the hymn where the poet-seers, *kaváyaḥ*, the first human characters, appear, not just as witnesses but as participants: "Inquiring in their heart, the poets succeeded in discovering / by their reflection the link between nonbeing and being (*sató bándhum ásati*)."

They are words that challenge, some centuries in advance, the Parmenidean prohibition on conceiving a passage from nonbeing to being. And they do so using the most precious word: *bandhu*, "nexus," "bond," "tie." Thought, for the *ṛṣis*, was itself none other than a way of ascertaining and establishing *bandhus*. This was the beginning, and the culmination. Thought could offer nothing else. And it was clear that the first of these *bandhus* had to be the one between *asat* and *sat*. Here, once again, if the two words *asat* and *sat* mean "unmanifest" and "manifest"—and not "nonbeing" and "being," which are too Greek—then the formula seems far clearer: because the manifest must continually draw upon the unmanifest, in the same way that the leg of a wild goose, of the *haṃsa* that will one day become a swan, must stay immersed in the wave. Otherwise the circulation of life would stop.

But the *bandhu* described above was only the threshold of the riddle. The three verses that follow are a breathtaking progression of doubts and flashes that it would be pointless trying to explain. The only clear thing is that we are entering an area of questions that do not have—and perhaps cannot have—an answer. First of all, the *bandhu* found by the poets inquiring into their heart is a "rope stretched across." Across what, we are not told. In fact, it is followed by the questions "What was below? What was above?" And immediately there is a reference to dark powers, which Renou has translated as follows, with evident perplexity: "Spontaneous impetus," "Gift of self." They are the last appearances of something that one might try to affirm. What follows is the boldest and most surprising declaration on the impotence of thought. An unparalleled example of sublime sarcasm: "Who knows, in fact, who could declare here / from where this secondary creation [*visṛṣṭi*, which presupposes the *sṛṣṭi*, "creation" before it] is born, from where it comes? / The gods [came] after, through the secondary creation of our [world]. / But who knows from where this emerged?" It is a compelling process, which makes the uncertainty even greater—and culminates in the last stanza: "This secondary creation, from where it emerged, / if it had been established or not, / he who oversees this [world] from the highest heavens, only he knows, or perhaps not even he."

The Vedic seers were masters at raising the stakes, taking them beyond reach. Here the *ṛṣi* wanted to show how esoteric knowledge culminates in complete uncertainty. And that alone would have been a magnificent result. But for him that was not enough. The gods also had to be cloaked in the same uncertainty, as beings who were born too late, born also from the "secondary creation," whose origin was unascertainable. The crucial step would be to extend the uncertainty—the suspicion of uncertainty and of ignorance—as far as the supreme, unnamed figure, "who oversees this [world]" from the highest point. No one had dared, no one would ever again dare, to deny the omniscience of this mysterious figure. But the *ṛṣi* does exactly that. Indeed, he leaves us in doubt using a more subtle cruelty, since, if he had claimed something with certainty about this figure, then he would already be going beyond what he was permitted to know. And so he suggests only the possibility of a supreme being, greater than the gods, who nevertheless *may not know.* And this is said as part of the Veda, which means Knowledge.

What happens after death? Silence, indistinctness of the elements. Then a voice is heard: "Come, here I am, your *ātman.*" It is the divine Self, *daiva ātmā*, that speaks, it is that which has been constructed over a long time, laboriously, piece by piece, through the acts of sacrifice. It is another body that was waiting in the other world—and was meanwhile taking form, because "whatever oblation is sacrificed here, becomes his *ātman* in the other world."

VIII

PERFECT WAKEFULNESS

J885

The wakefulness the Upaniṣads speak of (and the *Ṛgveda* before them) is a state opposed, not to sleep, but to another kind of wakefulness—inattentive, inert, automatic. Awakening means rousing oneself from that kind of wakefulness, as from a vapid dream. Philosophers have not regarded this swerve within the mind as worthy of consideration, but it became the focus of thought in one place and in one period: in India, in the time between the Veda and the Buddha—and then reverberated unremittingly through all the centuries thereafter.

The first reference, in the *Ṛgveda*, was clear, blunt: "The gods seek someone who crushes *soma*; they do not need sleep; tireless, they set off on journeys." Even if men cannot say what "journeys" the gods endlessly devote themselves to, their duty is clearly indicated: to remain alert and, with their labor, to prepare the intoxicating drug.

But what is the relationship between the Buddha and the Veda? It is a difficult, delicate, and intricate question. However much we may emphasize their opposing positions, there remains a vast, obscure common background on which every contrast is laid out. We can see this background in the name of the Buddha himself, in the verb *budh-*, "to awaken," "to pay attention." The primacy of *awakening* over every other mental action was not an innovation of the Buddha, who simply offered a version of it that was both radical and by and large destructive of all that had gone before. The concern for awakening and its centrality had always been present in the Vedic texts. Awakening was embedded in the ritual, in the moments when it was more vulnerable, more likely to fall to pieces. Deep attention (ours toward what is happening, and of the god toward us) is the support the officiant needs, even when he is obliged to perform "that which is incorrect"—and this occurs at various times, since life itself is incorrect. One instance arises when the sacrificial ashes are thrown into the water: "When he throws Agni into the water, he performs that which is wrong; now he apologizes to him so as not to harm him. With two verses connected to Agni he adores, for it is to Agni that he apologizes, and they will be such as to contain the verb *budh-*, so that Agni can pay attention to his words." The gesture with which the ash is thrown into the water is nevertheless an offense to the fire, since it interrupts a desire that is total. In fact, "it is for all his desires that he has prepared that fire." Here again, a healing gesture is also needed, which "rejoins and recomposes," in a perpetual labor of reconstruction and restoration. But what is needed to attract the benevolence of Agni, the injured party, in such a delicate situation? Only upon awakening can help be sought, at the crucial moment. And the first awakening is directed to Agni, at the moment when the fire has become ash and is scattered on the waters. The fire has been "all his desires." Awakening happens as soon as his desire is extinguished and returns to its watery abode. It alone can now act. It is as though this ceremonial conduct toward Agni contained, prearranged and prefigured within it, the whole of later history culminating in the awakening of the Buddha, under a tree that no flame could harm.

Awakening is the decisive act in life. We can see this from the passage in the *Bṛhadāraṇyaka Upaniṣad* where it is said that in the beginning there was only *brahman*, and *brahman* "was everything." Then "it [*brahman*] became the gods, as they gradually awakened [*pratyabudhyata*, where the root *budh-* follows the prefix *prati-*, which indicates a movement *forward*, as if rousing from sleep]." But the gods are only the first category of beings, those who set the example. They are followed by the *ṛṣis*, and lastly mankind: "So also [did] the *ṛṣis*, so also men." If becoming *brahman* is the target, then awakening is the appropriate instrument (the only one named: in this passage, for once, there is *no* reference to sacrifice). But this establishes a worrying proximity and affinity between mankind and the gods. And for this the gods use all possible means, even the lowest, to prevent man from reawakening. The text is abrupt. He who thinks that "divinity is one thing and I another," that person "does not know." The presumption is that men and gods are fundamentally one and the same thing. Nothing is more insidious and disturbing for the gods than this: "So they are not pleased that men know this." It is no surprise that the authorities in the Castle ensured that a torpid haze fell upon K. as soon as he came close to discovering their secrets.

What appears under the name *brahman* is arcane, far more so than the gods. If seen as a group, and not each in their own dazzling singularity, the gods appeared as beings who had been fortunate: they had succeeded in passing from the earth to the sky, they had succeeded in becoming immortal. And yet they were obliged perpetually to fight and continually defeat the Asuras, their elder brothers before being downgraded to demons. And this is already a diminution of their supremacy, which ought to have been continually protected and maintained. The Devas had to be allies of the *ṛṣis*, though not always regarded by them with benevolence—or even with mere respect.

But *brahman* is neuter, untarnished, untarnishable. The seven suggested translations of the word listed in the St. Petersburg Lexicon are all inadequate. But so too are more recent attempts, such as those of Renou and Jan C. Heesterman, which show keen insight but also end up in a disastrous paraphrase: "connecting energy compressed in enigmas" (Renou); "the link between life and death" (Heesterman). In the end, it can be said only that *brahman* is the peak from which everything else follows.

And yet *brahman* is also a "world," *brahmaloka*—and it is a world that can be *entered* ("he enters *brahman*"). But what allows access? Not power, nor piety, nor good works. But simple consciousness, contact with perpetual wakefulness: "He who is wakeful among sleepers, the mind that edifies the various desires, this one is pure, this is *brahman*, this is what is called the immortal. All worlds rest on it: no one goes beyond." At last, in this passage in the *Kaṭha Upaniṣad*, we discover—under the name of *brahman*—what constituted from the very beginning the Knowledge, which is the Veda. Though the Upaniṣads explain it (indeed: they are described as texts that seek above all to explain it), this secret of *brahman* as wakefulness and consciousness is already present, "unspoken," throughout the *Ṛgveda*. In a hymn such as 5.44, for example, which Geldner describes as "the most difficult hymn in the *Ṛgveda*." Here "divinity is everywhere unspoken (*anirukta*)." Here, according to Renou, "the phraseology, the esoteric intention, undeniably indicated the Viśvedevāḥ character" (meaning: this type of composition places the hymn among those to the Viśvedevāḥ, All-the-gods, a peculiarly Vedic entity). No single god is named, apart from Agni in stanza 15, at the end of a hymn where, wrote Geldner, "the final verses seem to be the solution to a riddle," adding: "and this is undoubtedly all it seeks to be." To a large extent it remains a riddle: Oldenberg, the father of all Vedists, had already laid down his arms in the face of such a tough obstacle ("Both the explanation and the textual analysis of this hymn remain for the most part doubtful and without solution"). And yet, even though the exposition of the riddle remains largely impenetrable, the "solution" speaks with marvelous clarity—and refers to the supremacy of wakefulness over everything. With these words: "He who is wakeful, the stanzas love him; he who is wakeful, the ritual chants also go to him. He who is wakeful, *soma* says to him: in your friendship (I feel as if) at home." Since the hymns are the very formulation of *brahman*—in other words the expression of *brahman* as a "word of power" (Kramrisch)—the nexus that connects power to the word is already acknowledged here in *wakefulness.*

"The life of sacrifice is therefore an infinite series of deaths and births," wrote Sylvain Lévi. And so will be, in the first place, the initiation that is implicit in the sacrifice. To celebrate a sacrifice, the sacrificer must first be consecrated. And the consecration is a form of sacrifice—an endless circle on which everything turns. But for the initiand, more than for the others taking part in the ritual, birth and death must be as literal as possible. This is what distinguishes the initiand. During one part of the ceremony he will be the one who is still unborn: "He then wraps his head. For he who is consecrated becomes an embryo; and embryos are enveloped by the amniotic fluid and by the outer membrane; so he covers his head." The veiled head, which we come across in Greek initiations and for which the texts give us no convincing justification, is explained here in a few brief words: the initiand, he who is consecrated, is an embryo—and the primary characteristic of an embryo is that of being hidden, veiled by a membrane. The turban therefore recalls that state of concealment, that of the initiand as an embryo, in the same way as its shape suggests Vāc's womb torn open by Indra.

Of course, for the initiand to be literally an embryo raises certain difficulties, which might seem frivolous, like many other details of the ritual. For example: what does he do if, during the ceremony, he feels an itch? The rules are very strict: "He shall not scratch with a splinter of wood or with a fingernail. For he who is consecrated becomes an embryo: and if an embryo is scratched with a wooden splinter or a fingernail, the amniotic fluid could escape and he would die. Thereafter the consecrated one might suffer from itchiness; and his offspring might also be born with itchiness. Now the womb does not damage the embryo, and since the horn of the black antelope is the womb, it does not damage it; so the consecrated one should scratch himself with the horn of the black antelope and with nothing other than the horn of the black antelope." The pictures conjured up by the rite are never *just* metaphors, in the sense of a lame literary device. They are invisible presences and at the same time are to be understood in a strict literal sense. If the consecrated one becomes an embryo, this must determine his behavior even at the most casual, unexpected, and insignificant moment: for example, when he feels an itch. And so we discover the subtle answer of the womb, which, with motherly concern, soothes the embryo within it. But how? With the horn of a black antelope, which, contrary to all evidence and appearance, is declared *to be* the womb. And so, the consecrated one scratches himself with the horn of a black antelope during the ceremony.

When the initiand is finally born, who is his father? The new birth that takes place through initiation makes it possible to escape the old worry of *pater semper incertus*. The father will now be one alone—and is neuter: *brahman*. And *brahman*, whatever it might be, is an intrinsic presence in the sacrifice, so that it could be said that "only he who is born from *brahman* is truly born," but at the same time that "he who is born from the sacrifice is born from *brahman*." Beyond this acquired paternity, anyone might also be the child or the descendant of one of those Rakṣas who wandered the land and went "hunting for women," like the angels in Genesis copulating with the daughters of men.

The night before the ceremony in which a person kindles his fires with the *agnyādheya* ritual is a most delicate moment. Until then he was a "mere man"—and what he did was unimportant. But now, if he wants to start building a relationship with the gods, the ritualists suggest he should remain awake through the night. And here lies the crucial point. What is the prime characteristic of the gods that we can emulate? Not power: ours will always be limited. Not immortality: we don't have it—at most we may fool ourselves into thinking we have gained temporary immortality, after long practice. But it's an immortality that gradually crumbles away, like every conquest gained by merit. Not knowledge, because it is far inferior to that of the gods: we don't even know the mind of our neighbor, while "the gods know the minds of men." So then, what? The pure fact of consciousness: of being awake. "The gods are awake": moving closer to the gods means being awake. Not performing good works, not pleasing the gods with homage and offerings. Simply being awake. This is what enables anyone to become "more divine, more calm, more ardent," in other words, richer in *tapas.* And was it not *tapas* that had enabled the gods to become gods? By isolating the pure fact of being awake and giving it supremacy over everything else, the ritualists made known their particular view with the utmost clarity. Everything could be traced back to this. And everything else could be eliminated, except this.

Becoming divine was not an ultimate experience reserved for the mystics: it was instead the experience of anyone who *enters* the sacrificial ceremony, immediately after having been consecrated: "He who is consecrated moves toward the gods; he becomes one of the divinities." This is the passage to which Henri Hubert and Marcel Mauss refer when they describe *entering the sacrifice* as follows: "All that touches the gods must be divine; the sacrificer is obliged to become a god himself to be able to act over them." Hidden in a hut built purposefully to keep him apart from the human world, shaved, washed, oiled, dressed in white linen and covered by a black antelope skin, the "consecrated one," *dīkṣita*, gradually transformed into a divine embryo. He was made to move back and forth around the fire like the fetus kicking in the uterus. As always, the ritualists note the most subtle details: it is essential that the consecrated one holds his fists clenched. But not out of anger or despair. With that gesture he tries to seize the sacrifice. At that moment he says: "With the mind I take hold of the sacrifice." It must be like this, because the sacrifice is invisible, like the gods: "The sacrifice is not visibly taken hold of, in fact, like this stick or a garment, but invisible are the gods, invisible the sacrifice." Every event will be accurately described only if the description includes two parts: the visible and the invisible. And so the correct moment to unclench the fists is indicated with precision. Then the fetus "is born to divine existence, it is god."

But even though the consecrated one, during the sacrificial journey, gradually moved closer to the gods, there still remained a vast distance. Revealed above all by one fact: the gods do not sleep, men are not granted sleeplessness. This, ironically, is enough to thwart human claims: not only do you have to die, but you are also unable to avoid sleep. And this again is why wakefulness was the highest good, the moment of greatest proximity to divine life. Otherwise, in ordinary life, when people found themselves in rites that lasted days and days, all they could do when overcome by sleep was to turn to Agni, the good awakener: may he rouse us, whole, after everything has abandoned us in sleep, everything but breath.

Having listed the other sacrifices, the sacrifice to *brahman* still has to be described. And so we read: "The sacrifice to *brahman* is the daily study of the Veda." There is a line that starts off with the sacrifice as a long ceremony, structured into hundreds of movements and actions—and therefore entirely visible—and which leads up to a later and invaluable variant, the sacrifice as an invisible and imperceptible activity, as it is performed through the study of the Veda.

Study of the Veda, known as *svādhyāya* or "inner recitation," had to be done beyond the confines of the village, to the east or north, where the roofs were out of sight. It was the first indication of a process by which the simple acquisition of knowledge would get gradually more distant from society and unshackled by it. But study could also be carried out in other ways, even in bed: "And, in truth, if he studies his lesson, even stretched out on a soft bed, oiled, adorned and completely fulfilled, he is burned by *tapas* up to the tips of his fingernails: and so the daily lesson must be studied." Here we see a figure we thought was modern: the reader, described much as the young Proust might have been described, given over to his *journées de lecture.* Once again we can see Vedic open-mindedness: to practice *tapas* we don't have to cross our legs or subject ourselves to those "mortifications" that some regard as the very meaning of the word *tapas.* No, even *luxe, calme et volupté* may help—or at least not hinder. It is enough that the fervor of the mind runs without respite, and burns "up to the tips of the fingernails."

IX

THE BRĀHMAṆAS

He who knew the taut thread on which all creatures are woven, he who knew the thread of the thread, would know the great Exegesis. —*Atharvaveda* 10.8.37 (trans. L. Renou, 1938)

He who knows the taut thread on which these creatures are woven, he who knows the thread of the thread, knows the great essence of *brahman.*

—*Atharvaveda* 10.8.37 (trans. L. Renou, 1956)

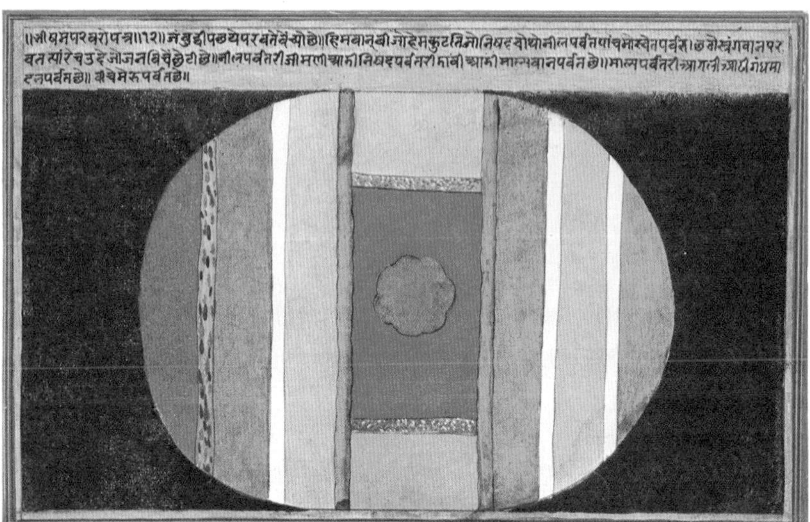

The Brāhmaṇas are the part of the Veda most neglected by scholars and most ignored by readers. In the second volume of Dandekar's *Vedic Bibliography*, the list of writings on the Brāhmaṇas fills eight pages, while thirty are taken up by the Upaniṣads and twenty-eight by the *Ṛgveda*. We can guess that not so many scholars, and even fewer readers, have taken any interest in them. And we might wonder why.

A first reason is to do with form, literary genre. The *Ṛgveda*, after all, can also be read as the most magnificent—and also most persuasive—example of Symbolist poetry, while the Upaniṣads, as Schopenhauer quickly recognized, can be read as outstanding metaphysical texts. But the Brāhmaṇas were neither poetry nor philosophy (only Deussen dared to put them at the beginning of his universal history of philosophy, but his example has not been followed). The Brāhmaṇas are continually laden with gesture: "He [the officiant] does *x* and *y*." This is the phrase that most often appears, each time prompting the thought: why does "he" do *x* and not *z*? The underlying assumption is that supreme importance is to be given to the liturgical gesture. And that ritual is given preeminence over every other form of thought, as if ritual were the immediate way by which thought itself becomes manifest. This, though, was exactly what the West wanted to shake off—starting with the Greeks and then through the whole of Christian tradition—like superstitious ballast. Liturgical reforms in the Catholic Church, over the centuries, mark a progressive, ruthless reduction in the range of ritual actions, and words accompanying these actions, up to the poor state of things in the wake of the Second Vatican Council. As for the Reformation, more than arguing particular points of theology, it urged a general rejection of the fripperies of worship. And yet, the heart of Christian doctrine is sacramental, linked to gestures that cannot be replaced by words. Hymns of thanksgiving, however lavish, can never substitute the gesture of the priest who *breaks the bread.* The sacramental act is the greatest obstacle for anyone wishing to adopt the regime of substitution. For it is an irreplaceable gesture, and a gesture that has immediate effect on the invisible. But if the invisible is to be discarded, then its intermediary must also be eliminated.

Witzel once observed, in passing, that the Brāhmaṇas are "one of the oldest examples of Indo-European prose." An invaluable comment, which very few seem to have given any thought to. In fact, if it is true that the Brāhmaṇas "are still regarded as incomprehensible and tedious by the very scholars who study them," then why take any interest in their form? And yet prose—this varied, flexible, prehensile form, capable of stretching to every level, from manuals on horse riding or hydraulics up to Lautréamont, this form that has become normality itself, so normal as to become transparent, to the point of being barely noticed—made its appearance on Indian soil through this unattractive and often incomprehensible literary genre. The Brāhmaṇas are not thought (or at least: they are not what people today are accustomed to consider as thought); and they are not stories (or at least: they are a series of fragmented and continually interrupted stories). Rather, they give instructions above all about ceremonies whose inner meaning, already obscure, often becomes even more obscure due to the explanations the Brāhmaṇas seek to provide. History has taken enormous trouble to chemically separate these elements, associating them with certain injunctions: thought cannot tell a story, a story cannot be a way of thinking, ritual is an obsolete activity that we can do without. To understand just how deeply these convictions are embedded in the mind, we need only listen to ordinary language. If something is described as a "myth," it is usually regarded as a baseless story; if something is described as a "ritual" act, it generally means it is a hollow and by now ineffective practice. This is diametrically opposed to the Brāhmaṇas, where "myth" is the very fabric of stories that have meaning, an everlasting meaning, and "ritual" is action in its most effective form. If there is such a misunderstanding—and it couldn't be greater—over the two words that are the foundation of story and gesture, it is no wonder if the people of modern times have developed such an aversion to this literary genre—more antiquated, jumbled, abstruse than any other—that is the Brāhmaṇas. Their first emergence is usually dated, at the latest, to the eighth century B.C.E. The dating is contentious, as it always is in India. But certainly earlier than those Greek sages of whom we know. Thales, the first of the pre-Socratics in the Diels-Kranz edition, lived between the seventh and sixth centuries. Moreover, a text like the *Śatapatha Brāhmaṇa* is so subtly arranged in its form as to suggest that it was elaborated over a long period. The Indian texts therefore clearly predate the earliest Greek speculation. But the subject matter is very similar—*phýsis*, the manifestation of that which is. It is a question of *giving names* to *phýsis*: in Greece it can take the form of poetry (Parmenides, Empedocles) or statements (Anaximander, Heraclitus). In India, it remains bound up with ritual, with gesture, even in the two longest and oldest Upaniṣads, the *Chāndogya* and the *Bṛhadāraṇyaka.* And, above all, the very form of the Upaniṣads—texts that were to be found *at the end* of a Brāhmaṇa—presupposes all the scrupulous, taxing, dauntless murmur of reasoning that precedes them.

The *Śatapatha Brāhmaṇa* belongs to the White Yajur Veda, a branch of the Veda devoted to the *yajus*, to the "formulas" recited by the *adhvaryu* during sacrifices. And the composition is painstaking, meticulous, always in danger of failing to keep a hold on the enormity of the material, all relating to the nature of the *adhvaryu*, this priest who works unceasingly and using every means—gestures, manual operations, words. While the other officiants spend their time chanting or watching in silence, the *adhvaryu* acts and makes the ceremony go on. He is its whirring engine.

When Renou had the chance, at Pune, to witness a Vedic sacrifice of the simplest kind, that of the Full Moon and the New Moon, he was struck by the activity of the *adhvaryu*: "One was able to gauge the overwhelming role of the manual officiant, the *adhvaryu*, on whom almost everything depends, gestures and words, despite the assistance he receives from two acolytes." While the *hotṛ*, the chanter, "appeared at the important moments, dominating everything with his tall stature and his vibrant voice," the *adhvaryu* provided the background to that "ample drapery of verses" with his "short, disjointed formulas," similar to the way of arguing in the Brāhmaṇas—always starting, being interrupted, being forced to change direction, weaving the fabric of the work by resuming it at different points.

The school of the White Yajur Veda is different from that of the Black Yajur Veda, above all because there is a clear-cut separation between the *mantras*—or verse "formulas," often taken from the *Ṛgveda*—and the commentaries on the ritual, which are in prose. We do not know and cannot guess what reasons lay behind this variance. But we can observe one result: the *birth of prose*, in the sense of a lengthy exposition, with no metric form, on a single subject: in this case the whole of the sacrificial rites. Until then, nothing of the kind had been seen in that form: of obstinate, meticulous, obsessive, relentless inquiry. Even if the Brāhmaṇas would one day become misused, spurned and reviled as a literary style, something of these origins would continue to energize prose, especially where that humble and practical form has revealed its intent to pervade every corner of everything, as in Proust. *À la recherche du temps perdu*, in fact, can be read as an immense Brāhmaṇa, devoted to expounding and illuminating the fabric of time within that long ritual (a *sattra*) that was the life of its author.

The "flavor," *rasa*, of the *Śatapatha Brāhmaṇa*, an unmistakable flavor that cannot be reduced to that of a metaphysical or a liturgical commentary, lies first of all in the uninterrupted sensation of *thinking the gesture* at the very moment when the gesture is performed, without ever abandoning or forgetting it, as if the spark of thought might be released only at that moment in which an individual being moves his body in obedience to a significant course. It would be hard to find other cases where the life of body and mind have coexisted in such intimacy, refusing to detach themselves for even a single instant.

The Brāhmaṇas do not offer *one* cosmogony, like the Bible or Hesiod or many tribal epic poems, but clusters of cosmogonies, juxtaposed, superimposed, and contrasted. This produces a feeling of bewilderment—and in the end of indifference. If the versions are so many and conflicting, might they not be regarded as lucubrations of the ritualists? The multiplicity of alternatives tends to lessen their meaning. Even Malamoud, who is used to treating texts with supreme care and discretion, in the end shows signs of impatience when referring to these "cosmogonies replicated, repeated, piling up, from one text to another, or within one and the same hymn, pushing back, overwhelming, penetrating, breaking up, like crashing waves"—a vivid and accurate description of these stories of "false beginnings or relative beginnings" that seem to give no hope of a fundamental solidity when describing origins, which are always veiled. And Malamoud quotes here a verse from the *Ṛgveda*: "You will not know he who created these worlds: something shields you."

Yet cosmogonies follow and overlap one another. But there is always the suspicion that they are "secondary creations." The gods are not there at the beginning, but almost at the end. Before them appeared the "mind-born children," *mānasāḥ putrāḥ*, of Prajāpati—successful attempts after many failures. And before them was Prajāpati himself, the Progenitor, though he—once again—was not a beginning. For Prajāpati to be created, the Saptarṣis had to meet and join forces, because they in turn felt unable to exist *alone.* A tangle of dark and tortuous stories, behind which always looms the outline of something else, perhaps only the "indistinct wave" to which the *Ṛgveda* refers.

On reaching the end of the tenth *kāṇḍa* of the *Śatapatha Brāhmaṇa*, after five *kāṇḍas* devoted to describing how the fire altar is to be built, covering an equivalent of 678 pages in Eggeling's translation, and after having negotiated a frenzy of additions and multiplications concerning the number of bricks to be used for building it and the way in which they are to be arranged, as well as various errors of calculation that have to be avoided during these operations, we come across three passages that are surprising for different reasons. After a final, breathtaking *excursus* on *arka*, a word in which a secret teaching is each time encapsulated, we immediately pass to a page that opens like a sudden clearing within the forest of numbers. It begins with these words: "Let him meditate on true *brahman*," which is linked, a little later, to a passage beginning: "Let him meditate on *ātman*." And it is followed by a few lines that already have the self-absorbed, final tone of the first Upaniṣads and end with the words: "Thus spoke Śāṇḍilya and so it is." Śāṇḍilya, according to tradition, is the author of *kāṇḍas* 6–10 of the *Śatapatha Brāhmaṇa* and these words of his are called the *Śāṇḍilyavidyā*, "the doctrine of Śāṇḍilya," as if the essence of his thought is revealed there. And it is here, in fact, that we find the precise meeting point, if ever this were needed, between the Brāhmaṇas and the subsequent and consequent Upaniṣads. This is the point where *ātman* is described as being like a "grain of millet" and like "this golden Puruṣa in the heart," after the five previous *kāṇḍas* had culminated in the description of how a minuscule human figure, the golden Puruṣa, was to be placed into the fire altar, whereas that same Puruṣa, that Person, is now to be found inside the heart and is revealed as being "greater than the sky, greater than space, greater than the earth, greater than all beings." This is the Vedic catapult that suddenly takes us from the smallest to the immeasurable and reveals where to find something that anyone, every meditator, can call "my Self." Here is a doctrine of enormous force, set out in a few clear, calm words, which will then extend throughout the Upaniṣads, for which it is the supreme teaching. "Thus spoke Śāṇḍilya and so it is." For Nietzsche's Zarathustra, the final clause—"and so it is"—would be missing. Nor could it have been otherwise.

An old problem for Indologists is the relationship between the Brāhmaṇas and the Upaniṣads. Agreement? Disagreement? Conflict? For guidance, there is a simple test: if we read the *Śatapatha Brāhmaṇa* as it is set out—and therefore followed immediately by the *Bṛhadāraṇyaka Upaniṣad*—we cannot avoid the impression of a perfect continuity of ideas. What changes is the stylistic register. After the incessant, detailed, stubborn exposition of the Brāhmaṇa, similar to the obsessive whirring voice of the *adhvaryu*, we now plunge into a dazzling *incipit*, which acts like a megavoltage discharge built up from the accumulation of nimbus clouds over the previous two thousand or so pages. It is as though, after a protracted compression and concentration of energies, we witness their release into bright fragments that instantaneously connect, without even a pause for verbs, as the Sanskrit language allows: "Dawn the head of the sacrificial horse, Sun its eye, Wind its breath, the open mouth Fire-of-all-men, the Year the Self," (where Dawn, Sun, Wind, and Fire are Uṣas, Sūrya, Vāyu, and Agni, all gods of the Vedic pantheon).

The unstoppable effusions of the Brāhmaṇa are followed and contrasted by the highly condensed Upaniṣad. What remains is the flash of equivalences: as dawn rises the young girl Uṣas is superimposed on the head of the sacrificial horse; the eye—anticipating Goethe—is the sun; fire and wind go deep into the body of every man. For all this we have been prepared by the "hundred paths"—intersecting, tortuous, rough and arduous—of the Brāhmaṇa. Only after traveling them does the view unfold in its full splendor.

There is no doubt, though, that in the Upaniṣads we see a tendency to give little value to knowledge gained through works and a parallel praise of knowledge detached from all action. It is the earliest gnosis, a model for all others. But it would be naïve and misleading to imagine that such a distinction was not already clear to the authors of the Brāhmaṇas, almost as if they were superstitious liturgical craftsmen, ignorant of metaphysics. The opposite was true—and from time to time they would refer with dry irony to what would, over the centuries, turn out to be the central point: "When they said 'either through knowledge or through work': it is the fire that is knowledge; it is the fire that is holy work." An apparently superfluous comment, which touches, however, on a key question. Two types of knowledge are thus established: the first is knowledge that need not be combined with visible acts; the other is knowledge as liturgical acts. At this stage, the shocking innovation lay in the first type of knowledge, which would then develop into the figure of the renouncer—and from there into every theoretical inquiry considered as the natural and appropriate condition of thought. In fact, what one day would become philosophizing, detached from any kind of ritual gesture, was the final outcome of a long process, a process in the course of which the crucial step was the internalization of the *agnihotra*, the first and most simple of sacrifices. And what could be done with the *agnihotra* could also be done with the most complicated rite, the *agnicayana*, the building of the fire altar.

But this step is important not only in distinguishing between the two regimes of knowledge. It is just as important in showing that the object of knowledge is still the same: the fire altar. When even knowledge is detached from every liturgical act, becoming pure construction and contemplation of relationships, such relationships would still remain the same ones expressed through that splayed wall of bricks built and then abandoned in a forest clearing. This is what the Vedic ritualists wanted to keep in mind; this would be the point on which they would clash with the Buddha, who wanted only to *extinguish* the fire.

The authors of the Brāhmaṇas paid meticulous attention to the world of desires (and of sacrifice insofar as it is based on desire), but they already saw perfectly well that the ultimate dividing line was between that world and what happens when desire no longer exists: "Regarding this there is the verse 'Through knowledge they ascend to that state where desires have vanished': one cannot get there with ritual fees and those practicing *tapas* do not get there without knowledge." With these words the paths of knowledge and sacrifice separate for the first time. Sacrifice, which arises out of desire ("Prajāpati desired" is said countless times—and every sacrificer, like him, says the same), cannot reach the point where "desires have vanished." Knowledge, which until then was equivalent to sacrifice, now appears as the path that allows access to a point that will never be reached by the sacrificial act. We are now in the realm of the Upaniṣads—if by this we mean that the question of knowledge is now to be posed in terms that will be followed by the Buddha (or Spinoza).

How do we heal an error that is always lurking in an imprecise gesture, in an inappropriate word? The gods were the first to ask the question, to Prajāpati. He replied with a concise and definitive lesson on methodology: "One heals the *Ṛgveda* with the *Ṛgveda*, the *Yajurveda* with the *Yajurveda*, the *Sāmaveda* with the *Sāmaveda.* As one would put together joint with joint, so he puts them [the parts of the sacrifice] together whoever heals by means of these words [the three 'luminous essences,' which are *bhūr*, *bhuvas*, *svar*, corresponding respectively to the three Vedas]. But, if he heals them in any other way than this, it would be like someone trying to put together something broken with something else that is broken, or as if a poison were applied as a balm for a fractured limb." This rule is also valid for the study and interpretation of the Veda. Bergaigne obeyed it in his *Religion védique*, illuminating the *Ṛgveda* with the *Ṛgveda* and nothing else. The *Śatapatha Brāhmaṇa* is waiting in the same way for a future scholar to fathom it in its entirety, as an immense opus dedicated to the opus of sacrifice. But the Brāhmaṇas have the peculiar characteristic of causing Indologists to lose their tempers. It's an age-old tradition. As old as the work of those intrepid scholars (such as Eggeling or Keith) who devoted several decades to translating and annotating them. We might imagine that the impressive quantity of studies amassed, beginning with Sylvain Lévi's illuminating *Doctrine du sacrifice dans les Brâhmanas* (1898), would have radically changed this attitude. But it hasn't. After more than a hundred years, it reemerges unchanged—paradoxically in an otherwise fascinating book by Frits Staal, one of the greatest experts on the Brāhmaṇas.

According to Staal, the Brāhmaṇas are an undigested hotchpotch, inside which the sober eye of the scholar has to "ferret out" (the verb is repeated within a few pages) some rare insight. The "most suspect" of all is the *Śatapatha Brāhmaṇa.* One has the feeling that Staal would like to go further in deploring these texts that contain "a great deal of what we may call magic but is better, more truthfully and less condescendingly or insultingly described as simple superstition." At this point he stops and asks, with haughty benevolence: "But should we not be charitable?" The answer follows immediately—and is less benevolent: "We should be, but there is a limit even to charity." We can infer from this that the Brāhmaṇas, after almost three thousand years, still have no right to the Western scholar's "charity." And yet, from what texts other than the Brāhmaṇas has most of the knowledge been taken that infuses the work of some of the greatest scholars on ancient India—Caland or Renou or Minard or Mus or Oldenberg or Malamoud? Or Staal himself?

We might ask why the Brāhmaṇas above all, among the whole of the Veda, arouse such irritation. Perhaps the answer is to be found in the word that Staal, with his vehement prose, would like to expunge not only from Vedic ritual, but from ritual in general: *meaning* (the intention is declared in exemplary fashion in the title of an important book of his: *Rules Without Meaning*). The assumption—unspoken, but increasingly apparent over the years—is that, *wherever* meaning appears (and not just in Vedic ritual, but everywhere and always), everything tends to become obscure and arbitrary, destroying the noble transparency of science. In Staal there is a violent and preposterous contrast between his devotion and expertise in studying Vedic ritual and his contemptuous and ill-concealed intolerance toward the oldest texts in which those rites are described and explained. This intolerance grows from the *hypertrophy of meaning* that marks the Brāhmaṇas, and induces him to take refuge in the opposite extreme, in the realms of algebra and formalization, areas uncontaminated by that unwelcome guest: semantics. Staal's theory, reduced to its bluntest and most provocative form, states that the rite is carried out *for the rite itself,* as if "art for art's sake" could be applied several thousand years retrospectively and could indeed serve as a prelinguistic basis for human activity. A bold approach that doesn't stand up to investigation. But Staal has used it because he has been struck by the very high degree of formalization (and a tendency toward algebrization) found in Vedic ritual. His studies of certain ritual sequences, above all those where recursive methods are applied, are in fact illuminating.

In that body of Vedic ritual, which is anomalous from every point of view, it is clear that two factors come together that elsewhere tend to remain separate: on the one hand a semantic excess, which leads to a proliferation of possible interpretations and can easily be passed off as an archaic remnant (as if it were a childish world where *anything can be said about anything*). On the other, a rigorous formalization that we are used to associating only with far more recent ideas (the very notion of a "formal system" is a twentieth-century acquisition).

If meaning is expunged from the Vedas, as Staal suggests, then at least two other words have to be expunged: *religious* and *sacrifice.* Staal, undeterred, does not shrink from the task. And his casualness applies not only to the ancient texts. Even when dealing with modern Indologists, in those rare cases where they are cited with approval, Staal has no qualms about carrying out corrective adjustments that guide the text toward the right theory: quoting an important passage by Renou on the "priority of the *mantras* and the liturgical forms which they presuppose," Staal frankly warns us that he is replacing the word *religious* with the word *Vedic.* Now, the word *Vedic* can mean either a vague chronological indication or the connection of something to "knowledge," *veda.* But Staal evidently wants to blot out anything religious from this "knowledge," as if it were a disturbing alien element. More than anywhere else, this is untenable when talking about ancient India, where it is pointless searching for even the tiniest detail that is not intertwined with religion. As Staal himself has noted elsewhere: "There do not exist, for example, any Indian category and words that correspond to the Western notion of religion." But they do not exist insofar as *everything,* in a Vedic context, is religious. Even so far as vocabulary is concerned, Staal seeks to intervene, presenting his own suggestions as an appropriate technical adjustment: "I prefer to use the word *ritual* rather than the word *sacrifice*, since I reserve this latter for describing the rituals that lead to the killing of an animal." A neutral tone, as if the matter ought to cause no problems. But that adjustment is enough to cancel out countless passages in the Brāhmaṇas that speak of the rite of the *soma* as a killing. A killing of a plant and of King Soma, who is a god, welcome on earth. The Brāhmaṇas are tireless in reaffirming that all offerings, including the libation of milk in the fire, the *agnihotra*, are sacrifices. And here comes the Indologist Frits Staal, three thousand years later, who decides this isn't so. And above all: that it mustn't be so. His zeal takes him to the point of correcting Hubert and Mauss's famous title: quoted by Staal, their *Essai sur la nature et la fonction du sacrifice* becomes *Essay on the Nature and Function of Ritual*. It is Western science, in its naïveté and its arrogance, that has decided this (and Staal has indeed entitled one of his books *The Science of Ritual*).

Even back in the times of Keith (1925) it could be suggested with a certain candor that *all is possible* (and that therefore *all is arbitrary*) in the Vedic texts: "If the waters can practice asceticism, it is not surprising that speech can speak standing in the seasons, or that the sacrificial consecration can be pursued by the gods with the aid of the seasons, or that the ascent of the meters to the sky should be visible." In short, in the Veda *anything goes*, declared Keith, at almost the same time as the première of the great musical of the same name. What offended a sane Westerner was above all "the notorious 'identifications' of the Brāhmaṇas which, since long, had been the laughing stock of occidental scholarship." This was an "identification technique that establishes links, equivalents, nexuses (or correlations) between, or identity of two entities, things, beings, thoughts, states of mind, etc. Both entities are unrelated, according to our way of thinking." Examples? "When the text says 'the *muñja* grass is strength' and 'the *udumbara* tree is strength,' or 'Prajāpati is thought' and 'Prajāpati is the sacrifice,' it will not be clear why some kind of grass (a living being, or dead material) could be the *same* as 'strength' (an abstract idea, or a force experienced); or, in the second case, why and how the god Prajāpati, 'the lord of creation,' could be the same as 'thought/thinking,' and, at the same time, the idea or act or ritual ('sacrifice,' *yajña*)." This passage is found in Witzel's introduction to his edition of the *Kaṭha Āraṇyaka* (an extremely rare instance of a Vedic text that can properly be described as published in a critical edition). And his intention is clear: to illustrate in a neutral and fair-minded tone why Vedic thought continues to be so disconcerting, but without adopting the usual voice of disapproval, in the manner of Keith or Eggeling or Max Müller. Yet, even in this very recent formulation, there is much that jars. What, indeed, is "our way of thinking" (almost as if the West were a seamless mass of unalloyed good sense)? And are the strange examples of identification that Witzel offers us indeed so inconceivable? Does saying that a certain grass "is strength" really sound any more incomprehensible than Jesus's words at the Last Supper when he says that a piece of bread is his body and some wine his blood? Is saying "Prajāpati is thought" any stranger than talking about the word made flesh? Is it possible to hold that "our way of thinking" is so barren and desolate that it doesn't embrace, at least to some extent, *thinking in images*?

We still, though, have to understand why the Vedic texts—and above all the Brāhmaṇas—continue to evoke such a feeling of vertigo and obscurity. Not because they involve thinking in images (without which all thought would be inert). But because they use it all the time, with extreme devotion, unperturbed about any implication, indeed putting every implication into action (through gesture). This is the intractable Vedic offense, that triggers so many reactions of rejection and fear. The Western attitude toward imagery wavers between minimization (*x* is *only* a metaphor, and therefore not binding) and the temptation to interpret metaphors literally (a practice leading to various basic psychic pathologies, above all paranoia and schizophrenia).

But in Vedic thought, identifications are *not* metaphors. As Witzel has rightly said, "the majority of sentences establishing identifications are simple nominal clauses of the type 'x [is] z' or 'x *vai* z'; they are frequently summed up by a statement 'x *eva* z' " (where *eva* and *vai* are words roughly corresponding to "indeed," "in fact"). The cautious and uncompromising way of metaphors is therefore ruled out from the very beginning. The identification (or equivalence) superimposes two entities without any exercise of caution. And here we sense the slight sneer of Western superiority, recalling Musil's description of the scientists in

Diotima's salon. Once the metaphor is gone, an irresolvable confusion would be created between the two entities whose equivalence is asserted. But it is obvious from a thousand indications that the Vedic ritualists were in no danger of confusing the multiple levels of that which is. Instead, they saw them at every moment and allowed thought to waver continually from one to the other. To cover themselves—and give an ironic nod to the effect that they were well aware of the rules and limitations of the game—they often resorted to the particle *iva*, "so to speak," "in a certain way." Far more subtle than the clumsy "like," which elsewhere (in the West) announces entry into the realm of the metaphor. *Iva* is more vague—and lets the unknown and the uncertain become involved at the very moment when a nexus, a *bandhu*, is established.

Iva, *svid*, two expressions that could even be left untranslated (as often happens), indicate that we are crossing the threshold of hidden thoughts. According to Renou and Silburn, "the word *iva* accentuates indetermination, evokes latent values." In the same way that *svid* above all accompanies questions in which enigmas are voiced. There were two ways of introducing into discussion that aspect of the *anirukta*, of the "unexplicit" that is destined to remain so, ever shifting but always encircling the spoken word like a halo. Since thought proceeded by way of identifications, comparisons, equivalences, *iva* was a reminder that everything said was to be understood "in a certain way," without becoming fixed in its identity. Which of itself does not exist—or at least only "so to speak," *iva*.

In the troubled history of the Brāhmaṇas, after much insult and abuse, the day of reckoning at last came. It happened in July 1959, at the Indological conference held at Essen-Bredeney. An eminent Indologist, Karl Hoffmann, stood up to deliver a few words that sounded like a long-awaited Supreme Court ruling: "The monuments of Vedic prose (the *saṃhitās* of the Black Yajur Veda and the Brāhmaṇas) are, as the immensity of the twelve principal works that they contain is already proof by itself, the literary precipitate of a significant period in the history of the spirit and religion, stretching from the *Ṛgveda*, India's most ancient literary monument, to the Upaniṣads. The contents of these monuments in prose are made up of theological discussions on the rituals of Vedic sacrifice. The arguments they present often seem devoid of meaning, which is why Max Müller could describe them as 'the twaddle of idiots and the raving of madmen.' This may be explained, however, through the magical vision of the world that dominates here (Stanisław Schayer). And they constitute furthermore, as a sort of 'prescientific science' (Hermann Oldenberg), the germ cell of the speculative thought of the Indians."

Unwieldy, solemn, perfectly right. The French school, in truth, from Sylvain Lévi to Mauss, Renou, Lilian Silburn, Mus, Minard, and Malamoud, hadn't felt the need to issue such a declaration of principle. They all knew that the Brāhmaṇas were an immense and largely unexplored mine of thoughts—and they were not concerned about declaring it. They concentrated instead on the task of bringing the texts to light and connecting them to one another. But we know that German science always needs legitimation. And so, on that July day, Karl Hoffmann assumed the responsibility of formally accepting, after almost three thousand years, the formless and semiclandestine corpus of the Brāhmaṇas among those works of thought that can be classed as indispensable to humanity. It was as if a group of patients had suddenly been moved from a mental hospital to an academy.

During the early years of the twentieth century, anthropologists were divided in two rival camps: one declared that ritual preceded myth, the other that myth preceded ritual. Childish squabbles—as became apparent a few years later. Mauss saw it as such from the very beginning. For him it was clear that "myth and ritual cannot be dissociated except in the abstract"—and he wrote this in 1903. The important thing was not to set illusory, unfounded precedents—on one side or the other—but to show "the interpenetration of ritual and myth, to reveal the living organism which they form through their union." And thirty years later he would devote an entire course, using Strehlow's evidence from Australia, to illustrate cases of perfect interdependence between ritual and myth, that showed "their solidarity, their intimacy." On the one hand, ritual appeared each time as a "dramatic representation (verbal and physical) of myth," whereas myth, if construed as a simple story and "detached from its cult necessities," ended up revealing itself to be "without real foundation, without practical essence and without symbolic flavor."

But it was exactly this that required an explanation. Why do particular gestures have meaning only if they are based on a story? Why do particular stories need to be told through particular gestures? Here we approach a riddle that lies hidden in the depths of the mind. It is the riddle of the *simulacrum*, of the *eídōlon*, of the image that *must* become visible in order to be effective. This is a characteristic not just of certain cultures, but of whatever culture, in the same way that Pythagoras's theorem, though formulated in Greece at a particular time, and in Mesopotamia even earlier, did not belong only to the Greek or Mesopotamian cultures, since it is universally applicable. Yet a certain degree of lucidity has to be achieved in a particular place and at a particular time over certain relationships. What Mauss described as the necessary "intimacy" between myth and ritual, the interaction between liturgy and story, had perhaps never been so clear and so effectively put into action as in the time and in the doctrine of the Brāhmaṇas. It should not, therefore, be a case of anthropology bending benevolently over the Brāhmaṇas to extract some still useful relic from the jumble. But the Brāhmaṇas themselves might help anthropology to recognize something on which its whole practice is based.

X

THE LINE OF THE FIRES

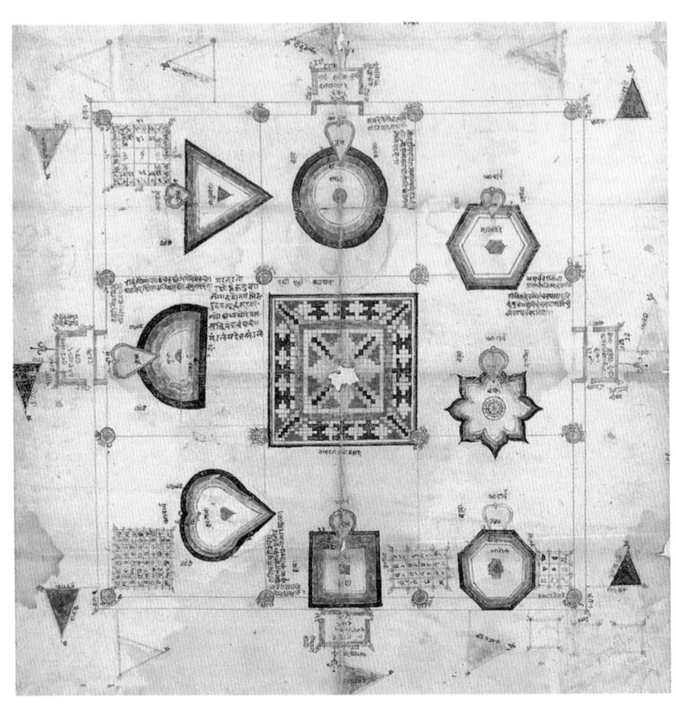

Man's initial state is formless, opaque, composite, and also "impure." Man is a being who "speaks untruth." He could carry on living like this, though leaving no significant trace. Otherwise he must compose a series of connected gestures that make an "action," *karman.* The quintessential action, the one that presupposes and assures that gestures have a meaning, is the sacrificial work.

But what is the origin of this work whose first peculiarity is that of being the model for all other work? Desire. Not a general, roving, multifarious, shifting desire—for "mortal man has many desires" and this plurality of desires dwells unremittingly within him from the first to the last moment of his life—but a *single* desire that seeks to detach itself from every other, to break its ties with the mesh of other desires and find the path to fulfillment. How? By becoming a "vow," *vrata.* Entering a vow is like entering another space, that of detached desire, which binds itself, barricades itself from the outside world, and builds a sequence of gestures within the new space that reaffirm it each time. What then is the first of these gestures? To touch water. But not anywhere. To touch it on a point of the invisible line that joins the *āhavanīya* fire and the *gārhapatya* fire. This is the *line of the fires.* The *gārhapatya*, "domestic," hearth is circular, sited to the west. There the fire is lit. There burn the embers with which the other fires will be lit. Not far away, to the east, on any type of ground, freshly swept with *palāśa* branches (*Butea frondosa*, Flame of the Forest, but it should also be thought of as *brahman*), a square hearth is built, called *āhavanīya.* On this fire the oblations will be offered—and it can be lit only with an ember taken from the *gārhapatya* fire. The *āhavanīya* fire is the sky, the *gārhapatya* fire is the earth (and it is circular since the earth is a circle at the center of other circles.) Between the two fires is the atmosphere, where we breathe, where we act. In the middle there is also "the trunk of the body," where the heart, life, beats. There are other fires, but these two must be set up first: *āhavanīya* and *gārhapatya.* They provide the tension on which everything rests. Everything is supposed to happen on the invisible line that connects them. The miracle behind everything else can happen only here—only here can things acquire meaning. If man wishes to escape from the untruth in which he is born, and in which he is destined to remain, he must tread that line, touch the water there and formulate a desire. In this way he will *enter the vow*, enter the hazardous state in which truth can be spoken, in which desire can be fulfilled, in which the gesture assumes a meaning. If every sacrifice is a "ship that sails toward the sky," the two fires, *āhavanīya* and *gārhapatya*, will be the sides of that ship, the limits within which the pilot (each and every sacrificer) must move, from the moment in which he begins to carry out certain movements: those movements, if they take place *between the two fires*, acquire a meaning that separates them from the ebb and flow of human actions.

The scene has to be observed from the viewpoint of the gods. Before a man (any man) crosses the line of the fires, the gods ignore him. Then, "having walked around the *āhavanīya* fire, from the east, he passes between it and the *gārhapatya* fire. For the gods do not know this man; but when he now passes between the fires they know him and think: 'This is he who is about to make an oblation to us.'" When the ceremony begins, the man must first make himself recognized. The gods, until then, seem not to notice him. His destiny seems unimportant to them, his essence—undefined. They are huddled around the altar, but this is all they know about the earth, and all that interests them. So to make himself noticed, and then recognized, the man passes between the two main fires. That is the line on which tension vibrates, giving meaning. When the gods see someone crossing it, they immediately know something is going on. At that moment the man is recognized and finally exists. And he exists only so far as it is he who will present an offering. Man's original lack of substance is gone and he becomes a being with whom the gods will deal. This is how relations between men and gods are established.

The sacrificer's first concern will still be not to act in vain: the oblations are offered, the complex liturgical machinery is set in motion, but the gods can still ignore him. They may not recognize the sacrificer. More than the Hegelian recognition between master and servant, Vedic men were worried about the recognition between gods and sacrificer. Hence the excited dialogue between *adhvaryu* and *agnīdh*, his assistant, who is responsible for lighting the fire: " 'Has he gone, *agnīdh*?,' and with this he means: 'Has he really gone?' 'He has gone,' replies the other. 'Ask that they listen to him.' " The officiants are those who are already familiar with the world of the sky. This is the basis of their existence. What is more, they depend on the ritual fees they receive from the sacrificer, who is, however, an ordinary man, someone whom the gods may even ignore.

The dialogue between the officiants takes place on a barren open space, marked out by three fires. The officiants had to understand whether the rite was *successful*. But how? By talking about the invisible, about something that was happening—perhaps—between the gods, between them and the sacrificer, along that aerial track which was the sacrifice. At that moment they might have seemed absorbed in monologues, participants in an identical hallucination.

According to Coomaraswamy, "the oldest Indian type of sacred architecture, both enclosed and roofed," is the *sadas*, the hut where the sacrificer or the initiand spends the night before starting the liturgical acts. "A place 'apart' (*tiras*, *antarhita*) to which the gods resort." A place that helps us to understand the reason for every closed space: for "the gods are segregated from men, and thus secret also is this which is closed on every side." The sacrificer sleeps there and, so long as he is there, "truly he comes close to the gods and becomes one of the divinities." But nothing is permanent: soon after the rite, the hut will be demolished. And yet it is in this empty, fragile, and makeshift place, before even the temple came into being, that contact is made with the gods. Emptiness and separation from the rest of the world are enough. The first image of what will one day be the *study*, not just of St. Jerome, but of every writer: that room which is a witness to writing and protects it with "the cloak of initiation and of ardor."

It is a premise of Vedic sacrifice that only while man is preparing and celebrating it can he become something more than human. It doesn't matter what he does up to the moment when the fire is set up: he will still just be human. So the night before the *agnyādheya*, the "setting up of the fires," he doesn't even have to remain awake: "Until he has set up a fire of his own, he is simply a man; so he can also sleep, if he so wishes." Certainly, as it says a little earlier, "the gods are awake"—and coming close to the gods implies participation in their vigil. But it would be pointless of him to do so unless he has his own fire, unless he enters into that opus which is the sacrifice. Wakefulness is the pivotal point of the Vedic world. But it operates only within the uninterrupted work that begins when he sets up his own fire. In any event, Vedic men knew that every evil sprang from a troubled state of mind. They wanted their enemies or rivals to be afflicted by "bad dreams" before every other infirmity (which they listed: "lack of offspring, homelessness, ruin").

The premise for every sacrificial act is metaphysical: entering the rite means entering the truth, leaving the rite means returning to untruth. A categorical statement, which ought to be placed beside the enunciation of the Way of Truth in Parmenides' poem. The ritualist's style is spare, abrupt, abrasive. There is no gradual progression and there are no moments of relief. The words are all the more penetrating: "Twofold is this, there is no third: truth and untruth. And the gods are truth, men are untruth. And so, by saying: 'I now enter from untruth into truth,' he [the sacrificer] passes from men to the gods. He shall speak only what is true. For the gods keep this vow: to speak the truth. And for this they are splendid. Splendid then is he who, knowing this, speaks the truth."

There are two extremities of existence, two poles between which tension flows: truth and untruth. Like being and nonbeing in Parmenides. *Tertium non datur.* And the space in which this occurs has the sky and the earth as its extremities—or the *āhavanīya* fire and the *gārhapatya* fire. But we immediately notice a peculiarity: "truth" and "untruth," in the text, are *satya* and *anṛta.* As if *anṛta* was the negation of *another* truth, indicated by the word *ṛta.* This takes us back to another open question: Heinrich Lüders, in his monumental, unfinished *Varuṇa*, devoted page after page to showing that *ṛta*, often translated as "order," primarily meant "truth." And his theory would seem to be borne out by the above passage, where *satya* and *ṛta* appear as equivalents. But synonyms do not exist. *Satya* is truth in relation to "that which is," *sat. Ṛta* contains within it a reference to order, to the *correct articulation* which is in the root *ar-* (from which the Latin *ars*, *artus*—and also *ritus*). In *ṛta* the *truth* is still visibly linked to an arrangement of forms, to a certain way in which they are connected.

It is the liturgy of the *agnihotra*—the morning and evening libations, the germ cell of all sacrifices—that sheds light on the relationship between *satya* and *ṛta*. In a passage in the *Maitrāyaṇī Saṃhitā* we read: "The *agnihotra* is *ṛta* and *satya*." Bodewitz translates this as "order and truth" and notes: "This of one of the passages which show that *ṛta*, 'order,' here occurring together with *satya*, 'truth,' does not mean 'truth,' as Lüders assumes in *Varuṇa* II." And so a vast body of investigation would seem to come to nothing in just a few short words. But does it really come to nothing? Or are both scholars perhaps right *in a certain way*—and is our conception of the word *truth* too limited? Let us now consider another passage in the liturgy of the *agnihotra*: before moving on to the oblation, the *adhvaryu* touches the water and says: "You are the thunderbolt; take my evil from me. From sacred order (*ṛta*) I enter the truth (*satya*)." That is how P. E. Dumont translates it. But according to Willem Caland: "From the just I pass to the true." *Ṛta* and *satya*, the Vedic ritualists would say, are a couple (like, as we will see elsewhere, *satya* and *śraddhā*, "trust in the efficacy of ritual") and their relationship is dynamic: from *almost* a superimposition we pass to a contraposition. Truth, in *ṛta*, is interlinked with order, above all with the order of the world watched over by Varuṇa. And in this sense the word, having fallen into disuse after the Vedic era, would be replaced by *dharma*, where the meaning of "order" is clothed by that of "law" (we are at the origin of *law and order*). In *satya*, on the other hand, truth is a simple statement of *that which is*, devoid of any other reference. And so from *order* (*ṛta*) we can arrive at *truth* (*satya*), as from one degree of the same truth to another, now entirely free of any cosmic reference.

The translation of *ṛta* will nevertheless remain a worry for Indologists, as Witzel has stressed: "There simply is no English, French, German, Italian, or Russian word that covers the range of meanings of this word." And yet a good approximation does exist, at least in Witzel's mother tongue—and it is *Weltordnung*, "world order." But, for confirmation, we need the help of Kafka. Anyone wanting an introduction to the meanings of *ṛta* might begin their personal initiation by reading the chapter in *The Castle* where there is a nocturnal dialogue between the counselor Bürgel and K.—a dialogue culminating in two sentences that could be attributed to one of the Seven Seers: "That is how the world itself corrects the deviations in its course and maintains the balance. This is indeed an excellent, time and again unimaginably excellent arrangement, even if in other respects dismal and cheerless." Wilhelm Rau observed that Renou himself wavered between two solutions when translating *ṛta*: "the cosmic Order" and "the regular 'course' of things = *ordo rerum*."

Questions of etiquette immediately arise: what should the sacrificer do as soon as he has taken his vow? What is the correct way to behave, so as not to defeat his purpose? First he must fast. Then, the night before the start of his planned rite, he should sleep on the ground, in the house of the *gārhapatya* fire. These are the first two rules of sacrificial etiquette.

But why is this? The vow is a way of welcoming the gods as guests—and is immediately perceived as such, for the gods see every movement in the mind of man. And so the first aim of the vow is to make space, to keep the area around the fire clear, since it is there that these new guests, the gods, sit waiting for their food. This is enough to link fasting with a rule of good manners: never eat before your guests. Then, when it is time to sleep, the sacrificer stretches out on the ground beside the fire. This is the first scene of the new life after taking the vow: a fire lit, protected by its house; invisible presences—the gods—who gradually gather around; a man sleeping on the ground: it is the sacrificer, who in this way starts to befriend the gods. He breathes together with them, he warms himself together with them. But he has to sleep on the ground, again as if by a rule of etiquette, reaffirming the immeasurable distance between the new guests and the man stretched out beside the new fire: "For it is from below, so to speak, that one serves a superior."

Once the "vow" (*vrata*) has been introduced, once the *āhavanīya* and *gārhapatya* fires have been introduced, once truth and untruth have been introduced, what is the next step? The act of *yoking* something to something else. The sacrificer "yokes" the water to the fire. And he announces it with an "indistinct" (*anirukta*) voice. Here, the yoking resembles what occurs in *yoga* ("yoke," "junction"). It is a gesture of the mind taking hold of itself. This assumes that the mind is always a double entity, where two parts act upon and yield to each other. This is the exercise (the *áskēsis*, "ascesis") behind all else. When, in the *Bhagavad Gītā*, Kṛṣṇa urges that it is good for the mind to be "yoked," *yukta*, this is what is meant. The immobility of the lone renouncer is only a final outcome of this discipline. Its first manifestation is in gesture, in the liturgical act. Indeed, any liturgy takes this yoking for granted. And this continual reference to a precise mental action is perhaps the distinctive, recurring feature in all Indian thought, from the Vedas to the Buddha—and up to the Vedānta. But how does this act occur, by which the mind (or two elements—water and fire—that represent it) begins to act upon itself? This is the first and last question: " 'Who (*Ka*) yokes you to this fire? He yokes you. For whom does he yoke you? For him he yokes you.' For Prajāpati is indistinct (*anirukta*). Prajāpati is the sacrifice: and thus he yokes Prajāpati, the sacrifice." Who, *Ka*, performs the act? The answer is given in the question: who acts is "who?," *Ka*, the secret name of Prajāpati, whose deeds the Brāhmaṇas are, in a certain way, recounting. And so elsewhere it can be said that "Prajāpati is he that yokes, that yoked, the mind for that sacred work." And we also learn that that gesture, in the liturgy, precedes another: "They yoke the mind and they yoke the thoughts." But before introducing himself with the name of Prajāpati, he steps forward, as if his shadow had appeared before he had, with the name Ka, the most mysterious, the most indefinite, the one that most radically expresses the difference between this being who preceded the gods and the gods themselves. And the name Ka arises in the most fitting way: murmured with an "indistinct" voice, *anirukta.* For all that is *anirukta* belongs to Ka: it is the implicit that can never become explicit, it is the "limitless unexplicit" (according to Malamoud's formula), the unsaid that can never be said, the indefinite that will always escape definition. The whole liturgy is a tension between the form that is expressed (*nirukta*) and the indistinctness (*anirukta*) from which it arises. The latter is Prajāpati's part. This is also because Prajāpati is made up of all the other gods, but without it being possible to say—as Sāyaṇa comments in relation to *Śatapatha Brāhmaṇa*, 1.6.1.20—that he is "this or that." He has to be remembered, he has to be taken into account, in every action, in every thought. Every action, every thought will be a move in the unresolved contest between those two ways of being.

With the first, simple action of moving forward carrying water, the sacrificer could already claim to have completed his task, since "with this first act he conquers all this [the world]." The liturgical setting begins to take shape. Meanwhile it is said that the water (*āpas*) is "all-pervasive"—playing on the root *āp-*, "to pervade"—and so reaches everything, and hence is used as a remedy to make up for the shortcomings of the officiants, in case they are ever unable to achieve everything. Then it is said that water is "a thunderbolt," as we can understand by observing that where it flows, it erodes the earth. And water as a thunderbolt has already been used by the gods to defend themselves from the Asuras and the Rakṣas, the evil demons who continually disturb them while they are celebrating sacrifices. These arguments ought to be enough to explain the use of water. And its dangers, since dealing with water is like handling a thunderbolt. But what then might be the purpose of water in the liturgy? Firstly sexual. Once set down to the north of the *gārhapatya* fire, its fruitful coitus with the fire begins. The sexual act is the first example of an action that is both yoking and yoked, an action underlying everything else that takes place in the sacrificial work. And so we read a little later: "Let no one pass between the water and the fire, so that in passing he does not disturb the coitus which is taking place." *Eros* is a certain state of tension that is only established if the distances are correct. The most common relationship, though, between water and fire is not erotic attraction, but rivalry. If the water was placed too far away, beyond the point exactly to the north of the fire, the fire itself would show its aversion. But also to stop too early, before the erotic tension is established, would be an error and a risk. It would in fact mean not reaching "the fulfillment of desire (*kāma*), for which he had carried forth the water." The final key word, *desire*, *kāma*, appears here. And its precariousness can immediately be seen. Placing the water jug in the wrong place would be enough to bring down the whole vast edifice of sacrificial acts.

The clearing used for celebrating the sacrifice was a setting where there was a risk at every step of offending or disturbing some presence. The water had to be placed to the north of the fire, not too far away. A short invisible line joined them. And the officiant had to take great care not to cross it. So powerful was the eroticization of the space—and above all that bare space where the officiants moved—that it is easy to see why they felt no need to make simulacra. The air was already crowded with them.

But fire and water were not the only powers that had to be heeded. The sacrificial ground was besieged by a mass of intruders—for the gods there were the Asuras, their brothers and enemies; for the officiants there were the Rakṣas. For the sacrificer, all of them were his rivals, his enemies. Nothing pleased these intruders more than interrupting the sacrificial work. To chase them off (over and over again, since they never let themselves be overcome once and for all) various stratagems were needed. The first was silence: the liturgy begins when speech is held back, for only silence assures continuity, unmarked by syllables and verbal forms. In the silence of mental discourse, such forms still exist, but as if reabsorbed in an aqueous element, from which they surface for just long enough to be submerged once again. Another stratagem is fire. Bringing the liturgical objects close to the flame is like beginning the process of *tapas*, "ardor," that constant production of heat, in the mind and in the liturgical act, which will encompass the whole rite and will defend it from outside. The intruders will be driven back, flayed.

The scene of the sacrifice is an empty open space on a slight slope, dotted with the fires and the altar. The bitter conflict of elements that is about to take place has to be mitigated. The tips of the bundles of grass are still wet: resting on the ground they dampen Aditi, the Limitless One who sustains us all. Another sheaf of grass, called *prastara*, is untied: it is Viṣṇu's braid. Yet another is strewn around the altar, since the gods sit here and they find it "a good seat." The sacrificer and his wife will also sit on a sheaf of grass, which has another name. Lastly there is a sheaf of grass with an awe-inspiring name (*veda*, "knowledge"). Its purpose is not clear. During the ceremony, while an officiant is reciting a *mantra*, it is handed from one officiant to another, and finally to the sacrificer as well as his wife. The spare and barren scene is becoming dappled with soft, damp grass. The sacrificial ground is now strewn with seven sheaves of grass, just as the earth had been strewn with plants. And the altar—a beautiful woman of perfect proportions, stretched out in her nakedness before the eyes of the gods seated around her, and of the officiants—also has to be dressed, attractively, veiled with a heavy, sinuous cloak of grass: in various layers, at least three (the number must be uneven).

Added now to the spoons and ladles, to the seven sheaves of grass, are three stakes around the *āhavanīya* fire. The scene is already animated in a vast hallucination: the sacrificer recognizes his body in the spoons and ladles, he feels it crossed by the breath of life; he recognizes Viṣṇu's braid placed on the altar that the officiants are busy clothing. He sees the grasses multiplying, as in the beginning of time, spread over the ground so that the gods find a comfortable bed. Lastly, three fencing stakes are added around the fire. Who might they be? Their closeness to the fire suggests something lofty and secret. They are the first three Agnis: the first *dead* gods. And dead through fear of themselves, of fire. Through fear of being unable to deal with the nature of fire. They are a first warning of death as bare absence. It is an example of how the gods bring back the dead: in the form of stakes. High pathos cloaks the figures of the first three Agnis. Mute, they have no wish to tell us what happened to them when they died. And neither will Agni comment on that act of restitution performed by the gods. But we know he is reconciled to it. Thus he has assumed the role of *hotṛ*, of "invoker"—and his ceaseless movement stimulates the very life of the sacrifice. Life itself.

The three stakes never told the story of their flight, their terror and their suffering, but they realized the gods were using them. Without their rigid presence, Agni would never have accepted his responsibilities. In this way they felt they could ask what the gods are accustomed to ask: a part of the sacrifice. And they had the part of the sacrifice that *is lost*, the part that is accidentally spilt. A subtly metaphysical solution: to those who are lost goes that which is lost. And at the same time a great relief for men who live in terror of being unable to completely offer what they are offering, of losing an essential part of it—through clumsiness, outside attacks, ignorance. At last they would know that nothing is lost: the earth receives it and transmits it to the three brothers who had themselves disappeared into the ground.

Finally, another three characters appear on the ever more populated and animated scene of the sacrifice. Once again three pieces of wood: but this time they are alight. The first brushes past one of the three brothers of Agni. With that slight contact, as with two old friends, the invisible fire is lit. Then it is the visible fire that has to be lit: the burning ember is brought close to the center of the altar while one officiant pronounces a verse in the *gāyatrī* meter. The fire cannot be lit unless he pronounces it, for only words spoken in that meter give power, give meaning to the action. At the same time, what the ember lights is the *gāyatrī* itself. And the *gāyatrī* in turn lights the other meters, one after the other. It is the first prodigy: the lighting of those verbal beings—the meters—which carry the oblation to the sky, like mighty birds. And from the sky they will come down among mankind. So enormous is this event that the other two embers must imitate it, in other kindling sequences: the second lights springtime, which lights the other seasons and sets in motion the circulation of time. Lastly, the third ember will kindle the brahmin, the last being who has to travel with the oblation toward the gods—and he too waits to be set alight. A meter, a season, a priest: the fire touches them and everything starts to exist.

Long before fire aroused fear, fire had felt terrified of itself, and of what men (and gods) would ask it to do. Agni's three older brothers had chosen to vanish, to disappear forever, rather than take responsibility for the fire. They knew that guilt and anxiety are created through dealings with the gods that would have to be nourished with the flame of sacrifice. And it was the task of fire to point out the way, the many stopping places between the sky and the earth, the routes that Agni would endlessly follow. This was to be life, the world. And Agni, as had also happened to other gods—even to Śiva, to Brahmā—had felt a strong aversion. He tried to hide. Every time we see life born like fire from water—or even just light glowing on water—we have to remember it is a sign of Agni's hiding place, from which Agni was snatched. This ought to be enough for us to understand that the first divine feeling toward life—life as it appears on earth—was simple anxiety and rejection. If this is not clear, it will never be clear later on why all ceremonial acts take place in an atmosphere of latent terror—as if handling something highly dangerous, something that has to be got rid of: guilt, similar to the Buphonia festival in Athens, when the axe that had slain the first ox was passed from hand to hand. With Indra—when he killed Viśvarūpa, the three-headed son of Tvaṣṭṛ the Craftsman—it was the three mysterious Āptyas who accepted the task of absorbing the guilt themselves. This wasn't enough, though, and for a long time, like an abandoned animal, Indra suffered the consequences of his crime: the killing of a brahmin, the most serious offense, which sticks in the throat of the assassin like a burning ember. The mad rush of guilt, rejected by all those who touch it, ends up in the *dakṣiṇā*, the "ritual fee" made to the priests, which is the origin of money and also a form of Vāc, Speech. It is a mystery that will pop up everywhere: punctual, penetrating, subtle.

It was not only Agni who was gripped by terror and fled, but also Indra, after having hurled the thunderbolt at Vṛtra. We find at a certain point that even Śiva disappeared. Not through terror, of course—Śiva can never be accused of feeling terror—but certainly as a refusal, a rejection of something that could also be the world. Indra even yields at the moment that ought to mark his triumph, the completion of his enterprise. In front of Vṛtra, Indra feels weaker, he doesn't trust his own thunderbolt. And the one who goes looking for him, to persuade him to return, is Agni, another fugitive, who in turn had not felt able to assume the role of messenger of the sacrifice. It might be said that all these gods occasionally feel paralyzed when faced with the task of existence—and of having a purpose. Such moments were—perhaps—the model for the radical rejection of the world that would later emerge in many forms among men in India.

"After which he should cast off the vow, saying: 'Now I am he that I really am.' " The sacrifice is complete. Hundreds of prescribed gestures have been performed. Hundreds of formulas have been spoken. What is to be done? It's a tricky situation. The sacrifice has to be treated like a skittish animal: first remove its yoke, which no longer has a purpose, and at the same time pour water—the water described as *praṇītāḥ*, "carried forth"—because "the sacrifice, while it is unyoked, backing away could injure the sacrificer."

The sacrificer then has to think about himself. He too has a yoke to remove: the vow. How does he express it? The sacrificer knows he ought to say: "I pass from truth to untruth," to describe exactly what he is doing. But it would be inappropriate, unseemly to acknowledge this, after the fervor of the liturgy. So he resorts to a formula that might seem tautological and yet is discreetly, humbly allusive: "Now I am he that I really am." In other words: an ordinary man who knows he is being ignored by the gods. And he returns with a certain relief—though he doesn't dare say it—to an anonymous, undisciplined, negligible life. But a life freed from the constraint of meaning.

What is the underlying presumption? Truth is an unnatural state for man. Man enters such a state only through the artificiality of the vow and the long sequence of actions (rites) connected to it. But he cannot remain there. The procedure for leaving the vow is just as important and delicate as that for entering it. In some way, man yearns to return to untruth, just as he yearns for sleep after the strain of a long vigil. Truth, whose name (*satya*) refers to "that which is" (*sat*), is an impermanent state for man, toward which he aspires and from which he slips away. Normality, the constant state of being, is in untruth, which immediately reenvelops man once he leaves the *vow*, the sacrificial action.

The most important step in the task of *setting up the fires* is the attempt to transfer the fires from the outside world to the remotest depth of the sacrificer's body. The whole doctrine of *yoga* rests on this operation, since in the beginning "the fires surely are these breaths: *āhavanīya* and *gārhapatya* are the exhaling and the inhaling." The origin of this difficult transposition was an episode in the war between the Devas and Asuras. The Devas were not yet gods then—and were therefore mortals, as the Asuras were. Between the two enemy forces there was only one immortal being—Agni—to whom everyone turned. So the Devas thought of infusing him into themselves. They let themselves be invaded by that immortal being—and so gained the advantage over the Asuras. It was a question of prefixes: they had chosen *ā-dhā-*, "to establish inside," rather than *ni-dhā-*, "establish below" (in the outside world, where grass is burned and meat is cooked), to which the Asuras were stubbornly attached. From then on, it became much easier to talk about inside and outside, about what happens visibly in the world and what happens invisibly in each person. *Tending the fire* was a single action that could just as well be carried out sprinkling butter on the flames or speaking words of truth. As Aruṇa Aupaveśi said one day: "Worship, above all, is truthfulness."

There is life when something is still also something else. There is death when something is only itself, a rigid tautology. This was one of the implications of the doctrine transmitted to Śvetaketu and his father, Uddālaka, by the king of the Pañcālas. That day, a warrior instructed a brahmin master and his son. The king didn't refrain from pointing out how unusual the event was. Not only was Uddālaka unfamiliar with the doctrine, but—said the king—"this knowledge, before you, had never reached the brahmins."

And yet Uddālaka had taught his son the doctrine that goes *beyond.* But the path of the esoteric is endless. Now it was for Uddālaka to present himself as a disciple, a *brahmacārin* just like his son. Each time, it was a question of starting over again. And it was he himself who suggested this. "We shall go back down and present ourselves as disciples."

There are two versions of what happened that day, one in the *Chāndogya Upaniṣad*, the other in the *Bṛhadāraṇyaka Upaniṣad.* They match each other, but with small, telling variations. The five questions put to Śvetaketu, not by a king but by one of his own followers, and which Śvetaketu was unable to answer, mostly related to the two ways that open up after death: the "way of the gods," *devayāna*, and the "way of the ancestors," *pitṛyāṇa.* But they also included a strange, apparently unrelated, question: "Do you know how, at the fifth oblation, the waters take on a human voice?"

In order to explain what ways there are for leaving the world and how they are reached, the king of the Pañcālas had first to explain how the world is made, starting with the celestial world. "That world," he said, was made of fire. But rain, earth, man, and woman are made of the same element, which is also a god: Agni. All are made of fire.

He then had to describe what fire is made of: logs, smoke, flame, embers, sparks. To explain *how* the celestial world, rain, earth, man, and woman were fire, he had to show in what way they were connected to each of their parts. The thought that operates by way of nexuses, correspondences, *bandhus*, is exacting, it does not allow for vagueness. And so, this time, man and woman appeared in the vision of the king of the Pañcālas: "In truth, O Gautama [as Uddālaka was often called], man is Agni: words are the logs, breath is the smoke, the tongue the flame, the eye the embers, the ear the sparks." Certain words in the *Bṛhadāraṇyaka Upaniṣad* version vary, but the essential nexuses are confirmed: "The word is the flame, the eye the embers."

As for the woman, her correspondence with the fire was entirely sexual: "Logs are her womb, her attraction to man the smoke, her vagina the flame, the embers coitus, the sparks pleasure." An erotic compendium. But we should not think that the Vedic vision of women is so limited, despite it being so acute. The point was this: the equivalences with Agni, relating in order to the celestial world, rain, earth, man, woman, were at the same time a sequence of oblations to Agni—and the woman served to make it possible to pass to the *fifth* oblation, for it is in the woman's fire that "the gods offer the seed; from that offering man is born." And only at this point—after the *fifth* oblation—can we understand what the answer was to the mysterious question put to Śvetaketu: "At the moment of what oblation do the waters take on human language, do they rise up and speak?" Śvetaketu's reply ought to have been: at the *fifth* oblation, because it is then that the waters protect the embryo for several months, until they become the voice of the human being that is born. It all fitted together. Not only the nexuses, the correspondences with fire and its constituent parts, but also—no less important—with the ritual order, therefore with the order of the oblations, which are each linked to the other like a sequence of equations.

But there was something that interrupted them: death. Man is conceived, then "lives so long as he lives. When he dies, he is placed on the fire. His fire is Agni, the logs the logs, the smoke the smoke, the flame the flame, the embers the embers, the sparks the sparks." Until a moment earlier, it seemed that the embers and the sparks might be transformed into anything whatsoever—and that everything was ready to be transformed into them. But now, all of a sudden, they were just embers and sparks, simple repetitions of themselves. Now, at the moment of cremation, it turned out that the logs were the logs, the flame was the flame—and, even if out of discretion it wasn't spelled out, the corpse was the corpse. It is difficult to imagine an *inference of death* that could be harsher, more unclouded, more clear-cut than these few tautological words.

"Thereupon he goes off, on foot or by cart; and, when he has reached what he considers to be the boundary, he breaks silence. And when he returns from his journey he maintains silence from the moment when he sees what he considers to be the boundary. And, even if there were a king in his house, he would not go to him [before having paid homage to the fires]." Behind the terse prose of the ritualist, we glimpse all the pathos of the journey: of any journey, as though Nerval or Proust were to recognize their own bedrock here. One has truly departed, and therefore can leave the silence that distinguishes the delicate phase of transition, only when the fires—or, according to another commentator, the roof of one of the fire huts—can no longer be seen. And the same when returning. Homeland, home—these are the fires. Even if a king were in your house, you have to pay homage first of all to the fires. There is something so intimate, so direct, so secret in each person's relationship with his fires that it seems to suggest a model for every personal relationship.

XI

VEDIC EROTICA

The altar is a woman with perfect proportions: "With broad hips, shoulders a little less broad, and narrow at the waist." Like a woman, it must not be naked. It is sprinkled with fine gravel or sand, so as to cover its body with a light gleaming film ("gravel is certainly an adornment, since gravel is fairly luminous"). Then with twigs and grass. The woman—the altar—makes herself beautiful, is helped to look beautiful, ready for the arrival of the gods. And so she passes a night.

At last she meets her lover, fire, "for the altar (*vedi*) is female and the fire (*agni*) is male. And the woman lies there embracing the man. And so a fruitful intercourse takes place. This is why he raises the two extremes of the altar on two sides of the fire." Every sacrificial act is interwoven with a sexual act. And vice versa. This is the nature of how things are. Arranged to attract the gods, so that the gods are aware of the sacrifice. How is it done? How can the altar be made "pleasing to the gods"? By ensuring as far as possible that it resembles a beautiful woman. The altar, then, cannot be just a roughly hewn stone. Instead "it should be broader on the west side, narrower in the middle, and broad again on the east side." Thus, looking at it, the gods cannot fail to feel attracted, as if by a beautiful woman lying motionless in a clearing. Awaiting her lover, her officiant, her victim.

The sacrificial setting was also an erotic one. One in which the intercourse didn't have to take place under the eyes of many, as in the horse sacrifice. Sometimes the appearance of a female was enough for the seed to be spilled. This was how some of the most powerful *ṛṣis* were born, owing to the superabundance of their mental life. They were born, in fact, without their father needing to touch the body of their mother. So pervasive was his desire, *kāma*, that Prajāpati—Kāma was another of his names—spilled his seed at the mere sight of Vāc during a long sacrifice. It was a three-year *sattra* that he was celebrating together with the Devas and even with the Sādhyas, the mysterious gods who had preceded the Devas: "There, at the initiation ceremony, Vāc arrived in bodily form. Upon seeing her, the seed of Ka and of Varuṇa spilled simultaneously. Vāyu, Wind, scattered it into the fire as he pleased. Then from the flames was born Bhṛgu, and the seer Aṅgiras from the embers. Vāc, upon seeing her two sons, while she herself was seen, said to Prajāpati: 'May a third seer, in addition to these two, be born as my son.' Prajāpati, to whom these words were spoken, said 'let it be so' to Vāc. Then the seer Atri was born, equal in splendor to Sun and Fire."

This occasion was not unusual among the many events we come across in the life of Prajāpati. On the contrary, it was a pattern that was set to recur, over and over again. Such episodes appeared frequently in the stories of the Devas and the *ṛṣis*. If it is not Prajāpati spilling his seed, it is his four sons—Agni, Vāyu, Āditya, Candramas—who spill it watching Uṣas passing before them. Mitra and Varuṇa spill it into a ritual bowl, during the *soma* rite, while they watch Urvaśī. And there are many stories of *ṛṣis* who spill their seed watching an Apsara (Bharadvāja watching Ghṛtācī, Gautama watching Śāradvatī, Nārada watching a group of Apsaras bathing). These scenes show one of the *ṛṣis* in solitary meditation, who is disturbed by the sudden appearance of a female being, generally an Apsara. But, for the gods, everything happens during a sacrifice, as if the erotic charge were always there and ready to be released at every liturgical scene. And the theory envisaged it. On various occasions, to justify the silence that has to accompany particular parts of the ritual, the *Śatapatha Brāhmaṇa* says: "For here in the sacrifice there is seed, and the seed is spilled in silence." From the moment when the fires are kindled to the end of the liturgy we find ourselves inside a field of erotic tension—and actions culminate in moments of silence in which the seed is spilled.

The *ṛṣis* born from the sacrificial blaze have a mother, because the flames are the vagina of she who has seduced that god or those gods who have procreated them. And so Vāc will demand another son from Prajāpati from the same flames that have produced Bhṛgu and Aṅgiras. Considering how persistently the theory and practice of semen retention has been developed in India, culminating in Tantrism, it is all the more astonishing how often scenes of semen emission without contact appear in the earliest texts. The *Ṛgveda* describes it with total clarity in relation to Mitra and Varuṇa before the appearance of Urvaśī: "During a *soma* sacrifice, excited by the oblations, they simultaneously spilled their seed in a bowl." This time the seed of the two gods isn't received by the flames, but by a ritual object, the *kumbha*, a clay pot that holds the "night waters," *vasatīvarī.* Thus one day Vasiṣṭha, the supreme *ṛṣi*, would be called Kumbhayoni, "He-who-has-had-a-pot-as-a-womb." But the *Ṛgveda* also says that Vasiṣṭha was "born from the mind of Urvaśī." The clay pot or the sacrificial flames were also the *mind* of the goddess or Apsara on which the gods who were watching her spilled their seed. An inseparable mixture of mind and matter. The seed of the gods spurted forth while the gods remained immobile. Urvaśī's mind was the vagina and the ritual bowl in which the seed was collected. Thus the hymn in the *Ṛgveda* addresses itself to Vasiṣṭha: "You, the squirted drop, all the gods kept through the sacred formula, *bráhman*, in the lotus flower."

If every act that happens in life is derived from a ritual gesture, then how can certain essential gestures that influence everything and are inextricably linked with everything, but have an unforeseeable and half-clandestine character, appear in the rite, how can they find a ceremonial position within it? The erotic gaze, for example, the exchange of glances between a man and a woman who do not know each other?

Movies, novels: these are the places where eyes meet, as part of a casual chain of events. But the Vedic ritualists, in their frenzy to include everything in the network of prescribed gestures, had even thought of this. There is a priest, the *neṣṭṛ*, whose main role was to escort and guide the sacrificer's wife—the only woman present—onto the scene of the sacrifice. The wife of the sacrificer, though, had no complicated duties. Only two subtle, erotic gestures, which the *neṣṭṛ* supervised. Three times she exchanged glances with the *udgātṛ*, the "chanter." That was enough for sexual union to take place, one of the many times it occurred during the rite. For the woman, at that moment, had thought: "You are Prajāpati, the male, he who gives the seed: place the seed in me!" Then she sat down and exposed her right thigh three times. Then three times, in silence, she poured over it the *pannejanī* water she had drawn that morning. Everyone was silent, all that could be heard was the gentle flow of water. Then she went back to hide herself in her tent.

At a certain point the sacrificer placed a bowl of ghee before his consort and told her to look at it. And so the woman "lowers her eyes to the sacrificial ghee." Now—we are told—"the ghee is seed." So what is happening, between the woman's eye and the ghee, is "fertile intercourse." At this moment the sacrificer's wife betrays her husband on his own instructions. But if the husband didn't ask her to look at the ghee, then his wife would be excluded from the sacrifice. There again, as soon as the wife looks at the ghee, their intercourse renders it impure, so the ghee has to be heated once again on the *gārhapatya* fire to remove its impurity before returning it to the *āhavanīya* fire. This is the formula that makes it possible to get around the difficulty: if the wife didn't look at the ghee, the sacrifice would be flawed, in that she would be excluded from it; if she looked at it on the *āhavanīya* fire, the offering would be rendered irredeemably impure. She can therefore look at it, but only on the *gārhapatya* fire. The ritualist is there first and foremost to show how to get around these conflicts, to avoid these paralyzing alternatives.

From a whole range of details we are reminded that what is occurring during the sacrificial liturgy is also a sexual act. The *sadas*, "hut," has many purposes during the ceremony, including that of accommodating the six *dhiṣṇya* fires of the officiants. But it is also a secret that has to be protected, since what it conceals is like intercourse between husband and wife—between the sacrificer and his wife. And "if a husband and wife are seen during intercourse, they immediately run away from each other, because they are doing something unbecoming." There is only one point from which it is permissible to see what is going on in the *sadas*: from the door, "because the door is made by the gods." Every other line of vision, every other angle of observation is illicit, like the act of a *voyeur*.

The oblation is preceded by a cry, an invocation, the *vaṣaṭ*: "May Agni conduct you to the gods!" That cry is the orgasm. If the oblation were presented before the *vaṣaṭ* it would be like seed not shed into the vagina, the cry of orgasm would not coincide with ejaculation. And so "the oblation is made either at the same time as the *vaṣaṭ* or immediately after it has been uttered."

The ejaculation, like immolation, can be regarded as the culmination of a process, but also marks its interruption, the beginning of a withdrawal from pleasure. If the pleasure is not interrupted, it would be as if the sacrificer were able to remain in his new body, intact, in the sky. But then he would have to leave his other body between the jaws of Agni and Soma, lifeless before the *āhavanīya* fire.

In the divine erotica, multiple seductions were frequent: Agni with the wives of the Saptarṣis or Soma with his sisters or Śiva once again with the wives of the Saptarṣis. Or Agni with the waters: "Agni once desired the waters: 'May I couple with them,' he thought. He coupled with them; and his seed became gold." When Alberich pursues the Rhine Maidens to possess the gold from which to make the Ring, he searches for Agni's seed, submerged there from remote times as a sign of the mutual penetration of opposites that makes life possible. "Gold's bright eye" is there, "which now wakes, now sleeps," writes Wagner in impeccably Vedic terms (Wellgunde in the Prelude of *Das Rheingold*). To snatch the gold from the waters brings disaster since it returns the world to a state where its elements are separated and thus cannot be regenerated. Neither the waters nor the gold will ever manage to regain the radiance that is the hallmark of elusive and everlasting life.

There is nothing more misleading than to think of the *Ṛgveda* as a work concerned only with sublime tone and enigmas, incapable of describing things directly. We also find irreverence toward the gods is already there, as well as every other trait later to be developed in Indian history. And no god is mocked and jeered more than Indra, the king of kings. In the tenth and last cycle of the *Ṛgveda*, which is also the one containing some of the loftiest enigmatic hymns, we find the hymn of Vṛṣākapi, the monkey-man. It is a hymn with multiple voices, divided between Indrāṇī (a sort of Mrs. Indra, who is given no name of her own), Indra himself, the monkey-man Vṛṣākapi, and his wife, Vṛṣākapāyī (a mirror image of Indrāṇī). It is not clear who the monkey-man is, nor to what extent he is an animal or a man. Perhaps he is a bastard son of Indra, produced with one of his concubines, whom his father keeps with him and protects. But the monkey-man shows disrespect (we don't know in what way) to the mistress of the house (Indrāṇī), who takes it out on her husband. The tone of the scene is exactly like that of the *commedia dell'arte*—or even Neapolitan comedy in the style of Scarpetta or De Filippo. The *trickster* Vṛṣākapi could be Punch. The scene is a family row, packed with sexual innuendo and bawdiness. The wife of the king of kings, furious because Indra won't intervene against the monkey-man, says to him: "No woman has a butt as fine as mine, no one fucks as well as me, no one grips tighter, no one can raise her thighs higher." No surprise that the dour Leopold von Schroeder should confess that the hymn "contains passages so obscene that I hesitated long before including it in this collection." Geldner resorts to euphemism in his translation. As for Renou, twice in this verse he resorts to ellipsis. So people of modern times, proud cultivators of low style, need have no worry. Even the Vedic seers were familiar with such language and used it when the situation arose. And they also understood the comic effect produced by the clash of conflicting tones. Throughout the hymn devoted to the pranks of the monkey-man every verse ends with the exclamation "*víśvasmād Índra úttaraḥ*," "Indra *über alles*."

In the *Atharvaveda* it is said that Earth "has black knees" like a child at play, but for another reason: because the flames have licked them, for Earth is "cloaked in fire." And, if we close our eyes, how do we recognize Earth? From its scent. It is the same fragrance that marked the fortunes of the Genies and the Nymphs, the Gandharvas and the Apsaras. He who invokes Earth also wants to acquire that fragrance. It is a fragrance associated with far-off memories: "That scent of yours that has penetrated the lotus, the scent which the immortal gods carried with them to the marriage of Sūryā, O Earth, that primeval scent, let me be entirely perfumed by it." The scent of Earth recalls one of the happiest moments in the lives of the gods: when Sūryā, daughter of the Sun, went to marry King Soma. The Earth's scent did not envelop Sūryā alone, but all girlhood splendor: "That scent of yours which is in human beings, female and male, which is their fortune, their pleasure, that which is in horses, warriors, that in wild animals and elephants, the splendor, O Earth, which is in the young girl, bathe us in it, so that no one wishes us harm!" All subsequent marriages, ever after, were a pale copy of what took place on Sūryā and Soma's wedding day. Even the hymn in the *Ṛgveda* that describes it begins by talking about Earth: "Earth is underpinned by Truth." And how could Earth be ignored on such an occasion? The hymn tells us straightaway that Earth—here called Pṛthivī, the Vast—"is great" thanks only to *soma*, to this intoxicating plant. Earth, for us, would not be so immense without *soma* to help us perceive it.

The bride soon appears: "Sūryā's fine dress was entirely embroidered with verses. The cushion was Intellect, the ointment was Gaze, the basket was Sky and Earth, on the day on which Sūryā went to her husband." Beside her, two handsome identical young men: the Aśvins, her brothers and attendants. Sūryā moved forward: "Her chariot was Thought, and Sky was the canopy." The chariot was drawn by the two months of summer. So summertime is auspicious for weddings. The effect of all that happened from the moment of Sūryā's arrival has reverberated down to today, though the daughter of the Sun is long forgotten. And from that day the psyche of the bride has received its imprint. This must encourage the husband to be humble. Even though he will be the first to touch his bride's body, he will be her fourth lover: "Soma had her first, the Gandharva had her second, her third husband was Agni, the fourth the son of man." Though the twentieth century would include psychology among its discoveries, no inquiry into the psyche of the young girl, the *kórē*, has reached such precision. When she reaches her wedding, even if her body is intact, every young girl has a long love story behind her. Her first lover was Soma—or Hades—since he is the ruler, as white as moonlight or as black as the darkness of the Underworld. For he is absolute and final. But after Soma comes the Gandharva Viśvāvasu, the wicked genie, the mental image of eros that besieges the young girl in her solitude, her dreams, her games. He is stubborn and wily, he knows how to wheedle his way into women's rooms and excite their fancy. Before the young girl can reach her marriage he has to be ritually driven out: " 'Leave here: this woman has a husband!' thus I addressed Viśvāvasu with the homage of my songs. 'Look for another young girl, who is still living with her parents: this is your fate: understand it.' " And if the Gandharva obstinately remains, he has to be told: "Leave here, Viśvāvasu! We implore you, paying homage to you, look for another, who may be lustful! Allow the bride to be united with her husband."

The third lover is Agni. Why? Agni is everyone's lover. Women, old and young, gathered around the fire and showed him the soles of their feet. From there the heat of the flames began to caress them, then climbed even farther, beneath their dresses, up to their thighs. If the Saptarṣis' wives betrayed them with Agni, what resistance could there be from an ordinary girl who had not yet been touched—and who is now being caressed in a way that no one else would ever equal? The fourth is "the son of man." His male arrogance is the most unfitting and unseemly. And yet, through the lengthy exercise of patience, with no claims to domination, he will have to find his way through the indelible memories of those lovers who have preceded him and whom he will try to emulate to succeed at last in being at least the fourth. And nothing will change when the young girl becomes a mother with many children. As the hymn says toward the end, invoking Indra: "Put inside her ten children, let her husband be the eleventh!"

XII

GODS WHO OFFER LIBATIONS

There is one gesture that inextricably unites the whole Indo-European world. It is the gesture of the libation. The pouring of a liquid into a fire that flares up, destroying a valuable or an ordinary substance in the flame. Libation is found back in the Minoan period, on the Hagia Triada sarcophagus. Homer's characters often carry it out as a necessary preliminary to their exploits. Sacrifices performed with no libation are extremely rare. And even Olympian gods are depicted on many vases in the act of offering a libation. Erika Simon has studied them—and has asked the inevitable question: to whom are they offering the libation? And why do gods feel they have to do it, just as much as humans?

In India, libation is to be found everywhere. The brahmin has to perform it each morning before sunrise, and each evening before dusk. It is the simplest rite, the *agnihotra*, which lasts about a quarter of an hour. Hundreds of times a year, thousands and thousands of times throughout a lifetime. But in the description given in the Brāhmaṇas, even the smallest rite is broken down into almost a hundred acts. And the texts tirelessly reiterate that this rite encapsulates all the others, and they describe it as the *arrowhead* of all rites: "What the arrowhead is to the arrow, the *agnihotra* is to the other sacrifices. For where the arrowhead flies, there flies the whole arrow: and so all the works of his sacrifice are released, thanks to this *agnihotra*, from that death."

It is not a social rite. The head of every family performs it alone. He needs no officiants, his consort is not present. Violence—which always leaves some mark, however much one tries to hide it—is absent here. But destruction is present, the irreversible yielding of something to an invisible presence. This action of abandoning something is called *tyāga*—and is often presented as the essence of sacrifice, of every sacrifice. Or otherwise: as its prerequisite. It is the gesture that indicates someone is approaching an invisible presence—showing submission or at least the willingness to *give way.* Marcel Granet, in *Danses et légendes de la Chine ancienne*, a work in which his genius shines, defined the virtue of *jang*, which is indispensable to the Son of Heaven, who wants to maintain his sovereignty, as a *yielding in order to get*, where it is essential that the gesture of yielding comes before everything else.

Libation: the act of pouring a liquid into the fire or onto the ground. Pure loss. Irreversibility. The gesture that most resembles the flow of time. The perfunctory Latins had only one word for it: *libatio.* The Greeks—three subtly different words: *choḗ*, *spondḗ*, and the verb *leíbō. Spondḗ* was the only way, in Greek, of saying "truce" or "peace treaty." At the start of the Olympic games, heralds ran through Greece shouting: *"Spondḗ! Spondḗ!"* All fighting would then stop. The Vedic people used fourteen terms to describe a particular type of libation, *graha*, in a particular type of liturgy: the *soma* sacrifice. But only for the morning libations. Another five names were needed for those at midday. And five more for those in the evening. And yet they said there was no simpler, more straightforward act for showing the sacrificial attitude. "The murmured prayer is a covert form of sacrifice, the libation is an overt form," we read in the *Śatapatha Brāhmaṇa.* For the prayer is murmured, while the act of pouring liquid cannot be hidden. Vedic men performed this act every morning, every evening. But so did the Greeks, according to Hesiod, who recommended the offering of libations "when you go to bed and when the sacred light returns." The Vedic people built a huge edifice of other ritual acts around this single act—and catalogued them in vast commentaries. The Greeks included it in their daily lives and in their rituals without any theorizing. Homer very often speaks about libations, since they formed part of the events he was describing. Their significance was implicit. The libation, as well as being the simplest form of worship, was also the oldest, if we are to believe Ovid. Water had been poured before blood: *"Hic qui nunc aperit percussi viscere tauri / in sacris nullum culter habebat opus."* "The knife that today opens up the entrails of the slaughtered bull / played no role in the sacrifices." And, once again according to Ovid, the libation came from India. Dionysus, or Liber, had introduced it on his return from his eastern expeditions: *"Ante tuos ortus arae sine honore fuerunt, / Liber, et in gelidis herba reperta focis."* "Before your birth the altars were without offerings, / O Liber, and grass grew on their cold hearths." But Dionysus, "having conquered the Ganges and the whole Orient," was said to have taught the offering of cinnamon, incense, and other *libamina.* From Liber also the name *libatio.* Through him the Vedic doctrine of sacrifice became meshed with that of the Romans.

Libation: the unrenounceable gesture of renouncement. Never so harrowing as the moment when we see Antigone before her dead brother, and "right away she lifted up with her hands the dry dust and a well-wrought bronze bowl to sprinkle on the corpse a triple libation." There is no need for fresh water—nor is it necessary to pour Oriental perfumes. Even the "dry dust" sprinkled by Antigone is just as good for a "triple libation." And the hopeless incongruity between that "dry dust" and the "well-wrought bronze bowl" that Antigone uses to pay homage to her brother goes back to the very origin of the gesture, which is the simple celebration of something that is forever lost.

The gods were great experts in the art of lengthening and shortening the rites. For the rite, like poetry, is greatly extendable or contractable. After having celebrated a *sattra* that lasted a thousand years, Prajāpati and the gods knew perfectly well that humans would be incapable of following them. Too weak, too incompetent. The gods said to themselves: "We have brought this [sacrifice] to an end with our divine, immortal bodies. Mortals will never be able to complete this. Let us try then to contract this sacrifice." And so the thousand-year *sattra* became the *gavāmayana*, the "march of the cows," which is still a *sattra*, but lasts only a year. But it could not be supposed, even then, that all people would spend a whole year on that rite. So the gods set about reducing it further and further. Until there were rites that lasted only three days, or two days—or just a few hours. And finally they arrived at the two *agnihotras*, for the morning and the evening. This was the nucleus that could be split no further. The rite consisted of pouring milk on the fire. Nothing could be simpler—even if the gesture was linked to dozens and dozens of others. Before this rite, below this rite there could be nothing more than formless life. Yet into those few minutes was concentrated the thousand-year *sattra* of the gods. "Therefore the *agnihotra* is unsurpassed. Undaunted is he who knows thus . . . therefore this *agnihotra* is unlimited."

Each morning and each evening, just before sunrise and again before the appearance of the first star, the head of the family pours four spoonfuls of milk into a larger spoon and then pours it into the fire, twice. All forms of worship emanate from this gesture, carried out by a single person, using the most ordinary of substances, with no need for the help of priests. And it is something that has no beginning and no end, since there would be endless arguments if anyone tried to establish that the morning libation or the evening libation had priority. One relates to the other, in a perpetual cycle. Nothing comes as close to the continuity of life. And so, "as hungry children press close to their mother, so do living beings around the *agnihotra*." The simplicity of this rite can only stir the boldest speculations around it. And, above all, the "limitless" nature of those gestures reassures those who perform them as to the limitlessness of their own being, however plain and simple such display might seem: "And in truth he who knows the limitlessness of the *agnihotra*, in this way is himself born limitless in prosperity and progeny."

The *agnihotra* is the occasion for making the distinctions on which all the rest will be built. The libation, however simple, will never be one alone, but double. Why? Because one does not exist. Even in the very beginning, there were always two beings: Mind and Speech, Manas and Vāc. Mind and Speech almost entirely overlap and allow themselves to be treated as "equals (*samāna*)." And yet they are "different (*nānā*)." When they become involved in the rite, both characters are to be remembered: so each of the libations appears as a replica of the other, yet at the same time they are different, since they are still two, and therefore with one preceding the other. And thus the relationship between two powers begins to take form. When Mind and Speech then free themselves from each other—as happens at the very moment in which the libation is repeated—it sets off the whole series of dualities with which we have to deal. And reproduced in each will be that tension between limitless and limited that already exists in the relationship between Prajāpati and the gods.

"For whichever divinity a person draws this libation, that divinity, being seized by this libation, fulfils the wish for which he draws it." This sentence appears in the passage that most clearly expresses the acrobatic play on the word *graha* throughout the *Śatapatha Brāhmaṇa.* Usually translatable as "libation," *graha* is always related to the verb *grah-*, "to grasp"—in a similar way as the German word *begreifen*, "comprehend" (from which *Begriff*, "concept"), is related to *greifen*, "grasp." A further difficulty arises with the continuous alternation, in the word, of the active and passive meaning: *graha* can be the one who grasps and the one who is grasped, what draws the libation and what is drawn by it. At this point Eggeling explained in a note: "The whole Brāhmaṇa is a play on the word *graha*, in its active and passive meanings of grasper, holder, influence; and draught, libation."

The libation is a way of grasping (of understanding) the divinity. And from it the divinity feels bound, grasped. This also happens with names: they are our libations to reality. They are used to grasp it: "The *graha* is in truth the name, for everything is grasped by a name. Why wonder, then, if the name is *graha*? We know the name of many, and is it not perhaps with the name that they are grasped for us?"

A crucial equivalence is that between Sun—"that one burning yonder"—and Death. Not only can the source of energy be a cause of death, but it is death itself. This is why the relationship between Sūrya and his bride Saraṇyū bears so many similarities to that of Hades and Persephone: for the *ṛṣis* did not regard Hades as the one who rules over the shades but the one who streaks the sky and spreads light. Yama, ruler of the dead, would be just a son of his—a consequence of his being, which itself is already Death.

The *ṛṣis*, tireless speculators, thought they could make a pact with Death. They had to find a way of going beyond the Sun—therefore beyond Death. How? Thanks to the *agnihotra.* They had to play on the relationship between fire and light, between Agni and Sūrya. And so they established a cyclical sacrifice, where Agni and Sūrya are alternated in the offerings, fire is offered in light and light is offered in fire—at the beginning of each day, at the beginning of each night, forever. They said: "In the evening he offers Sūrya in Agni and in the morning he offers Agni in Sūrya."

Everything, as always, went back to an episode at the very beginning. Agni, "as soon as he was born, tried to burn everything here: and so everybody tried to get out of his way." Those who existed at that time considered him an enemy. And so, "since he was unable to endure this, [Agni] went to man." And he proposed an arrangement: "Let me enter within you! Then, after having reproduced me, maintain me: and, as you will have reproduced and maintained me here, so then will I reproduce and maintain you in the world yonder"—"the world yonder" meaning the celestial world that is reached *beyond the Sun.* Man accepted: *agnihotra* is based on this agreement, and in this agreement man finds the only possibility of going beyond Death: using Death as a steed, making it possible to climb on its back, like a circus acrobat. And so in both daily libations of the *agnihotra*, at dawn and at dusk, man has to mount firmly on Death: in the evening "he mounts firmly on Death with his toes"; whereas in the morning "he mounts firmly on Death with his heels."

Implicit is the thought that Death is a cycle. What destroys is the simple passing of day and night. The new day means the destruction of the night. The new night means the destruction of the day. Together, they signify the destruction of the works carried out during the day and during the night. How can we escape from the cycle? By rising above it, looking upon it from on high, standing upright on the back of the sky: "In the same way as, when standing on a chariot, one looks down from above at the wheels that revolve, so he looks down from above at day and night."

But who can lift us up? The *agnihotra.* Then the Sun, which is Death, can allow us to be lifted onto his back, so we may see what lies beyond the Sun and are no longer touched by Death. How is it done? To escape Death, the feet have to be mounted firmly on Death. Then the journey begins. The Sun rises and carries us with it. Just by standing on Death—and only if Death helps us by carrying us on its back, as if it were a huge animal, without shaking us off—we will see the world that opens up beyond Death.

The Sun's first name was Mārtāṇḍa, Dead Egg. It so happened that Aditi, the Limitless, had given birth to seven children, who then became the main gods, the Ādityas. But appearing from her womb immediately after was a formless being, "as broad as it was high": it was Mārtāṇḍa, the Dead Egg. The gods decided not to throw it away because, they said: "that which is born after us must not be lost." And they began to give it form. When we think of the Sun as the origin of life, the image is mixed with the memory of a formless being, "a mere lump of bodily matter." Death and formlessness, which haunt life at every moment, are there from its very origin. Indeed, they are the foundation on which Vivasvat, the Radiant One, the Sun, rests, dazzling us with his light, who conceals first of all himself.

If the Sun is Death, what is night? Once the evening libation has been performed, the vast expanse of darkness opens up. But, once again, points of reference are reversed. The darkness appears "rich in lights," for the ceremony has lit it with the embers of Agni: "'O you, rich in lights, may I safely reach your end!' [the sacrificer] murmurs three times. She that is rich in lights (*citrāvasu*) is without doubt the night, since, in a certain way, she rests (*vas-*) after having gathered the lights (*citra*): so one doesn't see clearly (*citram*) from a distance.

"Now, it was by means of these words that the *ṛṣis* safely reached the end of the night; and because of them the Rakṣas did not find them: because of them he too [the sacrificer] now safely reaches the end of the night; and because of them the Rakṣas do not find him. He murmurs this while standing."

Long before the song of the Swiss Guards ("Notre vie est un voyage / Dans l'hiver et dans la Nuit, / Nous cherchons notre passage / Dans le Ciel où rien ne luit"), which Céline used as an epigraph to his *Voyage*, the *ṛṣis* had been murmuring very similar words—and every sacrificer since them. Ever at risk of ambush, moving forward in the darkness: this is the tension underlying every ritual scene: "Dangerous indeed are the paths between sky and earth." What we see is of little importance compared with the invisible maze, where the Enemy lies in wait, where the celestial waters open. The *ṛṣis* entered it, troubled and uncertain, like Céline's Bardamu, clinging to ritual words that showed them the route.

Socrates spent his last day—from the moment the prison gates were opened until dusk—talking with his disciples about how easy it is for a philosopher to die. Unlike the gods, who find it easy to live. He also talked about an "obstacle." He said: "The festival of the god has delayed my death." Athens, in obedience to a vow to Apollo, forbade anyone to be executed by the state during the period of the annual pilgrimage to his sanctuary at Delos. And Socrates' death sentence had been pronounced a day before the ship's departure for Delos. So he had spent his time during this period—a month, according to Xenophon—composing a hymn to Apollo and adapting some of Aesop's fables. Everyone wondered why. And Socrates replied that he had been urged in a dream to "compose music." A dream that had recurred through his life, which he had always interpreted as an encouragement to practice philosophy, since "philosophy is the greatest kind of music." But now, in that time of suspension before his death, Socrates had come to a different conclusion: perhaps the true meaning of the dream was its literal meaning. It would be "safer" to obey the dream without adding any interpretation to it. And so he had composed a hymn to the god whose festival was being celebrated (and, later the same day, he would also reveal that Apollo was *his* god). And so also—"since a poet, if he is really to be a poet, has to compose myths and not reasonings (*mýthous all'ou lógous*)"—he had devoted himself to those myths that were "ready to hand," the Aesop fables. Spoken on that day and with such tranquillity, they were words that would amaze his disciples—as well as the curious and spiteful Sophists. Socrates, as everyone knew, had spent his whole life elaborating discourses, reasonings, arguments: *lógoi.* Why should he now, at this moment, devote himself to *mýthoi*, which he had always treated with a certain disdain? Socrates had no wish to reply; instead he spent the whole day composing *lógoi*, no more or less striking than so many others that his disciples had heard in past years, in response to a question from Cebes, his most cautious disciple: "Why do you say, Socrates, that a man ought not to do violence to himself and, on the other hand, the philosopher does not want anything more than to follow someone who dies?" The question was well put. If the philosopher is so willing to die, why should he condemn suicide? Socrates' reply was a series of *lógoi*, but this time interspersed and subtly interwoven with terms and formulas of quite another kind: that of the Mysteries. And he immediately cited a *lógos*, but in the sense of a "formula" that is pronounced *en aporrḗtois*, "in the unnameables" (a traditional way of referring to the Mysteries). Socrates gave it as an example of "mythologizing about the journey yonder," which he proposed as the best way "of passing the time between now and sunset." It is as though his thinking, in this last dialogue, swerves in a way that exposes it to a bright light of indiscernible origin. But all now appears transformed.

This is the formula of the Mysteries: "We men are in a sort of garrison post (*phrourá*) and must not free ourselves or run away." Highly enigmatic, Socrates immediately recognizes. But he adds: "It is a sound way of expressing the fact that the gods are our guardians and that we men are part of the property of the gods." A brutal as well as pious definition: someone committing suicide would consequently be taking from the gods part of their property. Man is therefore *in debt* to the gods for his existence. This is the point that comes closest, in the West, to the Vedic doctrine of the four "debts," *ṛṇa*, that make up man. And here the differences between Plato and the Vedic ritualists become all the more apparent. What for them was a clear and binding doctrine is presented by Socrates as a doctrine that is secret and extreme, suitable for the "composing of myths" with which he wants to occupy his last hours.

Even though, a little later, Socrates would go back to reasoning with his disciples, as he had done so many times before, the halo of mystery over that initial formula would envelop his "hunting for that which is," as he described then his philosophy. And it would bring him as close as possible to a *katharmós*, a specific term used to describe the purifying transformation that took place in the Mysteries. To the point when Socrates goes as far as stating that "thought (*phrónēsis*) can itself be a *katharmós*." Never as in that phrase did Socrates' doctrine coincide so closely with the unrevealed, unrevealable doctrine of the Mysteries. Perhaps it was this—much more than arguments over the immortality of the soul, which are always open to doubt—that Socrates wanted to leave as his legacy to his disciples.

But the relationship between his philosophy and cult—in the Mysteries or in any other form—concealed some more secrets. Socrates' last words have been debated over the centuries—up until Nietzsche and Dumézil. "Crito, we owe a cockerel to Aesculapius. But pay the debt, don't forget it." Words in which he talks once again about *debt*. In their enigmatic exchange (" 'It shall be done,' said Crito. 'But have you anything else to say?' The question remained unanswered"), these words have distracted attention from Socrates' last *gesture*—which had no less weight.

When an official of the Eleven appeared with the hemlock, Socrates asked him a question, "looking up at him from below, as was his custom." He wanted to know whether he was allowed to use some of the drink to pour a libation. "We prepare just enough for it to be drunk," answered the official. Meaning: it is exactly the amount needed to kill. Socrates nods—and says that he will confine himself to offering a prayer to the gods "so that the change of residence from here hence may go well."

The implications of the scene are endless. Deep down, Socrates wants to preserve the sacrificial practice, which required part of the drink to be offered to the gods before being drunk. An established custom that went beyond practices of faith and was respected at every symposium. It was the gesture of giving way to the invisible.

At the same time, by doing so, Socrates sought to offer a deadly poison to the gods. All that would be written in future centuries about him being corrosive and disruptive is anticipated and underlined by that gesture. And the official, by declaring that the potion had been prepared with the exact amount needed to kill him, showed that state law contravened the age-old rule requiring a part of any drink to be poured off, to be destroyed as an offering to the gods. *"Speísas kaì euxámenos épie,"* "When he had poured a libation and prayed, he drank," says Xenophon, describing Cyrus. But the expression already appears in the *Iliad.* And every Homeric formula is firmly rooted in Greek life. The underlying principle: there is no prayer without libation, there is no libation without prayer. That was the most solid alliance between gesture and speech, in addressing the divine.

Thus the death sentence turned out to be murder. All that remained for Socrates was prayer, speech. But for the whole Athenian civilization it was assumed that speech and libation went together. One required the other. Whereas now there were only those spare words of hope for a peaceful "change of residence," *metoíkēsis*, fitting for a philosopher. Whose final wish had been refused. A pious yet blasphemous desire: offering a libation, sharing a poison with the gods. When the official of the Eleven refused to grant Socrates' request, the last wish of a man condemned to death, the link between gesture and word had, for the Greeks, been broken. From then on, the word stands alone, self-contained, orphaned and sovereign.

XIII

RESIDUE AND SURPLUS

In that place therefore the blessed god, all-present, sleeping on the ocean, cloaked his night with thick darkness. But a surplus of luminous quality awakened him and he saw the empty world.

—*Mahābhārata*, 3.272.40–41ab

The whole of Indian tradition, in its various branches, is influenced by a *doctrine of residue*, which can be embodied in three words, corresponding to three successive stages: *vāstu*, *ucchiṣṭa*, and *śeṣa*. It has a key role as a doctrine, similar to that of *ousía* in classical Greece, in that it suggests the inadequacy of sacrifice (but instead of sacrifice we can also say: *of any system*) in supporting the whole of existence. Something always remains outside—indeed, *has to* remain outside, because, if it were included in the system, it would disrupt it from within. On the other hand, the sacrifice or any system makes sense only if it extends to everything. A compromise therefore had to be established with what was left *outside*, what was left *behind*. So Rudra became Vāstavya, the ruler of the place and of the residue. This was the place the gods had left behind to get to the sky. But this place was the whole earth. So the whole earth was the residue.

The passage from one epoch to the other was described as being like an enormous fire, a funeral sacrifice in which the fire consumed the whole earth. In the end, all that remained was ash, floating on the waters. Once again, the residue. This ash took the form of a snake, called Śeṣa, Residue, and also Ananta, Infinite. What at the beginning had been thrown away turned out to be limitless, invincible. The snake arranged its coils into a soft bed so Viṣṇu could lie on it. The god slept—or meditated or dreamed. One day a surplus of *sattva*, that luminous thread woven within all that exists, shook him and woke him. And another world sprang forth while a long lotus stalk sprouted from his navel. At the top, a magnificent pink bud came into blossom. And resting on it was another god, Brahmā, who looked about him with his four faces and was puzzled, since "sitting at the center of that plant, he didn't see the world." Looking about in all directions he saw the vast lotus petals and then waters and sky, far away. The petals prevented Brahmā from seeing the other god, Viṣṇu, from whose navel the stalk had sprouted. Brahmā would one day drop down into that porous fiber to make a new world start.

The question of residue arises when at last "by means of the sacrifice the gods rose up to the sky." It could have been the happy ending to their troubled time on earth. But it was not to be so, for that moment marked the beginning of a convulsive, coruscating sequence that the *Śatapatha Brāhmaṇa* recounts in its masterly style: "The god who rules the cattle was left behind here: so they call him Vāstavya, because he was left behind on the sacrificial site (*vāstu*). The gods continued to practice *tapas* in the same sacrifice through which they had ascended to the sky. Now the god who rules the cattle and had been left behind here saw [all this and said]: 'I have been left behind. They are leaving me out of the sacrifice!' He pursued them and with his [weapon] held high he rose up to the north, and the moment when this happened was that of the Sviṣṭakṛt [He-who-offers-well-the-sacrifice]. The gods said: 'Don't shoot!' He said: 'Don't leave me out of the sacrifice! Leave an oblation aside for me!' They replied: 'Let it be so!' He withdrew and didn't shoot his weapon; and injured no one. The gods said to themselves: 'All portions of the sacrificial food we have prepared have been offered. Let us try to find a way of putting aside an oblation for him!' They said to the officiant: 'Lay out the sacrificial plates in the proper succession; and fill them, making an extra portion, and make them once again fitting to be used; and then cut a portion for each.' So the officiant lay out the sacrificial plates in the proper succession and filled them up, making an extra portion, and he made them once again fitting to be used and cut a portion for each. This is the reason he is called Vāstavya, because a residue (*vāstu*) is that part of the sacrifice that remains when the oblations have been made."

Sacrifice is a journey above all for the gods—the only way of reaching heaven. But who did the gods sacrifice to, when they rose up to heaven? The elements for the sacrifice had been obtained—desire, to remain in heaven; *tapas*, which the gods practiced; and the material for the oblation (ghee). But there was no one to sacrifice to. Heaven was apparently empty. On this point the texts, so complete in every other detail, are silent. One might suspect, then, that the sacrificial act was effective regardless of whom it was for. Indeed, one could arrive at the ultimate conclusion: that it was all the more effective because the recipient of the sacrifice was not there. One day, Kṛṣṇa taught a doctrine no less paradoxical, in the *Bhagavad Gītā*: of sacrifice where desire is eliminated. This is suggested as a path for mankind, a path that never reaches its destination and one therefore to be continually pursued. But the gods had set their minds on a journey that was to be taken only once. And so they had no wish to renounce desire. If anything, they were more concerned about something else: wiping out their tracks so that people couldn't follow them: "They sucked the sap of the sacrifice, as bees suck honey; and after having drained and wiped out its traces with the sacrificial post, they hid themselves." Spiteful gods. But they were equally spiteful toward one of their own. They had abandoned him on earth, at the very place of the sacrifice. He was a god they preferred not to name—and who is not indeed named anywhere in the whole passage except at the end, with a clever device in which his name appears as one of his epithets: Rudra, the Wild One. We can, thus, already see the strange impatience, tinged with fear and hostility, that the gods felt for two divine figures: firstly Prajāpati, the father, who in having intercourse with Uṣas had performed an act that was "an evil in the eyes of the gods," and then Rudra, this strange god, whom the other gods want to be rid of, for mysterious reasons that are never explained, at the point when they become fully fledged gods, inhabitants of the sky. Even if the texts are more reticent over Rudra than over any other god, the essential points seem clear: the Devas want to get away from Rudra, they want to leave him behind at the *place* (*vāstu*) of the sacrifice, which is also the *residue* (*vāstu*) of the sacrifice. But once the gods have risen to the sky, the whole earth can be seen as a *residue* of the sacrifice. And this residue is powerful and can attack the gods. And so its lord, who is Rudra, retains the capacity to *injure* the gods, as he threatens to do by shooting his unnamed weapon, presumably an arrow. For the gods, therefore, it is not enough to perform an effective sacrifice. They have to *reach a pact* with Rudra, who will otherwise strike them. And a pact, for the gods, is always a new division of portions. This time a division has to be made that includes *Rudra's portion*: *la part du feu*. And that portion, by definition, will be the *excess*, that surplus which the gods can forgo, so as to ward off Rudra's attack.

The question remains: how could the gods possibly think of leaving Rudra out of the sacrifice? And why did they want to leave him out? "They did not truly know him," says the *Mahābhārata*, thus revealing what older texts had been silent about. Perhaps they did not know him because in Rudra there was an element resistant to knowledge, of pure intensity, prior to meaning. The gods, though, had based their work—the sacrifice—on the pervasiveness of knowledge itself, on its transparency. They left Rudra out because they rightly suspected that he would have undermined their enterprise from within. But certainly not because Rudra was extraneous or hostile to the sacrifice. When Rudra appeared in the north of the sky, striking terror, bow in hand, his hair tied at the back of his neck in a black shell, the other gods saw straightaway that his lethal weapon was made of the same substance as the first and the fourth type of sacrifice. They also saw that the string of his bow was made of the invocation *vaṣaṭ*, which is heard every day in the sacrifices.

This much we can gather, but none of the texts give the reason for Rudra's initial exclusion. A reason, though, that will become much clearer when Rudra becomes Śiva in another eon and another story cycle, and the tale of his exclusion becomes the tale of Śiva's exclusion by Dakṣa from the sacrifice: another event that the gods would seek to hide, since it describes their own defeat. And here a suspicion arises: that the sacrifice claims to be everything, but fails to be so. Every sacrifice *leaves out* or *leaves behind* something that may turn against it: its site, its residue.

Śiva is excluded by Dakṣa because he has offended the brahminic laws, twice showing disrespect: in taking away Dakṣa's daughter Satī and, in a certain moment, not standing up in front of him. But at the same time Śiva cannot be regarded as being *against* the sacrifice. Nor can Rudra, who is called "king of the sacrifice" and "he who brings the sacrifice to its completion." It would therefore seem that the sacrifice performed by the Devas conflicts with a further sacrifice, that of Rudra and of Śiva, which threatens to harm and cancel out the first—and it may perhaps be the sacrifice that happens *in any case*, that forms part of the cycle of life, of its breath, and can sweep away everything, even the gods. Invasive and ever-present, this sacrifice doesn't follow an explicit doctrine, but is nevertheless performed. This happens all the time, whether we like it or not, just like the breath within us, which is a continual drawing in from the outside world and a continual expulsion into the outside world, even when it is not subject to yogic discipline. It can therefore be thought of as a continuous sacrifice, which coincides with life itself. When this form of sacrifice appears, there is no choice but to come to an agreement with it, to allow it its irreducible role. Only such a recognition enables the ordinary sacrifice of the gods to be *done well*, as is suggested by the term Sviṣṭakṛt, which is applied to this moment. In a certain way, then, the figure of Rudra and subsequently of Śiva, into whom he is transformed, is the most radical criticism of sacrifice to be found in the world of the gods. But it is a criticism that doesn't destroy. Indeed, in the end it provides confirmation, further extending the field of sacrifice to cover everything, encapsulating within it all residue.

Rudra's name is to be avoided. Anyone forced to name him must immediately touch sacred water, for protection. Better to call him Vāstavya, ruler of place and of residue. *Vāstu* means both: place and residue. "A disconcerting semanticism," noted Minard, eminent philologist. And yet there is just as much reason to be disconcerted over the Latin *situs*, which means site, place, but also powder, detritus, rust, mold, the bad smell built up over time. *Situs* implies that existence exudes a residue from the mere fact of being sited. There is something *stale* in existence, in that it has always been there. And this may produce a doubt that existence itself, that its site, are a residue, the detritus of a *désastre obscur*.

When oblations have been offered, something always remains. And, if nothing remains, the site itself of the oblations will remain, swept clean by the wind. Between order and the thing ordered, there is always a margin, a difference that is a residue: Rudra is there.

Any kind of order involves eliminating a part of the original material. That part is the residue. What is to be done with it? It can be treated as the principal enemy of order, as the constant threat of a relapse to the status that existed before order. Or as something that, going beyond order, ensures the permanence of a contact with the continuum that preceded order itself. The *soma* that issues from the body of Vṛtra is the most precious thing that order can offer. And it is a memory of something that already existed before order, before Indra's liberating attack.

What criteria can we use to compare two kinds of order? Two kinds of order can be considered as two formal systems. Alternatively we can look at them in relation to what surplus and residue they produce. To what degree do the two comparisons diverge? In the first case: we can evaluate the different extent, functionality, effectiveness of each kind of order, its capacity to remain consistent. Not much more can be said. To attribute a meaning to a formal system would be arbitrary. In the second case: we have to give a meaning to each kind of order, we have to evaluate it. But in relation to what? There ought then to be an order of reference that makes it possible to attribute meaning and quality to all other kinds of order. But this kind of order does not exist. Or at least: this is the condition in which the moderns found themselves, this is the situation in which they were obliged to think. But for Vedic men, surplus and residue were the prerequisites that made it possible to judge the kind of order that excluded them from it. And it could be world order itself, *ṛta*—or it could be any other kind of order undermined and disrupted by people unaware of what they are doing when dealing with surplus and residue.

"The officiant recites the verses continually, without interruption: and so he makes the days and nights of the year continuous, and so the days and nights of the year alternate continually and without interruption. And in this way he leaves open no way of access to the spiteful rival; but he would indeed leave open a way of access if he recited the verses in a discontinuous way: he therefore recites them continuously, without interruption." Here we see, with full immediacy, the Vedic officiant's main anxiety: the fear of time being split, of the course of the day being suddenly interrupted, of the whole world irretrievably disintegrating. This fear is far deeper than the fear of death. Indeed, the fear of death is only a secondary—one might say modern—concern. Something else comes before it: a sense of impermanence that is so great, so acute, so tormenting as to make the continuity of time seem an improbable gift, and one that is always about to be taken away. And so it is vital to intervene immediately with the sacrifice, which can be defined as that which the officiant *tends*, *extends*. This tissue of indefinite matter (the sacrifice) has to be "tended," *tan-*, so that something continuous is formed, with no breaks, no interruptions, no gaps into which the "spiteful rival" who is lying in wait might wheedle his way. It is something that, by reason of its elaborate construction, stands in opposition to the world—a place whose origin appears like a series of breaks, interruptions, fragments in which we may recognize the strips of Prajāpati's dismembered body. To overwhelm the discontinuous: this is the purpose of the officiant. Overcoming death is only one of the many consequences. And so the first requirement is that the voice of the *hotṛ* is as taut as possible, with a continuous emission of sound. How does he take in breath? "If he were to take in breath in the middle of the verse, it would be harmful to the sacrifice." It would be a defeat through discontinuity, like driving a wedge into the middle of the verse. To avoid it, the verses of the *gāyatrī*, the fundamental meter, have to be recited, one by one, without an intake of breath. This creates a tiny, impregnable cell of continuity in the boundless expanse of discontinuity. And so the *gāyatrī* meter one day became the bird Gāyatrī and had the strength to fly high into the sky to conquer Soma, that intoxicating and all-enveloping fluid in which the officiant recognized the supreme expansion of the continuum.

Such was the terror of discontinuity—and of the injury implicit in every interruption—that they resorted, in the end, to the ultimate weapon of etymology to make it clear: they derived the word *adhvara* ("worship," that which the *adhvaryu* practices) from the verb *dhūrv-*, "to injure." Meaning by this that "the Asuras, though desiring to injure them, were unable to injure them and were foiled: for this reason the sacrifice is called *adhvara*, not damaged, uninterrupted." And so the *adhvaryu* can only murmur, accompanying his constant acts with a buzz in which the individual words are unrecognizable. If he were to articulate them more clearly, he would risk losing his breath, which is life, since the formulas are breath—and the breath "resides in a silent abode." The power of the *adhvaryu* is concentrated in the indistinct: "All that he carries out in a very low voice, when it is finished and complete, becomes manifest." For something to assume its purest and clearest form, it has to be born out of something impenetrable, opaque, boundless.

Residue is the memory, the enduring presence of the insuppressible continuum. Whatever kind of order is established, in whatever context and of whatever kind, that order will leave something outside itself—and will have to leave that thing outside if it purports to be an order.

That something outside order is residue, but also surplus. Residue is what is left out, surplus is the part left out which is offered up. The meaning of order lies, first and foremost, not in the way the order itself is arranged but in what that order determines to do with the part that does not belong to it. Offer it up? Consume it? Throw it away? That is the part which is cursed and blessed. And depending on what is decided to be done with it, the newly established order acquires meaning. Taken by themselves, as a simple formal configuration, all orders are equivalents, insofar as all coexist at the same level, like crystals cut in various ways. Considered in terms of what is outside them—residue, surplus, but also nature, world—all forms of order are divergent and irreducible, no less than the timbre of one voice in relation to another.

Among the most memorable metaphysical disputations was the one in which the problem was whether the sacrifice is a curled-up dog. How did that happen? For some time the ritualists had been troubled by certain questions: "What is the beginning, what is the end of the sacrifice, what is its narrowest part, what is its broadest part?" There was no agreement about the answers.

One day a group of theologians belonging to the Kuru and Pañcāla clans, from the Land of the Seven Rivers, were arguing these matters. "Then they came across a curled-up dog. They said: 'May there be in this dog what will decide who wins.' The Pañcālas asked the Kurus: 'To what extent does this dog resemble the sacrifice?' They didn't know how to answer. Then Vasiṣṭha Caikitāneya spoke: 'In the same way as [the sacrificer] lies there joining the twenty-first verse of the *yajñāyajñīya* to the nine verses of the *bahiṣpavamāna*, so the dog lies there curled up, joining its two extremes. In this position the dog is the same as the sacrifice.' With these words the Pañcālas defeated the Kurus."

This is how the most difficult questions are tackled: they come across a curled-up dog *or any ordinary thing*—and they decide that the answer must be there. If the answer isn't *in any ordinary thing* then it won't be anywhere else. But the Pañcāla theologian was a learned man and his answer referred back to a very old story. In the beginning, when only the waters existed, Agni sang the verses of the *agniṣṭoma* so that the waters would recede and he could find food for himself. And it was then that the *sampad*, the "equivalence" or "correspondence," flashed before him, enabling him to carry on singing without interruption, thereby preventing the other gods from stealing his food. He *saw* then that the dreaded gap which appeared between a particular song (the *yajñāyajñīya*) and another (the *bahiṣpavamāna*) could be eliminated: if the last verse of the one also became the first verse of the other. With this, the *bahiṣpavamāna* came to consist of ten syllables, transforming itself into a *virāj* meter. And *virāj* is food. QED. And so Agni would never be short of food, and there would never be a break in the sacrifice. This is what Vasiṣṭha Caikitāneya was referring to. He thought that the dog curled up before their eyes was the sacrifice as it had become after Agni had seen his vision. This, then, was the precedent to which the theologian referred.

But something else was implied in the answer to the riddle. Above all, that the sacrifice has to be *continuous*. Any break whatsoever would make it worthless, allowing the gods to snatch Agni's food from him. But here they failed, since now the sacrifice "had become endless" in the words of the *Jaiminīya Brāhmaṇa*, which adds: "it was like a lighted ember in a pot." But if the sacrifice is continuous, with no end and no beginning, it also means it is not a human institution. There is no zero point at which a man begins a sacrifice. Sacrifice is something that is always happening. If this is so, the whole world must be seen as the field in which sacrifice is celebrated. The difference between gods and men is primarily this. Certain gods—such as Prajāpati, such as Agni, who *are* the sacrifice—ensured that the world came to function like an uninterrupted sacrifice. Humans are the last arrivals who become part of the ceremony and perpetuate it, as long as their strength allows them to do so. This, according to Vasiṣṭha Caikitāneya, was a first series of ideas that could be elaborated that day, observing the curled-up dog that a group of theologians from the Kuru and Pañcāla clans had come across as they walked along the road in discussion.

We can certainly know the world—and live there—observing only the dealings that occur between mankind and the thirty-three gods. But, if we also take into consideration all that is left out of these dealings, because it forms their background, the residue that does not belong to anyone, then everything changes, in the same way that it would change if, rather than looking at individuals, we look at the background against which they are gradually drawn. But we can better understand the implications of residue with the question of the Sāhasrī (which means "she who sees to it that the ritual fee is a thousand [cows]"). The Sāhasrī is a dappled cow, of three colors. Or alternatively red. Never approached by a bull. That cow is Vāc, Speech, and she appears along with nine hundred and ninety-nine other cows. In all, there has to be a thousand—and no more—because "with a thousand he [the sacrificer] gets all the objects of his desire." Three hundred and thirty-three every day. The Sāhasrī guides them, moving forward at the head of the herd, for three days. Or alternatively she follows them from behind. These cows are also the hymns of the *Ṛgveda* (though in fact there are a few more: one thousand and twenty-eight). The Sāhasrī, the supreme power of speech, is the thousandth cow: once again the remainder, the residue.

Then the unprecedented gesture occurs. They do not sacrifice it, they do not deliver it up to the priests as a ritual fee, but "they release it." In that instant the whole sacrificial edifice is in danger of collapsing. How can a domestic animal, destined for sacrifice or to be offered as a ritual fee to the priests, be released—to wander about once again like a forest animal? If this happens, it becomes an ordeal. Without human interference, the direction chosen by the released cow determines the fate of the sacrificer: "If, not being goaded by anyone, it goes eastward, let him know that this sacrificer has been successful, that he has conquered the world of happiness. If it goes northward, let him know that the sacrificer will become more glorious in this world. If it goes westward, let him know that he will be rich in servants and crops. If it goes southward, let him know that the sacrificer will soon depart from this world. These are the ways of finding out." The same happened to St. Ignatius of Loyola and his mule, whom Ignatius, still a layman and a warrior, allowed to choose between two roads: one of which would certainly lead to murder; the other of which would ultimately mean sainthood. If the Sāhasrī wanders southward, the sacrificer knows his death is imminent. The immense effort of the sacrifice has been worth nothing. And so too have been the nine hundred and ninety-nine cows given as a ritual fee to the priests. And all because that one, single cow went southward. "These are the ways of finding out."

However he was considered, Prajāpati always appeared unique. Even when the gods were counted: "There are eight Vasus, eleven Rudras, twelve Ādityas; and these two, Sky and Earth, are the thirty-second and thirty-third. And there are thirty-three gods and Prajāpati is the thirty-fourth." Prajāpati's supernumerary nature was his unfailing characteristic. Prajāpati was always *extra*—and it is precisely to this that the ritualists connected the link between surplus and residue. They saw that they were the same question. And the question was Prajāpati himself. Prajāpati is *that which remains.* Prajāpati is the superfluous part from which all that is necessary is born.

Surplus and *residue* are ever-present. Especially in time. The day that marks the climax of the year is the *viṣuvat*—and that is a *surplus* day. Without that day, the year would be divided into two equal parts, in which each rite could have its identical counterpart. But the *viṣuvat* places this perfect symmetry at risk. The question is: "'Does the *viṣuvat* belong to the months that go before or those that follow?' He must reply: 'Both to those that go before and those that follow.'" Why? "Because the *viṣuvat* is the torso of the year and the months are its limbs." And a body cannot do without its torso. And then again: the year is a great eagle. The first six months are one wing and the other six the other wing. And the *viṣuvat* is the body of the bird. That *surplus* day, the *viṣuvat*, is therefore indispensable: only this interval can keep time together, can enable it to spread out two perfectly symmetrical wings, that extra day alone gives completeness to the year, where the rites each occur in correspondence with their counterpart, in the first and in the second half. Only in that way, with the last ceremony (the stairway that is climbed emerging from the ocean of the rite) do we reach the "world of heaven, the place of quietness, of plenty."

Having reached the end of this crucial demonstration, since the proper conduct of the whole liturgy depends upon it, the ritualist allows himself a meditative *aside*, serious in tone, almost a confession by someone who has spent his whole life carefully, steadfastly, examining this subject: "These are indeed the forests and the ravines of the sacrifice, and hundreds and hundreds of days are needed to travel them by chariot; and if anyone ventures into them without knowledge, then hunger or thirst, marauders and wicked demons will assail them, in the same way that wicked demons would attack fools who wander in a wild forest; but if they who know do so, they pass from one task to the other, as from one river to the other and from one safe place to the other, and they reach bliss, the world of heaven." Then suddenly, as if he had become carried away for a moment in contemplating his life and all his past experience—and this was against the rule—the ritualist patiently returns to a technical detail of the liturgy, to preparing answers to those who are always asking pointless and captious questions about this and that.

"That is full, this is full. / Full gushes forth from fullness. / Even after the full has been fully drawn upon, / this full remains full."

We encounter the "stanza of plenitude" at the beginning of the penultimate *adhyāya* of the *Bṛhadāraṇyaka Upaniṣad.* Paul Mus wrote a masterly commentary on it. But, as the words of the stanza say, what it describes is boundless. And it might be placed at the very center of Vedic thought—even if the word *thought* may, in this case, seem reductive. The closest proximity to *full*, *pūrṇa*, mentioned in the text is a passage in the *Śatapatha Brāhmaṇa*, which reads: "The gods certainly have a joyous Self; and this, true knowledge, belongs to the gods alone—and indeed whosoever knows this is not a man but one of the gods." The real difference between gods and humans does not lie exclusively in the immortality that the gods have laboriously achieved—and which they want to keep only for themselves. It lies in a particular kind of knowledge, which corresponds to the joy gushing forth from the depths of Self. Ultimate knowledge is neither impassive nor immovable, but resembles the perpetual flow of plenitude in the world. The Vedic cult of knowledge is directed toward this image.

"When the yonder world overflows, all gods and all beings subsist on it, and truly the yonder world overflows for he who knows this." All is possible—even the existence of the gods—only because "the yonder world" is superabundant. Its bursting forth into the other world, which is ours, offers that surplus without which there would be no life.

XIV

HERMITS IN THE FOREST

The *saṃnyāsin*, the "renouncer," in whose traits Louis Dumont had the farsightedness to recognize the archetypal *individual* in the Western sense, is a figure who does not appear in the earliest stratum of the Vedic texts. The system, at that time, is compact and leaves no such space. Having once entered the process of cosmic interaction on birth, there is no way out. But on reaching the Upaniṣads, which take ritualist reasoning to an extreme, the *saṃnyāsin* makes his appearance—the first defector, not because he rejects the complex system of interaction on which ritual is based, but because he seeks to absorb it within himself, in the inaccessible space of the mind. So the *agnihotra* becomes the *prāṇāgnihotra*, the first case of the complete internalization of an event, an invisible ceremony that takes place in an individual's "breath," *prāṇa*. There is no longer any fire, there is no longer any milk to pour on it, the words of the texts are no longer to be heard. But all this still exists: in silence, in the activity of the mind. And so the *inner man* makes his first appearance in history. He is the "individual-outside-the-world," who has severed his links with society—and who will eventually prove to be enormously effective in his action *upon* society. Dumont recognizes in him the earliest figure of the *intellectual*, right up to his most recent awkward or lethal manifestations.

The *saṃnyāsin* can quite properly be described as the inner man, since it is he who first internalized the sacrificial fires. Thanks to a subtle elaboration of correspondences, the factors that made up the liturgy of the Vedic sacrifice are moved into the body and into the mind of the *saṃnyāsin*; and so he becomes the only being who need not keep fires burning, since he keeps them within himself. With the advent of the renouncer, sacrificial violence no longer leaves any visible traces. All is absorbed into this solitary, emaciated, wandering being, who would eventually become the very image of India. Not the man in his village or in his house. But the man of the forest—a place of secret learning, a place far removed from social constraints.

There is no mention of *saṃnyāsins* in the *Ṛgveda.* They hardly dominate the scene in the Brāhmaṇas, which are filled instead with the figures of mighty and forbidding brahmins like Yājñavalkya, virtuous warriors well practiced in dangerous disputations on *brahman*, the king's counselors and rivals. But, once again, it is in the liturgical literature—particularly the Sūtras—that we find the answer to a vital question that is rarely asked: how did the *saṃnyāsin* first come into being?

The answer is disconcerting when we think of the mild image, alien to any form of violence, that has been passed down to us: the *saṃnyāsin* originated from the *puruṣamedha*, the human sacrifice. Here almost all scholars prefer to stay on the safe side and suggest that this ceremony must have been described in the Brāhmaṇas and in the Sūtras only *for completeness*, in that it corresponded to the formal layout of the sacrifices, but was never practiced—or else practiced in earliest times but then abandoned. This is all possible, but it cannot be confirmed or denied with any certainty. What remains is a series of texts. And these texts describe *puruṣamedha* in the same way as various other kinds of sacrifice. But this is not proof that certain deeds took place. And it is plausible to raise a doubt over *puruṣamedha* in much the same way as we may doubt that certain other rites were celebrated, given their interminable duration and complexity. Yet here, as always, it is wise to follow the texts. It is the *Kātyāyana Śrauta Sūtra*, with its rugged concision, that reveals its points of connection. Above all: the *puruṣamedha* is modeled on the "horse sacrifice," *aśvamedha.* And so, whereas the rules governing the latter are set out in two hundred and fourteen aphorisms, those on the *puruṣamedha* require only eighteen, as if it were a secondary variation (which is in turn duplicated immediately after in the *sarvamedha*, the "sacrifice of everything"). But far more significant are the differences. Anyone wanting to celebrate an *aśvamedha* has to be a king or have a "desire of the Whole": it is the maximum expression of sovereignty. To celebrate a *puruṣamedha* it is enough to be a brahmin (or a *kṣatriya*) and "desire excellence." This already points us in the direction of the individual who is defined by his desire alone. Another indication comes from the requirement that the brahmin sacrificer has to give, as a ritual fee for the sacrifice, "all his possessions." What then will happen to him, stripped of all his belongings after having sacrificed a man? The answer comes in the penultimate aphorism: "at the end of the *traidhātavī iṣṭi* [a certain kind of oblation, to be offered at the end of the sacrifice], the sacrificer assumes the two fires within himself, offers prayers to Sūrya, and, reciting an invocation [which is specified], goes off toward the forest without looking back, never to return again." This is the moment where the figure of the renouncer emerges: when he takes his first step toward the forest, without looking back and knowing he will never return. In this instant, the brahmin cuts all links with his previous life. Never again will he have to celebrate the *agnihotra* at dawn and sunset, pouring milk on the fire, performing a hundred or so prescribed gestures, reciting formulas. Indeed, the renouncer no longer has to kindle and feed the sacrificial fires, since he will tend them within himself. Nor will he have to comply with countless obligations that make up his life as a brahmin. Now he will eat nothing but berries and roots when he finds them in the forest. His life will interfere only to a minimal extent with the course of nature. But what lies beneath all this? The celebration of a *puruṣamedha*, wanting a man to be killed in a sacrifice planned in order to establish the personal "excellence" of the sacrificer? We will never know whether this was ever carried out, even just once. Perhaps it was there only as a set of instructions, necessary for the formal completeness of the liturgical doctrine. But its significance still stands out in the text. And it is the supreme paradox of "nonviolence," *ahiṃsā*.

In the *puruṣamedha* the victims are chosen from all social classes, with no exceptions: there will be a brahmin, a warrior, a peasant—and lastly a *śūdra*.

The brahmin immediately recites the hymn to Puruṣa (*Ṛgveda*, 10.90) while seated to the right of the victims tied to the sacrificial post. More than any other, this detail may explain why the name Puruṣa—and not Prajāpati—appears in the hymn: for *puruṣa* is the word that describes man as sacrificial victim, tied to the post in exactly the same way as Puruṣa was in primordial times. With delicate cruelty, this is what the hymn describes. Afterward, we read, the officiants "passed with burning embers around the victims, but they had not yet been immolated."

This is when the miracle happens, corresponding to the voice of Yahweh's angel who stops the hand of Abraham already raised over Isaac: "Then a voice said to him: 'Puruṣa, do not put an end to these human victims (*puruṣapaśūn*): if you put an end to them, man would eat man.' And so, as soon as the ember had been carried around them, he set them free and offered oblations to the same divinities [to whom he had already dedicated the human victims] and thereby gratified those divinities, who, thus gratified, gratified him with all objects of desire."

No Kierkegaard, no Kafka has ever commented on this passage. But it would be no less difficult than the story of Abraham and Isaac. This time it is not one man, not the son of the sacrificer, but four men, chosen from the various classes of society and waiting to be killed. They have been tied to a post, alongside many animals tied to other posts and also waiting to be immolated. They have seen an officiant approach and walk around the post holding an ember. It is the most frightening moment: the announcement of the immolation. From that moment on, the victims can consider themselves already dead: strangled or suffocated. And then—"a voice" arrives. But how does it address the sacrificer? It calls him "Puruṣa" and asks him to save the *puruṣas*, the men who are about to be immolated. And Puruṣa, the primordial being whom the gods dismembered, had just been recalled in the recital of hymn 10.90. So the sacrificer, while he was preparing to immolate the four men, was Puruṣa himself whom the gods had immolated. This is why the voice turns to him calling him Puruṣa—and not by his own name.

But the ritualist offers no comment on this point. Unperturbed, he carries on describing the ritual acts that follow. It could be a ritual just like any other. Or does he perhaps not recognize the seriousness of what he has just described? It is always wrong to imagine such a thing when dealing with the authors of the Brāhmaṇas.

This is confirmed by the description of what happens at the end of the ceremony: "After having assumed the two fires within himself and after having celebrated the sun reciting the Uttara Nārāyaṇa litany, he [the sacrificer] shall go toward the forest without looking back; and that place is indeed far away from men." If this description is—as it seems to be—the beginning of the transition to the state of *vānaprastha*, of he who withdraws into the forest, the step prior to the state of renouncer, this means that the first renunciation is in not sacrificing another person. Having carried this out, he can—indeed in a certain way he must—leave society, "without looking back." If he is unable to do so, the ritualist immediately gives practical advice for anyone who wants to continue living in the village. But even for him there has been a break. Immediately after, with the usual abruptness, it is explained that the moment signals a watershed: "But in fact this sacrifice must not be imparted to everyone, for fear that it ends up being imparted to all and everyone, for the *puruṣamedha* is everything; but it must be imparted only to those who are known and to those who know the sacred texts and to whom they are dear, but not to everyone."

The figure of the renouncer indicates the path by which a highly detailed ceremonial practice could become invisible, transforming itself into an act of knowledge. The *saṃnyāsin*, thus, no longer kept fires, and withdrew from the community into the forest. Yet remaining a sacrificer, indeed enhancing this aspect of his character.

Several thousand years later, with whom would we now associate this figure? With all those who are driven by a powerful urge—they often prefer not to call it duty, but it is certainly something they feel obliged to do for someone, someone they may never know—and they concentrate their energies on some form of composition, which in turn is offered to someone unknown. They are the artists, those who study. They all find the origin and purpose of what they do in the practice of their art, in their studies. They are Flaubert, who roars in the solitude of his room at Croisset. Without asking for what reason and for what purpose. But absorbed in working out ardor, *tapas*, in a form.

"Mobile are the waters, mobile the sun, mobile the moon and mobile the stars; and, as if these divinities did not move and act, so will be the brahmin on that day when he does not study." Study is that which assures movement, which makes it possible to respond to the ceaseless activities of the divinities in the sky and on the earth. It is the closest approximation in defining that which is living, that which overcomes inertia. Study can also be reduced to reciting its smallest unit—one verse of the *Ṛgveda* or one ritual formula. That is enough for the thread of the vow not to be broken, to ensure "the continuity of the vow, *vrata*."

There is a subtle distinction between *renunciation* and *detachment*. To accept the life of the renouncer means following an *āśrama*, a stage of life like the three that have preceded it. And each stage brings its own guilt and restrictions. "Detachment," *tyāga*, is something else—a mental attitude that can pertain to any stage of life. Simone Weil is extremely clear on this point: "Detachment and renouncement: often synonyms in Sanskrit, but not in the *Gītā*: here 'renouncement' (*saṃnyāsa*) is the lower form that consists of becoming a hermit, sitting beneath a tree and moving no further. 'Detachment' (*tyāga*) is making use of this world as if not using it."

XV

RITOLOGY

Nothing actually left it and nothing entered from anywhere—there was indeed nothing else—and it [this all, *tónde tòn ólon*] nurtured itself procuring its own destruction, whereas all that it suffered and did in itself and by itself happened by art [*ek téchnēs*]. He who had created it felt indeed that it would have been better if it had been self-sufficient and not needy of anything else.

—Plato, *Timaeus*, 33 c–d

Even today, in some Indian airport lounges, we can find a billboard with the following words: "Lead me from nonbeing to being. Lead me from darkness to light. Lead me from death to immortality." Tourists either ignore it or read it with satisfaction, as a sign of age-old Indian spirituality. What are these words? They were part of a series of ritual formulas recited during the *soma* sacrifice, called *pavamānas.* While a priest intoned a chant, the sacrificer pronounced those words in a low voice, as we can read them in the *Bṛhadāraṇyaka Upaniṣad.*

For the Upaniṣad the meaning of those words is clear: *asat* (unmanifest), *tamas* (darkness), *mṛtyu* (death) all mean "death" in the same way. It is assumed that every life in its raw state is an amalgam of nonbeing, darkness, and death. To leave it, we need help. And to get help, we need ritual.

Giving stability to the earth was the decisive action, whether it was the gods who achieved it, during their battle for supremacy over the Asuras, or whether it was Prajāpati himself, as the *Taittirīya Brāhmaṇa* says. What appears to us today as "the vast one (*pṛthivī*)," motionless and calm, was in the beginning a lotus leaf battered by the wind. That beginning is the state in which every person finds himself before the sacrifice begins. He is a confused being, wavering, at the mercy of unpredictable gusts of wind. He can find nothing to rest on. And so he has to imitate the action of the Devas: he will take some pebbles and place them around the edges of the area where he wishes to build fires. First of all to mark out, circumscribe (it is the same as the Greek concept of *témenos*). And so the earth will become a "foundation," *pratiṣṭhā*, for any action whatever, for any thought whatever.

In dealing with the gods, there is an etiquette that justifies certain activities, without which nothing would happen. One of these is fence making. If it is true that "the whole earth is divine" and that sacrifices can be performed on any part of it, it is also true that the part chosen can only become a place of sacrifice after it has been closed off from the rest. The same happens when a hut is built to shelter the sacrificer during the time of consecration. "Now the gods are segregated from men and that which is enclosed on every side is also secret: this is why they enclose it on every side." What is the underlying assumption? "The gods do not speak with everyone," and so a way has to be devised to approach them: men must segregate themselves in the same way as the gods are segregated from men. Then perhaps the gods will pay attention. This is what the consecrator must do, so that he "truly draws close to the gods and becomes one of the divinities." An initial separation from other men is achieved through the preliminary actions of the rite. And it is only possible through this separation to establish a rapport with the gods. Secrecy, the need for secrecy, arose from the original segregation of the gods from men. The one who intends to break this secrecy (the sacrificer) must agree to segregate himself from everyone else. Secrecy is not a way of concealing something that would otherwise be obvious to all. Secrecy indicates that one is entering an area where everything, including meaning, is enclosed. The secret is the place cut off by the enclosure, as a picture by its frame.

One enters the ritual as if entering a circle in perpetual movement. A particular act is prescribed at each point and has to be carried out at the next point, until we get back to where we began. But where then is the beginning? There isn't one. Existence, all existence, begins *in debt* to something else, first and foremost to life itself. Between *ṛṇa*, "debt," and *ṛta*, "world order," there is a restless wavering. Debt is born out of order, and is given back to order. Otherwise the balance of things would be upset, life could not continue. It is a process that takes place at every instant, the elaboration and exchange of a substance that can be called *anna*, "food," but incorporates within it also the word, the thought, the gesture of offering, the "yielding," *tyāga*, of the substance itself. But if there is no beginning, will there ever be an end? No—for every offering leaves a "residue," *ucchiṣṭa*, and this residue sets off a further chain of acts. Nor must we think that the whole process relates only to man's rapport with the gods. For the gods must also sacrifice, perform ritual acts in the *devayajana*, the "place of offering of the gods," since they too have forebears, *pūrve devāḥ*, the "gods before." The circulation of substance is not limited to the earth or to the "intermediate space," *antarikṣa*, between earth and sky, but pervades the whole cosmos, as far as the "celestial ocean" that can be recognized in the Milky Way.

The ritual area has to be clearly marked out, for its boundaries are those of an *intermediate world*, which we may describe as the world of effective action. It is where we find, on the one hand, a relentless urge for dominion and control and, on the other, an anxious, intense feeling of impermanence. The homologous elements certainly correspond, in the various realms of that which is, but they are also spiteful, slow to obey, elusive. For this reason rituals always begin anew, for this reason they are interlinked, for this reason they tend to eliminate any gap in time where inertia might creep in. And here we touch upon the final obstacle: ritual serves to make life possible, but since ritual tends to occupy time fully (certain rites, such as the *mahāsattra*, can even last twelve years), life itself becomes impracticable. There is no time free of obligations, free of prescribed rules, in which to live it.

For the Vedic liturgists, any place, generally speaking, can become a *ritual scene*. It is enough that water is not too far away and there is sufficient space to mark out the lines between the fires. This is tantamount to admitting that the ritual opus can—indeed must—start each time from nothing. The first thing to do is find a neutral surface with no defects. Any trace that the past may have left has to be swept away. But for the Vedic people, with their marvelous literalism, sweeping away the past means that an officiant sets to work in the clearing, like an obsessive housewife: "When setting up the *gārhapatya* fire, he first sweeps the chosen space with a *palāśa* branch. For, when he sets up the *gārhapatya* fire, he settles himself in that place; and all the builders of fire altars have settled on this earth; and when he sweeps that place, with this action he sweeps away all those who have settled here before him, saying: 'To avoid settling myself on those who have been here before.' He says: 'Away from here! Away! Crawl away from here,' then:

'Go away, go and slip away from here,' he says to those who slither on their bellies. 'You who are here from ancient and recent times!' and therefore both those who are here from a remote time as well as those who have settled here today." The *palāśa* branch sweeps an area of level, featureless ground. A gesture that, if seen by a passerby, might seem like a domestic ritual moved outdoors for everyone to see, in a place that belongs to no one. Before anything can begin, every previous gesture, every mute connotation with the past, has to be swept away. It's an important and decisive moment, to the extent of being equated with an action through *brahman*: "He sweeps with a *palāśa* branch, for the *palāśa* tree is *brahman*: through *brahman* he sweeps away those who have settled there."

The ritual action is an imitation. Of other men, who lived in the beginning? Or of gods? But what actions of the gods, then? The answer appears during the building of the fire altar when certain bricks, known as *dviyajus*, "which require a double formula," have to be arranged. At that moment the sacrificer thinks the following words: "I wish to go to the celestial world following the same form, celebrating the same rite that Indra and Agni used to enter the celestial world!" Here it is not a matter of imitating the heroic or erotic exploits performed by the gods of the sky *in* the sky or in various forays *from* sky to earth. Here the first action to be imitated—*first action* meaning rite—is the one through which the gods found a way to the sky. What the sacrificer is imitating is the act of the god himself *making himself a god*; something far more secret than any other act that might be attributed to a god once he has become a god. What man seeks above all to imitate is the process by which divinity is gained. And it is highly significant that, to do it effectively, man seeks to imitate the "form" of gestures carried out by the gods. This will one day become the basis of that secular activity which is art. But to imitate the process by which the sky is conquered produces unpredictable results. Imitation might perhaps finally be so effective as to enable men to reach the sky, like so many unwelcome guests. This is why the gods look upon rites performed by men with satisfaction but also suspicion. There is always the risk that men will go *too far*, as far as the sky, as far as the gods themselves.

In the Vedic pantheon, there is no Apollo to whom poetry belongs with his own exclusive dominion. Bṛhaspati is the "poet of poets," though Soma, Vāyu, and even Varuṇa, the dark, remote, formidable Asuras, are also poets. And so too are the gods as a whole. Why? For one reason alone, one which has enormous consequences. Once having reached the sky and immortality, the gods continued to perform sacrifices. We are not told what "invisible fruit" they expected—now that they possessed all conceivable fruits—nor what desire motivated them. But perhaps this has to be accepted: "The mysterious plan of the gods when they meet together—of that we have no knowledge." The hymns certainly show the gods frequently in the act of sacrifice. But a sacrifice can only be effective when accompanied by the right formulas, which only the *kavi*, the "poets," know how to devise. Agni has to follow the worship as an "inspired seer who brings the sacrifice to completion." And here the texts use the word *vípra*, describing the poet who quivers from the tension of speech. And so, if the gods hadn't been poets, their divine life would have been inconceivable, unacceptable.

Ritual serves above all to resolve through action what thought alone cannot resolve. It is a cautious, timid attempt, made in spite of our own fragility, to answer dilemmas that arise every day, that besiege us, mock us. For example: what do we do with the ash produced by the sacrificial fire? Throw it away? Or use it in some other way? The question was put in this way: "The gods at that time threw away the ash from the hearth pan. They said: 'If we make this [ash], such as it is, part of us, we will become mortal carcasses, not freed from evil; and, if we throw it away, we will place outside Agni that part of it that belongs to the nature of Agni; discover then in what manner we should act!' They said: 'Meditate!'" And what will be the outcome of the meditation? The ash has to be disposed of (otherwise it would mean becoming matter that "is used up"). Yet at the same time, in disposing of the ash, an essential part of Agni must not be lost. So what happens? The ashes are thrown into water. And these words are spoken: "O divine waters, receive these ashes and place them in a soft and fragrant place!" Indeed, they say: "Place them in the most fragrant place of all!" And then: "May the consorts, married to a good lord, bow down to him." The "consorts" here are the waters, who have found a "good lord" in Agni. The waters are chosen as a place for ashes, because Agni was born from the womb of the waters. Now he returns to it. But with this act the ashes would simply be dispersed, though in their proper place. The doubt would remain that some intrinsic part of Agni's nature had been lost. And so the officiant, passing his little finger over the waters, collects a few specks of ash to be returned to the fire. So Agni will not be lost. And ritual, thought, and life can go on.

The ritualists' anonymous hero—and ideal author of the Brāhmaṇas—is the *adhvaryu*, the officiant who ceaselessly performs the prescribed actions and murmurs the sacrificial formulas during the rites. Without him nothing would happen, nothing would take form. Like an attendant, he goes from one task to the next. He does not experience the relief, the liberation of chanting. His is just a murmur. He is an artisan of liturgies, working away humbly, resolutely, under the fixed gaze of the brahmin who waits, motionless, to catch every error, every impropriety—and to punish it. Of the *adhvaryu* we read that "he is the summer, because the summer is, so to speak, fiery: and the *adhvaryu* leaves the sacrificial ground as something fiery." Parched and singed from his continual occupation around the fire, the *adhvaryu* was the first who could say, as did Flaubert (and Ingeborg Bachmann): *"Avec ma main brûlée, j'écris sur la nature du feu."*: "With my burnt hand, I write on the nature of fire."

The course of the sacrifice is punctuated with moments of drama—or even of comedy or subtle humor. So, for example, we find the story of Indradyumna Bhāllaveya (about whom we know little, but can presume he was a learned ritualist): "It happened that Bhāllaveya composed the incitative formula with an *anuṣṭubh* verse and the formula for the offering with a *triṣṭubh* verse, thinking: 'In this way I will receive the benefits of both.' He fell from his chariot and, on falling, broke his arm. He then began to reflect: 'This has happened because of something I have done.' Then he thought: 'It has happened because of some breach by me of the correct procedure for the sacrifice.' And so the correct procedure for the sacrifice must not be broken: and so the two formulas must have verses in the same meter, either both *anuṣṭubh* or both *triṣṭubh*." The sacrifice is a form that is composed in every single moment. And an error in form can be due to a certain greediness in desiring, to a wish to acquire *too many* benefits through the forms themselves. The result is immediate: Bhāllaveya falls from his chariot and breaks an arm. In the same way that the outside world is ready to offer the fruit of desire, so too is it ready to chastise any form that arises from a tainted desire. The prime purpose of the outside world is an ordeal. Depending on the meters that Bhāllaveya has selected and used, he either moves forward or falls from the chariot and breaks an arm.

The incident with Bhāllaveya clearly shows the Vedic attitude toward the world. There are three simultaneous passages, each included in the other: each event that occurs is significant; its significance is connected to an act performed by the person concerned; the ideal area in which every event takes place is the scene of the sacrifice. It is the scene of the action on which later actions depend. Bhāllaveya doesn't immediately think the accident is due to blameworthy acts he has committed in normal life. His first thought goes to what he has done *in the liturgy.* That is the area that bristles with significance, the first to which his thoughts turn. Normal life is a secondary consequence of it. It is no surprise, then, that there was no concern at the time about leaving records or chronicles, and that history as such was ignored.

The *sattra* is the most extreme, esoteric, all-pervading rite in the Vedic liturgy for its conception, for its form. Based on the number twelve, it has to last for a minimum of twelve days, otherwise a whole year or, in theory, twelve years (in the last case it is known as the "great *sattra*," *mahāsattra*). And this capacity to invade time, to fill it to its very limit, alone gives food for thought. Caland and Henry, with their usual clarity, immediately realized this and asked themselves: on what does the person celebrating a *sattra* live? And if the rite itself occupies a whole year, what life does he lead outside the rite? These were only their first questions: "One might at this point ask, not only what interest they had in celebrating [this rite]—for it would be irreverent to believe them incapable of holding a sincere faith and piety that would be self-sufficient—but at least on what these men lived, who, absorbed every day in the practice of a meticulous and taxing devotion, surely didn't have the possibility to create resources by other ways." The invasion of time, to the extent of forcing out every other form of life, was only one of the peculiarities of the rite. In the *sattra* there is no sacrificer: everyone is sacrificer and officiant at the same time. As a result, there is not even the ritual fee for priests. As a result, all twelve officiants have to go through the consecration, which is normally reserved only for the sacrificer. And they appear as a compact body, a group of beings consecrated for one single purpose. There are no divisions by categories or roles. The rite becomes absolute: it occupies the totality of time and is celebrated by beings consecrated for the sole purpose of carrying it out.

If a rite lasts a year and then begins immediately all over again, what time will there be for living life that is not part of a ritual? So the ritualists thought: if the game becomes untenable, fight back by raising the stakes. Are people afraid of rites that last a year? Let them listen then to a story in the life of the gods: "The gods were once celebrating the consecration ceremony for one [sacrificial session] of a thousand years. When five hundred years had passed, everything here was worn out, namely the *stoma* chants, the *pṛṣṭha* chants, and the meters.

"The gods then perceived the element of the sacrifice that cannot be worn out and by means of this element they obtained success in the Veda; and in truth, for him who knows this, the Vedas are intact and the work of the officiants is carried out with that inexhaustible, triple knowledge."

What then is the element that remains intact? Anybody would be impatient to find out. Impassive, the ritualist is ready with the answer. It consists of five exclamations that punctuate certain moments of the ceremony. Eggeling doesn't even translate them, as if they were simple interjections. But Minard, meticulous as ever in seeking to fix the "element of the sacrifice that cannot be worn out," translates them as: "Oh, come! Here, listen! Adore! We, the worshippers! Heave-away!" We seem to be eavesdropping on a scene of men at work. And yet they are the germ cells of the sacrifice, loaded with power. But there is a further argument, of crucial significance for the ritualist. The syllables of the five exclamations, added together, are seventeen in number. And Prajāpati is composed of seventeen parts. It is a perfect example of *sampad*, that "correspondence" which is above all a "numerical congruence." The *sampad* is the supreme weapon of the intellect, which Prajāpati finally resorts to in his duel with Death. When the gods realized this, they felt satisfied. They had isolated the inexhaustible element of the sacrifice—

and had established the glorious truth that the five exclamations, added together, made seventeen syllables. It was another way of saying: added together, they made Prajāpati, the Progenitor.

For once, then, they were concerned about mankind. They knew man was too weak to resist. He would never even manage to celebrate a rite of only five hundred years. They said to themselves: "Let us find a sacrifice that is a substitute for the thousand-year sacrifice." And they tried hard to combine and compress the forms. An activity they were most fond of. They invented accelerated rites, in the same way as accelerated courses would one day be invented for students who lag behind—and, for the gods, all humans lag behind. In the end, with a sense of relief, they established the minimum form of sacrifice, the shortest, most suitable form for human capabilities—as well as being arranged to correspond, in miniature, with the complete form. And so they said to each other: "When he [the sacrificer] spends one year celebrating the rites of consecration, in this way he is assured of the first part of the thousand-year ceremony; and when he spends a year celebrating the *upasads* [a particular *soma* rite], in this way he is assured of the central part of the thousand-year ceremony; and when he spends a year with the pressing [of *soma*], in this way he is assured of the final part of the thousand-year ceremony." All was now clear. People need no longer worry. The gods had found the abbreviated formula for the ceremony, gauged to fit man's capabilities. It was enough for them to sacrifice for three years in succession. And the gods, in their magnanimity, would accept the ceremony as if it had lasted a thousand years.

In describing one sequence of the *sattra*, when the *mahāvratīya* cup, the cup of the "great vow," is used, we read: "For what food is for men, the vow (*vrata*) is for the gods." Here at last, in the clearest terms, we see what the gods expect of men: to feed themselves on their "vows," to which some feel bound in relation to an invisible presence, which is nourished by that mental tension. Certainly not by the smoke and blood of sacrifices, as the theological opponents of the Vedic ritualists would one day suggest, above all the author of the Epistle to the Hebrews, who would still claim that the pagan gods, and even the God of Moses, were appeased "by the blood of goats and calves."

The Vedic ritualists were keen to make it clear that there is no way out of sacrificing. The sacrifice is like a secret formula that has to be protected in every way from the eyes of the enemy. This is true not just for men (such an assertion would be banal and tremendously limited): it had been just the same for the gods. As they hurled themselves into their repeated and indecisive conflicts with the Asuras, the Devas thought: if we are ever defeated, where could we keep the sacrifice? (Someone must have been tormented by the same concern during the Second World War, worrying about the formulas for the atomic bomb.) Their answer: on the moon. It would have been their place of refuge in the event of being defeated on earth.

Sacrifice accompanies us everywhere. We realize this even when we look up at the moon. What are those dark spots on the lunar disk? Places of worship. This has been so since the day the Devas decided to take various sacrificial altars to the moon. They set them down on the white dust, and the marks they left were of identical proportion to those of the fine body of a woman. From there they look down on us, from there they still make signs to earth and work on its behalf. The altars were lifted in the air toward the moon while the gods said: "Lifting up the earth that gives life, before the bloody battle." And they repeated: "Before the bloody battle."

That the sacrifice was a "controlled catastrophe," to use Heesterman's vivid expression, can be seen from certain marginal observations: "The houses of the sacrificer could easily collapse behind the back of his *adhvaryu*, when he goes away [from the cart] with the sacrifice, and could crush the family [of the sacrificer]." Here we see the sharp, piercing sense of impermanence that must have pervaded the Vedic world. When the sacrificer starts the ceremony, he turns his back on the old world, which is nevertheless the everyday world on earth. Sucked into another space, he can ignore all he is leaving behind, in a first *après moi le déluge.* And the mighty void which then opens up in the world could act like a tornado that whips and crushes man's flimsy shelters. But the sacrificer knows that one day he will have to *leave* the sacrifice—and he would like to leave it safe and sound, and find too that the world he had left behind is also safe and sound: above all his house. And so the sacrificer does not forget to plead: "May those who have doors remain secure on the earth!" Even if he is already swept away by the elation of roaming in the "atmosphere," he knows that one day not only will that elation come to an end but he himself will yearn to leave it, to return to ordinary, dull, secular life, as if returning to a haven of peace.

Whether it is the celebration of an *aśvamedha* or a *soma* sacrifice, all nevertheless ends with a purifying bath. Too much tension, contamination, guilt, horror, exaltation have been concentrated around the sacrifice. Now he thinks only of freeing, ridding himself of that excess energy, of returning to being an ordinary creature who lives in untruth. To do so, the sacrificer reveals that up to that moment he has felt like the victim: the first feeling he names is that of one who is "untied from the sacrificial post." And at the same time he gives no more weight to the sensation than someone who, feeling too hot, goes looking for cool, fresh water. So violent is the sense of liberation that his first thought is to let his clothes float away in the current. Now they float away, forever. The Vedic ritualists were certainly not worried about possessions. They made use of few objects, always as temporary vehicles, to be destroyed, abandoned, thrown away as soon as they were of no further use to the opus, to that unique sequence that appeared against the background of the invisible and flowed back to it. The only visible remains were an area of ground that had been trampled over, with ashes and charred logs and little else. Better for them to be rid of everything, starting with their own clothes, cast off like the dried skin of a snake.

One day—perhaps every day—someone woke up and conceived the "plan," *saṃkalpa*, for a sacrifice. He chose a suitable place, a clearing not far from running water, on a slight slope. He drew lines on the ground, or got someone else to draw them: rectangles, trapezoids. This was the place where he would say: "Now I pass from untruth to truth." But the ceremony didn't involve just one person. There had to be sixteen officiants—and the sacrificer's wife was also there. Then there was the *śamitṛ*, with the task of appeasing (in other words, strangling) the victims immediately outside the sacrificial area. Lastly, to celebrate a sacrifice, it had to be rewarded with the distribution of ritual fees to the officiants. If any one of these elements was absent, the sacrifice was ineffective, indeed harmful. The sacrifice turned against the sacrificer.

There was also another risk, an obstacle that could ruin the sacrifice.

It was vital that no other sacrificer was celebrating his sacrifice in a place too close. The *Āpastamba Śrauta Sūtra* gives clear instructions in this respect: "If the distance of a day's journey by horse, or a hill, or a river crossing the mountains separates the two sacrifices, or if there is a mountain between the two or if the sacrifices are celebrated in two different kingdoms, then there is no conflict between the two sacrifices. The text of a Kaṅkati Brāhmaṇa says: 'There is no conflict between the sacrifices if the sacrificers are not enemies.' "

There is a certain flavor of multiple delirium about imagining a number of open spaces, each in immediate proximity to a community (which couldn't have been numerous), where dozens of officiants were simultaneously circling around fires, reciting, singing, murmuring, each running the risk of overlapping or interfering with the others. The texts refer several times to such events, suggesting what to do, especially where the sacrificers are rivals. We can then also imagine that they are sacrificing with opposing desires, each bent upon the ruin of the other.

The desire forming the basis of the sacrifice thus meets various obstacles: it has to be capable of being formulated (to understand itself), it has to be capable of paying itself (for its own existence), it has to avoid colliding with the desires of others. The sacrifice originates from one person alone but broadens out into a community, where it can be affected by the opposing desires of others—desires that are either too close (danger of imitation) or adverse (which is why the texts continually refer to *spiteful rivals*).

But the Vedic ritualists were too subtle to think that, if anyone wanted to get rid of their rival, all they had to do was celebrate their sacrifice a sufficient distance away. The rival is a perpetual presence, lurking within, wrapped up in the gestures of the officiants. Among the materials for the sacrifice—the *sambhārāḥ*, "utensils" required for the liturgy—there are two identical wooden spoons. The first is called the *juhū*, the other the *upabhṛt*. Both are filled with ghee. Both are brought close to the fire. But the offering is poured from only one of the spoons, while the officiant holds the other directly below, with his left hand. Why? The ritualist (in this case Yājñavalkya) gives the answer: "Certainly the sacrificer is behind the *juhū* and he who wishes ill is behind the *upabhṛt*; and if [the officiant] should speak of two spoons, he would be letting the spiteful rival clash with the sacrificer. Behind the *juhū* is he who eats and behind the *upabhṛt* he who has to be eaten; and if [the officiant] should speak of two [spoons], he would be letting he who has to be eaten clash with he who eats. So speak of only one spoon."

What, then, will one see? In front of the fire of the oblations, the officiant is about to pour the ghee from a wooden spoon in his right hand, while in the other hand he holds an identical spoon, also full of ghee, but is careful not to use it. Why this complication? The second spoon is the shadow of the first, it is the double that emanates from the sacrificer and is bound to accompany him, threatening to overpower him.

The second spoon seems entirely superfluous. But if it were not there, it would mean that the presence of the spiteful rival is being ignored, making things even more dangerous. For the sacrifice to be perfect and complete, everything has to appear exactly as it is—evil as well as good, falsity as well as truth, disorder as well as order. To disregard just one of these powers means leaving it free to strike. Even *nirṛti*, which Renou boldly translated as "entropy," a power opposed to "order," *ṛta*, a nullifying power that lives in gaps, cracks, holes, crevices, has a right to its oblations, presented with no less devotion than that reserved for any other goddess (for that was how Nirṛti was portrayed: as a goddess "with a terrifying mouth"). During the stage in which the sacrificer is consecrated and initiated, he has to look for a crack or split in the ground, to make a special fire there and present the oblation with these words: "This, O Nirṛti, is your portion: accept it graciously, *svāhā*!" It is the only way to prevent Nirṛti from taking hold of the sacrificer when he is in the highly delicate condition of being consecrated and initiated—and so to avoid regression to the most helpless state of all, the embryo.

It should be no surprise, therefore, if the liturgical texts make continual mention of the risk of a spiteful rival bursting forth—or the possibility of the ceremony being usurped. And we should not imagine, as Heesterman suggests, that this corresponds to an historical phase in which the sacrifice, more than a religious ceremony, must have been like a tournament that often ended in death. The Vedic ritualists were accustomed to talking about the invisible as something very much present. They *saw* the gods huddled around the altar (around all altars, of all the sacrificers who celebrated a rite, over every valley and plain). And likewise they saw human enemies, those whose desires conflicted with those of the sacrificer and who sought nothing but his ruin. But in every crevice or hollow of the landscape they also saw the "terrible mouth" of Nirṛti, the goddess who disrupts every complete and well-ordered action and sucks it back into a vertiginous void. A goddess with powerful emissaries. Among these, dice and women. And so the person being initiated (and this is true for every sacrificer) abstained from gambling and sex during the days of the consecration.

At the end of the sacrifice, the sacrificer is empty, a wrinkled husk. For the underlying gesture throughout the ceremony is the *tyāga*, the "yielding," the act of abandoning something—and potentially everything—to the divinity. But what has been abandoned isn't lost. It travels, it is looking for its "place," *loka*, in the sky: there it recomposes a body, a being. And the task is repeated over and over again. The main concern now is to survive on earth, to come out of the sacrifice unscathed. This is the moment for three oblations that revive the sacrificer. But the gods are jealous and astute: even now, when the ceremony is finished, they remain there, saying crossly: "These he should really be offering to us!" The sacrificer then insists: "What was emptied he fills again." And so continues the skirmish between men and gods.

There was a very clear concern, during this last stage of the liturgy, to be rid of the gods. It was feared that they didn't want to leave the field. They had been invited to go, they had received their gifts. But now they had to return to their august abodes. To leave men to their lives. Some gods had arrived on foot, others by chariot. Now they had to leave in the same way, laden with their gifts. And the sacrificer, during this delicate phase, needed help. So once again he turned to Agni: "The willing gods that you, O god, brought here, speed them each to their own abode, O Agni!" The sacrificer, like an impatient host, even went on to say: "You have all drunk and eaten." In this way "he bids goodbye to the divinities." Dry, consistent, with no note of self-righteousness or bigotry: this is how the Vedic ritualists spoke.

In Vedic India, every sacrificial rite is a motionless journey, a journey within a room, if we regard the sacrificial area as a vast open-air room. Broken down into hundreds, into thousands of gestures accompanied by formulas, formulas without actions, actions without formulas, it ended with a "bath," *avabhṛtha*, that washed away all that was left of the journey and made it possible to return to normal life. In order to survive, that return was obligatory. The *Taittirīya Saṃhitā* says: "If they didn't return down into our world, the sacrificers would go mad and perish."

But there is one rite that is a real journey, a long journey lasting exactly a year. If a hypothetical sacrificer were immediately to start it all over again, his life would be an unending journey. It is the *sattra*, one of those rites where the sacrificer is also officiant. No ritual fee is therefore given to him. It would be like paying himself.

When the ritualists spoke about "those of times past" they were not referring to historical events but differences in liturgical practices. And the old days were always better. What they used to do then would always be beyond the capabilities of officiants today. Every rite contains moments of greatest concentration and tension. In a *sattra* lasting one year, "those of times past" used to celebrate three great days, called *mahāvratas*. But already by the time of the *Śatapatha Brāhmaṇa* only one day was celebrated. The ritualist notes bitterly: "Today, if someone celebrated in that way [like the ancients], he would surely crumble away like an unbaked clay pot would crumble away if filled with water." That is what men today are like: fresh clay that easily disintegrates. But even if what can be done today is a pale image of what ought to be done, there is always a way of establishing an exact correspondence between the weakness of today and the intact forms of times past. This requires the patient, meticulous work of the ritualists.

In the *sattras* lasting a year the officiants built up a new body, piece by piece, limb by limb. Each segment of the rite corresponded to a part of this body. The first ceremony produced the feet, "for with the feet he moves forward." On the day of the summer solstice, the *viṣuvat*, which divided the year in two, a new head was obtained. And, since the year consisted of two equal parts, in the first the fingernails had "the shape of grass and trees," while in the second they assumed "the form of the stars."

They knew very well that to celebrate a rite lasting one year was a risky business. Those who are consecrated to celebrate it "cross an ocean." The opening rite is therefore "a flight of steps, for it is by a flight of steps that one enters the water." This is the origin of the *ghats*, found throughout India even today, in every place where you enter the water: along the Ganges at Varanasi, but also on countless other rivers and lakes. The flight of steps, which in the West immediately evokes the ascent to heaven, for India was above all the proper way of descending into the waters, which mark every beginning. And so the second segment of the rite, the *caturviṃśa* day, was a point where the water reached as far as the armpits or the neck. A moment of rest before entering deep water. In the subsequent phases, which lasted more than five months, you had to swim, without a break. Until you reached a shallow bank, where the water became ever more shallow: until it reached the thigh, then the knee, then the ankle. It was the sign that you were reaching the solstice, the *viṣuvat*, which "is a base, an island." A moment of respite, before throwing yourself back into the water and passing through stages that were the exact mirror image of the first months of the rite. Then again there was a shallow bank, when you reached the *mahāvrata.* Another key point. Then you came out of the rite, once again by a flight of steps. You had to leave in the same way as you entered.

Śvetaketu—to whom his father, Uddālaka Āruṇi, had stated a doctrine in three words, three words that have come down through the centuries: *"Tat tvam asi,"* "This you are"—said to his father one day: " 'I want to be initiated for a one-year rite.' His father looked at him and said: 'Do you, you who have a long life, know the shallow banks of the year?' 'I know them,' he replied, for indeed he said this as someone who knows it."

XVI

THE SACRIFICIAL VISION

As for Numa himself, they say that he confided so much in the divine that one day, while he was celebrating a sacrifice, when told that enemies were approaching, he smiled and said: "And I am sacrificing."

—Plutarch, *Numa*, XV, 12

The sacrifice is a journey—linked to a destruction. A journey from a visible place to an invisible place, and back. The point of departure can be anywhere. And also the point of arrival, so long as it is inhabited by the divine. What is destroyed is the energy—an animate or inanimate being—that moves the journey. But it is always considered a living being—an animal or plant or even a liquid that is poured or an edible substance or an object (a ring or a precious stone or something that is perhaps precious only to the sacrificer).

This, in a minimum of words, was the doctrine of the Vedic ritualists, expounded in the Brāhmaṇas in thousands and thousands of words. And it didn't simply describe the Indian way of practicing sacrifice, comparable with countless others. The sacrifice, like the sexual act, can be practiced in many different ways, but it follows an immutable pattern.

Men are continually changing. Their basic physiology remains the same. If a certain interlinked sequence of gestures is to be carried out, certain ways will be constant. The sacrifice is not like the act of running or breathing or sleeping. But it is a sequence of acts that has a certain resemblance to them. It doesn't matter that the motives are various and complex. In each case they have to follow certain preexisting tracks.

The Vedic ritualists composed their treatises between the tenth and the sixth centuries B.C.E. Nowhere else was the theory of the sacrifice ever developed, varied, explained with such clarity. All other practices and other descriptions—in Polynesia or Africa, in Greece or Palestine—are just particular instances of what may be found in the labyrinths of the Brāhmaṇas.

One day, in late nineteenth-century Paris, an Indologist—Sylvain Lévi—set out to describe as precisely as possible the sequence of actions that govern the sacrifice according to the Brāhmaṇas. Lévi refrained from expressing his own thoughts on the doctrine, except in a few isolated instances. He was convinced that the scholar had only one duty: accuracy.

Very shortly after, two of his students, Hubert and Mauss, outlined a theory of sacrifice—hence of all sacrifices, in every age and in every place—stating at the outset that they would be following the lines traced out in the Brāhmaṇas and in the Pentateuch (though in fact referring almost exclusively to the Brāhmaṇas). This declaration was presented as a methodological warning that the authors wished to express at the very beginning of their study. But it was much more. Almost a hundred years later, Valerio Valeri observed that "perhaps more than any other work on sacrifice, that of Hubert and Mauss reflects a traditional priestly viewpoint." An observation that is not only true, but is to be taken literally. Mauss spoke as a Vedic ritualist disguised as a young sociologist of the Durkheim school, doing much as Sylvain Lévi had previously done, but this time extending his inquiry to the whole of history. And his arguments sounded right, even if they were set out in a form that could be accepted in the scholarly journals published in the West during the years of positivism. Thanks to this approach, the Vedic ritualists could be presented once again in a new guise, without any of their doctrine being left out. It was an indication that such a doctrine had immense vitality—and it was capable of containing within it any other form of what anthropologists called "sacrifice" but for the Vedic ritualists was *action* itself (in Latin it would have been described as *operari*, hence the German *Opfer*, "sacrifice").

We need only accept one of the most common metaphors—"life is a gift"—and already we are caught in the web that is implicit in the act of giving. Until we discover, at least where there is an exchange between a visible and an invisible subject, that *gift* and *sacrifice* are superimposed and amalgamated: *"Agnaye idaṃ na mama,"* "This is for Agni, not mine." The formula of the *tyāga*, of the "yielding"—or abandonment of the offering to an invisible presence—brings the gift and the sacrifice together once and for all, even in the simplest of rituals. Staal comments: "The *tyāga* is considered, more and more, as the essence of the ritual. The term will have a great destiny in the development of Hinduism. In the *Bhagavad Gītā*, *tyāga* denotes the fact of renouncing the fruits of actions and is recommended as the main aim of human life." But what are the consequences? Either that world which calls itself modern has to reject certain metaphors (and this would imply being reduced to a sort of muteness in regard to images)—or it has to agree to drag a whole uncontainable web of connotations with these metaphors, which oblige us to plunge into the farthest depths of time, thus reaching a point where only the metaphors remain, as if they had the power to cover the totality of existence.

The sacrifice is a gift that has to be destroyed. It would be impious for it to remain intact. Only destruction assures the rightness of the ceremony. Only destruction ensures that we will not be destroyed: "The sacrificer puts himself in debt to Yama in that he spreads grasses over the altar; if he went away without having burned them, they would wring his neck and they would drag him away into the other world."

At the origin of the sacrificial vision is the recognition of a debt contracted with the unknown and a gift that is bestowed upon the unknown. No epistemology can alter this view. The concept passes it by, leaving it untouched. What objection can be made to someone feeling in debt toward the unknown and at the same time wanting to offer it a gift? At most, such behavior might suggest a certain madness. But a feeling cannot be refuted. And, before becoming liturgical and metaphysical, the sacrificial vision was a feeling—a chemical reaction that can develop in anyone exposed to existence. This feeling forms the basis of everything—and casts its shadow over everything. Only if it is flimsy can it be dispelled by arguments—from which it could in any case make a quick escape, like an animal that disappears in the forest as soon as the hunter approaches.

A feeling can only be supplanted by a contrary feeling. It is pointless objecting to it with reasonable considerations. Far more effective, far more immediate is the outburst of an extreme eccentric, John Cowper Powys: "Toward these forces, which have summoned us forth from the deep, we have, as men and women, a perfect right to be hostile, to be vindictive, to be blasphemous, to be cynical. To worship these forces with tender solicitude is ridiculous. To prostrate ourselves before them in panic-terror is humiliating and degrading. To seek to propitiate them, to seek to get them 'on one's side,' is natural enough; but whether it is likely to make any difference is another matter!

"We owe them nothing. *We did not ask to be born.* They deserve no more from us than the rain deserves when it wets us or the sun deserves when it dries us.

"If we do have to invent incantations 'to get them on our side' we do not love them the better for that, or admire them the more! The account is equal between us. They to their ends. We to our ends."

There is a *debt* that finds its way into every feeling of gratitude. If at some moment—as a sensation underlying every other—the pure fact of being alive gives rise to a sense of gratitude, that is enough to establish a relationship with an unnamed counterpart to whom that feeling is directed. And even to outline an obligation, which may arise in a whole variety of ways. One of these is the sacrifice.

Sacrifice brings together *debt* and *desire.* Opposing powers: one that invites giving, the other taking. Colliding, they produce destruction. More accurately: the destruction of a living being, even if it is just a plant. This destruction is the element that cannot be removed from the sacrifice. By accepting destruction, desire is saved from itself, through *detachment.*

Sacrifice is a game where things are never entirely what they are. The sacrificer *is* the victim, but he is never entirely so. As Malamoud writes: "The sacrificer seeks to show that he is the victim and at the same time that he is other than the victim." When the victim is dismembered, Agni is called to bless it and at the same time to bless the sacrificer. But the ritualist immediately warns: " 'Uniting the blessings, not uniting the bodies.' By this he means: 'Unite the blessings but not the bodies'; for if he were to unite the bodies, Agni would burn the sacrificer." In that case the sacrificer would die, whereas the sacrificer has to make his life longer and better. But the game is all the more perfect when this superimposition appears. The higher the risk, the better the sacred work.

This game in which each element, each entity that has a name, is and at the same time is not another entity, to which it is tied by a kinship, by a bond, by a connection, is the very game of Vedic thought. Every single step, every gesture described there, every formula is an application of it. But how can all this be translated into the language of the Westerner? Is there a word that at least resembles that game and can be used without awkward periphrases? There is such a word—and only one: *analogy.*

Apart from liturgy, apart from metaphysics, the sacrifice is a character. "The sacrifice . . . is not just a series of acts, it is also a structure, an organism." Sometimes it appears as a fleeing antelope, sometimes we hear only its voice: "The sacrifice said: 'I am afraid of nakedness.' 'What is it for you not to be naked?' 'That they spread sacrificial grass around me.'" We might ask why the sacrifice is afraid of nakedness, but we immediately feel it has good reason: there is something frightening about nakedness, all the more if it is the sacrifice itself that is naked, in other words something that in a certain way can only be naked, because it is performed *in the open.* The sacrificial grass, which the sacrifice invokes here, lessens the impact of the truth, of its unbearable intractability. But at the same time the sacrifice is "afraid of thirst": it is afraid of drying up to the extent of being inert and therefore unable to act.

The sacrifice is an alternation of two gestures: scattering and gathering. The gods sucked the essence of the sacrifice, which for them was as sweet as honey. Then they scattered the shells with a pole. They didn't want people to reach them. Happy with the "victory" they had gained through the sacrifice, they thought: "May this world of ours be unreachable by men!" Then the *ṛṣis*, the perennial counterpart of the gods, appeared and collected up the *disiecta membra* of the sacrifice. That "collect," *sambhṛ-*, also means "prepare," lay out the objects—the spoons, the wooden sword, the antelope hides, and other items that are the "equipment," *sambhārāh*, for the sacrifice. The gathering up, on a desolate scene, of the empty shells of the sacrifice, to which the *ṛṣis* devote themselves, is also a refinement of the tools of the trade, an exercise in meter, a series of piano scales. That the sacrifice is an alternation, a combination, a superimposition of two gestures—scattering and gathering—also explains why it is inevitably and immediately conceived of as breathing, systole and diastole, alchemical *solve et coagula.*

The gods continued to sacrifice even after—thanks to it—they had conquered the sky. This might lead us to think that the sacrifice is the model for every action that is an end in itself, as someone will one day claim in relation to art. Every form of opus would then be an indirect descendant of sacrifice, which—in exactly the same way as alchemy—can claim to be effective only if it exceeds a certain degree of complexity. This is what Prajāpati taught people when he said that they could build the fire altar only by piling a certain number of bricks in a certain way. The right form was therefore a boon, revealed by that being whom the gods sought to reassemble. Prajāpati's behavior to the gods was like that of a master craftsman with his apprentices. Here you are building too much, here too little. In this way you'll never succeed. Even though the Vedic liturgists—and Prajāpati before them—never spoke about art, it was exactly that. When, at the opposite end of history, in places and times far removed from any form of liturgy, people began to talk about art in terms of an *absolute*, the memory of Prajāpati was once again revived—and in a way congenial to him, as if such memory were cloaked in a boundless cloud, nourished by what Bloy called "prophetic recklessness." He was speaking about Lautréamont—one of the first to do so—and wrote: "The undisputable sign of the great poet is *prophetic recklessness*, the disturbing faculty of uttering words without precedent, regardless of people and times, of whose effect he himself is ignorant. This is the mysterious mark of the Holy Spirit on certain sacred or profane foreheads."

One of the more tormenting paradoxes that the Vedic ritualists had to consider was this: "Those who presented oblations in former times touched the altar and the oblations in that moment, while they were sacrificing. Thus they became more guilty." Meanwhile those who refused to sacrifice did not increase the burden of their guilt. This was intolerable. And so "unbelief took hold of men: 'Those who sacrifice become more guilty and those who do not sacrifice become more prosperous.' "

This led to an extremely serious crisis: "No sacrificial food then came to the gods from the world." Life itself was in danger of becoming extinct. It was Bṛhaspati, the chaplain to the gods, who suggested a solution to the problem by spreading a layer of *darbha* grass over the altar. And so, "thanks to the sacrificial grass the altar is appeased." Life then resumed, but the episode was etched into the memory as one of the moments of great danger and uncertainty. Behind that episode was a nagging concern that would remain and that nothing—not even the *darbha* grass—could allay. This was the thought that the substance of the sacrifice—the oblation and the altar—is impregnated with contagious guilt. Sacrifice is above all the place where evil dwells—and from where it can infect those who come into contact with it. The brahmin, as can be seen from this passage, is the one who possesses sufficient strength to absorb the evil, transmitted through contact, in himself. A brahmin is he who, more than anyone else, boldly allows his body to be exposed to evil. Yet over the course of time the brahmin was to become the opposite: the one who most strictly observes the rules that prevent contact with impurity. Continuing along this path, anyone who avoided exposing themselves to evil could become a model of good, hence anyone who avoided performing sacrifices: the most undeserving, cowardly, insignificant beings. And so unbelief took root: through purity. But at this point communication broke down between gods and humans: an example of a stalemate from which the liturgy had to point the way out. How? By following the suggestion of Bṛhaspati, performing sacrifices once again, but spreading a layer of grass over the altar, like a cushion that prevented immediate contact with the guilt. This is one of the many sublime *half measures* by which the liturgy showed how to do something, and at the same time how not to do it. If this way out through gesture was not good enough, all that was left was logical impossibility, which paralyzes and prevents any further thought. The whole of Vedic India was an attempt to *think further.*

If no one celebrates the rites any longer, if there are no longer any places fit to celebrate them—apart from open countryside, but then the very notion of "open countryside" has become archaic—what is left of the sacrifice? The Vedic ritualists had thought even of this possibility. And their answer: there are still two syllables, *svāhā* (an invocation, something like "hail!"). "*Svāhā* is the sacrifice; thus he makes everything here immediately ready for the sacrifice." All the differences, ramifications, variations take us back, in the end, to one question: whether or not there is a sacrificial attitude in thought, in action, whether or not the act of making any offering to any invisible presence has meaning. That which indicates the sacrificial attitude, prior to any act, prior to any thought, that which holds it like a sound cell, is a two-syllable invocation: *svāhā*. The presence or absence of those two syllables shows that action and thought have set off in one or other of the two fundamental directions. That's why it might be said that "*svāhā* is the sacrifice": that tiny vibration is enough to announce that we have arrived in the world where something will be offered. What is to be offered, and to whom, is in a way secondary to the gesture of that preliminary invocation.

And so it might also be said: "It is only with the offering that a brick becomes whole and complete." In those words we may find an answer to the question of what is the object of the gesture—an inevitable question, given such a profusion of liturgical gestures. An object—therefore also the object of knowledge—is never just that which is enclosed within a perimeter of matter or within the limits of a definition. To be complete, the object must also include within itself the gesture of the offering—and the entire liturgy is an immense variation on that gesture.

"The sacrificer being the sacrifice, he thus heals the sacrifice by means of the sacrifice." Hidden in a sequence of invocations, we find an all-embracing formula, which describes the essence of that action—the sacrifice—which claims that it is everything. In this autistic and tautological vortex, only one word is added: the verb *heal.* The rest consists of grammatical variations on the word *sacrifice.* And if the verb *heal* is the only other word, this already indicates that everything proceeds around a wound, which coincides with life itself.

The sacrifice is a wound. Which has to be healed by inflicting another wound, but *in a certain way.* And, since wound is added to wound, the wound never closes. And so the sacrifice must be performed over and over again.

The sacrifice is an interrupted, incomplete suicide (Sylvain Lévi, with his masterly concision: "The only authentic sacrifice would be suicide"). But the ritualists were used to thinking to the extreme. What would happen if, on that journey toward the sky and coming back from the sky, which is the sacrifice, someone refused to *come back*? It would be a new rite, the *sarvasvāra* (the ritualists were relentless classifiers). A rite befitting an old man "who wishes to die." It will begin with a series of actions and chants that make up the first part of the sacrifice, the part that moves toward the sky. When it is complete, the sacrificer lies down on the ground, with his head covered. Other chants follow. At the end of which the sacrificer *must* die. But if he doesn't die? The ritualists also thought of this: "If he remains alive, he shall celebrate the last oblation of the *soma* sacrifice, after which he will seek to die of hunger."

And there is yet one more eventuality: what if someone, before reaching old age, wishes to reach the sky through the sacrifice and not come back to earth? The ritualists advised against it: "People say: 'A life of a hundred years leads to heaven.' And so one ought not to yield to one's desires and die before having reached the last term of life, for this does not lead to heaven." And we know why: the gods don't like intruders.

In thought, there is no evolution but rather an occasional concentration, accumulation, crystallization in particular places at particular times. For *ousía*, it occurred in Greece between the sixth and the fourth centuries B.C.E.; for *sacrifice* in India, between the tenth and sixth centuries B.C.E.; for *hunting* in certain tribes, in various parts of the world, we know not when. Each of these peoples was the most tenacious, most lucid, most obsessive in thinking about what is hidden behind those words. Then time served above all to unlearn, to obfuscate these elements of knowledge. But they remained there, waiting to be picked up once again, expanded, worked out, connected.

Sacrifice is a system that can have countless, uncontrollable variants. Always belonging to the same set. More than being a system, it is an attitude: the sacrificial attitude. It is to be found (or not) at every moment in a person's life. And according to the teachings of the Brāhmaṇas, it is present throughout life, in its perpetual pulsation.

In the theories of sacrifice, after many twists and turns, we reach a final fork: either sacrifice is a device used by society to ease certain tensions or to satisfy certain needs, in which case it has to be said that it is a ruthless institution based upon a collective illusion that is perpetuated from generation to generation; or it is an attempt by society to blend with nature, taking on certain irreducible characteristics, in which case it must be seen as a form of metaphysics put into action, celebrated and displayed in a formalized sequence of gestures. In the first case, sacrifice would be an official part of society to be rejected without any second thoughts: a society that, in order to sustain itself, needs to choose arbitrary victims, simply because it *must* kill someone, is a society that no enlightened thinking could put forward as a model. In the second case, sacrifice would be a form of metaphysics to be refused or accepted. And an experimental form of metaphysics, based not just on certain propositions, but on certain acts.

Rudra is the most powerful objection to the sacrificial world of the Vedas. He accompanies it like a shadow, he watches its disruption. In the Black Age, that patient, noble work of sacrificial builders would no longer be feasible. Rudra, the nameless, was to become the ever-present Śiva, already multiform in his names, ruler over every cult. For only Śiva, as obscure as the primordial archer, the unnameable Rudra, resembles the obscurity of time. Only Śiva can absorb time into himself—time which kills without remedy.

Desire, Kāma, swirls about with his sugarcane bow and his five flower-arrows. The only one who can reduce him to ashes is Śiva. This was the obsessive thought: desire that provokes action, that produces fruits. One of these fruits is the world itself—its enchantment. The one who incinerates desire is therefore the destroyer of the world. But does this mean that Śiva would become an enemy of desire? Such a conflict would be too simple, too crude. On the contrary: Śiva is also the one who, more than anyone else, is susceptible to desire, who continually exasperates it, who pushes it to the extreme, who lets it run in his veins—to the point that sometimes we might think that Śiva *is* desire, that Śiva is Kāma.

When Brahmā curses Kāma, he incites him to turn on Śiva, because he knows that only Śiva can crush Kāma. In the same way that he knows that only Kāma can wound Śiva. By bringing Kāma and Śiva together, Brahmā knows that in this way he can avenge himself against the one who has subjugated him (Kāma) and the one who has mocked him (Śiva). And he hopes they will torment each other endlessly, like two warring brothers.

XVII

AFTER THE FLOOD

Noah left the Ark, obeying Elohim's command. And with him all other creatures, one by one, countless pairs of animals of every species. Long processions, especially of insects. As many left the Ark as had entered, since none of them had had intercourse during the voyage. Intercourse was forbidden in times of calamity. And during the long months of the voyage, even death was held in abeyance, even for those whose lives were fleeting. Noah didn't know what Elohim intended to do now. His last manifestation had been a disaster that had wiped away the land. And now his voice was inviting him to set foot once again on land that was barely dry. But what if Noah had got it wrong, from the very start? What if he himself had incurred the wrath of Elohim, as had happened to the rest of his generation? So Noah decided to do something that had never been done before. He built an altar. No more than a block of stone. But no one had thought of doing such a thing until that moment. Then Noah made a choice "among every clean beast and of every clean fowl" and killed them, beside the altar. Then he laid out the various pieces of flesh on the altar so that they burned completely. This is what we must assume, since the chronicler says that he "made holocausts rise on the altar."

It was a strange, systematic slaughter of single animals. And their corpses were laid out on the same stone block. Yahweh was satisfied. The smell of the burnt flesh, horrible to men, was sweet to his nostrils. When Utnapištim did the same as Noah in Mesopotamia, after the flood, "the gods gathered like flies around the officiant." Yahweh, on the other hand, did not move but began to think. He decided he would not "curse the ground any more for man's sake." Had his opinion of man perhaps changed? No. He thought then, as he had done before the flood, that "the object of man's heart is evil from his youth." This was how man was made. But this was no reason for man and the earth to be destroyed, as had almost just happened. Nevertheless, man had to follow certain rules. And his life had to undergo certain changes. First of all, from that day forth, men would inspire "fear and dread" in all creatures. This was itself something new, since, immediately before creating Adam, Elohim had thought only of offering him and his descendants "authority" over all the creatures of the earth. Between "authority" and "fear and dread" there was a distinct difference. But it was now the era *after the flood*—and this was a sign of it. Elohim then proclaimed another innovation: "Every moving thing that lives shall be food for you, like the green herb: I have given you all this." Only one proviso was attached: "But you shall not eat flesh with its soul, which is the blood." There were then a few words about killing. Any being that has killed a man—whether the killer is an animal or another man—would in turn be killed. We are not told by whom, hence it would not necessarily be revenge. The only certainty was that the killer would be killed, even if it was an animal that had killed a man. The killing of a human was a cycle from which there was no escape. And Elohim added: "For in the image of Elohim, Elohim has made man." They were the same words that Elohim had thought before creating man, but which perhaps he had never spoken to him. About this, the chronicler doesn't tell us. But those words are now spoken to Noah, immediately after the moment in which Yahweh had thought that "the object of man's heart is evil from his youth." And so that being which had been formed in the image of Elohim kept in his heart the desire for evil. Thus it was, and thus it must continue to be, thought Elohim. It was one of his thoughts that men most ignored.

In making his first "covenant" with mankind, Elohim limited himself to two actions: eating and killing. He made no mention of idols, adultery, stealing, or respect for parents, as if the only possible guilt serious enough to violate the covenant was centered on eating and killing. Eating also came within the sphere of killing, since Elohim now allowed flesh to be eaten. More precisely, the flesh of slain animals. But if the blood, being the soul, was eliminated from that flesh, then the killing would not have been a true killing. It involved Elohim in a line of reasoning that was very similar to that of certain Vedic ritualists in relation to sacrifice.

Finally, Elohim declared that the rainbow would be the seal of the covenant. It was a pact containing very few rules. When, over the years, Elohim felt the need to renew the covenant, all would be expanded. But for now, with Noah, he wished to add nothing else, as if those meager instructions included all the others that would be added in the future. In the first place, man was granted dominion over nature. He was allowed a surplus of force over all other beings. At the same time Elohim reserved life to himself. So man would therefore never be self-sufficient. So man could kill animals, but not eat their blood. So man had to perform sacrifices, because only after sacrificing had he become once again agreeable to Elohim. There was an obvious difficulty in these precepts, for man—in order to sacrifice as well as to eat—had to take the life of other creatures. But Elohim thought this could be overcome: to eat the flesh of animals, all that man had to do was drain the blood away. And in the sacrifice? Noah had celebrated a holocaust, where the animal was wholly consumed by fire. More than losing its life, it disappeared from the face of the earth—and passed on in its entirety to Elohim. For the moment, human life could proceed on that basis.

Anyone wishing to approach the phenomenon of sacrifice through the Bible will come up against two questions: why did Abel, "after a certain time" and after his elder brother Cain had offered to Yahweh "the first fruits of the earth," wish to kill "the firstlings of his flock" to offer them with "the fat thereof" to Yahweh? And why did Noah, as soon as he set foot on dry land, want to kill examples "of every clean beast and of every clean fowl" to offer them to Yahweh?

The word *offering* or *oblation* appears for the first time in the Bible in reference to Cain. And Cain's offering—"fruits of the earth"—can be interpreted as a gesture of homage of someone who offers a guest the finest that he has. At that time man was allowed only to feed on the fruits of the land. And so to offer it to Yahweh was a pious and evocative gesture, *as if* Yahweh wished to share those fruits with man.

The case of Abel is quite different. Until then the Bible had never mentioned the act of killing. And the eating of flesh had not yet been permitted by Yahweh. It is therefore strange that Abel should feel the need to kill some of his animals to offer them to Yahweh. If his gesture was to be interpreted as an imitation of that of his brother Cain, it was *as if* Abel were offering that animal flesh to Yahweh ("with the fat") that Yahweh himself had not yet allowed man to eat.

While the *offering* is linked to the figure who will become the epitome of malice, the *killing* is the gesture of two men about whose goodness there is no doubt. Yet at the same time the gesture of offering is an essential characteristic of the devout man, while killing is the first of all evils. Sacrifice and murder, offering and killing: a conundrum from the very beginning, which history cannot unravel. Indeed, history will be marked by failed attempts to unravel it.

Sacrifice is powerful, but it does not remedy all guilt. If someone sins "with his hand raised (*be-yad ramah*)," going deliberately against the law, it is stated in Numbers that no sacrifice can redeem it. He will then be "cut off" from among his people. The sacrifice of atonement, *haṭṭa't*, can therefore serve only to remedy sins committed "unwittingly" by the individual or by the community. But how can the whole community be aware of sins that it has committed "unwittingly"? Neither Leviticus nor Numbers tells us. The answer is implicit. The sacrifice of atonement presupposes the attainment of awareness. Indeed, the sacrifice itself *is* awareness, as if the act of becoming aware were also to imply the act of killing. This is the hardest and most mysterious point of sacrifice. And, consequently, also of awareness. Why does becoming aware of something make it necessary to kill an animal? For the sins of the community it was a bullock, for those of an individual a ram.

When the sin is deliberate, the simple sacrifice of an animal—of greater or lesser size and strength depending on who has committed the sin—will no longer be applicable. Then the line is crossed between sacrifice and sentence of death. An obscure point on which a story, the cruelest and most eloquent in Numbers, casts light: "While the children of Israel were in the wilderness, they found a man gathering sticks on the Sabbath day. And they who found him gathering sticks brought him to Moses and Aaron, and to all the community. And they placed him under guard, because it had not yet been decided what should be done to him. Then Yahweh said to Moses: 'The man should surely be put to death: all the community should stone him with stones outside the camp!' And all the community brought him outside the camp, and stoned him with stones, and he died; as Yahweh had commanded Moses."

This unknown man who dared to gather sticks on the Sabbath marks the dividing line between the sacrificial system and the judicial system. An unclear and ill-defined dividing line that certainly doesn't suggest we are entering a more enlightened and evolved field. It is, indeed, as if the sentence carried out by the community has not removed us from the realms of sacrifice but, on the contrary, has taken us to its harshest and most unfathomable inner core. The episode stands in abrupt isolation, not least because we find it at a juncture between two passages in which Yahweh speaks to Moses—the first of these dealing with the various types of sacrifice required of the children of Israel (sacrifice of the first crop, holocausts of atonement, insufficiency of the atonement sacrifice for anyone who sins "with his hand raised"), and the second dedicated to the "fringes on the border of garments," always containing "a band of purple color," that the children of Israel shall carry for all future generations, in remembrance of the commandments of Yahweh. Between these two fundamental discourses, the text of Numbers suddenly stops to record something that once happened in the life of the children of Israel. A man is found gathering sticks on the Sabbath day. The people do not know what to do with him. What follows is through the direct intervention of Yahweh. And it would be difficult to put it in a more conspicuous place. The commandments that Yahweh had just given on particular sacrifices were, it seems, insufficient to cover every eventuality. There were cases where the children of Israel didn't know what to do. And then Yahweh speaks once again, before Moses asks for his instructions. The story offers an example of what could and should happen when people don't know how to decide for themselves. Divine law clearly cannot cover every eventuality. So Yahweh intervenes and decides the fate of the wood gatherer: "The man should surely be put to death." It is also stated where and how he is to die: *extra castra*, "outside the camp," as would happen one day for Jesus.

The rules set out in Leviticus and Numbers lack the scrupulousness, the tireless urge to classify, the metaphysical nitpicking that distinguish the Brāhmaṇas. Even in the single category of atonement sacrifices, the terms overlap and get muddled together so that their area of application cannot be clearly defined. Scholars struggle diligently, without much success, trying to distinguish *haṭṭa't* from *asham*. Is one perhaps the "sin sacrifice" and the other the "reparation sacrifice"? But there are cases where their meanings seem to be reversed and the differences are lost. There is only one fixed point that is emphasized each time: the blood. What to do with the blood. In the *haṭṭa't*, "if the sacrifice is offered for the high priest or for all the people . . . having gathered the blood, the officiant enters the Holy Place, and seven times makes a sprinkling before the veil which shuts off the Holy of Holies, then he rubs with blood the horns of the altar of perfumes which is before the veil, and finally he pours the rest at the foot of the altar of holocausts. These are the only bloody sacrifices where something of the victim is introduced inside the Temple." This last sentence is like a brief pause in Fr. Roland de Vaux's detailed list of what happens with the blood in the various rites called *haṭṭa't* and *asham*. For this seems to be the real distinction: where and how the blood is poured and smeared.

Here a high doctrine of slaughtering was being described. It is impossible to ignore or omit what happened to the blood. It is impossible to forget the words of Yahweh to Noah and then one day to Moses: "For the life of the flesh is in the blood: and I have given it to you upon the altar to make an atonement for your souls: for it is the blood that makes an atonement for the soul." Salvation, or even just the readjustment of the continually fraught relationship with Yahweh, comes from blood. And they are inconceivable without blood.

The Jews discovered how blood was essential to their salvation on the night when Yahweh *passed over* those houses whose doorposts were smeared with blood, as he proceeded to exterminate all the firstborn in Egypt, men and beasts. That was the historical—and therefore the only—Passover. Before that, it had been a festival for seminomadic shepherds, repeated every year on the first full moon of spring. Then, too, the blood of slain animals had been smeared on doorposts and lintels. But, at that time, nobody could know that this blood would mean salvation—and farewell to Egypt. It was believed to protect homes from the *mashḥit*, the Destroyer, the evil power that was always lying in wait. Then came history—the sacred history that absorbs within itself the overwhelming plurality of stories—and that recurring feast became one single night, at one single moment of history. From a recurrence it became a memory. Every father, from then on, eating unleavened bread, could tell his son: "This is done because of that which the Lord did unto me when I went out of Egypt." The feast that was repeated every year, when the full moon rose in the month of Nisan, was transformed all of a sudden into one *single* night, which became part of the life of every father and was told to his firstborn son, saved by the blood smeared on the doorposts of his house, long ago.

XVIII

TIKI

The idea that the web of correspondences constitutes a foundational element in a society was recognized and accepted in the most rigorous academic circles at the beginning of the twentieth century, with the essay by Émile Durkheim and Marcel Mauss, *"De quelques formes primitives de classification"* (1903). But a confusion immediately began that reflected the two-headed nature of that paper, the result of a collaboration between a born analogist (Mauss) and a born determinist (Durkheim), related through family ties (Mauss was Durkheim's nephew). That was the beginning of the tendency to affirm that *first* came society and *then* correspondences. Which were therefore *determined* by the social structure. The realm of analogy was certainly recognized, but was considered as a consequence of the main cause, which was society itself. And so it came about that the most formidable investigator and identifier of correspondences—Marcel Granet, who followed in the tracks of Mauss—could declare on several occasions, almost as if to close the matter, that there was no doubt that every form of thought was dependent on and subject to the structure of society.

It was, in fact, a vicious cycle that could never be resolved: correspondences presuppose society, but society presupposes correspondences. Thought and society are fashioned and shaped insofar as (and thanks to the fact that) they are each based on the other.

In 1933, exactly thirty years after their essay on the primitive forms of classification, and now free from Durkheim's guidance, Mauss went back to express his own view on correspondences (the realm of analogy). And he did so in one of those marginal and preliminary writings of his where he often expressed his most radical thoughts. Intervening in a session where Granet had delivered his enlightening study *"La Droite et la gauche en Chine,"* Mauss used the occasion to make an undisguised and blatant retraction. He said: "Wrongly we have been too ritological and too worried about practices." This had originally been Durkheim's error, since the *practices* (basically: the rites) offered secure ground, insofar as they were established and rooted in society, whereas all the rest (especially myth) could also disappear among the mists of beliefs and folk tales. But now, Mauss added, the scene was changing: "The progress made by Granet consists of introducing some mythology and some 'representation' into all this." Continuing in this vein, Mauss arrived at other surprising conclusions, which could be glimpsed between the lines. First of all by firmly shifting the sphere of research in the Durkheim school, to which he had never denied belonging: "The great effort we have made on the side of ritology is unbalanced because we have not made a corresponding effort in mythology." Here Mauss introduced a word (*ritology*) that has become particularly valuable today, and he attacked the very bases of the anthropological work that he and his colleagues had carried out in Paris over the previous thirty years. And that criticism could just as well have been applied to English anthropology over the same period. Thus he gave advance warning of what years later would be referred to as a change of paradigm. And, as a last coup de théâtre, to represent it he named someone who had never apparently questioned the school's precepts—Marcel Granet. Mauss now wished to make him into something highly suspect: a mythologist. Mauss wrote: "But we have one mythologist left, and this is Granet." The reference, though unstated, was to the masterpiece that Granet had published seven years earlier: *Danses et légendes de la Chine ancienne*, an unsurpassed example of how mythology can be put into practice.

Mauss was concerned about something else in these impromptu comments. That was correspondences. This vast subspecies of classifications has acted in a whole variety of ways in giving meaning to the world, from the very earliest times up to the plates of *signaturae* in Athanasius Kircher and Robert Fludd, at the height of the seventeenth century, which is to say up until very recent times. "These ways of thinking and at the same time of acting are, besides, common to a very large mass of humanity," wrote Mauss—introducing another extremely important phrase (what do the whole of the Brāhmaṇas speak of if not of "ways of thinking and at the same time of acting"?). But how to unravel the immense tangle that had been formed well before all documented history? Here Mauss intervened with *his* mythopoetic power—and deliberately referred to the fact that, for him, the key did exist: it was a small jade plaque, gray or dark green in color, that the Maoris call *hei tiki*, and that their noblewomen wear around their necks as a talisman. Tiki was also their name for the Progenitor of the human race, their Prajāpati. What do these enchanting small objects represent? "They depict a fetus—highly stylized—, the most beautiful ones with a red stone eye." But not only that: "These *tikis* also represent the phallus, the first men, the act of creation; these *tikis* are above all depictions of the macrocosm and of the microcosm, of God."

Each time that Mauss has occasion to speak about these jade plaques we can feel his mind vibrating, as if he were holding the very first cell of correspondences, condensed into these tiny, untarnishable objects, which Western invaders had simply taken for ornaments and resold as exotic trinkets.

Mauss had come across an illustration of Tiki while working with Hertz at the British Museum one day, in a plate attached to the first volume of John White's *Ancient History of the Maori*, with the list of correspondences connected to individual parts of its body: "We copied carefully: Tiki . . . was a little man with a tuft of hair, naked, his virile member modestly hidden. Inserted immediately into their place are the names of the gods to his right and to his left, the god of war and the god of peace. Also, the gods of intelligence, of dreams and of the sky that are on his head, the gods of feet and of magic . . . etc. This we found immensely interesting."

But the story doesn't end here. Years later, Mauss presents a paper on Tiki at a conference on anthropology and he decides to go back to the British Museum, he says, "to have another look at the text I had cited. Then, to my great amazement, thirty years later, I found myself in front of something that went far beyond what I had noted down. I had before me an enormous folded plate, which had been drawn by experts and summarized the sayings of the high priests of New Zealand, for White, in obedience to Grey and White's instructions. They are documents dating back to the years 1859–1886. Consequently, they are completely beyond all contamination on the part of professional ethnography, ethnology and all the sociologies you care to imagine [it is impossible not to express a note of admiration and delight for that "all the sociologies you care to imagine"]. Around all the limbs of Tiki, and all the body parts of Tiki, on this large folded illustration, is set out the complete classification of the world, that of times and spaces and of all the species of things with the gods that rule over them. It is therefore the picture of the microcosm, together with the complete development of the macrocosm, and I am not the one who has made it! There is no possible doubt, it is much clearer than all the texts of the great theorists of divination, of Antiquity and of the Renaissance. With these words, I deliver this fact to the materials of René Berthelot. The Maori priests have outlined the macrocosm and the microcosm." This scene of recognition, in which first Mauss and Hertz, then Mauss alone, bent over the plate of a book, come across the subject matter that was to occupy their most intimate and constant thoughts, was recounted by Mauss in 1937, during a discussion that followed Paul Mus's lecture *"La Mythologie primitive et la pensée de l'Inde"* at the Société Française de Philosophie. On that occasion, Mauss did not say so explicitly, but seemed to suggest that Prajāpati, the Puruṣa, the lone figure that dominated the scene of the Brāhmaṇas, might have a counterpart farther east in New Zealand, in those jade pendants that Maori noblewomen wore against their skin, while the Vedic Prajāpati had left no tangible image of himself. Everything, in India, began and ended with fire.

The underlying significance of the *tiki* had been more fully stated four years earlier, in response to Granet's lecture (the occasion remains important, establishing the link between Mauss and a particular scholar). Mauss had stated in clearest detail what was implied in the question of the *tiki*, and where—very far indeed—it might lead. The *tiki*, wrote Mauss, "is literally the world picture, a sort of barbarian version of one of the fundamental notions of East and West, that of macrocosm and microcosm in a human figure. Because, as in our ancient systems of *signaturae*, the limbs of the *tiki* and of man 'correspond' to beings, things, events and parts of the world. Everything is divided between 'powers and natures' not only to left and right, but also above and below, to front and back, in correlation with a center." We can still feel, in those lines, the excitement of someone convinced he has finally found—and, we might say, actually touched—the "barbarian version" of an immense, multifaceted text of thought. Indeed, not only of thought, but of all experience. He says here, in a few words, that in East and West—and therefore with no geographical limitation and in spite of all the sacred principles of anthropology—a certain way of thinking had guided "a very large mass of humanity."

A wide and variegated procession of beings had populated the vast realm of analogy, from the jade plaques of the Maoris to the plates of *signaturae* in the books of the last pansophists of seventeenth-century hermetism—and onward, up to Baudelaire's web of *correspondances*, where "fragrances, colors and sounds respond to each other."

What was all this about? Thought—but certainly a kind of thought no trace of which was to be found in the histories of philosophy, except on odd occasions. Why? Mauss never posed the question, but he gave one of those brilliant answers that we find scattered among his dispersed writings: "Philosophy leads to everything, provided there's a way out of it." It is a phrase applicable to all times—to the past as well as to what would be the future when Mauss wrote it (in 1939). It was tacitly assumed by the leading anthropologists of the twentieth century that philosophy—at least in the form it had assumed at universities after the French Revolution—is not thought itself, but only one of many forms of thought, a kind of springboard. An assumption, however, that should never be declared. Such an idea was well respected up until Lévi-Strauss. But it was Mauss himself who revealed the hidden goal in *his* conception of anthropology: "I will even go as far as saying that comprehensive anthropology could replace philosophy, because it would include within itself the very history of the human spirit that philosophy presupposes."

If a jade pendant that adorns the breast of a Maori noblewoman can gather within itself all the heavens, all the worlds, and all the gods, and even God—as Mauss ventured to suggest—then what would come of the various distinctions between primitive and civilized, between people who had no writing and those who did, between simplicity and complexity? Things would have to be thought out and described in another way. For the French anthropologist, who had grown up in a period and atmosphere of positivism, that "little man" of hard stone which he had discovered in a large folded plate at the British Museum would become a talisman, as it was already for the Maori noblewomen. It could be said that Mauss's whole body of work, his tireless, ragged, ramified inquiry toward a "comprehensive anthropology," had found its demon protector in that small being.

If the Maoris, whom Mauss's predecessors had regarded as exemplifying primitive man, had developed "a complete classification of things of a type no less clear and incisive that any of the other cosmological mythologies produced in the ancient world," then in what way might those systems of correspondences be judged? First of all, the Maoris were placed on the same level as not only ancient China and the Mesopotamian civilizations, but also the Hermetic tradition in Europe. It brought together a prodigious mix of times, places, and circumstances. And a problem immediately arose: how, by what criteria, can systems of correspondences be evaluated? The usual answer among anthropologists, that those systems were to be judged according to their social function, was not enough. It was clear that, in their subtlety and intricacy, they went far beyond any application in society. In them was an irreducible superabundance of thought. Exactly as in the prescriptions of the Vedic ritualists. Those systems were a mode of thought. They were the substance of thought—and that thought was waiting only to be recognized as such: in the same way as the thought of Spinoza or Leibniz is considered or judged. At this point it seemed clear what a subversive gesture Mauss had made toward the traditional way of thinking when he placed himself under the protection of Tiki. And perhaps it could now be seen what really lay hidden behind some of his apparently innocuous phrases. Such as these: "Philosophies and sciences are languages. Consequently, it is a matter only of speaking the best language."

The first step, when considering systems of correspondences, is to recognize their vastness, complexity, precision, subtlety, and their arrangement on multiple levels. The second is to ask why, in such different situations and times, thought has felt it necessary to take on these forms. Mauss also tried to get to this second step, but made only the gesture of doing so. Only newly accepted into the Société de Philosophie (the circumstances are always telling in Mauss's life), he found himself—in his own words—"paying for it [that honor] by immediately providing the spectacle of two sociologists savaging each other." The incident involved Lévy-Bruhl, who had just read a paper, *"La Mentalité primitive,"* and Mauss, who then proceeded to attack him.

For Lévy-Bruhl, the word that opens all doors was *participation.* And this was what Mauss found objectionable. Not because the word did not point in the right direction. But because Lévy-Bruhl used it with a vagueness and haziness that he suggested, wrongly, was part of the notion itself. And this gave Mauss the chance to touch a central nerve: "'Participation' is not only a confusion. It presupposes an effort to confuse and an effort to make things similar. It is not a simple resemblance, but a *homoíōsis* [assimilation]. From the very beginning there is a *Trieb* [a drive], a violence of the mind on itself in order to overcome itself; from the very beginning there is the wish to bond."

Using for once, quite strangely, a Freudian word such as *Trieb*, Mauss is pushing toward the source of the *bandhus*, those "nexuses" that make up the web of correspondences. And, with this desire to connect, he discovers a *violence* of the mind toward itself. A moment of suspense, astonishment, fear, as if he were setting foot in forbidden territory. Here we were approaching the childhood amnesia of knowledge, a barrier of fire and darkness. Mauss said no more on that occasion. But he resorted to an ethnographical object, as he would do with the Maori *tikis.* When he found himself at a crucial junction in knowledge, which threatened to overturn it, Mauss adopted a peculiar strategy, without declaring it: he abandoned the role of anthropologist and took on the role of a museum guide pointing out various exhibits. This time it was not jade jewels but masks: "At the Trocadéro museum there are certain North-West American masks on display on which totems are carved. Some have a double shutter. Open the first and behind the public totem of the 'shaman-chief' appears another smaller mask which represents his private totem, and then the last shutter shows highest-ranking initiates his true nature, his face, the human and divine and totemic spirit, the spirit that he incarnates. For, let us be clear, in that moment it is supposed that the chief is in a state of possession, of *ékstasis*, of ecstasy, and not just of *homoíōsis.* There is rapture and confusion at the same time."

Mauss does not stop to indicate the implications of his *argument through imagery.* But those repercussions go a very long way. First, because they point to a knowledge arranged by strata, on various levels, as if passing from one face concealed in the mask to the next. And each of these levels is firmly connected to the other, since they are the faces of the same shaman: an eloquent example of the firmest correspondences.

But there is another point: in referring to the use of the shamanic mask, worn at ceremonies marked by possession, Mauss suggests that the *homoíōsis*, the process of "assimilation" through which the mind relates like with like, would not be the first act of thought, but almost the consequence of a *state*: a state of possession. Thus the rapture, the fusion of like with like, find their driving force in an upheaval of the psyche. On the other hand, the notion that possession is the origin of knowledge was the very foundation of Delphi. And Mauss, though telegraphic in style, goes further. If Lévy-Bruhl's "participation" goes back in the end to possession, it is not just because this is a rudimentary (Lévy-Bruhl himself would have said "prelogical") form of knowledge. But also the saintly Reason of Kantian and Comtian *instituteurs* (well represented by Durkheim) would come from the same origins. And here Mauss dealt the hardest blow to his readers, to his discipline, and to his illustrious uncle, while maintaining an impeccably neutral formulation: " 'Participation' thus implies not only a confusion of categories, but it is, from the beginning, as it is for us, an effort to identify ourselves with things and to identify things among themselves. The reason has the same deliberate and collective origin in the most ancient societies and in the most incisive forms of philosophy and science."

It is a delightful irony that Marcel Mauss, at the beginning of his academic career, was appointed to the Chair of History of Religions of Uncivilized Peoples. And already on the eighth line of his inaugural lecture the new professor declared, stressing the words in italics: *"Uncivilized peoples do not exist."* Mauss had been appointed to teach a subject that he declared did not exist.

Thirty years later, at the beginning of a course at the Collège de France, Mauss would go as far as not only avoiding all reference to that annoying expression "uncivilized," but also abolishing a more obstinate word: *primitive.* Explaining: "All the rest of humanity, who are called primitive and are still living, deserve instead the name archaic." Having cleared away those ungainly remnants of the positivistic and progressive vision, it remained to be seen what dignity and power of thought was to be given to the *archaic.* For even the archaic could be considered a crude rehearsal for something to come or as a chaotic repertory upon which, having become *compos sui*, history would later draw. This is how Durkheim explained his interest in studying religion, which he would otherwise have been embarrassed to admit—and he said it in the true manifesto of the French school of sociology, the 1898 Preface to the *Année sociologique*: "Religion contains within itself, from the very beginning, though in a confused state, all the elements that, in dissociating themselves, in determining themselves, in combining themselves together in a thousand ways have given birth to the different manifestations of collective life." Underlying Durkheim's words, and very difficult to erode, is the conviction that the complex is explained through the simple, the superior through the inferior, the perfect through the imperfect. If there is a dogma people today are not prepared to do without, it is precisely this one. It needed the lucidity of Simone Weil to throw sand—a deadly sand—into the workings of that speculative machine: "The imperfect proceeds from the perfect and not the other way around."

Hidden among the reports of the *Annuaire de l'École Pratique des Hautes Études*—usually put together as a *pensum* to explain the academic curriculum—a few words announce the fact that, for the 1934–1935 course, "the Director [Mauss] has managed to procure White's *Ancient History of the Maori* (six volumes plus one volume of plates)," and so lectures were to be dedicated to the study of Maori cosmology. Some highly revealing words then followed, despite the limited importance of that publication: White's work contained "one of the most coherent bodies of cosmogonic myths that we know." For example, the Tiki cycle, "macrocosm and microcosm, great male god, phallus and fetus, creator of All," is now presented as being "most important and best coordinated, and in the end almost better documented than any other cycle of any other known mythology." A statement brimming with implications. What was glimpsed here was a Copernican upheaval: no longer was it a question of Egyptian, Greek, Mesopotamian, or Vedic mythology offering opportunities for understanding certain aspects of rudimentary and obscure Maori mythology, but—on the contrary—perhaps the immense and well-articulated corpus of Maori mythology was capable of holding within itself the mythological systems of more advanced civilizations, as particular examples and extensions. And even arranging them indeed *in their proper place*, as part of an ordered sequence. Or at least this seems to be the implication of an extremely bold sentence: "All the themes of the great ancient cosmogonies have found their logical place there."

Words that were enough to explode the basic assumptions of anthropology, then and now. Here the mythologies are presented as one single tree—a tree-forest, consisting of countless other trees, arranged in logical and consequential relationships with each other. And the closest possible approximation, in seeking to perceive this tree-forest to its full extent, would be found in the evidence of Maori mythology. So New Zealand, always cited as an example of a lost island, a place unconnected with *advanced* civilizations, would be the place to which some of the greatest mythological and cosmological systems could be traced, as if to a matrix. Mauss could in no way publicize this idea, since it would certainly have caused problems with his colleagues. But he must have thought about it very often: the figure of Tiki and of the *tikis*—of the god and of the jade pendants that depict him—continued to appear in his papers, including one of 1937–1938 now lost.

Mauss always used rather fewer words than the required minimum. And so his declaration on Tiki and *tikis* is like the outline for an essay. He could have developed it more or less along these lines: mythology is a particular and irreducible modality of knowledge. Its materials are pictures, stories, and combinations of them, in the same way that Newtonian science is a particular modality of knowledge that uses numbers, functions, methods of calculus as its materials. But, unlike Newtonian science, which is practiced every day, mythology is something that has fallen into disuse. Its images, its history have become "empty words." What, then, is the anthropologist's task? Exoterically: to investigate the inextricable link between all living forms and the society that holds them, obeying one single principle: "Myths are social institutions." An easy task, that Mauss was able to perform brilliantly. Yet at the same time he used it as a cover for what was most important to him: an esoteric inquiry that sought to trace the elements of that lost knowledge found in the evidence of scattered fragments of mythologies, rites, and systems of correspondences. This time it was an extremely difficult, almost hopeless, task. It drove Mauss to make sad admissions: "We are still at the stage of preparing the materials of a mythology and very often we are only in a position to demonstrate that the myths are social phenomena." At this point, Mauss found himself doing two jobs: on the one hand, that of a strict scientist of *society*—this all-embracing entity that had never before been studied in all its ramifications; on the other, that of a shaman or medicine man of an extinct tribe, trying to reconstruct its doctrines step by step. And it is through this very superimposition of roles that Mauss's work still transmits a secret energy that anthropology itself, in its various schools and branches, seems to have lost.

Mauss could also be brusque when discussing Tiki. What could the West offer, in comparison? Hesiod's *Theogony.* But if the two texts were put side by side, what would be the result? "Comparisons have been made with Hesiod's *Theogony.* The Maori version (and the Polynesian version in general) appears more coherent, better developed, closer to living institutions than that sort of Greek compilation." What effrontery . . . Not only are the Maoris and the Greeks presented on the same footing. But here indeed the crude, formless text is Hesiod's—or "that sort of compilation" which is passed off under his name. It was a subversion of Wilamowitz's conception of classical antiquity, a liquidation of all claim to European hegemony in matters of the spirit. But where was this epoch-making event declared? In Mauss's (half-page) course summary for the year 1937–1938, describing "relations between certain games and certain ancient cosmologies" in the *Annuaire du Collège de France.* Not many people noticed it.

XIX

THE ACT OF KILLING

If, in digging out the ground for the altar, there was already a fear of hurting the land and its creatures, the killing of animals must have seemed horrific.

—Julius Schwab, *Das altindische Thieropfer*

The question to be answered: Why does the imbalance between divine and human have to be corrected with a killing?

Killing is present everywhere in the food chain that runs throughout the animal kingdom. In each link particular species have to kill others in order to survive. With man, the chain is not broken, indeed it expands. But man is the only being who reflects upon killing, who builds up the act into a sequence of prescribed gestures. As the Vedic ritualists say, man is the only one of the sacrificial victims who also celebrates sacrifices. This happens not because man occupies a final, culminating position in the food chain. Above him are alpha predators who have terrorized and hunted him for millennia—and can still get the better of him. The capacity to reflect upon killing is therefore an anomaly in the food chain, an unexpected divergence that occurs only in that link of the chain. Above it and below it, everything continues and proceeds as always, unchanged. The repertory of gestures is fixed in advance and takes no account of history, which is really a history of that anomaly: the transformation of a being who is basically vegetarian into an omnivore. It is a history of the various ways in which that anomaly appears in actions and gestures. If the food chain were observed from far away in space, human history would appear like a deformed link that assumes a multiplicity and variety of forms compared with the geometrically rigorous fixity of all the other links.

The greatest risk for sacrifice is that it too closely resembles the simple slaying and butchering of an animal. It is essential to anticipate this question: why invent the highly complex ceremony of sacrifice, if in the end everything is to be reduced to dividing up pieces of meat? Here is the answer given by the *Aitareya Brāhmaṇa*: the sacrificial victim shall be divided into thirty-six parts, *because* the *bṛhatī* meter consists of thirty-six syllables: "By dividing it in this way, the victim is made into a celestial being, whereas those who proceed in another way tear it apart like rogues or criminals."

When the sacrificial rite comes closest to the crude, uncontrolled, formless course of things, then the last defensive barrier—the only one that can still separate behavior conducive to order from the behavior of "rogues or criminals"—is meter. And here we see the great role that meter plays in the Veda, as the primary articulation of form, as the first effective device for breaking away from the meaningless and arbitrary succession of existence. And thus the tireless development of correspondences between particular meters and particular gods. Here it is said, among other things, that "the *bṛhatī* is the mind." And so, if the mind coils within itself the thirty-six fragments of the sacrificial victim, this alone is enough to transform those pieces of flesh into fragments of a whole that has a life of its own—and is perhaps also "a celestial being."

There is no doubt: the dividing line is extremely fine. But the suspicion arises that this was perhaps an essential element in the game. In the end, it was much nobler and much simpler to pour something—even an ordinary liquid such as milk—to dedicate it to the gods. A solitary, highly potent, bloodless ceremony, the origin of every sacrifice. We might therefore imagine that, even when a precious liquid such as the *soma* was offered to the gods, it followed the gestures of the *agnihotra*. But this was not the case. The *soma* rites had to be accompanied by a sacrifice of animals. It was as if at that point sacrifice sought to put itself to the test, sought to show how close it was to what necessarily happened in normal, nonritual life, which is always a life of "rogues or criminals." And, at the same time, how distant it was, as was shown by the mind-boggling complication of the whole *agniṣṭoma*, the *soma* sacrifice where animal killing was only one of the many sequences of prescribed gestures.

Puruṣa is a most mysterious figure. The name is often translated (even by Renou) as "Man." Yet in the *Ṛgveda* it is not the word normally used to describe Man. Whereas in the Brāhmaṇas, human sacrifice is called *puruṣamedha* (a word not found in the *Ṛgveda*). *Manu* is much more frequent in the *Ṛgveda*—and the origin of the word (from *man-*, "to think") much clearer. Puruṣa, however, appears in hymn 10.90, which tells how his body, dismembered in the sacrifice, gives birth to the various parts of the universe, but in the rest of the *Ṛgveda* the word appears only in passing, in another two hymns. As for its derivation, the only plausible explanation is from *pūrṇa*, "full." It can therefore be associated with the "stanza of plenitude" in the *Bṛhadāraṇyaka Upaniṣad*. The *Ṛgveda* presents Puruṣa and the dismemberment of his body only once, to show how order is established: "These were the first laws." In the same way, Prajāpati appears only once, in hymn 10.121, to answer the question on *ka*, on *who* must receive the sacrifice. It is irrelevant whether or not the last stanza, where his name is spoken, was added later. The crucial element is that the figure on whom everything depends—whether Puruṣa or Prajāpati—is mentioned in only one hymn out of the thousand and twenty-eight hymns of the *Ṛgveda*. On the other hand, Puruṣa and Prajāpati are referred to endlessly in the vast and rugged plains of the Brāhmaṇas and the Upaniṣads.

It can be said that, in the *Ṛgveda,* the two figures are used, first of all, as support for two phrases that have a formidable capacity to be expanded, as will be seen throughout the rest of the Veda. For Prajāpati, it is the question repeated at the end of every verse, before his name is spoken: "To what god shall we offer the oblation?" For Puruṣa, the phrase appears in the last stanza: "The gods sacrificed the sacrifice through the sacrifice (*yajñéna yajñám ayajanta devā́s*)." The particularly dense and solemn nature of the formula is confirmed by the fact that it is repeated in identical terms, together with the whole of the next verse, at the end of hymn 1.164, the dizzying hymn of Dīrghatamas, the *ṛṣi* called Long-Darkness. Here too, scholars seem to hesitate when dealing with such a bold form of words. Geldner translates: "With the sacrifice the gods sacrificed to the sacrifice." But *yajñám* is an accusative, not a dative. Renou translates: "The gods sacrificed the sacrifice through the sacrifice." And the meaning obviously changes. But even Renou is still evasive. This is how he comments on the verse: "In other words, Man is at the same time the object offered (victim) and the object to which one aspires (divinity)." But at least one further explanation is needed: in the

Vedic verse the endless circle of self-referentiality is outlined, which men have been obliged to pursue since then, up to Gödel and beyond. An endless circle that is not a defect of thought, but a foundation of thought itself. The *ṛṣis* were sure of it: "To this the human *ṛṣis*, our fathers, adhered when the original sacrifice was born in primordial times. With the mind's eye it seems to me that I see them, those who first sacrificed this sacrifice."

As to Puruṣa: it is true that the gods behaved toward him like the officiants who tie the victim to the *yūpa*, the "post." And it is stated clearly: "When the gods, in laying out the sacrifice, had bound Puruṣa as victim." And the following passage is also true—that the gods cut Puruṣa into pieces, as happens with every animal victim ("when they had cut up Puruṣa"). But at the same time Puruṣa was already the sacrifice, as the Brāhmaṇas fully explain. Together with Prajāpati he had appeared from the golden egg that floated on the waters: "After one year, from it was born Puruṣa, this Prajāpati." And Prajāpati, as is repeated insistently, *is* the sacrifice. So the gods, who operated on his body, were none other than his tools. And the same would one day be the case for men, who imitate the gods in their acts. Only this could lighten the guilt for having killed the one from whom, piece by piece, everything was born: meters, stanzas, chants, but also the sky, the sun, the moon. Guilt that the gods heaped onto men, before men, in turn, heaped it onto the gods.

During his endless vicissitudes, Prajāpati seemed sometimes to ignore what he himself had done. After having generated the worlds of men and gods, he happened to look upon them as if they were something strange and unknown:

"Prajāpati desired: 'Would that I might conquer the two worlds, the world of the gods and the world of men.' He saw the animals, the domestic and the wild ones. He took them and by means of them took possession of the two worlds: by means of the tame animals he took possession of this world and by means of the wild animals he took possession of the other world: for this world is the world of men and that other is the world of the gods. And so, when he takes the tame animals, with them he takes possession of this world and when he takes the wild animals, with them he takes possession of the other world.

"Were he to complete the sacrifice with the domestic animals, the roads would converge, the villages would have boundaries close to each other, and there would be no bears, men-tigers, thieves, assassins, and rogues in the forests. Were he to complete the sacrifice with the wild animals the roads would diverge, the villages would have boundaries far from each other and there would be bears, men-tigers, thieves, assassins, and rogues in the forests.

"As to this they say: 'Certainly this, the wild animal, is not part of the cattle and should not be offered: if he were to offer it, the wild animals would soon drag the sacrificer away dead into the forest, for the wild animals belong to the forest; and if he were not to offer wild animals, it would be a violation of the sacrifice.' And so they release the wild animals after having passed fire around them: thus, indeed, it is not an offering and nor is it a non-offering, and thus they do not drag the sacrificer away dead into the forest and there is no violation of the sacrifice."

Prajāpati seemed momentarily to have forgotten having made the world, which appeared to him from the very beginning split in two: this and that, the world of men and the world of the gods. That is: a world of untruth and a world of truth. Prajāpati wanted to find a way of taking possession of these worlds. Then "he saw" the animals. That *to see* has a disturbing implication in this case, for it is always connected to an action. And the action is one alone: killing. In that "he saw," there is still the perception of the prehistoric hunter.

To go ahead and conquer the world of men and the world of the gods, he had to use animals. Animals are the keyboard of the two worlds. At one and the same time, between animals themselves there is a gap that corresponds perfectly to the one between men and gods: men are equivalent to domestic animals, gods to wild animals. We might think, then, that Prajāpati (the model of every sacrificer) would perform a double sacrifice. But he didn't. On the one hand, the only means of action is sacrifice. On the other, sacrifice of wild animals would bring ruin to the sacrificer: the victim, being too powerful, would kill the killer and drag him away into *his* world. Here we have the metaphysical spark, at the point, as ever, where we are about to come up against the irresolvable contradiction. Reason would be crippled at this point, and would dare to go no further. Not so with the liturgy. The solution found—to release the victim, but first to carry a burning ember around it, a gesture performed only as a prelude to immolation—is not a childish attempt at compromise nor the indication of a collapse in reasoning. On the contrary, it is an indication that thought, in its inquiry into life, has encountered something that does not allow one straight, unambiguous solution but demands two conflicting responses. On the one hand, sacrifice can be nothing less than total—and must therefore include wild animals—because sacrifice corresponds with life itself. On the other hand, the sacrifice of wild animals would mean the end of the sacrificer—and therefore interruption of the sacrificial activity.

This situation should be compared with that of the modern world over a very similar issue: the killing of animals. On the one hand, such killing is practically unlimited, based on an alleged social need (the vegetarian diet cannot be imposed by law). On the other hand, all attempts at moral justification fail miserably, even by a civilization that prides itself on giving moral justifications for everything. The conflict rings out loud and clear. But it has not become part of the general awareness. Indeed, the issue is regarded as distasteful and is avoided. It is left to professional agitators like Elizabeth Costello to raise it in academic circles, as J. M. Coetzee, her chronicler, recounts. The reaction is a series of muffled coughs of embarrassment.

The first action of sacrifice personified is to flee. It runs away from the gods before running away from men. And its flight from the gods takes place while the gods are not yet gods. Only the sacrifice can, in fact, make them into fully fledged gods. We are never told exactly *why* the sacrifice runs away. But we know that being the sacrifice means first of all agreeing to be killed. There is a deep revolt, in every being, in the face of this—and more than any other, in that being who is the sacrifice itself.

Nothing in the sacrifice is immediate and certain: indeed, it is the result of an action of recovering, of calling the sacrifice back with words. The gods had to beg the sacrifice: "Listen to us! Come back to us!" And the sacrifice then agreed. But agreement came after a blunt refusal. Aware of the delicacy of the matter, the priests pass this creature, fragile as a seed, from hand to hand—"like a bucket of water," in the words of Sāyaṇa. And so a tradition is established.

Sacrifice is an animal ready to escape. Maintaining silence is like shutting that animal inside an enclosure. And this gives the impression of possessing it. But if the sacrifice escapes, becoming spoken word, then the sacred formula—*ṛc* or *yajus*—will reveal its nature as a remedy extracted from evil itself: "When he withholds speech—since speech is sacrifice—he therefore closes the sacrifice within himself. But when, after having withheld speech, he emits some sound, then the sacrifice, once allowed its freedom, escapes. In that case, he should then murmur a *ṛc* or a *yajus* addressed to Viṣṇu, for Viṣṇu is the sacrifice; so he captures the sacrifice once again; and this is the remedy for that violation."

At the center of the sacrifice we find an obscure word: *medha*, the sacrificial essence that circulates in the world like water and accumulates in a hundred beings fit for sacrifice. "Essence" here is not to be understood (only) in the metaphysical sense: *medha* means "marrow," "juice," "sap." "In the beginning the gods offered man as a victim. When he was offered up, the sacrificial essence, *medha*, left him. It went into the horse." And, after the horse, into the ox, into the sheep, into the goat, and lastly into rice and barley. Sacrificial substitution therefore implies that a life-giving substance continues to flow, even though it is housed in different receptacles. The passage from animal to vegetable is only one of these passages. But we should not imagine that this happens because sacrifice is being made more and more innocuous. On the contrary: the fact of killing is also claimed for rice and barley. *All* of that which possesses sacrificial essence, *medha*, is killed. Rice and barley no less than man or ox. The process is one, the cycle is the same, for "he who knows thus."

"Now when they lay out the sacrifice, celebrating it, they kill it; and when they press King Soma, they kill him; and when they obtain the victim's consent and cut it up, they kill it. It is by means of a pestle and mortar and with two millstones that they kill the offering of grain." The Brāhmaṇas have often been accused of being "immensely monotonous." And yet at times—indeed so frequently as to rebut any accusation of monotony—we find sentences or passages in those texts that describe with great clarity and concision what others elsewhere have been loath to put in writing. The scriptures in many different civilizations have always been reticent about the act of killing. It is indeed a favorite opportunity for euphemism. Not so in the *Śatapatha Brāhmaṇa.* The act of killing, generally a natural part of sacrifice, is applied here first of all to the sacrifice itself: celebrating a sacrifice implies the killing of the sacrifice. What this means is not immediately clear, but it can be linked to the stories where the sacrifice runs away from the gods in the guise of a horse or an antelope. The sacrifice can be an abstraction—and sometimes runs away in the face of similar abstractions, such as "priestly sovereignty." But likewise, a plant that is a king—Soma—can be killed. Or a simple offering of grains of barley. Or an animal victim. Most people would use the word *kill* only for the last of these. Whereas for the Vedic ritualists the killing of the animal victim is only one of many instances in a series of killings. This procedure could be read as the opposite to euphemism. Instead of toning down the violent occurrence, it is extended to apply to everything, since what happens in the sacrifice involves the whole of existence and is to be found at every level, among abstract concepts just as much as among plants.

In Sanskrit, in Greek, and in Latin, killing was defined as a "consent" by the animal to be immolated. In India, killing took place outside the sacrificial area and was not to be seen by anyone except the *śamitṛ*, the slaughterer who performed the act. And even where a vegetable substance such as *soma* was sacrificed, the pestle had to strike it in the presence of someone who was blindfolded.

In factory farms, right now, millions of animals spend a life of agony crammed together in spaces that prevent them from any movement, before being killed as hastily as possible. According to food industry ideology, this takes place with the "consent" of the animals themselves, who are supposed to feel *more secure* in such conditions.

When certain crucial stages were reached, various actions served to sidestep or surmount a contradiction that would otherwise have been crippling. When the animal chosen as a victim is taken for immolation, could the sacrificer touch it or not? He must not touch it—it is said—because it is being taken to its death. He must touch it—it is said—because "that [victim] that they are taking to the sacrifice is not being taken to its death." Which argument is right? Both are. But which should be followed? If the sacrificer touches the victim, he makes contact with death. If he does not touch it, he is cut off from the sacrifice. So what should he do? Watching the sacrifice, we would have seen the *pratiprasthātṛ* guiding the victim, touching it from behind with two skewers, the *adhvaryu* holding the hem of the *pratiprasthātṛ*'s robe, and then the sacrificer holding the hem of the *adhvaryu*'s robe. Moving forward in a line, in silence, like Bruegel's blind men. But slightly bent in concentration. This was the answer. In this way the sacrificer touched and at the same time didn't touch the victim. And in this way they thought to escape logic by means of ritual gesture.

At the moment of immolation, those present are to avert their eyes. The animal is killed beyond the sacrificial boundary, next to the *śāmitṛ* there is fire where they will cook the victim's limbs, outside the trapezoidal area marked out for the sacrifice, to the northeast. As in Greek tragedy—and with a perfect correspondence of meaning—the killing takes place *offstage.* The rite and the tragedy are complex ceremonial activities that make it possible to work through that intractable event, which must not be witnessed.

And here is the main point at which the use of euphemism inherent in every sacrifice emerges. Before striking the victim, they cannot say: "Kill it!" because "that is the human way." They have to say: "Make it consent!" Some regard this instruction as hypocritical; others as sublime. It is both. And, above all, it is what happens in any case, as soon as the mute act is clothed in words. But it would be naïve to think that the Vedic ritualists were eager to cover up or mitigate something. That certainly was not their style. When necessary, they knew how to spell things out very clearly: "When they make the victim consent, they kill it."

The formula in the Brāhmaṇas corresponds precisely with the Roman ritual that required the meek consent of the victim in order for the ceremony to be faultless. And before that, the Delphic oracle had recognized that "if an animal consents by bowing its head toward the lustral water . . . it is right to sacrifice it."

The worry continues even after the killing—or after the consent, if we want to use the language of the gods. At that moment the victim has become food for the gods. But "the food of the gods is living, immortal for the immortals," whereas the victim is a lifeless animal, strangled or with its throat slit. The contradiction is intensified especially around the killing of the sacrificial victim, like specks emerging in various places on a canvas, marring its perfection. What should be done, then? At this point, the sacrificer's wife was to be seen coming forward. She would turn to the sacrifice, praise it. Then she would approach the victim and begin to clean its orifices with water. The vital spirits passed out—had passed out—from there. But "the vital spirits are water." And so that motionless body, freshly bathed, now returned to being "truly living, immortal for the immortals." Another obstacle had been overcome.

The first tangible form of evil is created by the anguish of the victim who is about to be killed. That anguish deposits itself in the heart. But the primary characteristic of evil is that, like energy, it cannot be eliminated, but only transformed, moved elsewhere. And so the evil passes from the heart of the victim to the spear that pierces it. But what will happen to the spear? The officiants would like it to be swallowed up in the current, near to the sacrificial ground. And so they cautiously approach the waters—seeking to assuage them, asking for their friendship. But as soon as the waters see them approaching with the spear, they draw back. Negotiation then begins. The officiants know they have to make a pact with the waters. They will agree not to throw the spear into them after the sacrifice to Agni and Soma—nor after that to Agni alone. And in exchange they will obtain an agreement that once the barren cow has been killed they can then, at the end of the ceremony, throw the spear into the waters. The ritualists felt satisfied with this, because with the barren cow "the sacrifice is completed." And that which completes—they thought—has the power, due to its strategic position, to transfigure all that has gone before it. By freeing themselves from that extreme part of the evil, they could believe they were free of all evil. It would have been hard to achieve more than this.

The gods were the first to feel a sharp sense of guilt over the sacrifice. When the first victim was seized, they were filled with fear: "They did not feel inclined to that." They knew what they were about to perform was the model of all guilt. They would pass this on to mankind. And so, whatever sacrificial speculation might one day be raised over guilt, to the point of wandering into abstraction or into the remotest realms of heaven or creation, at the end of the ceremony the perception of guilt would once again emerge, even more sharply, more insistently—and be concentrated on one object: the spear that pierces the heart. How can it be eliminated? Guilt does not decay, diminish, disappear. Like radioactive matter, it continues to emit radiation. Once again, it was a question of finding an answer to the unanswerable: "He shall bury the spear at the point where the dry and the damp meet." A mysterious, indefinable point. A point—we can suppose—where the elements neutralize each other, where even anxiety would be suspended, inoperative, even if not entirely removed. This is what can be achieved: an impermanent balance. The anxiety remains. To get rid of the spear as soon as the barren cow has been slain: this pact remains valid even until today. The most effective measure has always been to forget it.

At the end of the sacrifice, rites are necessary in order to leave it. They correspond point by point with the rites celebrated to enter the sacrifice. The form A-B-B-A, known to anyone who studies music, originates here. The same also goes for any structure where the end must correspond with the beginning. And since, at the beginning, there was nothing on the sacrificial ground, all traces must be destroyed, removed, wiped away. The grass used as a cushion for the invisible gods is burned, various utensils are destroyed, the sacrificial post is burned. Only one object remains intact—the spear that has pierced the victim's heart—but it is concealed, for "the instrument of the crime or of the suffering must be hidden."

The final dilemma over the sacrifice emerged when Soma was killed. There was then an exchange between the gods and Mitra, whom the sacrificer recalls at the moment when *soma* is mixed with milk:

"He mixes it [*soma*] with milk. The reason he mixes it with milk is this: Soma was really Vṛtra. Now, when the gods killed him, they said to Mitra: 'You kill him too!' But he did not like it and said: 'I am certainly a friend (*mitra*) of all; if I am not a friend, I will become a nonfriend (*amitra*).' 'Then we will exclude you from the sacrifice!' He said: 'I also kill.' The cattle moved away from him, saying: 'He was a friend and has become a nonfriend!' He was left without cattle. Mixing [the *soma*] with the milk, the gods then supplied him with cattle; and likewise now this [officiant] supplies it [to the sacrificer] mixing [the *soma*] with the milk.

"And to this they say: 'Surely he did not like killing!' So the milk that there is in this [mixture] belongs to Mitra, but the *soma* belongs to Varuṇa: and so it is mixed with the milk."

Sacrificing implies complicity in the killing. Only in this way is it possible to avoid being excluded from the sacrifice. And this must be a far more serious threat, if Mitra, the Friend, the one who represents the brahmin's purity, is prepared to take part in the killing, so as not to be excluded from the rite. But what is to be lost by being excluded from the sacrifice? Everything—if what there is to be gained is a result of action. And if action comes from desire. Anyone who accepts the action—and the desire that prompts it—also accepts the killing. It is the inflexible rule of sacrificial society, in this respect similar to—and perhaps the model for—every secret society, every criminal society. The group is based on complicity—and the most solid complicity comes from killing. That this then consists of pressing the juice of a plant can offer no form of reassurance. Indeed, it allows us to see how the realm of killing is larger than we might imagine, as large as the world.

Any reference to *the invisibles* in Vedic times is not to be interpreted as a metaphysical allusion, but as referring to a situation that recurs in all "solemn," *śrauta*, rituals. Those present belong to four groups: the sacrificer, for whose benefit the rite is celebrated (he is present, but, once he has been through the consecration, he plays no active part); the officiants (sixteen: the *hotṛs*, the *udgātṛs*, the *adhvaryus*), who have to pronounce the verses of the *Ṛgveda*, chant the melodies of the *Sāmaveda*, murmur the formulas of the *Yajurveda* while the countless gestures that make up the ceremony are performed (this being the exclusive task of the *adhvaryu*); the brahmin, a priest who watches every detail and intervenes only when errors are made, otherwise remaining silent. But a last group is also there: the gods, invisible presences. Or more exactly: those who are crouching around the *āhavanīya* fire, on fragrant layers of *kuśa* grass, entirely invisible apart from Agni and Soma. Agni is always visible, for he is the fire. King Soma is visible in the *agniṣṭoma*, because in that rite it is the *soma* itself that is offered.

After being purified with the *pavitra*—the "filter," which in this case is made of stalks of a sacred herb—for "impure, indeed, is man; he is foul within, insofar as he speaks untruth," the sacrificer folds his fingers one by one toward his palm, evoking a different power for each, because he wants to *take hold* of the sacrifice. And the commentator adds: "The sacrifice is not in fact to be taken hold of visibly, as this staff or a garment, but invisible are the gods, invisible the sacrifice."

Every sacrificial practice, beneath every sky, implies a relationship with the invisible, but never as in the India of the Vedic ritualists has that relationship been declared, celebrated, studied down to the tiniest details, including even the movements of the little finger. Thus we discover that the little fingers are the first to be moved in the gesture of taking hold of the sacrifice, and represent nothing less than the mind. This continual fluctuation between minuscule and huge, with equal attention to both, is the primary hallmark of Vedic liturgy. And such is the tension and the precision of that intense, ceaseless relationship with the invisible, that it is no surprise that the visible scene of Vedic life remained so bare, so unimpressive, so averse to all monumentality. And it is no surprise that its inhabitants had such a lack of interest in leaving behind any trace that was other than textual or whose object was not to be found in that invisible which could not be grasped like a staff or the hem of a garment, but was nevertheless to be grasped. The invisible is like the onetime forest animal—it is the prey that the liturgy teaches us how to hunt, showing us how to prepare the ground, how to stalk it, how to catch it. And finally how to kill it, as happened in hunting, and is now repeated in sacrificing.

There is one ultimate question on sacrifice, after all the others: why does the offering to the invisible have to be killed? Suffocating the animal, pressing the *soma*, grinding corn: all these are considered acts of killing. And already this suggests an intensity of thought, a concern to clarify that elsewhere was not felt necessary. But for the Vedic ritualists this was only the penultimate question. It was bound up with another, which they asked repeatedly: why is the celebration of a sacrifice also the killing of the sacrifice? Why, in the case of the sacrifice, does its performance have to involve not just the execution of the victim, but that of the sacrifice itself? Why is the sacrifice an act that not only kills, but kills itself?

Here we enter the most arcane area of Vedic liturgical speculation, an area in which it becomes increasingly difficult to find parallels in other civilizations. And it is an area where we have to move with caution, since "the gods love what is secret," as the texts never tire of repeating, as soon as we cross the threshold of the esoteric.

Why then does the sacrifice itself have to die, every time it is performed? And why does it then have to be performed again? The sacrifice is never a single act, nor can it ever be. The single act is the killing: the knife that slashes a body, the arrow that pierces it. But the sacrifice is—and has to be—a *sequence* of acts, a composition, an opus. Everything converges slowly, meticulously toward the oblation or the immolation. Hours, days, even months (or years) at one extreme; just a few seconds at the other. The sacrifice requires time. And it requires the existence of time as something clearly marked out. But we know from what happened to Prajāpati that the articulation of time is the same as the disjointing of the Progenitor, his dismemberment into the Year, therefore his death: "When [Prajāpati] became disjointed, the vital breath went out from within him." And, what was even more serious for the Progenitor of the gods, Prajāpati felt a dread of death: "Having created all existing things, he felt emptied and was afraid of death."

Life Below requires death Above, in the same way as life Above demands death Below. For the gods to continue living, it is necessary to perform a killing. For men to continue living, the Progenitor has to be dismembered in the world. This is the *ṛta*, "world order"—or, at least, it is one of its fundamental principles. But this is not enough—and points to something else. There cannot be a smooth flow, an undisturbed exchange, between the visible and the invisible. There is a sudden gap between the two poles, which can only be bridged through precise and complicated measures. Measures so complicated that they can absorb a whole lifetime. Sacrificial killing is the most apparent and most serious of these. If the offerings circulated between sky and earth, if they didn't have to be accompanied by a violent act, there would be an immediate correspondence between the visible and the invisible. The invisible would appear at any moment in the world, which would thus come to lose its opacity, its harsh muteness. Life would be a great deal easier—and less hazardous. But it is not like this. Every awakening is matched by a radical uncertainty over everything—and, if the *agnihotra* had to be celebrated every day just before sunrise, it was because there was no guarantee that this would happen. Perhaps Sūrya, the Sun, needed help.

Violence—though limited, mitigated, described by way of euphemism—could not be eliminated, insofar as it was the only adequate, irreversible signal of that hiatus, of that discrepancy between visible and invisible which nothing could heal. Between the two extremes there was a cavity, an open wound. Which could be—temporarily—healed only on condition that it was reaffirmed in the violent action of the sacrifice: "He thus heals the sacrifice by means of the sacrifice." If this happens, the unbridgeable ravines of the sacrifice are transformed into a celestial flight path. That hawk, which until a moment earlier had been an altar built with ten thousand eight hundred bricks, as many as the hours of the Vedic year, would then rise up and fly. An altar made of time. And time could not be deprived of the power, indeed the obligation to kill.

It is never clearly stated in the Vedic texts that there is a swerve, a gap, a break between visible and invisible, that the visible ends up suspended over the void. Not all of the *forest doctrine* (an expression used to indicate esoteric teaching) was to be enounced—or to be enounced in certain terms. There remained something precipitous, looming, which corresponded to the makeup of that which is. If sacrifice were only an illusion of particular groups of people living in remote times and conditions, then the life that ignores it would not feel compelled to remember and rediscover it, disguised, subtly recurrent and evasive, like a blackbuck antelope in the midst of traffic.

Certain ideas of the Vedic ritualists could be set out without resorting to their categories and reasoning, but using words acceptable even in a twenty-first-century university lecture hall. Like this, for example: the relationship between the visible and invisible is superimposed onto that between the discrete and the continuum. In the same way that the visible will never manage to penetrate the invisible, however much it expands and however transparent and significant it becomes, so too the discrete will never manage to coincide with the continuum, which envelops and surpasses it. There is a break point, between the two series, often recognizable by some trace of blood. The invisible and the continuum belong to the mind and express its sovereignty. The visible and the discrete are the expansion of what is outside the mind, innervated by the mind but not reducible to the mind. All that takes place is an exchange and an uninterrupted passage between the four corners of this quadrangle. The point where the paths meet and cross is the center of the quincunx, the fifth stone on which are laid the stalks of the *soma* before the other four stones strike it, rip it apart, so that the intoxicating juice can drip from it.

XX

THE FLIGHT OF THE BLACK ANTELOPE

The blackbuck is considered by many to be the most beautiful of all antelopes because of the male's striking black and white pelage and his long spiral horns. The species once roamed in huge herds throughout the open woodlands and cultivated tracts of India, making it one of the most conspicuous and most hunted members of the country's fauna. These large herds are now gone, and the animal clings to the last vestige of its former range in small scattered groups.

—G. B. Schaller, *The Deer and the Tiger*

Mṛga means first of all the black antelope. But the word *mṛga* describes any wild animal. What happened to the black antelope implicated the whole world of nondomestic animals, a world once synonymous with *hunting*. Mention of the black antelope stirred the feeling of a whole way of living and thinking, which had already been erased by the Vedic period, and yet continued to pulsate within every thought. Karl Meuli went too far in his attempt to trace the phenomenon of sacrifice in its entirety back to hunting. But no theory of sacrifice would be complete unless it involved hunting—and the age of the hunter.

Āryāvarta, "the Land of the Aryans," is the space where "by nature the black antelope roams"—making it "the country fit for sacrifices." Civilization is the place for sacrifice, and sacrifice can be celebrated only where the black antelope—an animal that *cannot* be sacrificed—roams freely. At the same time, the *Śatapatha Brāhmaṇa* states six times: "The skin of the black antelope is the sacrifice." And the ritualists did not waste words.

The black antelope is, indeed, not sacrificed but is killed all the same. Indeed, the scene of its primordial killing can be seen every night in the sky, where the antelope is Orion, shot by Sirius's arrow. Meaning: the antelope is Prajāpati, shot by Rudra's arrow. But then, when the antelope was shot by Rudra, "the gods found it and stripped its skin, carrying it [the skin] away with them." On that occasion, it is said, "the sacrifice escaped from the gods and, having become a black antelope, it wandered." Rudra's attack on Prajāpati was therefore *already* a sacrifice. But not only that: the skin of the antelope, an animal that cannot be sacrificed, becomes part of the sacrifice, indeed it is used "for the completeness of the sacrifice." Without the aid of that skin, the sacrifice would be incomplete. And it would lack exactly what was *forbidden* in the sacrifice. And yet the sacrifice is not effective unless it covers everything. The impasse seems irresolvable. But what is the purpose of rituals if not to resolve through gestures what thought cannot resolve? And so the antelope skin will become "the place of the good work."

At every point during the ceremonies it is taken for granted that every event belongs to at least two worlds—the heaven and the earth, the invisible and the visible. But how can this be shown to the person who is consecrated? How can he stay in both worlds? Two black antelope skins are laid on the ground, "joined along the edge, so that these two worlds are, in a certain way, joined along the edge." Almost as if these skins were two worlds of equal extension and not dissimilar appearance, which are stitched together along the edge and then communicate violently through holes through which a thong is made to pass. They are the two ways of contact: osmotic adjacency, along the edges of the world, where things seem no longer to belong to one but to two worlds; and incursion (the holes), which explains the sudden suction occasionally exercised by one world on the other. The sacrificer can be consecrated only if he places himself on those two antelope skins stitched together.

At a certain point the sacrificer will take a black antelope skin and will sit on it: "Its white and black hairs represent the *ṛc* and the *sāman* verses: in other words, the white the *sāman* and the black the *ṛc*; or vice versa, the black the *sāman* and the white the *ṛc*. The brown and yellow hairs, on the other hand, represent the *yajus* texts."

Sitting on a black antelope skin: only this gesture enables the sacrifice to be complete. And, since the sacrifice is everything, it cannot be incomplete. And so there is an acute and ever-recurrent anxiety about incompleteness: will the sacrifice have a head? Or will it, in any case, be complete? These questions ring out, they pulsate. Only the act of sitting on the black antelope skin can bring a satisfactory answer. Why? There is, of course, a story behind it: a very obscure and ancient story. The pact between the gods and sacrifice is not immediate, indeed: "The divine nature . . . shows no particular affinity with sacrifice." But the gods know it is only through sacrifice that they can defeat their adversaries: the Asuras, the Rakṣas. They also know that it is only thanks to sacrifice that they are now immortal. But sacrifice is not knowledge that is revealed and absorbed once and for all. Nor is it a well-defined corpus. The sacrifice, by its nature, extends in every direction: but how far? According to the *Maitrāyaṇī Saṃhitā*, "the gods saw the sacrifices one by one." It was a gradual, uncertain, laborious achievement. And often, where the gods did not succeed, the *ṛṣis* did—as happened, for example, to a serpent-like *ṛṣi*, Arbuda Kādraveya, who taught the gods how to drink *soma* without being overcome by the intoxication. The gods then had to humbly follow what a seer had known before they had. This, for a long time, was life, before humans appeared—and before they too tried to gain everything through sacrifice. But the path was far more treacherous. If sacrifice had fled from the gods, this occurred far more often with men. And why, from the very beginning, had the sacrifice fled and, "having become a black antelope, started to roam freely"? No text gives a satisfactory answer. But an underlying point has to be borne in mind: the antelope is an animal that cannot be sacrificed. The antelope is the wild animal par excellence, the hunter's prey. Yet only domestic animals can be sacrificed—five of them, to be precise, including man. There again, we read several times that "the black antelope skin is the sacrifice." This is therefore how things are: the animal that "is more or less the emblem of the sacrifice" cannot be sacrificed. At the same time, we read that "where by nature the black antelope roams is the place fit for sacrifices; beyond that is the land of the barbarians." Or again, with great conciseness: "Heed the laws of the country where the black antelope is." The boundaries of civilization are marked by where the black antelope roams freely, which corresponds with the places where sacrifice is practiced. Only a wild animal can mark out the perimeter of the land where the law rules.

The antelope flees because the gods want to sacrifice it (the antelope, in fact, *is* the sacrifice)—and the antelope knows it is an animal that cannot and must not be sacrificed. The antelope has just two invisible counterparts: the predator and the hunter—two single beings who kill in a flash, with their claws or their arrows, without any ceremonial niceties. They are what is immediate. So the opposite of a throng of beings—the gods—who choose their victim and around it elaborate a long ceremony that has to be performed with a sequence of acts. But in the thinking of the ritualists, using the brilliant words of Malamoud, "when the sacrifice is executed—executed in the sense of carried out—there is an execution, in the sense of a putting to death, not only of the victim but of the sacrificial act itself." This is why the antelope escapes from the gods. No one tells us what happened after, when the gods chased it. But one day they returned with the black antelope skin. They had killed and flayed it, as hunters do. From that moment on, they never went hunting again. They spent their time contriving and celebrating sacrifices. As for the officiants, they always had to gird their loins with a black antelope skin. Or at least to have one within reach and to touch it, as if to remind themselves of something. Or the person being initiated had to sit on it, as if contact with the ground had to be mediated by those animal hairs, in which they claimed to recognize the meters. Contact with the antelope skin did not only serve to recall that escape and pursuit which none have recounted. But also other pursuits, other flights, of which certain scenes have been described—or mentioned in passing. Two scenes stand out.

Prajāpati approached the body of his daughter Uṣas and, as he touched her, he was transformed into an antelope, as was she. It was then that Rudra shot him with his three-knotted arrow. It looked like a hunting scene—and at that moment Rudra became *mṛgavyādha*, "he who shoots the antelope." Prajāpati, who "is the sacrifice," then rose, wounded, to the sky. He escaped from the gods, his children who had plotted against him. He escaped from Rudra, the Archer, who had shot him at the peak moment of pleasure. The antelope that was Prajāpati ran away, too late, from an attack. This was not part of a ceremony: his children—now his adversaries—simply wanted to kill him, like one of the many beasts of the forest. The sacrifice ran off in the face of pure, instant killing, of the kind that strikes down its prey through the hunter's hand. And it ran off too late. But Prajāpati had his place to go to: an arc of sky, where he settled and formed a constellation: Mṛga, the Antelope, which the Greeks called Orion. And not just the prey but also the hunter went off toward the sky. The archer became Sirius, the antelope hunter. The three stars that the Greeks called Orion's Belt formed the three-knotted arrow shot by Rudra. That scene therefore became the background for every other scene. And thus it could illuminate every scene: at night the Antelope, Mṛga, signaled the way, "track," *mārga*, for its companions that roamed the forest. From then onward, no one has yet fully understood the meaning of that scene. Still we raise our eyes to contemplate it and discover something new.

So far as the story of men is concerned, one of the meanings was this: hunting is the background to sacrifice. Sacrifice is a response to hunting: it is a guilty act that is superimposed onto the guilt of hunting. Man sacrifices because he has hunted, because he hunts. And he hunts because he recognizes that killing is an irreparable and unsuppressible act, for at least as long as he has been eating meat, imitating the predators that once used to devour him. So he became more powerful, but he also forever exposed himself to the "greatest danger," which is this: "Man's food consists only of souls. All the beings we have to kill and eat, all those we have to strike and destroy to make our clothing have souls like us, which do not disappear along with their bodies and have to be pacified, so that they won't take revenge on us because we have carried away their bodies." This is what Aua, an Eskimo, told Knud Rasmussen with unequalled clarity. This was the mystery about which no one wished to talk. It raised too much terror—and nothing had managed to cancel it out. It was a blinding threshold, the place of guilt, where ceremonies drove people back each time to commit another guilty act—sacrifice—to heal the first guilty act: killing. The officiant who continually touches the skin of the black antelope throughout the ceremony, with no apparent reason, mysteriously retraces all this, as if the whole of human history were condensed into that gesture. His contact with the black antelope skin seems, above all, to hark back to that part of history that is most remote, most distant, most obstinate.

Then there was another antelope escape. It happened during the sacrifice of Dakṣa, the sacrifice that was the catastrophe latent in every sacrifice thereafter. Dakṣa, the officiant, had not wanted to invite Śiva, the seducer and abductor of his daughter Satī. He wanted the sacrificial order to exist without this god who had gone beyond it. The missing invitation was the cause of the ruin. In all other ways, no one had ever been such an impeccable officiant as Dakṣa—and no sacrifice had ever been prepared with such care and such magnificence. But precision and strict order are not enough. To exclude is something that a sacrifice can never do. If the sacrifice does not embrace everything that exists, it is nothing more than a massacre. Or rather: it becomes a massacre. And so the gods, scourged by Śiva's fury, found themselves crawling across the ground around the altar, bleeding and suffering. The sacrifice then fled, in horror, together with the fire. This time it was not just because they were about to sacrifice the sacrifice but also because the sacrifice had failed, it had shown itself unable to support everything that is. And so it fled to the sky. Without the sacrificial fire, no rite would now be possible. The antelope was seen rising up from Dakṣa's altar and rushing toward the sky and into the sky. But there it was reached, once again, by Rudra's arrow. The sacrifice could be interrupted, suspended, it could escape: but it could not escape being killed. This was the message lodged with the arrow in the flesh of the antelope. A certain observation became inevitable at this point: there is always an urge to escape from the sacrifice. Either because the sacrifice is being performed or because it cannot be performed. Whatever happens, there is no way out of being shot by an arrow. Is this a return to hunting? Or an extension of the sacrifice itself? Is there any need to ask? All that remains is written in the sky—and there the arrow perpetually strikes the antelope. Under that image we live, witnesses to the escape and to the wound.

Śiva, as successor of Rudra in another eon, maintains a close relationship with the antelope. He is accustomed to sitting on a black antelope skin. The antelope is the only animal, apart from the snake, that Śiva keeps in contact with his body. In bronze statuettes, it is often to be found between the fingers of the god's hand, ready to rush off. When Śiva wanders in the forest as a beggar, an antelope often approaches him and raises its head toward him, and he offers it leaves with his left hand, while in his right he holds a bowl, which is the skull of Brahmā. Like Rudra, Śiva is called *mṛgavyādha*, "he who shoots the antelope," but also *mṛgākṣa*, "he who has the eyes of an antelope." He is the hunter and the prey. Not because anyone is able to strike Śiva (how could they?), but because Śiva is the totality of sacrifice: that which is performed according to the rites, close to the village, along with that which takes place according to no rules, in the forest of the world.

The journey of the black antelope was also the journey of a remote thought that crossed the passes of Afghanistan to settle on the plains of the Ganges. The Vedic people apparently wished to go no farther. They continued to worship a plant that grew in distant mountains. It was increasingly difficult to get hold of. Less and less frequently could they press its juices. Through that plant, they worshipped rapture. It was the ultimate thing to conquer.

Where the black antelope roams is civilization. And the black antelope has fled from the sacrifice, which is the foundation of civilization. Civilization thus extends as far as where a creature that has fled from civilization roams, a creature that did not want to be killed by civilization.

XXI

KING SOMA

Thousands of pages in the Brāhmaṇas, and all the hymns in the ninth cycle of the *Ṛgveda*, are dedicated to *soma*. Of the few *realia* mentioned in the texts, *soma* is the most present. We cannot be sure what it was, except for saying: it was a "juice," *soma*, which produced intoxication. Attempts at identifying it, from the mid-nineteenth century up to today, have all been rather awkward and unreliable. Nor do they explain why *soma* was already spoken of in the Vedic era as something from the past, for which a substitute had to be found in the rites. But how can its intoxicating effect be substituted? This is one of the many sharp ironies that anyone venturing into the Vedic world encounters. Not surprisingly, it is ignored, intentionally or otherwise, by many scholars who continue to treat *soma* like an algebraic symbol. It is more important—they argue—to make a precise reconstruction of the rites that celebrated *soma*, and less important to know what exactly they celebrated. The moderns, as a rule, are proud when they make statements of this kind, since they are indifferent about substance in general and concerned only with getting the procedures clear. In this way they think they have risen high up the evolutionary ladder.

But not knowing what *soma* was is like not knowing what fire is. For Agni and Soma are two gods, but they are also a flame and a plant—and, through that flame and that plant, they are the only gods in a continual voyage backward and forward between earth and sky. Not to know any more about the plant called *soma* is a grievous gap in our knowledge.

The expanding of the mind caused by *soma* did not stop at the *flammantia moenia mundi*, the blazing walls of the world. It went beyond. The mind darted beyond every barrier and watched everything from high above: "I extend beyond the sky and this great earth," proclaims Indra (or anyone who feels like Indra). And in the meantime, at the end of every stanza, he repeats, as an obsessive murmur: "Have I drunk *soma*?" The speaker is no longer part of the world, but observes it from outside, as if watching a game or a puppet show. Intoxication, omnipotence, effortlessness: "I want to put this earth here or there," "Soon I want to push this earth here or there." The Vedic ritualists measured power on this sensation. In normal life, they lived in temporary huts and migrated with their herds. But when they tasted *soma*, the whole earth and sky became their faithful subjects, ready to let themselves be shaped or annihilated by a sovereign touch. When they spoke of power, they did not mean empires, which they ignored, but that sensation of a single person, of every individual who had taken part in a *soma* sacrifice and had taken a sip from one of the rectangular wooden cups, *camasas*, in accordance with the rules of the liturgy.

Childlike and grandiloquent, Indra was the first to sing of *soma*—and only *soma* could inspire the fervor that allowed him to perform his heroic deeds. One of which was the capture of the *soma* itself, thanks to an inversion of time that was intrinsic in Vedic logic. One day the other gods spitefully refused Indra the *soma*. He had committed too many crimes, beginning with the beheading of the three-headed Viśvarūpa, who after all was a brahmin. But if Indra was to be refused the *soma*, then this should apply as much to the *kṣatriyas*. The juice that gives the feeling of sovereignty was forbidden to the king of the gods himself and to the men who modeled themselves on him.

Meanwhile the brahmins drank *soma*—and kept silent. Indra celebrated *soma*—and could no longer drink it. Suddenly, in a flash, a secret, obstinate, unending conflict broke out between the two sovereign powers, between priest and king, who were required to work together. The Veda, unlike the rest of the world that would follow, was always biased in favor of the priests, without it being too apparent.

Who is noble? Anyone who can boast "ten consecutive ancestors who drank *soma*." But, to drink *soma*, you had to be invited. Indra's offense—greater than any other—was that of having tried to drink *soma* by force. Tvaṣṭṛ had refused to invite him. This was understandable, since Indra had just killed his son. But Indra should nevertheless have been invited by another brahmin, if not by Tvaṣṭṛ. This is the fundamental weakness of the *kṣatriyas*: their king has to be invited to drink *soma*. And only a brahmin can invite him. It is a question of intoxication, even of pure power. It is said that brahmins who drink *soma* can kill with their eyes.

The life of Soma—"the least understood god of the Vedic religion," Lommel once wrote—has been left in obscurity because many have thought it enough to identify him with the *soma* plant or (later on) with the moon. But being an intoxicating juice, a celestial body, a king, and a god, all at the same time, is not in itself a problem for Vedic thought. In his royal manifestation, Soma was the head of a dynasty—the *lunar dynasty*—that cuts through the whole of Indian mythical history up to the *Mahābhārata*.

Soma's father was one of the Saptarṣis: Atri, the Devourer. For three thousand years he had practiced *tapas* with his arms raised. He seemed like "a piece of wood, a wall, or a rock." So heightened was his consciousness that he never blinked. And one day a juice began to trickle from his eyes and illuminated every corner: it was Soma. The goddesses that kept control over all directions gathered together to receive that glow in their wombs. But the light spilled over. Soma's fetus fell to the ground and Brahmā placed it on a chariot drawn by white horses, which began to roam the skies, spreading a pearl-like glow. They said: "It is the moon." At that time Dakṣa, the chief brahmin, had to marry off his sixty daughters. He looked up at the lunar radiance and decided to entrust twenty-seven of them to Soma. Soma would receive them, night after night, on his journey through the sky. And each daughter was to enjoy him in equal measure. They became the houses of the moon, the first silver-sequined corps de ballet. Then Soma was consecrated king with the celebration of a grand rite, where the future sovereign offered the three worlds as recompense to the *ṛṣis* who had officiated over the sacrifice.

At the end, Soma cleansed himself in the *avabhṛtha* bath that marked the conclusion of the rite. He immediately felt relieved, buoyant, free of responsibility at last. All the gods, all the *ṛṣis* had worshipped him. He was sovereign over all. What did he lack? Liberty. That strange intoxication that flows from liberty. He felt that new waves were crashing in his mind: arrogance and lust. What would the worst outrage be? To abduct the wife of a brahmin. Soma knew very well that "even if a woman has had ten non-brahmin husbands, if a brahmin once takes her hand then he alone is her husband to the exclusion of all others." But no one could resist Soma, the fluid that penetrates everywhere and makes all desirable. And so he set his eye on Tārā, wife of Bṛhaspati, chaplain to the gods. It wasn't difficult to snatch her, and it was thrilling to have intercourse with her, with her exquisite round, moon face.

The result of her abduction could only be war, in the heavens. It was the fifth war between the Devas and the Asuras. Amid repeated massacres, with the final outcome still uncertain, many forgot the original reason for the conflict. But not Bṛhaspati, known as "the vulture" for the keenness of his gaze. He realized straightaway that Tārā's womb was swelling (in the meantime she had been returned to him). He looked at her in disdain, and said: "Never will you be able to hold a fetus in your womb that belongs to me." Then he ordered her to abort. But Tārā was stubborn and hated nothing more in the world than brahminic arrogance, of which Bṛhaspati was the epitome. She refused.

Questioned by the Devas, she admitted that she was about to give birth to Soma's child. When Budha was born, he condensed in himself the luminescent beauty of both his mother and his father. Meanwhile Soma was wasting away. The sovereign of the heavens, the perfect lover, the repository of rapture, was suffering from consumption. He felt weaker, his light grew dim. He then returned to his father. Inert, all skin and bones, Atri did not deign to look upon him. But later, little by little, as he humbly served that motionless and silent being, Soma felt he was recovering. The sap slowly began to flow once more through the veins of the cosmos.

Tārā's betrayal was all the more blasphemous and outrageous since King Soma was the *only* king for the brahmins, and therefore for Bṛhaspati. For the *kṣatriyas* everything can become food, except the brahmin, because "his king is Soma." And so the brahmins cannot be touched by the *kṣatriyas*, but it is their fate to be deceived and mocked by their own sovereign: Soma. The most treacherous enemy is within one's own power, even if it were *brahman. "Spiritualia nequitiae in coelestibus,"* as Paul would one day say. The greatest impiety comes from the sovereign god.

The seating position is most revealing: "And therefore the brahmin, during the king's rite of consecration, sits below the *kṣatriya* . . . *Brahman* is the womb of royalty (*kṣatra*), and so, even if the king reaches the highest position, in the end he can only rest on *brahman*, his womb. If he should damage it, he would damage his womb." An inextricable blend of subordination (the brahmin places himself *below* the king) and preeminence (the king can be born only from *brahman*).

Soma is pure quality on the threshold of the realm of quantity. Only thanks to *soma* is the existence of quantity justified: "Since he buys the king, everything here below can be bought"; "Since he measures the king, there is therefore a measure, the measure among men as well as any other measure." Money, measure: to enter the world they need to have King Soma, the only material that is quality alone, immeasurable, irreplaceable, the origin of every measure, of every substitution. If this knot is cut, order falls apart.

Exchange is a violent act because there is no secure, guaranteed fluidity between sky and earth. The flow is obstructed, continually diverted. Sacrifice, and consequently exchange, serve to reestablish the flow, but through an action that has something forced, disturbing, about it, a restoration that presupposes a wound and adds a new one to it.

Soma was to be approached with desire, but also with fear: "Do not terrify me, O king, do not pierce my heart with your radiance." The risk was apparent at every moment. *Soma*, liquid fire, had to make its way toward the head, where the Saptarṣis waited for it, crouching. But at the same time there was the plea: "Do not go below my navel." If that happened, one would have been overpowered.

The first to abuse *soma* was also he who seized it: Indra. Eager, impatient, headstrong, he snatched the liquid from Tvaṣṭṛ and drank it without ritual, without mixing it, without filtering it. His body "fell apart on all sides." The intoxicating liquid came out of every orifice. Then Indra vomited. He no longer knew what to do, so "he turned to Prajāpati." "Indra lay on the ground, devastated. The gods gathered around him and said: 'In truth, he was the best of us; evil has befallen him: we must heal him!'" This would one day lead men to perform the *sautrāmaṇī* rite, to remedy Indra's illness and his crime against *soma*. From that time on, men prayed for draughts of *soma* adding a modest request: "Like the harness of a chariot, thus keep together my limbs." And they made sure to add humbly: "Let these juices protect me from breaking a leg and preserve me from paralysis." Drunken and precise.

Soma and Agni are linked by an affinity more powerful and secret than any other, above all because they are the only gods who allow themselves to be seen: Agni is in every fire that blazes; King Soma in every *soma* plant that someone collects on remote mountain slopes and then sells to be offered in sacrifice. They are also linked by their origins: when both still belonged to the Asuras and—in the words of the *Ṛgveda*—breathed in the "long darkness," which was the belly of Vṛtra. They were born or came out of the monster, whom Indra had then killed with the help of Soma himself (Indra had ordered him: "Let us both strike Vṛtra, come out, Soma!"). But the story would become even more disturbing when it was discovered that Soma had not only left Vṛtra's belly, but *was* Vṛtra. The *Śatapatha Brāhmaṇa* leaves no doubt: " 'Soma was in fact Vṛtra: his body is that of the mountains and of the rocks where the plant called Uśānā grows,' so said Śvetaketu Auddālaki. 'They go to fetch it and press it; by means of the consecration and of the *upasads*, by means of the *tānūnaptras* [ceremonies that form part of the *soma* sacrifices] and the invigoration they make it into *soma*.' " They are words that summed up the whole life of Soma, from when he had hidden himself inside himself up until when he had become a plant transported among men, and transformed and killed by men.

Agni and Soma, so far as their origins and their history, are highly mysterious elements that have to be flushed out of the dark, and yet at the same time they are the most apparent, the elements that are visible in the sacrifice, in the fires and in the favorite oblation of gods and men. Bergaigne rightly separated Agni and Soma from the Devas as a whole, not only because Soma is *"fire in a liquid state,"* not only because the characters of the two gods are to a large extent interchangeable, but because their entire existence belongs to a secret stratum of that which is, in the same way as rapture invades consciousness carrying with it something more remote, overwhelming and indecipherable.

In comparison with Agni and Soma, the Devas have something of the *parvenus* about them: born on the earth, the Devas reached the sky through sacrifice, and therefore through Agni and Soma. Agni and Soma, on the other hand, were born in the sky, and from there were conveyed to the earth: Soma being *śyenabhṛta*, "carried by the eagle," Agni being delivered by Mātariśvan, the Vedic Prometheus. The *Ṛgveda* narrates it as follows: "Mātariśvan carried the one [Agni] from the sky, the eagle snatched the other [Soma] from the [celestial] mountain." There is therefore a cross-movement, between the gods, which corresponds with two lineages. The gods, no less than men, could be different *by birth.*

"Now Soma was in the sky and the gods were here on earth. The gods desired: 'May Soma come to us: we would sacrifice with him, if he came.' They created these two apparitions (*māyā*), Suparṇī and Kadrū. In the chapter on the *dhiṣṇya* fires we read how the affair of Suparṇī and Kadrū came to pass.

"Gāyatrī flew toward Soma, sent by those two. While she was carrying him away, the Gandharva Viśvāvasu stole him from her. The gods realized this: 'Soma has been carried away from yonder, but he does not come to us, for the Gandharvas have stolen him.'

"They said: 'The Gandharvas are fond of women: let us send Vāc to them and she will return to us with Soma.' They sent Vāc to them and she returned with Soma.

"The Gandharvas pursued her and said: 'Soma for you, Vāc for us.' 'So be it,' said the gods. 'But if she prefers to come here, do not take her away by force: let us woo her.' And so they wooed her.

"The Gandharvas recited the Vedas to her, saying, 'See how we know them, see how we know them.'

"The gods then created the lute and sat playing and singing, saying: 'Thus we will sing to you, thus we will amuse you.' She [Vāc] turned to the gods; but, in truth, she turned to them frivolously. Since, to go toward the dance and the song, she went away from those who sang hymns and prayed. And so even to this day women are only frivolous beings: for it was in this way that Vāc returned, and other women do as she did. And it is for this that they most readily take a fancy to he who dances and sings.

"And so Soma and Vāc were with the gods. Now, when someone buys Soma to obtain it, it is to sacrifice with the [Soma] obtained. He who sacrifices with [Soma] not bought, sacrifices with Soma that is not truly obtained."

Here is the story of the conquest of Soma, the basis for every liturgical act, told with the usual sobriety and making punctual reference to another passage—much as a Western scholar could do—where there is a full account of the story of Suparṇī and Kadrū. What would the rite be if it didn't have this radiant substance at its center, which is also the most sought-after celestial guest on earth? The gods are the first for whom life would lose all meaning without him. But the gods, alone, would not be able to capture Soma. They need the help of a being that is both a meter and an animal: Gāyatrī, who appears as a large bird. The power of form was never, and will never again be declared as boldly as in this passage: the gods could not have taken off from the earth without the help of a sequence of twenty-four syllables, which is a living being. The story of how the capture took place will continue later on. Here the emphasis is on what happened *after* the capture. First, the celestial obstacle: the Gandharvas, who live in the heavens, do not let Soma escape. Viśvāvasu snatches him from Gāyatrī. Once again, the gods wouldn't know what to do without the help of another female being: Vāc, Speech. The story that follows is not just a primordial comedy of the sexes, that perhaps only Aristophanes would have known how to stage with equal skill. Here it is a metaphysical game—and for the first time, with great clarity and concision, an equivalence is established: Speech-Woman-Money. Lévi-Strauss would reach the same conclusion in *Structures élémentaires de la parenté*. And didn't Western science, in its most noble form, speak through him? It is an equivalence full of ambiguities and pitfalls. But also of immense power. And the access path to all modernity: all that is needed is for exchange to expand and free itself from all respect—and we will be in the new world, preordained and perhaps even outlined in the mould of antiquity. This alone would be extraordinary: but even greater is the corrosive criticism that the civilization founded on *brahman* exercises here upon itself. If the frivolous Vāc had not gladly agreed to be used as barter, like a *putain au grand cœur*; if the gods—to heighten even more the outrageousness of the scenario—had not chosen to dance and sing to get her back, rather than chanting the Vedas, as the Gandharvas do, touchingly in their innocence, then Soma, the hypostasis of the Vedas, would never have reached the gods.

Lastly, if Soma had not been bought—as the ritualist punctiliously states at the end—then it would not be the real Soma, the effective Soma, the Soma "obtained" that makes it possible to "obtain." The deliciously erotic and mocking scene of the contest for Soma between the innocent Gandharvas—as innocent and fond of women as only celestial beings can be—and the wily gods is also the scene that introduces us to the realm of the value of exchange, all too familiar to any modern reader. There is no interval between the eventful arrival on earth of Soma, a self-sufficient and radiant substance, and the universal establishment of exchange, where Soma even takes on the role of hidden guarantor and surety, like gold to currency for Marx. The archaic and the ultramodern are here described at the same time, in the same terms. Perhaps this is the secret of the Gāyatrī meter.

The text of the *Śatapatha Brāhmaṇa* had already told us: "In the chapter on the *dhiṣṇya* fires it is said how the affair of Suparṇī and Kadrū came to pass." At last we reach it—and we read this:

"Now Soma was in the heavens and the gods were here [on the earth]. The gods desired: 'Would that Soma might come to us; we could sacrifice with him, if he came.' They produced two apparitions, Suparṇī and Kadrū; Suparṇī in truth was Vāc (Speech) and Kadrū was this [Earth]. Disagreement broke out between them.

"They then argued and said: 'Whichever of us can see farthest will have the other in her power.' 'So be it.' Kadrū then said: 'Look over there!'

"Suparṇī then said: 'On the yonder shore of the ocean there is a white horse by a post, I can see it, do you also see it?' 'Of course I see it!' Then Kadrū said: 'Its tail hangs down [from the post]; now the wind blows it, I see it.'

"Now, when Suparṇī said: 'On the yonder shore of the ocean,' the ocean in truth is the altar, with this she meant altar; 'There is a white horse by a post,' the white horse, in truth, is Agni and the post means the sacrificial post. And when Kadrū said: 'Its tail hangs down; now the wind blows it, I see it,' this is none other than the rope.

"Suparṇī then said: 'Come, let us fly there to see which of us has won.' Kadrū said: 'Fly there yourself, you say which of us has won.'

"Suparṇī then flew there; and she saw that all was as Kadrū had said. When she returned, she [Kadrū] said to her: 'Have you or I won?' 'You!' she replied. This is the story of Suparṇī and Kadrū.

"Then Kadrū said: 'I have won your Self (*ātmānam*); over there is Soma in the heavens; go and fetch him for the gods, and with this redeem yourself from death.' 'So be it!' replied [Suparṇī]. Then she produced the meters; and Gāyatrī seized Soma from the sky.

"He [Soma] was closed between two golden cups; the sharp edges closed together at every blink of an eye; and those two cups were, in truth, Consecration and Ardor (*tapas*). Those Gandharva guardians watched over him; they are these hearths, these fire-priests.

"She [Gāyatrī] snatched one of the cups and gave it to the gods. This was the Consecration: and so the gods consecrated themselves.

"Then she snatched the other cup and gave it to the gods. This was Ardor: and so the gods practiced ardor, namely the *upasads* [triple offerings of ghee to Agni, Soma, and Viṣṇu], for the *upasads* are ardor."

What Kadrū (Earth) sees and her sister Suparṇī (Speech) does not see—in the far distance beyond the ocean where that horse appears who is Agni—is the rope that ties the horse to the sacrificial post: "None other than the rope." Speech, in comparison with Earth, is she who does not see with total precision. And total precision is a rope that is tied to death. And so Kadrū challenges her sister to carry out the very action that can redeem her from death: the theft of *soma.* It is as if Kadrū had said: Since you are like this—and you do not see what ties you to death—you have to fly off into the heavens and carry out that brave task which alone can redeem you from death. Otherwise, not seeing the rope that ties you to the sacrificial post means being already dead—or at least having lost your Self.

Existence becomes complete only in the presence of *soma.* The story of the abduction of *soma* is therefore, so far as humans are concerned, the basis for everything else. A story of release and at the same time of redemption, of a gift which is at the same time the extinction of a debt. It is no surprise, then, that the story of Suparṇī holds within itself the principle that has governed everyone's life since then: "As soon as he is born, man is born as a person owing a debt to death; when he offers sacrifices, he redeems his person from death, in the same way that Suparṇī redeemed herself for the gods." These few lines explain with great clarity the reasons behind the radically different assumptions that separate Vedic India from the West. Or at least from the unspoken assumption that, after long elaboration, has ended up becoming Western *good sense*: that vision of man as a *tabula rasa*, the wax tablet to which Locke referred. This is the only assumption that allows the complicated mechanisms of society to operate (and for what else—some say—is thought required?). Certainly, the West is also Plato, for whom an equivalent to Vedic "debt" is the recovery of memory. But here we are talking about assumptions that support living in society. And, in particular, of those that are only rendered explicit with the beginnings of the modern age (starting with Locke). At that moment, what had previously worked covertly becomes evident. And it converges in the principal idea of empiricism: the individual as an entirely unprejudiced perceptive apparatus, a being that takes form on the basis of what gradually has an impact on his senses—and nothing else.

"Debt," *ṛṇa*, is a key word for Vedic man. His whole life is a continual attempt to settle four debts that weigh upon him from birth: debt to the gods, to the *ṛṣis*, to his ancestors, to men. They will be paid off, respectively, through sacrifice, through studying the Veda, through procreation, and through offering hospitality. The fact that there are four debts must not lead to confusion. They originate from one debt alone—the debt toward death and its god, Yama. Yet the text here doesn't name the god, but speaks only of "a debt toward death (*ṛṇaṃ mṛtyoḥ*)."

Life is an asset that death has left in trust for all humans (to be used while it lasts). An asset whose restitution death requires, making man return to death. This is the basis of every life, its innate imbalance. But to this imbalance there is a counterbalance, from the part of the gods: when man offers the oblation to certain divinities, "whoever the divinities are, they consider it as a debt for them to fulfill the desire of the sacrificer at the moment in which he makes the oblation."

Here, another key word appears: *śraddhā*, "trust in the effectiveness of ritual." Which is the Vedic way of expressing our "belief." And above all, as Benveniste observed, "the exact formal correspondence between the Latin *crē-dō* and the Sanskrit *śrad-dhā* is the proof of a very ancient heritage." The sacrificer, with his defect as an innate debtor, faithfully offers the oblation, in the belief that at that same moment the gods will begin to recognize they have a debt to him. Only the institution of a double obligation—of people to the gods and of the gods to people—ensures that flow which is life itself. By obtaining a credit with the gods, man (namely the sacrificer) delays, postpones, defers the moment when he will have to settle his debt with death. Every action is founded on this double imbalance. On the basis of this imbalance every action acquires meaning.

Malamoud observes that the word *ṛṇa*, "debt," apparently has no etymology. The four innate debts, and the very notion of debt, are presented baldly, without explanations—and are destined to go far, remaining alive and powerfully felt much later on, in the world of *bhakti*, of "devotion," which claims to do without ritual orthodoxy. To this Malamoud adds, by way of a parallel, that "there is no mythology of indebtedness." This is surely true, in fact, though with one exception: the story of the two sisters Kadrū and Suparṇī (or, in other texts, Vinatā) and the capture of Soma—a story that is, by no coincidence, the basis for all other Vedic stories. That story is enough to establish the perpetually unequal system of exchange between men and gods. But also between life and death.

How can men imitate the complex scenario of the capture of Soma? By replicating the last stage: the barter between Vāc and Soma. They offer a cow to a mysterious character (the trader who brings the *soma* on his cart) so as to *purchase* that prized item. Everything happens through an equivalence: the cow is Vāc. And the cow is milk. And the milk is gold: "Milk and gold have the same origins, for both are born from Agni's seed." The human repetition has nothing of the overwhelming divine theatricality. But it reveals a point that had remained hidden before: that barter—between a female being and a substance—is more accurately a sale, which is carried out through gold, the source of all currency. The first exchange, the first substitution, takes place with something that cannot, by its very nature, be substituted: *soma*, the substance that is a state of being, a state of mind that can be attained only through it.

But with the purchase of *soma* not everything is resolved. Another scene is included as a grotesque and enigmatic prelude. The first sale was a sham. In just the same way that Vāc had been offered in barter to the Gandharvas to obtain Soma but then—thanks to the wooing ploy—had to be returned to the gods, so too the cow that men use to buy the *soma* from the trader returns in the end to them. How? Because, at the end of the haggling, the *soma* trader is given a thrashing and the cow is led away. That which on the divine stage was a delightful and subtle exchange of words becomes an act of pure violence on the human stage. It is as if the act of selling was too serious to be entirely accepted. A brutal act must cancel out its consequences. But this only makes things worse—it is a fatal step.

Selling and measuring, those two irreversible gestures, can be carried out only after the arrival of the royal guest, the *soma* plant on the trader's cart, as if only *soma* was capable of providing a standard, to which every exchange, every measure can be related: "He [the *adhvaryu*] then spreads out the cloth folded in two or in four, with the fringe toward east or toward north. On it he measures the king: and, since he measures the king, there is therefore a measure, the measure among men as well as any other measure." Soma, the being that is pure quality, discernible only as an intensity of mind, exalted by the juice of that plant, guarantees and establishes the world of quantity, where everything is measured and is sold. What would happen without *soma*? Selling and measuring would continue, but dictated by the rule of "false weight," as Joseph Roth would say.

The *adhvaryu* who officiated at the *soma* ceremony kept a piece of gold tied to his finger. Why? In the human world—the world of untruth—*soma* bursts in like a palpable truth, the only substance flowing from the other world, the world of the gods, who are truth. This justifies the precautions, the ways they use to approach it. The officiants move around it as if it were a red-hot mass. They know that every gesture of theirs can harm it, but can also harm the truth, which is there before them, defenseless like any plant. And it's a guest.

And therefore before touching the *soma* with their fingers they touch it with gold, a divine intermediary since it is the seed of Agni, "so that [the sacrificer] can touch the stalks [of the *soma*] with truth, so that he can handle the *soma* with the truth." In order to deal with *soma*, so as not to upset it, men have to transform themselves into bearers of truth, going against their nature. This is what the rite is all about. All the more evident, in contrast with this delicate care, is the brutality that marks the purchase of the *soma*, when the trader who had sold it ended up being beaten with staffs.

"He buys the king; and, since he buys the king, everything here can be bought. He says: '*Soma*-seller, is King Soma for sale?' 'He is for sale,' says the *soma*-seller. 'I will buy him from you.' 'Buy him,' says the *soma*-seller. 'I will buy him for one-sixteenth [of the cow].' 'King Soma is certainly worth more than that,' says the *soma*-seller. 'Yes, King Soma is worth more than that; but great is the greatness of the cow,' says the *adhvaryu*."

This scene is the basis for every economy. But why *must* the *soma* be purchased—and why does it have no effect unless purchased? Why, if not simply for emphasis, does the text explain several times that it is referring to "bought *soma*"? Because the debt comes before the gift. We are born in debt, we make offerings and then—in time, through ritual—we receive the gift. The trader represents the Gandharvas who intercept Soma, a primordial clash between sky and earth. This reminds us that Soma does not arrive as a simple gift, even for the gods. They have to redeem him from the Gandharvas. They had to become "debtless" toward them. And, even earlier, the *soma* itself had been captured by Gāyatrī to ransom Suparṇī (or Vinatā) from slavery. There is always a payment to be made before anything is obtained. This is because nothing ever happens between sky and earth without some obstacle. There is always at least the shot of an arrow, something is always snatched away. The consequences of that act then weigh upon life on earth. Anyone who disregards them knows nothing about the heavens.

The sacrificer approaches a priest sixteen times and tenders his ritual fee. The *dakṣiṇā* can be of four kinds: "gold, a cow, cloth, and a horse." The distribution of fees is made following a strict order. The last to be paid is the *pratihartṛ* priest, entrusted with the simplest task: to keep the cows, "so that he [the sacrificer] does not lose them."

Watching this scene, in its meticulous arrangement, one might think it is the most recent part of the rite—almost an addition aimed at sealing the closure of the ceremony with the offering of a payment to the priests who have performed it. A naïve, modern notion. The first to distribute ritual fees had been Prajāpati. The world, the gods, humans had only just begun to exist. Everything had just arisen from Prajāpati's sacrifice. But Prajāpati was concerned all the same about distributing ritual fees, almost as if exchange had been there from the very beginning. To such an extent that this distribution of ritual fees could diminish the world—or even exhaust it, unless it were stopped.

This, at least, was the view of Indra, king of the Devas, who were always frightened of being ousted: by their brothers the Asuras, but also by men who tried to reach the heavens through sacrifice—or even, it was now discovered, by the ill-considered magnanimity of the Progenitor. "Indra thought to himself: 'Now he is giving everything away and will leave nothing for us.'" Indra realized at that moment that the power of exchange and substitution, if left to itself, is uncontrollable and corrosive, like the power of a central bank that goes on printing money. So he stepped in with his thunderbolt, in this case a simple formula: the invitation to pray to him.

Indra obtained relatively little satisfaction for his troubles, compared with the solemnity and severity of the obligation connected with the ritual fees. Its principle is set out and repeated in this form: "There should be no offering, as they say, without a ritual fee." This phrase comes close to being a postulate. And the implications that can be drawn from these few far-reaching and allusive words are endless. The postulate itself is only occasionally recalled, when it is appropriate—and is always accompanied by the phrase "as they say," the simplest and quickest way of appealing to the authority of tradition. In this way we learn that you cannot offer something, thus perform a gesture (indeed *the* gesture) that is essentially gratuitous, without at the same time giving a *dakṣiṇā,* which is exactly the opposite: a fee, a payment for a particular work carried out by another. Thus implying that gratuity has a price. And not only does it have a price, but it *has* to have one. Gratuity must be connected with exchange (because the fee is given in exchange for the opus, the priest's labor). But the exchange can arise only from the gratuitous act, with the simple offering, with the *tyāga*: the decision to "yield," to abandon something, to let it disappear in the fire, while watching it, attentively.

In the story of King Soma, those who lose out overall are the Gandharvas. It is they whose main mission was to be the keepers of Soma who are now left as keepers of the void. It is a position that would have to be remedied, if the world wants to maintain its equilibrium. And so it was: "The gods officiated with him [man]. Those Gandharvas who had been the keepers of Soma followed him; and having come forward they said: 'Allow us to have a part of the sacrifice, do not exclude us from the sacrifice; let us also have a part of the sacrifice!'

"They said: 'And then, what is there for us? As in the yonder world we have been his keepers, so will we be his keepers here on earth.'

"The gods said: 'So be it!' Saying: '[Here is] your retribution for Soma,' he assigns them the price of Soma."

Soma has to be purchased because it was stolen from the heavens—and the price is paid so as to silence its keepers, the Gandharvas. Devastating violence first, then an exchange that gives an illusion of fairness: this is not only the relationship that men have with the sky, but also that of the gods when they still had to conquer it.

The exchange appears in relation to an injury. More to cover it up than to heal it. The violence that took place in the heavens with the abduction of the *soma* cannot remain unanswered, but the answer can only be a reasonable and misleading one: a price for something that could not be substituted. The substitution arises in relationship to something it does not have the power to substitute. The *hýbris* of exchange is fully revealed when it claims to bring about substitution of something that cannot be substituted. And what is it that cannot be substituted? The *soma.* Only in relation to *soma* does exchange show itself in all its greed forcing into submission the totality of all that is.

If we first ask ourselves what are meters, the answer has to be that they are footprints. Footprints in which someone else puts their feet. And in putting their feet there they enter into the being of the one who has left the first footprint. This happens with the tracks of the cow that is used to obtain the *soma*: "He follows her, stepping into seven of her tracks; thus he takes possession of her." The cow is Vāc, Speech: as a resplendent woman she charmed the Gandharvas and finally abandoned them, preferring the frivolous songs of the gods to their pious liturgical chants. But Vāc has to be wooed—and so too the cow that is sold to obtain *soma.* Among its gifts there is this: to have marked out the first rhythm, a step, which men would then imitate. But it is essential that such a measure is external to man, that it originates from another being. Speech is a desirable woman or an animal that is used as currency. In any event, the sound that erupts from the depths of man, and would seem to be a part of him like a groan, is instead external, indeed it is the first visible being that he desires, even if she is now no more than a succession of tracks.

To win over the woman who is Speech they were forced to carry out a series of acts that might conceivably appear mad, but they were simply strictly following instructions: having placed their feet in six tracks in succession, they sat in a circle around the seventh track left by the right front hoof of the cow that was to be sold to obtain *soma.* They then took a piece of gold and placed it inside the track. They now poured ghee over it, until the track was full. If the piece of gold had not been there in this hoof print, they could not have made any offerings, since an offering is made only into fire. But gold—like milk—is Agni's seed. And so pouring ghee over the gold was the same as pouring ghee into the fire. And since ghee is a thunderbolt, the cow into whose track the offering is poured was freed, because the thunderbolt is a shield. Once again, everything is consequential. Finally, they shook the dust of the track over the sacrificer's wife. Then they made sure that the cow looked into the eyes of the sacrificer's wife. It seemed as if two females were exchanging glances. But it wasn't like that. The cow is female, but *soma* is male. Since the cow was exchanged for *soma*, the cow was the *soma.* So the gaze became the gaze of a male. And by exchanging glances with the sacrificer's wife, a "fertile coitus" took place. The sacrificer's wife then spoke: "I have seen eye to eye with the far-seeing divine *dakṣiṇā*: do not take my life away from me, I will not take yours away; may I obtain a hero under your gaze!" "A hero," the ritualists add, here means "a son."

The *soma*, purchased and loaded on a cart, arrives and is greeted like a royal guest. When the officiant handles a plant that is *soma*, he dresses it, moves it—and in the meantime talks to it. The plant is king, guest, friend. When he lays it down on his own right thigh, which is now Indra's thigh, *soma* is "the beloved on the beloved one," "propitious on the propitious one," "tender on the tender one," for "the ways of men follow those of the gods." Even sacrifice, at this point, is presented as an obligatory celebration for a high-ranking guest: "In the same way that one would place a large ox or a large he-goat on the fire for a king or a brahmin, so he prepares for him [Soma] the guest-offering." But a king is unlikely to arrive alone. Who then forms his retinue? The meters do.

Like K.'s assistants in *The Castle*, the meters go where Soma goes: "The meters act around him [Soma] as his attendants." What is seen is a cart that carries the stalks of a plant that "is in the mountains." But those who know also see, beside the cart, the shimmering of meters, similar to the rays of the sun.

Sweet, affectionate words are murmured to it—like those murmured to the horse just before it is killed during the *aśvamedha*—to persuade it that no one wants to harm it and it will not suffer, and so the *soma* plant, the newly arrived royal guest, is told why it has been bought. For a noble purpose, certainly, though a mysterious one: for "the supreme sovereignty of the meters." Then, straight after, we read: "When they press him, they kill him." The proximity of these two phrases is in the purest Vedic style. First the esoteric formula (the "supreme sovereignty of the meters," about which the text has actually given no explanation); then the dry, rugged, clear-cut description: "When they press him, they kill him." It is the very tension of all liturgical thinking.

Before reaching the moment of the pressing, problems of etiquette arose. The king was brought down from the cart and laid on the stones that would crush him. The stones are eager, they are already open-mouthed. King Soma, who is nobility, descends to his people of stones. This already raises a doubt in the mind of the ritualist—is it improper, a breach of etiquette, to invite King Soma to descend? Certainly—and (here we detect a sigh from the ritualist) "so people today confuse good and bad." Every complaint about how times are getting worse seems to originate from this brief aside. But the ritualist immediately recovers: this excessive magnanimity of King Soma, who *descends* to his people, eventually to be killed, must be answered by a gesture from the people, who have to maintain their distance, still placing themselves *beneath* him. How? By going down on their knees: "And so, when a noble approaches, all these subjects, the people, kneel down, sit lower than him."

Now the stones surround the *soma* with their mouths gaping. The sacrificer prays in succession to Agni, then to the *soma* bowls, and lastly to the stones themselves, since they know the sacrifice. Only those who know speak. "The stones know." And they "know" because the stones *are* Soma. Not only is Soma killed, but he is killed by his own body, by fragments of his body, by rocks that have been broken from the mountains that form him ("those mountains, those rocks are his body"). What happens? A murder or a disguised suicide?

And here, at this solemn moment, we are reminded that "Soma was Vṛtra." The noble King Soma, the being abducted from the heavens to spread rapture on the earth, had also been (in some way—in *what* way?) the primordial monster, the main obstacle to life.

There is always something *prior* to the gods. If it is not Prajāpati, from which they originated, it is Vṛtra, an amorphous mass, mountain, snake on the mountain, goatskin, a repository for the intoxicating substance *soma.* The gods knew that, in comparison with that indeterminate being, their power was too young and insecure. Even Indra, agreeing to fight a duel with Vṛtra, was by no means sure what would happen as he hurled the thunderbolt. He still feared he was the weaker. He immediately hid. The gods crowded behind him. Vṛtra lay dying on one side. The gods hid themselves in fear on the other. They sent Vāyu, Wind, to investigate. He blew on Vṛtra's bloated body. There wasn't a quiver. Once reassured, the gods then threw themselves on his corpse. Each wanted a larger portion of *soma* than the others. They brandished their *grahas*, cups, to fill them to the brim. But Vṛtra's vast corpse, upon which the gods clambered like parasites, was already giving off a powerful stench. The intoxicating substance, which they drew from the defenseless body, had to be filtered and blended with something else to become ingestible even for the gods. They still needed the help of Vāyu, of a breeze that blended with the liquid *soma.* This was the Vedic version of the Spirit that revives: Vāyu who disperses Vṛtra's stench and transforms the liquid within his body into an intoxicating and enlightening drink.

So Vāyu ended up winning the right to taste some of the first *soma.* Indra felt left out. He was the hero, the one who alone, shuddering, had accepted the challenge. It was he who had hurled the thunderbolt. And now he had to give way to the vain Vāyu. They took their dispute to Prajāpati. This was his ruling: Indra would always have a quarter of Vāyu's share. Indra said he wished, through *soma*, to have language—indeed, the articulated word. From that time on, through Prajāpati's decision, of all the languages throughout the world, only a quarter are articulated, and therefore intelligible. All the rest are indecipherable, from the warbling of birds to the noise of insects. Indra thus did not gain the upper hand. He lowered his head, in sadness. Yet the decision followed a general rule: that most things remain hidden. Only just a quarter of Puruṣa is visible. And the same goes for *brahman*. The unmanifest is much greater than the manifest. The invisible than the visible. The same also with language. We must all know that when we speak, "three parts [of language], kept in concealment, are motionless; the fourth part is what people use." Speech conserves and renews such a fascination only because language throws an inaccessible shadow much larger than itself.

Certain filters, called *pavitra*, are essential in worship—either two *kuśa* blades, used for purifying water, or two strips of white wool, used for the *soma*. Their use recalls the cosmic drama between Vṛtra and Indra. Vṛtra's nature was that of covering (*vṛ-*), enveloping, enclosing within him, obstructing every "evolution," a word that in Sanskrit corresponds with *pravṛtti*, the word that indicates life being lived. This *monstrum* par excellence, since he held everything within himself, also held supreme knowledge—the Vedas—and *soma*, the intoxicating drink. For Indra, killing him meant not only making life possible, but also conquering what could make life inextinguishable: knowledge. And it also meant that the waters flowed, brimming over into the world, where they produce the surplus that is life itself. Yet, even though Indra's gesture implied salvation, it was also a guilty act, one of immense guilt, commensurate with the enormity of his victim. The first sign of guilt is the impurity that has poured into the world since then, through Vṛtra's wound. This liquid is precious but also putrid. And it is enough to contaminate everything, except for those waters that rose up in disgust to escape evil contact, becoming *kuśa* grass. The waters, though immediately contaminated, at the same time escape impurity—at least in part. So they will be used to sprinkle, and then consecrate, every element. And here a subtle theological problem appears: how can those who have not been consecrated consecrate? This too is a guilt for which the officiant "makes amends": already a first sign that guilt extends up to the peak of purity.

The presence of filters enables us to understand that the world is an impure mass. If this were not so, it would not be alive, but would still be closed up in Vṛtra's vast belly. Now, when even the waters are suspect, since they are in part contaminated, what will allow the return to purity? The world has to be *filtered*, in the same way that the prodigious *soma* has to be filtered, which otherwise would not be tolerable. And here is a crucial step: the only element that can provide help, in this scenario of a cosmic swamp, is the stirring breeze. The wind that "blows purifying (*pavate*)" corresponds with the two blades of grass that filter, *pavitra*: but why are there two blades of grass but only one wind? Here follows another decisive step for Vedic theology: there are two filters because there are two basic breaths (inhaled and exhaled), which, by entering the body and leaving it, make it live. So the wind is those breaths and those breaths are the two filters of *kuśa* grass. This dazzling equation introduces the supreme function of breath (from which the whole of *yoga* and countless reflections on breathing follow) and explains why the world, this formless and fetid mass of elements where the liquid held in Vṛtra's wounded body continues to flow even today, needs a breath of wind to filter it, to give life to it, to make it usable in a ceremonial act.

In the beginning, the gods lost the *soma*; men did not have it. But they both found themselves performing the same gestures when they recovered it (or bought it): practicing *tapas*, fasting—with ever greater rigor. In the meantime, men as well as the gods "heard its sound," the sound of *soma*. What was this sound for the gods? We are not told. But we know what it was for people. The sound of the lost *soma* said: "On such and such a day the buying will take place." For the gods, an undefined sound; for men, the announcement of an exchange, a sale. This is the passage from divine to human: abrupt, curt. But we are made to understand that, without exchange, man does not exist. Or, at least, he can never obtain *soma*. As for immortality, it would be naïve to think that for men it may mean an endless duration. So it is made clear: "This assuredly is immortality for man: when he attains a full life." The most important thing for man is to give form to life, making it whole, perfect, in the same way that the fire altar must be whole, perfect. There is no answer to the question that worried Prajāpati's creatures: does the perfect life include Death in it? On this there is no answer, either positive or negative.

The "comedy of innocence" is just the same for the bear about to be killed by hunters as it is for Soma. When the stones are on the point of striking the stalks of the divine plant to bring out the juice, the intention to kill must be directed toward any enemy or being that is hated. Then the sacrificer can say: "Here I strike *x*, not you." The guilt therefore resides not in the act—the killing of Soma—but in the mental picture accompanying it. And if the sacrificer has no enemies? If he hates no one? Then he directs this thought, with hatred, to a blade of straw: "If he hates no one, he can even think of a straw, and thus no wrong is incurred." Corollaries: the act is a necessity, an inevitable step. And it is in itself a guilty act. But anyone who doesn't want to increase his own guilt, which belongs already to the fact of existing, has to separate their mind from the act, to direct it toward an object that mitigates the guilt. The straw indicates that we are approaching the nonexistent and the invisible. Does anything exist beyond the straw? The detachment that Kṛṣṇa will teach Arjuna in the *Bhagavad Gītā*, the nonadherence to the act. This is one step higher than simply diverting the act onto another object.

"And he [Soma], insofar as he is generated, generates him [the sacrificer]": a phrase that rings out three times. It touches on a delicate and crucial point: mutual procreation. A general rule among the gods, it now finds a ritual counterpart. Nothing exists in itself, all is the result of work. Likewise for *soma*: the plant from the heavens does not exist until it is pressed, filtered, and sprinkled by the sacrificer and by the priests. But, at the point when *soma* comes into being, it produces the sacrificer. The existence of the *soma* brings about a transformation in the person who with his actions has brought it into being.

And at the end of the ceremony, in the same way that King Soma is a bundle of crushed stalks, reduced to a "body unfit for offering," so too the sacrificer, tired out, a shadow of his former self, makes his way toward the water that flows just below the sacrificial ground. There the cleansing bath, *avabhṛtha*, awaits him. The *soma* and the sacrificer: both yearn for new sap. They want to immerse themselves in the water, to forget.

"Thereupon both [the sacrificer and his wife], having gone down, bathe, and wash each other's back. Having wrapped themselves in fresh clothing, they leave: like a snake that sloughs its skin, so he frees himself from all evil. In him there is no more guilt than in a toothless babe."

Anyone entering the rite is burdened with gestures, acts, and *karman*, which literally means "ritual action." There is no doubt: he sees the light, immortality, he touches the gods. But at the end he nevertheless wants to forget, exhausted. He wants to return to dull, insignificant, straightforward normality. And the sacrificer and his wife retrace the steps they took to arrive at the sacrificial site. They bathe in flowing water. The objects used in the sacrifice are thrown into the water, as if no one wanted to remember they ever existed. Everything must now be new. The innocence of the newborn child is never something given. On the contrary, it is hard fought for. And is short-lived. For the action immediately starts all over again. And the action, every action, and above all that sacred action that makes it possible to attain the light through *soma*, is a form of guilt. Not because it hurts or injures someone or something, even if it inevitably does hurt and injure, but simply because it is action. On the other hand, without *that* action any life is formless and empty. But from time to time we need to return to that formlessness, that meaninglessness, because we do not bear too much meaning, too much light, or too much guilt. The sacrificer no longer wears his own clothes. They too are part of an episode now swallowed up. But how will he dress, now? He covers himself with the cloth in which the *soma* stalks had been wrapped, in which they had appeared in the distant past, a few hours earlier, when the *soma* had still to be pressed. Tied around his wife is the cloth that had wrapped the cloth in which the *soma* lay. Then they leave, silently, passively, cleansed, empty. All that remains is a barely discernible fragrance—perhaps discernible only to them—coming from the two cloths in which the *soma* had for some time been kept.

"When Gāyatrī flew toward Soma, a footless archer, aiming at her, shot off a feather, either of Gāyatrī or of King Soma; and the feather, dropping down, became a *parṇa* tree." Elsewhere we are told that this mysterious footless archer is called Kṛśānu, but we learn little more. His appearance and attitude suggest a being on the margin of the unmanifest—or of "fullness," *pūṛna*, which is another name for it. Like another archer—Rudra—Kṛśānu tries to stop a deed that goes against the order of the world, and thereby creates life as we know it. In the case of Rudra, it was Prajāpati's incest with Uṣas. In his case, it is the abduction of the *soma*, which will enable men to become drunk on it. Kṛśānu's nature is perhaps also implied in his being "footless," *apād*, a characteristic that links him with another enigmatic figure: Aja Ekapād, the one-footed goat. If we go back to the "unborn," *aja*, to the "self-existing," *svayambhū*, the last two figures that let themselves be recognized—though only in flashes and glimmers, without ever being described—are a Goat (Aja Ekapād) and a Serpent (Ahi Budhnya). We can distinguish nothing beyond them. The Goat has to stand up because it is the "supporter of the sky," but if we look closer we see it is resting on only one hoof (*ékapād*). At times it appears as a column of fire speckled with black, the black of the darkness against which it stands out. And beneath it? The Serpent of the Deep, Ahi Budhnya. No text dares to say any more about it. Only its name is mentioned—five times, in the Vedic hymns, along with that of the Goat, as if these two figures hint at something beyond which we cannot go: the Unborn, the Deep. The inevitable and almost imperceptible channel for all that exists.

The world owes its existence to the infinitesimal delay of an arrow. Or of two arrows: that of Rudra, which pierced Prajāpati's groin, but did not prevent him from spilling his seed, and that of Kṛśānu, which grazed the wing of the hawk carrying the *soma* and made one of its feathers drop to the ground, but did not stop the *soma* from reaching mankind. That particle of time was all time, with its uncontainable power. It was the way out of plenitude closed up within itself, the passage to plenitude brimming over into something else, into the world itself. But that superabundance had happened thanks only to a wound. The rites Vedic people sought to establish were primarily an attempt to treat and heal that wound, thereby renewing it. And burning one part of the superabundance that enabled them to live.

Soma not only induced intoxication, but encouraged truth. "For the man who knows, this is easy to recognize: true and false words clash. Of these two, the true, the just, is what Soma protects. And he fights untruth": This is hymn 7.104 of the *Ṛgveda*. This double gift—rapture and the true word—is what distinguishes Vedic knowledge. If Soma did not lead to rapture, it could not fight for the true word either. And much the same happens to anyone who receives Soma into the circulation of their mind. Dionysus was swept into rapture and used sarcasm against anyone who opposed him. He never claimed to protect the true word. It was as if the word passed among his retinue of Maenads and Satyrs, but without being much noticed. Dionysus was intensity in its purest state, that overcame and destroyed every obstacle, without dwelling on the word, whether true or false. Possessed by the god, the bacchant declared: "Make way, make way / let lips not be contaminated with words."

"Now we have drunk *soma*; we have become immortal; we have attained the light, we have found the gods." Sudden, lightning words, the opposite of the sequence of riddles that makes up so much of the *Ṛgveda*. Men need *soma* so that they can *find* the gods; but the gods, in turn (and primarily their king, Indra) need *soma* in order to be gods. They chose *soma* one day as their intoxicating drink because "the vigor of the gods" is due to *soma*.

If *soma* is desired just as much by the gods as by men, it will also become their factor in common. Only in rapture can gods and men communicate. Only in *soma* do they meet: "Come toward our pressings, drink *soma*, you *soma* drinker." This is how people address Indra, in the first hymn dedicated to the god in the *Ṛgveda*. Only insofar as people are able to offer rapture to the gods can they hope to attract them to the earth. What people offer the god is what the god himself has conquered for them—and for the other gods—committing the gravest of crimes, the killing of a brahmin, when he cut off the three heads of Viśvarūpa. There is a secret understanding between Indra and men, for Indra is the god who most resembles men (and several times he will be mocked for this): he has killed a brahmin to obtain the *soma*, in the same way that people kill King Soma to obtain the intoxicating liquid from which he is made. Killing, sacrifice, and rapture are bound together, both for god and man. And this makes them accomplices, it obliges people to celebrate long, exhausting *soma* rites. But it is also the only way of attaining a life that—for a while—is divine.

ANTECEDENTS AND CONSEQUENTS

When you gods were in the waves, holding each other tightly,
thick foams then rose up from you, as from dancers.

—*Ṛgveda* 10.72.6

This book was started quite a number of years ago out of the rash idea of writing a commentary on the *Śatapatha Brāhmaṇa*, the *Brāhmaṇa of One Hundred Paths*. The *Śatapatha Brāhmaṇa* is a treatise on Vedic rituals that dates back to the eighth century B.C.E. and is made up of fourteen *kāṇḍas*, "sections," which add up to 2,366 pages in Julius Eggeling's five-volume translation in the Sacred Books of the East series, published in Oxford between 1882 and 1900. This is at present the only complete translation (that of C. R. Swaminathan has so far reached only the eighth *kāṇḍa*). The Brāhmaṇas—and the *Śatapatha Brāhmaṇa* stands out among them—contain thoughts that cannot be ignored yet rarely find a place in the philosophy books. Thus, very often, they were treated with impatience, as being a sort of intrusion.

The *Śatapatha Brāhmaṇa* is a powerful antidote to current existence. It is a commentary that shows how one can live a life totally dedicated to passing into *another* order of things, which the text dares to call "truth." A life that is impossible to live, since almost everything is worn down in the strains of that transition. But a life that certain people tried, very long ago—and of which they wanted to leave some record. It was a life based above all on particular gestures. We should not be led astray by the fact that some of those gestures still survive today in India and are commonly performed by a great many people who know almost nothing about how they originated, while other great civilizations have left no comparable legacy: the civilization of the Vedic ritualists did not withstand the test of time—it fell apart, remaining for the most part inaccessible, incomprehensible. And yet all that still shines out of it has a power that stirs any mind not entirely enslaved to what surrounds it.

People at the beginning of the twenty-first century speak much about religion. But very little in the world is religious in the strict and rigorous sense. And not so much with regard to individuals as to social structures. Whether these are churches, sects, tribes, or ethnic groups, their model is an amorphous superparty that lets people go further than the idea of the party had previously allowed, in the name of something that is often described as "identity." It is the revenge of secularity. Having lived for hundreds and thousands of years in a condition of subjection, like a handmaiden to powers that were imposed without caring to justify themselves, secularity now—sneeringly—offers all that still makes reference to the sacred the means to act in a way that is more effective, more up-to-date, more deadly, more in keeping with the times. This is the new horror that still had to take form: the whole of the twentieth century has been its long incubation period.

If one wants to talk about anything religious, some kind of relation has to be established with the invisible. There has to be a recognition of powers situated over and beyond social order. Social order itself must seek to establish some relations with that invisible. All this does not seem to be of great concern to religious authorities at the beginning of the twenty-first century. In the higher ranks of Christian or Islamic hierarchies, or among the pandits of Hinduism, it is easy to find keen sociologists or social engineers who use the sacred names of their respective traditions to impose or sustain a certain collective order. But it would be hard to find anyone who could speak the language of Meister Eckhart or Ibn 'Arabī or Yājñavalkya—or could even remind us of such a voice.

In the face of this, the *Śatapatha Brāhmaṇa* offers the picture of a world made up *only* of what is religious, with no apparent curiosity or concern about anything that is not. As the Brāhmaṇas see it, the religious pervades every tiny gesture—and even pervades all that is involuntary and accidental. For Vedic ritualists, a world without such characteristics would have appeared meaningless, in exactly the same way as their writings have often appeared to readers of today. The incompatibility between the two views is total. And the disparity of forces is overwhelming: on the one hand a chain of procedures that has succeeded in covering the entire planet for the first time with an invisible digital network; on the other hand a body of texts, partly accessible only in a dead, perfect language, which describes actions and entities that seem no longer to have any importance. Yet the thinking of the Vedic ritualists, in its sometimes unfathomable eccentricity, had this peculiarity: it always posed crucial questions, in the face of which all thinking going back to the Enlightenment shows itself to be clumsy and inadequate. The ritualists did not offer solutions, but they knew how to isolate and contemplate the knots that cannot be undone. It is by no means certain that thought can do much more.

It would be pleonastic to use the word *symbol* in a world where multiple meanings could be found in every tiny fragment. What, for example, would water be a symbol of in the Veda, other than—almost—everything? To apply the Western notion of "symbol" to the Vedic world would rapidly produce a general state of meaninglessness through an excess of meaning. Indeed there is no exact word in Sanskrit for "symbol." *Bandhu*, *nidāna*, *sampad*: these are words that indicate an affinity, tie, bond, correspondence, nexus, assimilation, but cannot be reduced to official functions, as happened in the case of the symbol.

In the ordinary Western mind, as it has developed over centuries of elaboration before producing hordes of anonymous Bouvards and Pécuchets, it is generally assumed to be quite unnecessary for the vast majority of things to be a symbol of something else, except in certain clear-cut cases where such a role is considered legitimate—and also useful. The *flag* is a good example. But the Vedic world would then be a boundless expanse of flags.

At the same time, a modern Western mind is able to navigate the Vedic texts, though with some difficulty—finding itself at times before obstacles that seem insurmountable—and discover something vital that can be found nowhere else. And the difficulties it encounters are not that much greater than those that a present-day Indian has to face. The distance between Indian and Western cultures of today, though obviously great, becomes negligible when compared with the astral distance of both from the Vedic world.

How does contact become possible? Analogically. In the silent plains of the past, the Veda is most probably the widest, most complex, most ramified area, where people lived granting sovereignty and preeminence to only one pole of the mind: the analogical pole. A pole that works perpetually (and cannot fail to work) in every being, at whatever time, in the same way as its corresponding pole: the digital pole. Under whose dominion the entire world now finds itself living—an experimental condition that is unprecedented. But, though the preeminence of the digital pole is solid and secure, this does not mean the analogical pole is disappearing. And in fact it has no option but to continue working, since physiology demands that it does. Yet at times it works secretly, or in disguise, or at least without letting itself be noticed. On the other hand, digitality was also present and active in the Vedic world, though bridled and trampled upon. And it cannot be otherwise, since this is how our brain and our nervous system are made. This implies, among other things, that nothing can in principle stop them from trying to act and react in ways they once used to, over several millennia. On the scale of the brain, those times are not even so very far distant.

Behind the *Ṛgveda*, behind the swarming of gods, behind the seers who saw the hymns, behind the ritual acts, we glimpse something that could approximately be called *Vedic thought.* If this thinking was the most hazardous and consistent attempt at ordering life in obedience to the analogical method alone, that attempt could not last—and we can only be amazed that it has managed to survive in particular places and particular periods, like a wedge of alien material. Yet it is also true that this attempt, vulnerable though it might have been, has also had the strength to keep some of its features alive over a distance of millennia, when other grandiose constructions had sunk. In Greece today, its gods and their rituals speak only through the silence of their stones. The same is true for Egypt, the most hoary of civilizations. But the Vedic *mantras* continue to be recited and sung, intact, sometimes in the same places where they were formed—or even in Kerala. And particular ritual gestures, to which Vedic thought had devoted obsessive attention, continue to be carried out in the *saṃskāra*, in the sacramental ceremonies that are part of countless lives in India.

The gods dwell where they have always dwelt. But on earth, certain indications about those places have now been lost. Or we no longer know where to find them among old sheets abandoned and dispersed. Meanwhile, life goes on as if nothing had happened. Some think those sheets will one day be rediscovered. Others that they were of no particular importance. Others, yet again, have no idea they ever existed.

Humanity does not have a superabundance of *modes of thinking.* And two—*connective* and *substitutive* thinking—stand out like inimical brothers. Each is based on a statement: "*a* is connected to *b*" and "*a* stands for *b*" (where "*a* implies *b*" is a subset of "*a* is connected to *b*"). There is no form of thought that cannot be subsumed into one or other of these two statements. And they are in a relation of chronological succession, because the *connective* has always preceded the *substitutive* in every place or time, if we take *connective* as referring to the Vedic *bandhus*, and therefore to those "bonds" and "nexuses" that link the most disparate phenomena by affinity, resemblance, and analogy.

The more mature thought is—in the sense of it being multifaceted, all-embracing, precise—the more it practices *both* of its modes to the very end, to the full extent of their potential. To choose one or the other, as if they were two political parties, would be puerile. But it is essential to distinguish their respective fields of application. Neither the *connective* nor the *substitutive* have the capacity to extend to everything. In certain spheres, they become vacuous and inert. The more subtle and effective the activity of one of the modes of thinking becomes, the more it can identify and accurately delineate the areas to which it applies.

Connective and *substitutive*: the two *modes* of the mind can be so defined by referring to their dominant characteristic. But, if we are referring to the implementation of their workings, they could also be described as *analogical* and *digital*, insofar as the principal way of substitution is through codification—and the number is what enables it to act with maximum ease and efficiency. And the digital mode is applied above all to the realm of quantity, where the result of an operation is a number that substitutes an initial number. Whereas the analogical mode is based on similarity, thus on the connection between entities of whatever kind.

Convention and *affinity* are other useful terms for defining the two poles of the mind. *Convention* means that, whatever *a* is, it can be decided that "it stands for *b*," therefore it substitutes it. An impositional principle, not based on argument—and highly effective. *Affinity* means that, for reasons not necessarily clear or apparent, there is something in *a* that it shares with *b*, so that anything said about *b* will in some way involve *a*. At the beginning it is a largely obscure terrain—and destined to remain so to some extent even at the end of any investigation. The perception of affinities is never-ending. We can say where the process begins, but not where it can be ended. The *convention*, on the other hand, begins and ends in the act with which it is established.

This is what we are made of. In the same way that the binary number system, in its simplicity, allows an endless series of applications, so the two modes of the mind lend themselves to supporting the widest variety of constructions that combine or mix together, or repel each other. And each continually referring to the other. Every decision that claims to divide them or declares the predominance of one over the other is useless, because both continue to operate, consciously or otherwise, at every instant, for anyone and in anyone.

The connective mode and the substitutive mode correspond to two irreducible elements of nature—and of the mind that observes it: the continuum and the discrete. The continuum is the sea; the discrete, the sand. The connective mode assimilates itself to the continuum, in that it produces a never-ending amalgam, an uninterrupted strip of figures where each enters the other. The substitutive mode multiplies indefinitely the grains that, seen from a certain distance, compose a single distinct figure, in the same way that the halftone screen allows things photographed to be recognized. More than categories, the continuum and the discrete are dimensions with which the mind works nonstop. And through them the world works. They are "the poles of a fundamental complementarity of thought throughout all time." The mind and the world draw upon that obscure, inexhaustible background, like craftsmen in the same workshop.

There is nothing pleasant about the picture of someone taking an animal, tying it to a post, and then strangling or suffocating it, or slitting its throat. And yet that gesture formed the centerpiece of solemn rituals, in India and elsewhere. Clearly it must have been considered necessary, inevitable. Instead of concealing it, they flaunted it, surrounding it with bold and mysterious speculations. Then that same gesture, at a certain point during the Christian era, became unacceptable as a public spectacle. But the number of animals killed each day—strangled, suffocated, their throats slit (other methods of killing also came along in the meantime)—never diminished, indeed it steadily grew. There was no more talk of *sacrifice*, except in books. And yet, in laboratories, they talked about test animals being *sacrificed.*

Sacrificial practices all have a familiar nature, whether they are celebrated in Cameroon or among the Australian Aborigines, in the American Northwest or in the Temple of Jerusalem, in Mexico or Iran or in Imperial Rome. Examining documentary evidence or archaeological finds, it is impossible to deny that we know—in an obscure way—what they consist of. They are words and fragments of phrases that belong to dialects of one and the same language, of which nowhere is the grammar and syntax worked up to the degree of perfection that we find in the India of the Vedic ritualists. We can say of Vedic sacrifice what was said about the *Mahābhārata*: in it is found all that exists elsewhere—and what is not to be found there does not exist anywhere else. Every detail of the sacrificial rites of every part of the world can be illuminated from a passage in the system of Vedic sacrifice, yet there are many details of Vedic sacrifice that can be illuminated only by themselves. Behind the disparate, ramified, discordant practices of sacrifice—so disparate and so discordant that various scholars today, out of speculative cowardice, are tempted to treat sacrifice itself as an invention of anthropologists—the outline of a sacrificial vision can be recognized, and it involves everything. This vision, though ubiquitous and persistent, also has the following characteristic: if it is not accepted, it can dissolve away instantly. There is no obligation to describe, to interpret the world in sacrificial terms. There is nothing to prevent thinking in a way that totally ignores the sacrificial vision. Sacrifice itself can easily be described as a mental disorder. And yet its language cannot be expunged. Irritatingly, it remains and returns. The sacrificial practices have gone. But the word is still used—and everyone seems to understand it immediately, even without being anthropologists. At the opposite extreme, in Vedic India the sacrifice was like breathing. It is therefore a phenomenon that continues to exist even unconsciously—indeed it is an implicit condition of our own lives, in whatever place or time.

In the battle between sacrificial and anti-sacrificial stances, the most plausible result could be that the former is gradually defeated, abandoned, repressed, forgotten, superseded in Hegelian manner. It would remain, if at all, an *archaic survival* (it could be said of almost everything that it is an archaic survival) and some scholar would take it upon himself to search out traces of it.

But this is not the case. In its Vedic variant—the most complex, intricate, subtle, staggering—the sacrificial stance contains an implication that goes very far: it is quite possible to ignore the very thought of sacrifice, but the world will continue just the same—whatever happens—to be a huge sacrificial laboratory. In the words of Paul Mus: "Beginning from *Śatapatha Brāhmaṇa*, 10.5.3.1–12, a closer examination of sacrificial doctrine shows that, if sacrifice is the reason for every life, life itself, even if it is not redeemed by it, is like a sacrifice which ignores itself." Now, if any life whatsoever is "a sacrifice which ignores itself," every attempt to overcome sacrifice will turn out to be illusory. But why should the whole world be a sacrificial laboratory? Simply because it is based—every part of it—on an exchange of energies: from outside in and from inside out. This is what happens with every breath. And likewise with eating and excreting. Interpreting physiological exchange as sacrifice is the critical step, on which all else depends. And it is a step that, reduced to its most elementary form, implies only that between everything internal and everything external there is a relationship, a communication that can have a meaning—and a wide diversity of meanings, up to the hypermeaningful fervor of the Veda.

The sacrificial attitude implies that nature has meaning, whereas the scientific approach offers us the pure description of nature, in itself devoid of meaning. And this absence of meaning in the description is not due to an imperfect state of knowledge that can one day be remedied. Indeed, from description it will never be possible to reach meaning. Knowledge about a neural pathway, however perfect, will never be translated into the perception of a state of consciousness. This is the ultimate, insurmountable obstacle that the sacrificial attitude sidesteps at the very beginning. Perhaps arbitrarily. Indeed, most certainly arbitrarily, so far as the detailed correlations that it then sought to establish. But is it not an equally arbitrary gesture if, starting with a particular point of scientific investigation, we seek to introduce meaning into what is described?

Meaning is a work of the mind—and we might say that the mind always keeps company with primordial doubt, when "in the beginning this [world], as it were, existed and did not exist: then there was only the mind." For the Veda, "mind," *manas*, has a sovereign position, but only insofar as it corresponds to a state in which the world itself did not know whether it existed or not. In a certain way, the Vedic absolutism of the mind is much more ready to entertain radical doubt about itself than is scientific empiricism, which always offers its results—however provisional and perfectible—as a verified (and therefore *true*) transcription of that which is.

In many different times and places, a *rite* was created that practiced the *destruction* of something in connection with an *invisible counterpart.* If one of these elements is missing, there is no sacrifice. And, if all three are present, the ceremony can have many different—and even conflicting—meanings. But all will share at least one characteristic: *detachment*, yielding, abandoning something to an invisible counterpart. If such an action were performed onstage, half the stage would remain empty—the half featuring those for whom the sacrifice was made.

What is more, sacrifice has to have a *destructive* element. There can be no sacrifice unless something is consumed, dispersed, discharged, poured. And in a large number of cases the ceremony calls for a killing, the spilling of blood. To understand sacrifice we have to understand why, in offering something to an invisible entity, the offering has to be killed.

While the reason for the gesture of offering itself is not too difficult to find (made out of fear or respect, in order to corrupt, to establish a relationship), the reason justifying the act of killing is not at all clear. First, it is not clear why the entity or entities to which sacrifice is made require the offering to be destroyed. Nor is it clear why, even when the sacrifice is centered around the offering of a precious substance (*soma*), the offering must be accompanied by the killing of various animals.

No theory about sacrifice manages to cover the phenomenon in its entirety. The rite is too plastic, changeable, adaptable to the various motives. Yet there is no difficulty in describing as *sacrifices* all those acts carried out in remote times and places. What holds them together is not so much the specific meaning as certain preconditions, which are unfailingly there.

And they are the following: that every sacrifice is a formalized sequence of actions addressed to an invisible counterpart; and that every sacrifice implies a destruction—something must be separated from what it belonged to and be dispersed. It may be life, for the animal that is killed; or money, for the taxpayer who is invited to make "sacrifices" (in this case we are no longer talking about ritual, but the word continues to be used in a broader sense); or it may be a liquid, even just water, which is poured as a libation; or a perfume, such as incense, which is dispersed; or the life of the sacrificer himself, as in the Roman *devotio.* The variants are many and subtle. The motives mean or sublime. The ceremonies age-old or improvised—the *Śatapatha Brāhmaṇa* described them as "supreme action (*śreṣṭhatamaṃ karma*)." In any case, it still has to be understood why, over thousands of years and in places far apart and unrelated to each other, it was felt necessary to turn to an invisible counterpart, performing a series of gestures that, without exception, include a destruction—and in any case the *detachment* of something from the animate or inanimate being to which it belonged. Sacrifice is in the first place a *caesura*, in the original sense of the word, which comes from *caedo*, to cut, a verb used in sacrificial killing. But, if the sacrifice introduces a *caesura* into life (into any life), then we must ask what happens if that *caesura* does not occur. There would then be another *caesura*, but this time in the sense of *interruption*, after an incalculable series of acts. The whole history of mankind can be seen from this standpoint, if we consider that evidence of sacrifices can be found from the Paleolithic age onward, long before any verbal testimony. Meanwhile, in certain places, on certain days, blood sacrifices are still performed, even today.

Abdellah Hammoudi, a professor of anthropology at Princeton, a Moroccan of Sunnite family, decided one day in 1999 to make a pilgrimage to Mecca, as numerous relatives, friends, and co-nationals had done. He wanted to understand, as an anthropologist. And to discover what remained of his education as an Islamic believer. The pilgrimage to Mecca imposes various obligations, including the task of choosing a lamb and slitting its throat at the Feast of the Sacrifice. Hammoudi wanted to avoid it. He paid a "charitable works corporation" to perform the act in his place. Hammoudi would be just a spectator.

When the day approached, "in Mina, the sheds looked like a giant concentration camp for animals: two, three, four million heads or more. An immense crowd of pilgrims was preparing to sacrifice them as an 'offertory,' along with the sacrifices of expiation or alms . . . We were gathered here to save our own lives, a salvation requiring that we kill these animals. The mass of pilgrims, who had reached the peak of renunciation—after the station at Arafa, the prayer at Muzdalifa and the stoning at Mina—was about to snuff out millions of lives . . . Modernization of the *hajj* certainly had something to do with it: the optimal-productivity animal pens, closed-off areas, grid-like arrangements of space, failsafe security and surveillance systems. Each domain had its own camp: the masses of animals in their sheds and, not far off, the masses of humans in their camps surrounded by high chain-link fences stretching ad infinitum along the straight streets . . . Police vehicles on the ground and helicopters constantly circling overhead completed the picture. This order would allow the human masses to annihilate the animal masses in the name of God."

So far as secular society, sacrificial ceremonies are not allowed. Even though the word is still in common use, like a poisonous snake accidentally applied for therapeutic purposes. And then it is always pronounced in worthy contexts, in reference to noble gestures of abnegation and self-denial. But above all it will come back into frequent and timely use in wartime, to describe those killed, all of those killed, including those who were most averse to being killed in a war.

The ultimate question that sacrifice poses: why, in order to establish contact between human and divine, does a living being have to be killed? Or at least, why does a certain quantity of a certain material have to be destroyed—burned or poured away? Strangely, this very question, which lies at the root of all others, has been avoided in the various conflicting theories about sacrifice. Girard doesn't avoid it, but this is because he regards sacrifice purely as a social fact, where the divine is just a convenient façade. And sacrificial violence then becomes the outlet for general violence. But if the divine, as the ancient theologians meant it, existed—indeed were the fullness of existence—how could we explain the continual repetition of bloody acts devoted to it?

Secular society, in its purity, ignores ritual ceremonies. But ridding itself of them is not easy. To achieve this, squads of protestants had to clear the way, leaving as a legacy, among other things, the religious wars, a model for every civil war, and a certain way of behaving, a model for that chimera that was later to be called "secular morality." Rituals survive in secular society for certain legal necessities: the swearing of oaths in trials, the preset pattern of words in marriages. All the rest are ingrained customs, such as birthdays. The same with military processions or New Year speeches by heads of state. Customs that come and go, practices that we can—if we wish—ignore. Strictly speaking, with a little care and planning, we could avoid being involved in any kind of ritual, from the cradle to the grave. For death there are no rites. Not even at funerals. At such moments even established customs seem particularly feeble.

Waking up each morning, rain or shine, and knowing there are no duties to follow. Making coffee, looking out the window. A feeling of blankness. Indifference. To reach this state, various millennia had passed. But nothing remained of it, apart from an opaque curtain, on all sides. No one celebrated this fact as an achievement. It was normality, reached at last. A characterless state, prior to desires. A mute foundation to existence. There would be no shortage of time for whims, plans, survival strategies. And this was the central point: time was not taken up, measured, assailed by obligatory gestures, without which there was a fear that all might fall apart. This might well have produced a feeling of exhilaration. But it was not to be. Indeed, the first sensation was of emptiness. And with it, a certain tedium. The metaphysical animal looked around, not knowing what to grasp hold of.

So secular society has not learned how to value its discoveries. It has felt no sense of relief. Instead, looking at itself, it has found itself insubstantial. Immediately it has felt the need for some *cause* to espouse, to give itself substance and regain solidity. And with causes once more there are obligations. A network of ready-established meanings has settled once more on the world. Why then have rituals been abandoned? *Causes* are always cruder than rituals. They are *parvenus* of meaning. Rituals, on the other hand, brought together the whole of the past, certain gestures repeated innumerable times, until they became part of human physiology, as a strange trust in their effectiveness grew. The fall of ritual also brought with it a heavy aesthetic decline. Free expression was always more awkward, more imprecise than the prescribed gesture. And forms tended to become uncertain and inert, now that they could develop unimpeded.

Secular society (and this would potentially include the whole planet) has therefore lost a great opportunity. It could have rediscovered a sense of wonder at the world, though this time from a safe distance that prevented it from being overwhelmed. But something else happened. A potent compound has been formed between technical procedures and ignorance of powers, which has left its mark on everyday life.

How might we define a *secular society*? Before resorting to complicated theories, we might say that such are societies that share the same airport boarding procedures. Therefore a network of societies that covers the planet. Essential in defining the *secular society* is the acceptance of a certain number of procedures. Those of airports are among the simplest, but in other cases the procedures can reach a dizzying complexity, especially where money is concerned. Once applied, the procedures may then be associated with very different forms of societies: tribal or authoritarian or cosmopolitan or libertarian or communist or theocratic or democratic or feudal. The range is vast, with unforeseeable opportunities for hybridization. But the basis doesn't change—and is made up of procedures. This is the crucial innovation, compared with every previous form of society. As for the social forms themselves, they can also consider themselves mutually incompatible and fight each other with lethal expedients. Nevertheless they have much more in common than what we are prepared to admit. And that common basis could also have a greater heft than all the religious and ideological differences. From the point of view of procedures, secular society is the first *universal society*, marred by numerous civil wars, wars that seem to have been part of its physiology from the very beginning.

Substitution, exchange, value: pivotal elements around which the world we call modern revolves. Their origin lies in sacrificial practices—and in the metaphysics of sacrifice. There is no sacrifice that does not involve exchange; there is no sacrifice that does not acknowledge substitution; there is no sacrifice that does not have a value at its core. But what happens when sacrifice is no longer allowed, as the modern world is proud to declare? Where has it ended up? As a superstition? How can we get to understand that the three categories (substitution, exchange, value), of which no one would dare suggest they are superstitions, were created and formed as part of one and the same superstition (sacrifice itself)?

The ban on practicing blood sacrifice in Western societies grew up and developed alongside the ban on capital punishment. But the latter is a legal issue that is accompanied by long, passionate debate and is crystallized into laws. Whereas the ban on blood sacrifice is almost never mentioned. It is implicit—and the issue is avoided, with a certain embarrassment. Yet, if a certain ethnic group in London or New York today, in obedience to its traditional practices, seeks openly to perform a blood sacrifice, the police immediately step in. Applying what laws? They would have to rely on regulations against cruelty to animals. And those regulations are found on the periphery of the law, as basic rules of public order. The question is not dealt with in major legal textbooks. Blood sacrifice is something to be cast aside, preferably without any accompanying words. Killing animals has to be the prerogative of those who work in slaughterhouses, in the same way that only the police are authorized to use violence. But any decision that regards the monopoly of violence is a fundamental aspect of society and treated with meticulous attention to detail (the police can use violence only in certain specific circumstances), whereas what happens in slaughterhouses slips out of control (apart from certain *humanitarian* measures toward animals—and the word itself immediately sends shudders down the spine) and is regulated only in terms of effectiveness and practicality. There is a remarkable omission when it comes to the killing of animals, today. And there is no more direct way of discovering how thought can become so subtle and can agonize over the question than by reading the Vedic texts. Texts from a remote civilization that celebrated innumerable—and often bloody—sacrifices.

The dominant view in twentieth-century anthropology, heightened and taken to an extreme in the thought of René Girard, was that every society, in order to survive, needs sacrifice, either as an institution that produces a homeostatic effect, or as a mechanism that makes it possible to concentrate the violence produced within it on a victim, ostracized from society itself.

The thesis of the Brāhmaṇas was that the world is based on sacrifice, which is performed when the surplus of available energies is burned. Vedic society seeks to superimpose itself, point for point, moment for moment, upon this process—and offers the energy burned to powers that have a name. The different ways in which a society chooses to burn the surplus end up giving it its shape.

The two approaches have one area in common: that area where guilt is developed. In the case of society as viewed by Girard, the guilt is based on the fact that the victim is innocent—and his killers know it. In the case of the Brāhmaṇas, the guilt is based on the fact that every destruction of excess is a killing. And killing recalls the decisive step in the creation of society: the transformation of the human animal from prey into predator. Before becoming a hunter, man had been the animal who was hunted. And before settling as a farmer who lives off the land, man had been a hunter who lived on the flesh of the animals he killed. This is linked to another crucial step in the memory of the species: the transition to a diet of meat, in which a primate that was fundamentally vegetarian changed into a carnivore, assuming a character that is typical of his own enemies. It was a radical change that had a lasting effect on his psyche. There is therefore a lasting memory of how the sacrifice took form. And that secret history, infused with guilt, leaves its traces in the actions of the sacrifice. And so guilt constitutes the basis of sacrifice, in any version.

Girard's fallacy was to think that sacrifice in the brahminic version was a disguising of the other sacrifice, which seeks to banish a scapegoat. Thus, with the boldness of the debunker—a boldness much like that of Freud's and, at one time, of Voltaire's, which the West proudly regards as one of its singular, irreplaceable qualities—Girard proceeded to unmask first Greek tragedy and then, little by little, other literary and religious forms, including finally the speculations of the Brāhmaṇas.

But in pursuing this illusion, Girard was doing nothing more than tracing back the movement in secularized society that can no longer see nature or any other power beyond itself and believes it is itself the answer for everything. A movement that is still active today and has made the world into a secular totality dotted with islands and streaks of fundamentalist religion. And here there is good reason to think that even the secularized world is prone to fundamentalism, in that the only one on which it adores lavishing offerings is society itself. Offerings that ought to give a lustrous shine: first of all advertising, the endless, ever-changing stream of images that covers every surface, the only laboratory that continues nonstop and covers the totality of time, like a *sattra.* Apart from some isolated cases, such as occasional glimpses in Simone Weil, attention has not yet been focused on the *religion of society*, which is the highest form of superstition. And yet this should be our challenge, this immense object of contemplation, so boundless and pervasive that it is not even perceived as an object.

Nature, for urban man, is a barometric variation and a few leafy islands scattered across the urban fabric. Apart from this, it is raw material for manufacture and a scenario for leisure. For Vedic man, nature was the place where the powers were manifest and where exchanges between the powers took place. Society was a cautious attempt at becoming a part of those exchanges, without disturbing them too much and without being annihilated by them.

As soon as war became total, and therefore far bloodier than any previous war in terms of death toll and weapon power, it absorbed within itself the lexical legacy of sacrifice. Victim, self-denial, consecration, redemption, trial by fire—all words and expressions recurring in war reports. Where the dominant word is *sacrifice* itself. A phenomenon that reached its peak—as if European history had converged toward that point—in the First World War. Never had the language of sacrifice been so squandered, in the absence of sacrificial *rites.* The Second World War brought a further growth in weapon power and the number of dead. But a new factor would be added: the extermination of Jews and other enemies for racial reasons by Hitler's Germany. For several years, just after the war, language faltered: there was an uncertainty about how to describe these events. By 1948, Raul Hilberg was already working on a book that would become one of the leading works on the question, entitled simply *The Destruction of the European Jews*, published in 1961. But another word soon began to spread: *holocaust.* A word that did not belong to the language of the time and describes one of the two basic types of Jewish sacrifice: *'olah*, the offering "that goes up" to the altar where the victim is completely burnt. A sacrifice quite different from the "peace offerings," *shelamim*, ceremonies where the officiants were allowed to eat a part of the sacrificial meat. And so the extermination of six million Jews by the Nazis was described using a word that suggested certain sacred ceremonies, celebrated from the time of Noah by the ancestors of those killed. Someone pointed out that this was an enormous blunder, but no one listened and the word became established by force of use in the various European languages. Something irreversible had happened: in fact, as was being discovered in all its horrendous detail, the extermination of the Jews had not been carried out as an operation of war, but as a process of disinfestation. And that process, in which the Jews had been the victims, was now being described using a word that Jews themselves, as officiants, had used for certain ceremonies to please Yahweh. The immensity of that misunderstanding was a sign that history had entered a phase where muddle and misconstruction between ancient and modern would be pushed far—much farther than ever before.

And yet, in the inappropriate and jarring choice of the word *holocaust* to describe the extermination of the Jews, an invisible hand was at work that was not just the hand of ignorance. That word was indicative of something that was lurking mysteriously. War had taken over from sacrifice, but now sacrifice was about to take the place of war. The extermination of the Jews, in the way it was carried out by the Nazis, had been something halfway between the slaughterhouse and a decontamination process. And it could have happened in peacetime, like a gigantic waste disposal operation. So military terms were no longer appropriate. And for this reason it was natural—horribly natural—to fall back on the terminology of sacrifice.

Several years would pass, and the twenty-first century opened its eyes watching the collapse of the Twin Towers. Here again, an uncertainty in language. The attackers were immediately called "cowards." But cowardice is the oddest accusation to make against someone who kills himself with full determination and maximum violence. Or the suicide attackers were called *kamikaze*. But the Japanese *kamikaze* were soldiers carrying out acts of war. Whereas the attackers in New York were civilians acting in peacetime. At work once again was a subtle wish to deflect attention, fixing it on an exotic and inappropriate word. It would have been better to open the pages of Livy and note that the Islamic suicide-killers had much in common with a mysterious sacrificial institution in ancient Rome: the *devotio*.

It is everyday experience at the beginning of the third millennium that sacrifice has become the new feature of war. Islamic suicide-killers follow variations on the Roman rite of *devotio* recorded by Livy in the case of the consul Decius Mus. In 340, while fighting against the Latins under Mount Vesuvius, having taken a vow to the gods of the underworld, he plunged on horseback into the enemy ranks and after being stabbed several times, fell *"inter maximam hostium stragem,"* among a great heap of enemies. His death had the purpose of dragging the whole army of the Latins to defeat, through its contagion.

More than the warrior, it is the figure of the suicide-killer that has brought trouble for the entire American and allied military-industrial apparatus. And this is because the lethal weapon of sacrifice is voluntary death. Much more to be feared when it conceals *substitution* within it. *Devotio*, in principle, was reserved for those who exercised supreme *imperium*, as in the case of the consul Decius. But Livy explains: *"Illud adiciendum videtur, licere consuli dictatorique et praetori, cum legiones hostium devoveat, non utique se, sed quem velit ex legione Romana scripta civem devovere; si is homo qui devotus est moritur, probe factum videri"* ("It seems proper to add here that the consul, dictator, or praetor who formulates the *devotio* for the legions of the enemy need not designate himself for the *devotio* but may also choose any citizen from a regularly enlisted Roman legion; if the man designated for the *devotio* dies, it is deemed that all is well"). The only problem might be where the soldier whom the leader designates for the *devotio* does *not* in the end die. In that case a sacrifice of atonement has to be performed: "a seven-foot-high image of the man is buried and an atonement victim is killed."

Devotio unites within itself the two extreme, most devastating possibilities of the sacrifice: the sacrifice of the person who has the charisma of power and the substitution of a human victim with another human victim, with *any* other human victim. Today, the only form of sacrifice universally visible on television screens, almost every day, is this last variant of *devotio.*

The *devotio* of Decius Mus occurred during a war that, according to Livy, much resembled a "civil war." The Romans and the Latins were too much alike "in language, customs, weapons, and military institutions." It was an ideal occasion for *devotio* to be used.

A civil war is a war where any battlefront disappears. Now the front is everywhere—and the attack can come from anyone, as happened in Iraq and Afghanistan after the Twin Towers. But *devotio* sought to drag a whole army to ruin, magically contaminated by the death of an enemy. Whereas Islamic suicide-killers cause the instant death—along with their own—of a group of people who are similar to the attacker "in language and customs." The Roman consul—or his substitute—had to fight to the death. The Islamic suicide-killer has to blow himself up. Ordeal is replaced by a death that strikes at random, as if by inscrutable decree. And above all, the *devotio* is no longer a single act that strikes a single group. Essential now is the plurality of acts, multiplied in every direction. This implies that an exclusive form of *devotio* is turned into one in which a succession of various unknown individuals substitute the absent leader. In the war against the Latins, the impulse to carry out the *devotio* had come in the silence of a night, when two consuls had been visited by the "apparition of a man of greater than human stature, and more majestic, who declared that the commander of one side, and the army of the other, must be offered up to the Manes and Mother Earth; and the army and the people whose leader has devoted the enemy legions, and himself, to death would have the victory." A divine name always has to be evoked to encourage or instigate the act.

And we continue to resort to the names of gods when it comes to weapons regarded as decisive, as if they still had an irresistible attraction. Saturn and Apollo were immediately recruited by NASA. Agni is an Indian long-range missile. Saturn could have been a valid name because of his fatal aura, and Apollo for his epithet of "he who strikes from afar," *hekatēbólos*, but for Agni the correspondence is even more convincing. Agni is Fire, the very element of which the weapon is built. And he is the first messenger, he who wove the perpetual flow between earth and sky, between the place of men and that of the gods. Agni, indeed, points toward the sky even today. But, once it has disappeared from sight and become an imperceptible dot in the atmosphere, Agni will turn around and seek out its objective on earth. A vertical voyage, up and down, which was the basis of the sacrifice, has become a horizontal movement, where the sky serves only as an obstacle-free terrain. This is the comparison that best represents the current state of affairs: the compulsion to resort to the gods, but wiping them from existence and using their names to evoke deadly power. A trick of infidels who cannot resist using the family crest.

The religion of our time is the religion of society, within which even Christianity or Islam are vast enclaves. Its herald, though he was not entirely aware of it, was Émile Durkheim, who crystallized the notion in *Les formes élémentaires de la vie religieuse*, first published in 1912. More than with elementary forms of religious life, the book dealt with the transformation of society into a religion of itself. But it is part of its nature that the religion of society does not seek to describe and identify itself as such. Its conduct is similar to that of the religions of the past: pervasive, omnipresent, like the air we breathe.

According to Durkheim, the "moral ascendancy" of society, given the pressure it exercises over every individual, would be sufficient to explain the origin of religion. As for religion itself (*any* religion—and not just that of the Australian Aborigines with which he had been concerned from the very beginning), Durkheim describes it as "the product of a certain delirium."

And if religion dies out? This would not mean that the delirium would die out. Durkheim is consequential—no one can deny it—and immediately he ventures to suggest: "Maybe there is no collective representation that is not in a sense delirious." Including therefore also the secular, skeptical collective representation of those at the beginning of the twentieth century who sought to explain the "inexplicable hallucination" they considered religion to be.

Seen from a distance of a century, this view, set out in spare and austere prose, could itself be plausibly described as a calm delirium. Society is more clinging and pressing than ever, but it is difficult to recognize a "moral ascendancy" in it. One cannot see, for example, through what argument such "moral ascendancy" could be denied to Hitler's Germany. Was it not perhaps a *society* like so many others? Conversely, there seems no doubt that life carries on, more and more, within a "fabric of hallucinations," which are the irrepressible secretions of society itself (of *any* society, in the same way as Durkheim referred to any religion): thin layers of pixels that wrap the world tighter and tighter, like a new kind of mummy, where the corpse itself tends to crumble away under the layers of bandages.

What Durkheim was describing was not the explanation of every religious phenomenon as an inevitable product of society ("the god is only a figurative expression of the society"). On the contrary: it was the founding charter for the transformation of society itself into a new all-encompassing cult, compared with which every previous form would seem inadequate and childish. But this was the overwhelming historic phenomenon that was being developed at the time of Durkheim—and which now dominates the planet. So omnipresent and so evident that it is not even noticed. Paradox: the totally secular society is one that turns out to be less secular than any other, because secularity, as soon as it extends to everything, assumes within itself those hallucinatory, phantasmal, and delirious characteristics that Durkheim had identified in religion in general. And this is what Durkheim was talking about, without meaning to and without recognizing it, when he wrote: "Thus there is one region of nature where the formula of idealism is applicable almost to the letter: this is the social kingdom." The "formula of idealism" was an antiquated way of suggesting what, a little earlier, Durkheim had described, more perspicuously, as a "fabric of hallucinations." But the crucial point was another: it was all in that "almost to the letter." Life continues from then on, and forever more, within a "social kingdom" where hallucinations have to be understood "almost to the letter."

What are rituals? Durkheim asks this in the manner of someone spying on certain unintelligible sequences of gestures. And he immediately comes to the point: "Whence could the illusion have come that with a few grains of sand thrown to the wind, or a few drops of blood shed upon a rock or the stone of an altar, it is possible to maintain the life of an animal species or of a god?" Everything points to the view that "the efficacy attributed to the rites" is no more than "the product of a chronic delirium with which humanity has abused itself."

Up to this point the reasoning is consequential. But Durkheim goes one step further. For him, rites (*all* rites) are senseless delirium, but they have a sense. Indeed, they have *one sense only*, which is found everywhere, among Australian Aborigines as much as in ancient Greece: "The effect of the cult really is to recreate periodically a moral being upon which we depend as it depends upon us. Now this being does exist: it is society." In one well-prepared move, Durkheim has managed to pull out of his magician's hat something that might seem even more hallucinatory and delirious than a god or a totemic animal: nothing less than a "moral being," who must be presumed identical everywhere and capable of embracing any form of existence insofar as it is a supreme and total being: society ("the concept of totality is only the abstract form of the concept of society"—it can be no surprise that people began talking a few years later about *totalitarianism*).

Perhaps Durkheim's view will one day appear no less improbable than that of the Urabunnas who broke off pieces of rock and threw them randomly, in all directions "in order to secure an abundant production of lizards." And yet for the whole of the twentieth century Durkheim's voice was the voice of science, of a sober and cautious learning that dispels all delirium, even though it studies its forms with diligent benevolence. And this could not happen except by way of an act of faith that conferred divine status on an invisible entity (society).

In the end, the question of rituals could be expressed in this way: society celebrates them to sustain, reaffirm, or give credence to itself—and in this case nothing marks them better than military parades on national holidays, tributes at war memorials, or speeches by heads of state at New Year (and from these rites, examples of the highest kind, all others should be inferred); or alternatively, society celebrates rituals to establish contact with something outside itself that is largely unknown and certainly powerful—something of which nature itself is a part. In this case, the model rite would also be the least visible, performed by an individual, in silence, not corresponding to fixed moments of time, as with festivals, celebrations, and commemorations. The two paths are divergent and incompatible. Separated by one essential difference: the second path can never include the first, due to the unyielding disparity between those for whom the ritual is performed. But the first can include the second: for this to happen, it is enough that the very notion of society manages to become the entity that is *largely unknown and certainly powerful* to which certain rites are directed. If this is a god—and a god who demands human victims—society has no difficulty in taking its place, as we have seen on so many occasions. Countless human beings have become victims for the benefit of society.

The word *sacrifice* has now assumed a psychological and economic meaning: this is clear to anyone. Someone *makes sacrifices* for the family. A government *asks sacrifices* from its citizens. But if the same government were to ask citizens to *celebrate sacrifices*, whether or not involving killing, the suggestion would sound very odd. It would seem like a fit of madness.

Yet mankind, for most of its history, has *celebrated sacrifices*. In

Egypt, in Mesopotamia, in India, in China, in Mexico, in Greece; in Rome and Jerusalem; in various parts of Africa, Australia, Polynesia, the Americas, central Asia and Siberia; sacrifices have been celebrated everywhere. Why then have such acts become unthinkable, at least for an entity that still calls itself the West but now extends across the whole earth?

"The great tasks of government are sacrifices and military action," we read in the *Zuo zhuan.* But "the most important task of government is sacrifice." And, in a period not so distant from this Chinese text, Plato wrote in his *Laws* that "the noblest and truest rule" was this: "For the good man, the act of sacrificing [*thýein*, a specific word for sacrifice] and engaging in continual communion with the gods through prayers, offerings, and devotions of every kind is the thing most noble and good and helpful for a happy life." Both the *Zuo zhuan* and the *Laws* seek to define the proper way of living, for the community and for the individual. And both texts immediately point to sacrifice. Something so essential might change somewhat over time (like the art of war) but it is very hard to believe that it could disappear, becoming unimaginable. And yet this is exactly what has happened with the *celebration of sacrifices.* A caesura separates the last few centuries of the secular and Christian West (and secular because previously Christian) from all that had happened previously. And this caesura is what should be studied, contemplated.

Sacrifice is a word that creates immediate embarrassment. Many use it casually when they talk about psychological considerations, money, or war. Linked always to some noble sentiment. But, if we are referring to the ritual ways of what in the past was called *sacrifice*, there is a sudden repulsion. *Sacrifice* is, by definition, something that society will *not* accept, belonging to an age that is dead and gone forever. *Sacrifice* is regarded as something barbarous, primitive, the stuff of peplums. Why, then, is the word continually used? Especially in key issues where there is nothing, it seems, to take its place.

The reasons for the sacrifices described in the *Śatapatha Brāhmaṇa* or in Porphyry's *De abstinentia* or in Leviticus remain just the same if we have a perception of the *numina*, the divine powers to whom the rites were addressed. But that perception has become confused over time. So the ceremonies seem no more that a sequence of foolish gestures, generally culminating in the killing of an animal. And this is the only point on which there is no possible blurring, since it is patently obvious to anyone today that the world depends upon the daily killing of millions of animals. Killings that take place in many different ways, but all, without exception, in obedience to one single rule: they should not take place in public. This rule is enforced in very different cultures as inviolable and inalienable, without any real voice of opposition. The killing of animals during sacrifices ought therefore to stir a universal feeling of repulsion. And so it does—yet at the same time sacrifice is associated with a series of fine and noble images. Indeed, the word itself is still used, metaphorically, in situations where it inevitably denotes something dutiful and commendable. This tangle of very strong and contradictory feelings becomes evident as soon as we begin to look at the world today, which pretends to ignore sacrifice. And perhaps in that tangle, more than anywhere else, we notice how this world of today is detached from and, at the same time, dependent on all that has preceded it. The inevitable embarrassment of anyone who approaches the question of sacrifice is only a symptom of the persistence of that tangle, which seems to become even more tightly knotted whenever we try to unravel it. And above all, for most people, it remains invisible. The simple act of being aware of it would itself bring a radical change.

It wasn't just the difference between consubstantiation and transubstantiation that worried Luther when it came to the Eucharist. There was another question to be answered. Was the Last Supper to be interpreted as a divine and human gathering, which the Mass had simply commemorated? Or was it a sacrifice, celebrated by a priest who was also the victim? And a sacrifice that heralded another sacrifice—this time a blood sacrifice—the crucifixion?

Luther had reached a point where he could no longer contain himself and, with his innate vehemence, he declared that to interpret the Mass as a sacrifice was "the most impious abuse (*impiissimus ille abusus*)" and all such teachings produced "monsters of impiety (*monstra impietatis*)." That moment marked the watershed in the Western history of sacrifice. A voice was finally saying that sacrifice could be abandoned. Or rather, that it was something barbarous and incompatible with the true religion, in which *iustus ex fide vivit*, the just man lives by faith, without resorting to particular gestures, particular acts, as a way of seeking justification through pious works. And on this point Luther was inflexible.

But so too was the Roman Church. Here it was not a question of deploring or defending indulgences, something blamable on weaknesses that were human, all too human. Here the entire liturgy was at stake, and the very framework of religious life. And so on September 17, 1562, forty-two years after Luther had proclaimed his terrible words, the Council of Trent promulgated nine canons. The first of these was that of: "Anathemizing anyone who shall say that in the Mass no true and proper sacrifice is offered to God," whereas the third obstinately condemned "anyone who shall say that the Mass is a sacrifice only of praise and thanks or bare commemoration of the sacrifice of the cross, and not propitiatory, or that it benefits only they who receive it and must not be offered for the living, for the dead, for sins, suffering, satisfactions, and other needs." Here was a rejection, therefore, not only of the negation of sacrifice but also of that form of euphemism that meant transforming the Mass into the *commemoration* of a sacrifice. Because commemorating is not the same as performing, it no longer belongs to that sphere of actions that are efficacious. Here once again, after so many empty disputes, was the arcane and archaic wisdom of the Roman Church, its capacity to recognize when a founding principle of its very existence was at stake. But it was a battle already lost. Luther was not just suggesting that a part of religious society wanted to be rid of sacrifice, but that the whole of secular society, in its expansion over the world scene, would look upon sacrifice as a meaningless institution, to be consigned to the lumber room. Four centuries later, it is no surprise that a Catholic theologian, Stefan Orth, ends his inquiry into various recent writings on sacrifice by saying that nowadays "many Catholics are in agreement with the verdict and the conclusions of the reformer Martin Luther, according to whom speaking of a sacrifice in the Mass would be 'the most great and tremendous horror' and an 'accursed idolatry.'" It is a sort of delayed surrender of arms, as if world pressure has forced the Catholic Church to abandon even this doctrine. Without which, however, the entire edifice of St. Peter would inevitably collapse.

Jesus's gesture of breaking bread during the Last Supper and speaking the words *"Hoc est corpus meum"* is a dazzling ray of light that opens up two horizons, behind and ahead. Behind Jesus himself we can look back to the beginning, to the situation when the officiant and the oblation are the same (*"ipse offerens, ipse et oblatio,"* in the words of Augustine). A situation to which every sacrifice alludes, but which is reserved for the deity. Ahead of Jesus is a view that goes beyond the observer, toward that which has still to take place. In fact, the sacrifice announced by the *fractio panis*, which prefigures the dislocation and fracturing of his joints in the crucifixion, is not a sacrifice but a death sentence confirmed by the voice of the people. Therefore it is something belonging not to the religious domain but to the secular domain and, ultimately, to the domain of public opinion. Two extremes are therefore set: on one side the sacrifice that no man can celebrate, except by committing suicide; on the other the abandonment of sacrifice, substituted by a judicial sentence and by the majority choice of a community. The Eucharistic innovation suggests the opening up of two conflicting and incompatible perspectives. The sacramental bread will assume the name of *hostia*, which is the technical term describing the oblation in sacrifices of atonement. But Jesus's trial and the carrying out of his sentence will follow a procedure imposed by the Roman state, alien to the religion of Jesus's own people. There remained only one point of contact with the sacrifice: the killing would take place *"extra castra,"* outside the city.

Reading the *Śatapatha Brāhmaṇa* is like making a journey to the radiant heart of India. But the idea—later abandoned—of a commentary certainly did not aim to do that. On the contrary, it was an attempt to move away from any specific coordinates of time and place to return to observing certain simple gestures, of which we may be aware or unaware, but are always with us and without which we could not exist: the actions of breathing, swallowing, copulating, cutting, killing, evacuating, speaking, burning, pouring, thinking, dreaming, watching—and more. Cultures have practiced each of these actions, indeed they have become identified with the methods and techniques used to develop them. But, once the anthropologists had seemingly concluded the work of listing all of these configurations, a sense of indifference and atony took over. All of these cultures marched off, in formation, like lead soldiers each dressed in different uniforms. Marching off not to war but to a World Exposition—one respectful of all diversity and futile in its foundation, which was simply this: all diversity is to be respected, because, within a particular culture, it serves to maintain social balance. But, since we are concerned here with techniques, each placed on the same level, how do we work out which will be the right technique? And what could it mean for a technique to be *right*? Every technique, by its nature, recognizes only one criterion, that of effectiveness. But effective in relation to what? The only acceptable technique is that which relates to material power and conquest. But what if we are aiming for an effectiveness of another kind? Then, perhaps, the Brāhmaṇas might be helpful. Because they deal only with irreducible gestures, eliminating any other concern. And because they introduce techniques and criteria of effectiveness that very often seem to be ironic and impatient glosses on what, three thousand years later, has established itself as common sense. Such an abrupt and disorientating shift of perspective might well be beneficial in itself, like a sudden change of air.

The gods appear like foam, ready to be blown away. Their waves persist. "A divine vitality, infinitely agile and deceptive," wrote Céline in a letter of 1934, thinking of the America that was around him. He was also referring to the world.

In the end, we might well ask: what can be the relevance of all we read in the Veda, seeing that it has nothing to do with modern life in a secular society? None, we could say. But then quantum mechanics has no correspondence whatsoever with modern life, whereas Newtonian physics has ended up becoming the very model of common sense. And should we then perhaps think of quantum mechanics as unimportant? The Veda might be more comparable to a microphysics of the mind than to other categories (archaic or magic or primitive thought or other descriptions of that kind, now inert). The impressive vividness of those writings, even though nothing of them is borne out by common experience, might indicate that something of that-which-is continues to appear as the Vedic seers saw it. Or at least it resembles nothing so much as what the *ṛṣis* have passed down to us.

In the present world there are so many brands that strive to become myths. But the expression "myths of today" is a lexical abuse. A myth is one fork in one branch of a vast tree. To understand it we need to have a view of the whole tree and the great number of other forks that are hidden within it. That tree has not existed for a long time—well-honed axes have chopped it down. Modern stories that most resemble myths (Don Giovanni, Faust) therefore have no trunk on which to attach themselves. They are stories that are orphaned, self-sufficient, but have none of that sap which flows inside a tree of myths and whose composition is constant in every part of it—a sap that contains a certain coefficient of truth. And it is that very coefficient of truth that enables us to understand and make use of stories from the most distant times and places. What these stories offer is something that, once found, remains unscathed by any further investigation or discovery. Anyone who has entered the flow of mythical stories can let himself be swept anywhere, knowing that one day the very same current will bring him back to the land from where he first set off. And from where he may, at any moment, set off once again.

NOTES

The first number refers to the page, the second to the line of text where the quotation ends. The translations of Vedic and classical texts are the author and translator's own unless otherwise indicated.

I. REMOTE BEINGS

4, 34 *Ṛgveda*, 10.68.12.

4, 35 *Viṣṇu Purāṇa*, 4.6.9.

5, 2 Ibid., 4.6.32.

5, 10 *Ṛgveda*, 10.109.4.

6, 23 *Śatapatha Brāhmaṇa*, 10.5.2.6.

7, 7 Ibid., 3.1.1.2.

7, 36 Joseph Conrad, *Chance* (1913), Oxford University Press, Oxford, 1988, p. 4.

8, 14 *Śatapatha Brāhmaṇa*, 4.2.5.10.

8, 36 Ibid., 1.2.4.4.

9, 33 Louis Renou, "L'Ambiguité du vocabulaire du Ṛgveda" (1939), in *Choix d'études indiennes*, edited by N. Balbir and G. J. Pinault, Presses de l'École Française d'Extrême-Orient, Paris, 1997, vol. I, p. 113.

9, 37 Louis Renou, *Langue et religion dans le Ṛgveda* (1949), in *Choix d'études indiennes*, cit., vol. I, p. 11.

11, 6 *Śatapatha Brāhmaṇa*, 13.3.3.6.

11, 10 Ibid., 13.2.10.1.

12, 2 Ibid., 3.6.2.26.

13, 2 Louis Renou, *Religions of Ancient India* (1953), second edition, The Athlone Press, University of London, 1972, p. 1.

13, 33 Frits Staal, *Rules Without Meaning*, Peter Lang, New York, 1989, p. 65.

16, 21 Michael Witzel, *Das Alte Indien*, Beck, München, 2003, pp. 28–29.

16, 26 *Ṛgveda*, 3.26.5.

16, 30 Ibid., 1.88.1.

16, 31 Ibid., 5.59.2.

16, 33 Ibid., 5.60.3.

17, 9 Paul-Louis Couchoud, *Sages et poètes d'Asie*, p. 6, cited in the Introduction to *Hymnes et prières du Veda*, edited by Louis Renou, Librairie d'Amérique et d'Orient, Adrien-Maisonneuve, Paris, 1938, p. 1.

17, 14 Letter from Stéphane Mallarmé to Paul Verlaine, November 16, 1885, in *Correspondance*, edited by H. Mondor and L. J. Austin, Gallimard, Paris, 1965, vol. II, p. 301.

17, 23 *Ṛgveda*, 4.58.1 (trans. Louis Renou).

18, 18 Arthur Schopenhauer, *The World as Will and Representation* (1818), trans. E.F.J. Payne, Dover Publications, New York, 1966, p. xv.

19, 7 *Ṛgveda*, 4.5.3.
19, 8 Louis Renou, "Les Pouvoirs de la parole dans le Ṛgveda," in *Études védiques et pāṇinéennes* (1955), second edition, Collège de France, Paris, 1980, vol. I, p. 10.
19, 22 *Śatapatha Brāhmaṇa*, 1.4.1.13.
20, 6 Ibid., 5.1.1.1.
20, 21 *Ṛgveda*, 8.48.3.
20, 30 Ibid., 8.48.9.
20, 34 Ibid.
21, 3 Ibid., 8.48.5.
21, 5 Ibid., 8.48.7.

II. YĀJÑAVALKYA

25, 12 Frits Staal, *Discovering the Vedas*, Penguin, New Delhi, 2008, p. 77.
26, 6 *Śatapatha Brāhmaṇa*, 11.3.1.2–4.
26, 18 Ibid., 1.1.2.17.
26, 33 *Jaiminīya Brāhmaṇa*, 1.19 (trans. Louis Renou).
26, 33 *Bṛhadāraṇyaka Upaniṣad*, 4.2.1.
27, 1 Ibid.
27, 8 Ibid
27, 10 Ibid.
27, 23 Ibid., 4.2.2.
27, 28 René Guénon, *Le Règne de la Quantité et les Signes des Temps*, Gallimard, Paris, 1945, p. 114.
27, 35 *Bṛhadāraṇyaka Upaniṣad*, 1.4.1.
28, 5 Ibid., 4.2.3.
28, 10 *Śatapatha Brāhmaṇa*, 10.5.2.11.
28, 18 *Bṛhadāraṇyaka Upaniṣad*, 4.2.4.
28, 31 Ibid.
29, 9 Ibid., 4.3.1.
29, 26 Ibid., 4.3.33.
29, 34 *Śatapatha Brāhmaṇa*, 11.6.2.5.
30, 5 Ibid., 11.6.2.10.
31, 14 Ibid., 1.3.1.21.
31, 30 Ibid., 3.1.1.4.
32, 3 Ibid., 3.1.1.5.
32, 19 *Bṛhadāraṇyaka Upaniṣad*, 3.1.2.
32, 37 Ibid., 3.1.3.
33, 14 Ibid.
33, 29 Ibid., 3.1.4.
34, 5 Ibid., 3.1.3.
33, 13 Ibid.
35, 7 Ibid.
35, 20 Ibid., 3.1.6.
36, 10 Ibid.
36, 20 Ibid., 3.9.26.

36, 28 Ibid., 3.6.1.
37, 10 Ibid., 3.8.2.
37, 13 Ibid., 3.8.3.
37, 14 Ibid., 3.8.4.
37, 15 Ibid., 3.8.7.
37, 19 Ibid., 3.8.1.
37, 22 Ibid., 3.8.10.
37, 23 Franz Kafka, *Nachgelassene Schriften und Fragmente II*, edited by J. Schillemeit, in *Kritische Ausgabe*, edited by J. Born, G. Neumann, M. Pasley, and J. Schillemeit, S. Fischer, Frankfurt a. M., 1982, p. 124.
37, 31 *Bṛhadāraṇyaka Upaniṣad*, 3.8.8.
38, 7 Ibid., 3.8.11.
38, 9 Ibid.
38, 14 Ibid., 3.8.10.
38, 38 Julius Eggeling, Introduction to *The Śatapatha-Brāhmaṇa*, Sacred Books of the East, Clarendon Press, Oxford, 1900, vol. V, p. xiii.
39, 9 Plato, *Republic*, 614b (trans. H. P. Lee), Penguin Classics, 1955.
40, 4 *Śatapatha Brāhmaṇa*, 1.9.3.16.
40, 7 Ibid., 1.4.3.1.
40, 9 Ibid.
40, 22 Ibid., 2.3.2.13.
40, 24 Johann Wolfgang Goethe, "Epirrhema," line 6, in *Gedenkausgabe der Werke, Briefe und Gespräche*, edited by E. Beutler, Artemis, Zürich-Stuttgart, 1950, vol. I, p. 519.
41, 6 *Śatapatha Brāhmaṇa*, 4.1.3.8.
41, 21 Ibid., 4.1.3.3.
41, 23 Ibid., 4.1.3.4.
41, 27 Ibid., 4.1.3.6.
41, 28 Ibid., 4.1.3.7.
42, 9 Ibid., 5.1.3.6 (Kāṇva recension).
42, 18 *Bṛhadāraṇyaka Upaniṣad*, 1.4.1.
42, 21 Ibid., 1.4.3.
42, 22 Ibid.
42, 27 Ibid.
42, 30 Ibid.
42, 34 Ibid., 1.4.4.
42, 38 Ibid.
43, 5 Sophocles, *Antigone*, 781.
43, 11 *Bṛhadāraṇyaka Upaniṣad*, 4.3.21.
43, 13 Ibid., 1.4.1.
43, 14 Ibid., 1.4.3.
43, 21 Louis Renou, "Le Passage des Brāhmaṇa aux Upaniṣad" (1953), in *Choix d'études indiennes*, cit., vol. II, p. 906.
43, 23 Ibid.
43, 28 Ibid., p. 907.
44, 3 *Bṛhadāraṇyaka Upaniṣad*, 4.5.1–2.
44, 15 Ibid., 4.5.6.

44, 16 Ibid., 4.5.7.
44, 22 Ibid., 4.5.15.

III. ANIMALS

47, 9 *Śatapatha Brāhmaṇa*, 11.6.1.3.
47, 14 Ibid., 11.6.1.7.
47, 25 Ibid., 11.1.6.19.
49, 14 Ibid., 11.7.1.2.
50, 2 Ibid., 3.7.3.2.
50, 2 Ibid.
50, 31 Ibid., 3.7.3.1–5.
52, 24 Ibid., 3.7.3.4.
52, 36 Ibid., 3.7.4.2.
53, 1 Ibid.
53, 2 Ibid., 3.7.4.1.
53, 8 Ibid., 3.7.4.3.
53, 13 Ibid., 3.7.4.5.
53, 16 Ibid.
54, 24 Ibid., 3.1.2.13–17.
55, 2 Ibid., 3.1.2.14.
55, 17 Ibid., 3.1.3.7.
56, 9 Ibid., 3.1.2.17.
56, 13 Ibid.
56, 15 Ibid.
57, 6 Ibid., 3.1.2.13.
57, 6 Ibid.
57, 34 Ibid.
58, 9 Ibid., 3.1.2.18.
59, 11 Ibid., 3.1.2.21.
59, 14 Ibid.
59, 20 Ibid.
59, 27 Ibid.
59, 30 Ibid.
60, 14 Ibid., 3.6.3.19.
60, 24 Ibid., 3.6.4.14.
60, 25 Ibid., 3.6.4.10.
60, 28 Ibid., 3.1.2.7.
60, 28 Ibid., 12.9.2.6.
60, 29 Ibid., 3.6.4.15.
60, 30 Ibid., 3.6.4.13.
60, 30 Ibid., 3.6.4.19.
60, 32 Ibid., 2.1.4.16.
60, 32 Ibid., 3.6.4.7.
60, 38 Ibid., 3.1.3.18.
61, 13 Ibid., 3.6.4.6.
61, 17 Ibid., 3.6.4.7.

62, 9 Ibid., 3.6.4.18.
62, 20 Ibid., 3.6.4.26.
63, 25 *Odyssey* XII, 129–30.
63, 27 Ibid., XII, 130–31.
63, 36 Ibid., XII, 341–42.
64, 8 Ibid., XII, 343.
64, 17 Ibid., XII, 297.

IV. THE PROGENITOR

67, 5 *Aitareya Brāhmaṇa*, 3.21 (trans. Charles Malamoud).
67, 6 Ibid.
67, 7 *Taittirīya Brāhmaṇa*, 2.2.10.1.
67, 9 *Ṛgveda*, 10.121.1.
67, 10 Ibid., 10.121.8.
67, 18 *Śatapatha Brāhmaṇa*, 4.5.7.2.
67, 27 *Ṛgveda*, 10.121.2.
68, 8 Ibid., 10.121.7.
68, 23 *Śatapatha Brāhmaṇa*, 11.5.8.1.
68, 27 Ibid.
68, 30 Ibid., 6.1.1.1.
69, 16 *Pañcaviṃśa Brāhmaṇa*, 20.14.2.
69, 21 *Śatapatha Brāhmaṇa*, 6.1.2.6.
69, 27 Ibid., 6.1.2.8.
70, 8 Ibid., 6.1.1.1.
70, 14 Ibid., 6.1.1.2.
70, 22 Ibid., 6.1.1.3.
70, 27 Ibid., 6.1.1.5.
71, 7 *Jaiminīya Brāhmaṇa*, 2.159 (trans. Willem Caland).
71, 16 *Pañcaviṃśa Brāhmaṇa*, 24.13.2.
71, 22 Ibid., 24.13.3.
71, 37 *Śatapatha Brāhmaṇa*, 13.3.1.1.
72, 28 *Maitrāyaṇī Saṃhitā*, 1.8.1.
72, 33 *Jaiminīya Brāhmaṇa*, 1.283.
73, 3 Paul Deussen, *Allgemeine Geschichte der Philosophie*, third edition, 1, Brockhaus, Leipzig, 1920, vol. I, p. 190.
73, 5 A. Berriedale Keith, *The Religion and Philosophy of the Veda and Upanishads*, Harvard University Press, Cambridge, 1925, vol. II, p. 442.
73, 31 *Jaiminīya Brāhmaṇa*, 1.357 (trans. Jan Gonda).
74, 11 *Śatapatha Brāhmaṇa*, 10.4.4.2.
74, 19 Ibid., 10.4.4.3.
74, 37 Ibid., 2.2.4.4.
75, 4 Ibid.
75, 14 Ibid., 2.2.4.6.
75, 17 Ibid.
75, 26 Ibid., 2.2.4.9.
77, 30 Ibid., 1.7.4.1–8.

78, 1 Ibid., 1.8.1.10.
78, 18 Ibid., 1.7.4.4.
78, 26 Ibid., 1.7.4.9.
79, 15 Ibid., 1.7.4.15.
79, 18 Ibid., 1.7.4.19.
80, 4 Charles Malamoud, "Tenir parole, retenir sa voix," in *L'inactuel* 5, Autumn 2000, p. 223.
80, 14 *Śatapatha Brāhmaṇa*, 1.7.4.18.
80, 30 Ibid., 10.4.4.1.
81, 23 Ibid., 10.6.5.1.
81, 32 Ibid., 10.1.3.1.
82, 15 *Jaiminīya Brāhmaṇa*, 2.69.
82, 20 *Śatapatha Brāhmaṇa*, 10.4.3.3.
82, 23 Ibid., 10.4.3.4.
82, 28 Ibid., 10.4.3.6.
82, 32 Ibid., 10.4.3.20.
83, 3 Ibid., 10.4.3.9.
84, 3 Ibid., 10.5.2.3.
84, 7 Ibid.
84, 15 Ibid., 11.4.3.1–2.
86, 2 Ibid., 10.4.4.5, which cites *Ṛgveda*, 1.179.3.
86, 34 Ibid., 9.4.1.4.
87, 6 Ibid., 9.4.1.15.
87, 12 Ibid., 2.5.2.2.
87, 18 Ibid., 2.5.2.13.
88, 2 Ibid., 6.1.2.23.
88, 6 Ibid.
88, 24 *Chāndogya Upaniṣad*, 4.10.3.
88, 28 Ibid., 4.10.5 (trans. Émile Senart).
88, 31 Ibid. (trans. Émile Senart).
88, 36 *Bṛhadāraṇyaka Upaniṣad*, 5.1.1.
89, 2 *Śatapatha Brāhmaṇa*, 7.1.2.1.
89, 5 Ibid.
89, 30 *Chāndogya Upaniṣad*, 3.12.7–9 (trans. Émile Senart).
90, 8 Armand Minard, *Trois Énigmes sur les Cent Chemins*, Les Belles Lettres, Paris, 1949, vol. I, pp. 80–81.
90, 10 *Śatapatha Brāhmaṇa*, 10.3.4.3.
90, 13 Stella Kramrisch, "Pūṣan" (1961), in *Exploring India's Sacred Art*, edited by B. Stoler Miller, University of Pennsylvania Press, Philadelphia, 1983, p. 171.
90, 17 *Śatapatha Brāhmaṇa*, 10.3.4.5.
90, 21 Ibid.
90, 25 *Bṛhadāraṇyaka Upaniṣad*, 1.1.1.
90, 35 Ibid., 1.2.1.
91, 1 Ibid., 1.2.2.
91, 6 Ibid., 1.2.4.
91, 12 Ibid., 1.2.6.
91, 16 Ibid., 1.2.7.

91, 19 Ibid.
91, 23 Ibid.
91, 31 Ibid.
91, 36 *Śatapatha Brāhmaṇa*, 10.1.3.1.
92, 2 Ibid., 10.4.2.2.
92, 2 Ibid.
92, 11 Ibid., 10.4.3.3.
92, 18 Ibid., 11.5.4.1.
92, 20 Ibid., 11.5.4.2.
92, 25 Ibid., 4.5.5.1; 4.5.6.1; 4.5.7.1.
93, 24 Ibid., 1.2.4.21.
93, 28 Ibid.
93, 35 Ibid., 4.6.1.4.

V. THEY WHO SAW THE HYMNS

97, 16 Hermann Oldenberg, *Vorwissenschaftliche Wissenschaft*, Vandenhoeck & Ruprecht, Göttingen, 1919, p. 54.
98, 6 Ibid.
98, 20 Ibid., p. 224.
98, 31 Louis Renou, *La Poésie religieuse de l'Inde antique*, P.U.F., Paris, 1942, p. 4.
98, 34 Ibid.
100, 15 *The Poem of Erra*, 162.
100, 16 *Ṛgveda*, 1.164.15.
100, 32 *Śatapatha Brāhmaṇa*, 2.1.2.4.
101, 31 Ibid., 1.4.3.6.
102, 5 Ibid., 3.4.4.27.
102, 36 *Ṛgveda*, 7.33.5.
103, 7 Ibid., 7.83.7.
103, 20 *Devībhāgavata Purāṇa*, 6.12.26.
103, 23 *Taittirīya Saṃhitā*, 3.5.2.1.

VI. THE ADVENTURES OF MIND AND SPEECH

107, 5 *Vājasaneyi Saṃhitā*, 34.1 (trans. Louis Renou).
107, 7 Ibid., 34.2.
107, 8 Ibid.
107, 9 Ibid., 34.4.
107, 10 Ibid., 34.6.
107, 12 Ibid., 34.1–6.
107, 18 Ibid., 34.6.
107, 26 *Ṛgveda*, 10.129.1.
107, 27 *Śatapatha Brāhmaṇa*, 10.5.3.1.
108, 3 Ibid., 10.5.3.2.
108, 31 *Taittirīya Brāhmaṇa*, 2.2.9.1.
109, 3 Ibid., 2.5.11.4.

109, 3 *Śatapatha Brāhmaṇa*, 4.1.1.22.
109, 35 Ibid., 1.4.4.2.
110, 10 Ibid., 1.4.4.9.
110, 12 Ibid.
110, 14 Ibid., 1.4.4.5.
110, 18 Ibid., 1.4.4.7.
111, 7 Ibid., 1.4.5.9–12.
111, 21 *Iliad*, II, 205; II, 319; IV, 59.
111, 37 *Śatapatha Brāhmaṇa*, 3.2.1.18.
112, 36 Ibid., 3.2.1.19–22.
113, 25 Ibid., 3.2.1.24.
113, 28 Ibid.
113, 34 Ibid., 3.2.1.26.
113, 37 Ibid., 3.2.1.27.
114, 11 Ibid., 3.2.1.28.
115, 29 *Chāndogya Upaniṣad*, 7.3.1.
116, 4 Ibid.
116, 8 *Śatapatha Brāhmaṇa*, 3.4.3.14.
116, 16 Ibid., 3.4.3.16.
116, 18 Ibid., 3.2.1.25.
116, 24 Ibid., 3.4.2.15.
116, 25 Ibid., 3.4.2.16.

VII. *ĀTMAN*

119, 8 *Ṛgveda*, 1.164.20.
120, 16 *Śatapatha Brāhmaṇa*, 12.3.4.11.
120, 21 *Bṛhadāraṇyaka Upaniṣad*, 1.4.1.
120, 35 Ibid., 1.4.5.
122, 31 *Chāndogya Upaniṣad*, 7.1.1.
122, 34 Ibid.
122, 37 Ibid., 7.1.2.
123, 8 Ibid.
123, 15 Ibid., 7.1.3.
123, 20 Ibid.
123, 24 Ibid., 7.2.1.
123, 32 Ibid.
124, 11 Ibid., 7.4.2.
124, 16 Ibid., 7.5.1.
124, 26 Ibid., 7.5.2.
124, 34 Ibid., 7.6.1.
125, 5 Ibid.
125, 9 Ibid., 7.7.1.
125, 16 Ibid., 7.8.1.
125, 27 Ibid., 7.15.4.
125, 33 Ibid., 7.16.1.
126, 3 Ibid., 7.22.1.

126, 6 Ibid., 7.1.3.
126, 10 Ibid., 7.23.1.
126, 12 Ibid., 7.25.1.
126, 18 Ibid.
126, 28 Ibid., 7.25.2.
126, 31 Ibid., 7.26.1.
126, 37 Ibid., 7.26.2.
127, 3 Ibid.
127, 22 Ibid., 7.23.1.
128, 6 Ibid., 7.25.2.
128, 15 Ibid., 7.1.1.
128, 19 Ibid., 6.1.2.
128, 27 Ibid., 6.2.1.
128, 29 Ibid., 6.2.3.
129, 2 Ibid., 6.4.5.
129, 5 Ibid., 6.8.7.
129, 13 *Ṛgveda*, 10.72.2.
129, 15 *Taittirīya Upaniṣad*, 2.7.1.
129, 17 *Chāndogya Upaniṣad*, 3.19.1.
129, 36 *Ṛgveda*, 10.129.1 (trans. Louis Renou).
129, 37 Ibid., 10.129.3.
130, 1 Ibid., 10.129.2.
130, 2 Ibid., 10.129.3.
130, 3 Ibid., 10.129.2.
130, 7 Ibid., 10.82.6.
130, 8 Ibid., 10.129.2.
130, 10 Ibid., 10.129.3.
130, 17 Louis Renou in *Hymnes spéculatifs du Véda*, edited by Louis Renou, Gallimard, Paris, 1956, p. 254.
130, 18 Karl Friedrich Geldner, *Der Rig-Veda aus dem Sanskrit ins Deutsche Übersetzt*, Harvard University Press, Cambridge, 1951, vol. III, p. 360.
130, 21 *Ṛgveda*, 10.27.4.
130, 30 Ibid., 10.129.4.
130, 38 Ibid.
131, 19 Ibid., 10.129.5.
131, 21 Ibid.
131, 23 Ibid.
131, 30 Ibid., 10.129.6.
131, 34 Ibid., 10.129.7.
132, 15 *Śatapatha Brāhmaṇa*, 11.2.2.6.
132, 20 Ibid.

VIII. PERFECT WAKEFULNESS

135, 11 *Ṛgveda*, 8.2.18.
136, 6 *Śatapatha Brāhmaṇa*, 6.8.2.8.
136, 9 Ibid., 6.8.2.11.

136, 10 Ibid.
136, 26 *Bṛhadāraṇyaka Upaniṣad*, 1.4.10.
136, 28 Ibid.
136, 35 Ibid.
137, 1 Ibid.
137, 20 Louis Renou, "Sur la notion de 'brahman'" (1949), in collaboration with L. Silburn, in *L'Inde fondamentale*, edited by Charles Malamoud, Hermann, Paris, 1978, p. 114.
137, 20 J. C. Heesterman, *The Broken World of Sacrifice*, University of Chicago Press, Chicago, 1993, p. 156.
137, 23 *Bṛhadāraṇyaka Upaniṣad*, 4.4.23.
137, 24 Ibid., 4.4.6.
137, 29 *Kaṭha Upaniṣad*, 5.8.
137, 36 Geldner, *Der Rig-Veda aus dem Sanskrit ins Deutsche Übersetzt*, cit., vol. II, p. 46.
137, 36 Ibid.
138, 1 Louis Renou, *Études védiques et pāniṇéennes*, De Boccard, Paris, 1958, vol. IV, p. 69.
138, 5 Geldner, *Der Rig-Veda aus dem Sanskrit ins Deutsche Übersetzt*, cit., vol. II, p. 46.
138, 9 Hermann Oldenberg, *Ṛgveda. Textkritische und exegetische Noten*, Weidmannsche Buchhandlung, Berlin, 1909, p. 340.
138, 15 *Ṛgveda*, 5.44.14 (trans. Louis Renou).
138, 16 Stella Kramrisch, *The Presence of Śiva*, Princeton University Press, Princeton, 1981, p. 3.
138, 20 Sylvain Lévi, *La Doctrine du sacrifice dans les Brâhmaṇas* (1898), P.U.F., Paris, 1966, p. 81.
138, 30 *Śatapatha Brāhmaṇa*, 3.2.1.16.
139, 13 Ibid., 3.2.1.31.
139, 30 Ibid., 3.2.1.40.
139, 33 Ibid.
140, 1 Ibid., 2.1.4.7.
140, 11 Ibid., 2.1.4.1.
140, 12 Ibid., 2.1.4.7.
140, 15 Ibid.
140, 24 Ibid., 3.1.1.8.
140, 28 Henri Hubert and Marcel Mauss, "Essai sur la nature et la fonction du sacrifice" (1899), in Marcel Mauss, *Œuvres*, Minuit, Paris, 1968, vol. I, p. 213.
140, 36 *Taittirīya Saṃhitā*, 1.2.2.3.
141, 2 *Śatapatha Brāhmaṇa*, 3.1.3.25.
141, 6 Hubert and Mauss, "Essai sur la nature et la fonction du sacrifice," cit., p. 214.
141, 21 *Śatapatha Brāhmaṇa*, 11.5.6.3.
141, 34 Ibid., 11.5.7.4.

IX. THE BRĀHMAṆAS

146, 10 Michael Witzel, *On Magical Thought in the Veda*, Universitaire Pers, Leiden, 1979, p. 20.

146, 13 Ibid.

147, 33 L. Renou, "Cérémonies védiques dans l'Inde contemporaine" (1949), in *Choix d'études indiennes*, cit., vol. II, p. 845.

147, 36 Ibid.

149, 3 Charles Malamoud, "Sans lieu ni date," in *Tracés de fondation*, edited by M. Detienne, Peeters, Louvain-Paris, 1990, p. 188.

149, 4 Ibid., p. 190.

149, 8 *Ṛgveda*, 10.82.7 (trans. Louis Renou).

149, 10 Malamoud, "Sans lieu ni date," cit., p. 188.

149, 18 *Ṛgveda*, 10.129.3.

149, 31 *Śatapatha Brāhmaṇa*, 10.6.3.1.

149, 32 Ibid., 10.6.3.2.

149, 34 Ibid.

150, 4 Ibid.

150, 9 Ibid.

150, 12 Ibid.

150, 14 Ibid.

150, 32 *Bṛhadāraṇyaka Upaniṣad*, 1.1.1.

151, 16 *Śatapatha Brāhmaṇa*, 10.4.3.9.

152, 7 Ibid., 10.5.4.16.

152, 11 Ibid.

152, 29 Ibid., 11.5.8.6.

153, 15 Staal, *Discovering the Vedas*, cit., p. 151.

154, 26 Louis Renou, "Les Connexions entre le rituel et la grammaire en sanskrit" (1941–1942), in *Choix d'études indiennes*, vol. I, cit., p. 366.

154, 27 Frits Staal, *Jouer avec le feu*, Collège de France, Paris, 1990, p. 80.

154, 35 Ibid., p. 6.

155, 3 Ibid., p. 5.

155, 23 Berriedale Keith, *The Religion and Philosophy of the Veda and Upanishads*, cit., p. 483.

156, 1 Michael Witzel, Introduction to *Kaṭha Āraṇyaka*, edited by Michael Witzel, Harvard University Press, Cambridge, 2004, p. xxxi.

156, 32 Ibid.

157, 17 L. Renou and L. Silburn, "Nírukta and ánirukta," in *Sarūpa-bhāratī*, edited by J. N. Agrawal and B. D. Shastri, Vishveshvaranand Institute Publications, Hoshiarpur, 1954, p. 76.

158, 7 Karl Hoffmann, "Die magische Weltanschauung im Veda" (1959), in *Aufsätze zur Indoiranistik*, edited by S. Glauch, R. Plath, and S. Ziegler, Reichert, Wiesbaden, 1992, vol. III, p. 709.

158, 27 Marcel Mauss, "Introduction aux mythes" (1903), in *Œuvres*, cit., vol. II, 1969, p. 271.

158, 30 Marcel Mauss, "Mythologie grecque et théorie des mythes selon Gruppe" (1903), in *Œuvres*, cit., vol. II, 1969, p. 283.

158, 33 Marcel Mauss, "Leçons sur l'unité des systèmes mythiques et rituels" (1932–1933), in *Œuvres*, cit., 1969, vol. II, p. 289.
158, 37 Ibid.

X. THE LINE OF THE FIRES

163, 2 *Śatapatha Brāhmaṇa*, 1.1.1.1.
163, 9 *Ṛgveda*, 1.179.5.
163, 20 *Śatapatha Brāhmaṇa*, 2.3.3.13.
164, 3 Ibid., 7.1.2.14.
164, 13 Ibid., 2.3.3.15.
164, 24 Ibid., 2.3.3.13.
165, 7 Ibid., 1.8.3.20.
165, 23 A. K. Coomaraswamy, "An Indian Temple: The Kandarya Mahadeo" (1947), in *Selected Papers*, edited by R. Lipsey, Princeton University Press, Princeton, 1977, vol. I, p. 3.
165, 26 *Śatapatha Brāhmaṇa*, 3.1.1.8.
165, 27 Ibid.
165, 34 Ibid., 3.1.2.20.
166, 4 Ibid., 2.1.4.7.
166, 4 Ibid.
166, 11 *Atharvaveda*, 9.2.2.
166, 12 Ibid., 9.2.3.
166, 24 *Śatapatha Brāhmaṇa*, 1.1.1.4–5.
167, 7 *Maitrāyaṇī Saṃhitā*, 1.8.7.
167, 10 H. W. Bodewitz, *The Daily Evening and Morning Offering ("agnihotra") According to the Brāhmaṇas*, Brill, Leiden, 1976, p. 118.
167, 17 *Āpastamba Śrauta Sūtra*, 6.5.3 (trans. Paul-Émile Dumont).
167, 18 Ibid. (trans. Willem Caland).
167, 33 Michael Witzel, "How to Enter the Vedic Mind? Strategies in Translating a 'Brāhmaṇa' Text," in *Translating, Translations, Translators: From India to the West*, edited by E. Garzilli, Harvard University Press, Cambridge, Mass., 1996, p. 172.
168, 6 Franz Kafka, *The Castle*, chapter 18, translated by Willa and Edwin Muir, Penguin, London, 1957, p. 254.
168, 9 W. Rau, Review of Louis Renou, "Études védiques et pāṇinéennes," vol. XVI, De Boccard, Paris, 1967, in *Orientalistische Literaturzeitung* LXIV, 1/2, 1969, col. 72.
168, 32 *Śatapatha Brāhmaṇa*, 1.1.1.11.
168, 36 Ibid., 1.1.1.13.
168, 37 Ibid.
169, 16 Ibid.
169, 20 Ibid., 6.3.1.12.
169, 22 Ibid., 14.1.2.8.
169, 29 Charles Malamoud, "Tenir parole, retenir sa voix," cit., p. 223.
169, 36 Sāyaṇa on the *Śatapatha Brāhmaṇa*, 1.6.1.20.
170, 5 *Śatapatha Brāhmaṇa*, 1.1.1.14.

170, 7 Ibid.
170, 10 Ibid., 1.1.1.17.
170, 23 Ibid., 1.1.1.21.
170, 30 Ibid.
171, 28 Ibid., 1.3.3.11.
174, 24 Ibid., 1.9.3.23.
174, 30 Ibid., 1.9.2.32.
174, 33 Ibid., 1.9.3.23.
174, 37 Ibid.
175, 19 Ibid., 2.2.2.18.
175, 34 Ibid., 2.2.2.20.
176, 6 *Chāndogya Upaniṣad*, 5.3.7.
176, 11 *Bṛhadāraṇyaka Upaniṣad*, 6.2.4.
176, 20 *Chāndogya Upaniṣad*, 5.3.3.
176, 23 Ibid.
176, 34 Ibid., 5.7.1.
176, 36 *Bṛhadāraṇyaka Upaniṣad*, 6.2.12.
177, 2 *Chāndogya Upaniṣad*, 5.8.1.
177, 9 *Bṛhadāraṇyaka Upaniṣad*, 6.2.13.
177, 12 Ibid., 6.2.2.
177, 22 Ibid., 6.2.13–14.
177, 37 *Śatapatha Brāhmaṇa*, 2.4.1.6.

XI. VEDIC EROTICA

181, 2 Ibid., 1.2.5.16.
181, 5 Ibid., 3.5.1.36.
181, 11 Ibid., 1.2.5.15.
181, 15 Ibid., 1.2.5.16.
181, 18 Ibid.
182, 12 *Bṛhaddevatā*, 5.98–101.
182, 29 *Śatapatha Brāhmaṇa*, 6.6.1.11; 6.2.2.22.
183, 6 *Ṛgveda*, 7.33.13.
183, 18 Ibid., 7.33.11.
183, 37 *Śatapatha Brāhmaṇa*, 4.4.2.18.
184, 8 Ibid., 1.3.1.18.
184, 28 Ibid., 4.6.7.9.
184, 30 Ibid.
185, 2 Ibid., 1.7.2.14.
185, 14 Ibid., 2.1.1.5.
185, 18 Richard Wagner, *Das Rheingold*, Prelude.
186, 9 *Ṛgveda*, 10.86.6 (trans. Louis Renou).
186, 12 Leopold von Schroeder, *Mysterium und Mimus im Rigveda*, Haessel, Leipzig, 1908, p. 304.
186, 23 *Atharvaveda*, 12.1.21.
186, 30 Ibid., 12.1.24 (trans. Louis Renou).
186, 37 Ibid., 12.1.25.

187, 2 *Ṛgveda*, 10.85.1 (trans. Louis Renou).
187, 4 Ibid., 10.85.2.
187, 10 Ibid., 10.85.6–7.
187, 12 Ibid., 10.85.10.
187, 20 Ibid., 10.85.40.
187, 34 Ibid., 10.85.21.
187, 37 Ibid., 10.85.22.
188, 7 Ibid., 10.85.40.
188, 14 Ibid., 10.85.45.

XII. GODS WHO OFFER LIBATIONS

191, 21 *Śatapatha Brāhmaṇa*, 2.3.3.10.
192, 21 Ibid., 3.1.4.1.
192, 26 Hesiod, *Works and Days*, 339.
192, 36 Ovid, *Fasti*, I, 347–48.
193, 3 Ibid., III, 727–28.
193, 4 Ibid., III, 729.
193, 12 Sophocles, *Antigone*, 429–31.
193, 27 *Jaiminīya Brāhmaṇa*, 1.3 (trans. H. W. Bodewitz).
194, 2 Ibid., 1.4.
194, 14 *Chāndogya Upaniṣad*, 5.24.5.
194, 19 *Śatapatha Brāhmaṇa*, 2.3.1.13.
194, 25 Ibid., 2.3.1.17.
194, 38 Ibid., 4.6.5.5.
195, 11 Julius Eggeling in *The Śatapatha-Brāhmaṇa*, cit., vol. II, p. 432.
195, 17 *Śatapatha Brāhmaṇa*, 4.6.5.3.
195, 20 Ibid., 2.3.3.7.
195, 35 Ibid., 2.3.1.36.
196, 5 Ibid., 2.3.3.1–2.
196, 13 Ibid., 2.3.3.9.
196, 22 Ibid., 2.3.3.12.
196, 35 Ibid., 3.1.3.3.
196, 37 Ibid., 3.1.3.4.
197, 2 Ibid., 3.1.3.3.
197, 9 Ibid., 2.3.4.22.
197, 19 Ibid., 2.3.4.22–23.
197, 26 Ibid., 2.3.4.37.
197, 36 Plato, *Phaedo*, 61a.
198, 6 Ibid.
198, 8 Ibid.
198, 11 Ibid.
198, 16 Ibid., 61b.
198, 28 Ibid., 61d.
198, 33 Ibid., 62b.
198, 36 Ibid., 61e.
199, 5 Ibid., 62b.

199, 16 Ibid., 66c.
199, 21 Ibid., 69c.
199, 30 Ibid., 118a.
199, 32 Ibid.
199, 36 Ibid., 117b.
199, 38 Ibid.
200, 3 Ibid., 117c.
200, 16 Xenophon, *Cyropaedia*, VII.1.1.
200, 26 Plato, *Phaedo*, 117c.

XIII. RESIDUE AND SURPLUS

204, 1 *Bhāgavata Purāṇa*, 3.8.16ab.
204, 8 *Śatapatha Brāhmaṇa*, 1.7.3.1.
204, 31 Ibid., 1.7.3.1–8.
205, 13 Ibid., 1.6.2.1.
205, 22 Ibid., 1.7.4.2.
206, 3 *Mahābhārata*, 10.18.3.
206, 29 *Ṛgveda*, 4.3.1.
206, 30 Ibid., 1.114.4.
207, 17 Armand Minard, *Trois Énigmes sur les Cent Chemins*, De Boccard, Paris, 1956, vol. II, p. 309.
208, 26 *Śatapatha Brāhmaṇa*, 1.3.5.16.
209, 10 Ibid., 1.3.5.14.
209, 24 Ibid., 1.4.1.40.
209, 28 Ibid., 10.3.5.15.
209, 31 Ibid., 10.3.5.16.
210, 18 *Jaiminīya Brāhmaṇa*, 1.258 (trans. Willem Caland).
210, 29 Ibid.
211, 17 Ibid., 1.238.
212, 6 *Śatapatha Brāhmaṇa*, 4.5.8.14.
212, 14 Ibid., 4.5.8.11.
212, 25 Ibid.
213, 2 Ibid., 4.5.7.2.
213, 16 Ibid., 12.2.3.6.
213, 26 Ibid., 12.2.3.11.
214, 1 Ibid., 12.2.3.12.
214, 8 *Bṛhadāraṇyaka Upaniṣad*, 5.1.1.
214, 9 Ibid.
214, 17 *Śatapatha Brāhmaṇa*, 10.3.5.13.
214, 26 Ibid., 14.3.2.23.

XIV. HERMITS IN THE FOREST

217, 16 Louis Dumont, "La Genèse chrétienne de l'individualisme moderne," in *Le Débat* 15, September–October 1981, p. 126.
218, 35 *Kātyāyana Śrauta Sūtra*, 20.1.1.

218, 37 Ibid., 21.1.1.
219, 3 Ibid., 21.1.15.
219, 9 Ibid., 21.1.17.
220, 3 *Śatapatha Brāhmaṇa*, 13.6.2.12.
220, 12 Ibid., 13.6.2.13.
220, 23 Ibid.
221, 2 Ibid., 13.6.2.20.
221, 15 Ibid.
221, 34 Ibid., 11.5.7.10.
222, 3 Ibid.
222, 14 Simone Weil, *Cahiers*, Plon, Paris, 1953, vol. II, p. 429.

XV. RITOLOGY

225, 3 *Bṛhadāraṇyaka Upaniṣad*, 1.3.28.
225, 18 *Taittirīya Brāhmaṇa*, 1.1.3.6.
226, 3 *Śatapatha Brāhmaṇa*, 3.1.1.4.
226, 9 Ibid., 3.1.1.8.
226, 10 Ibid., 3.1.1.10.
226, 14 Ibid., 3.1.1.8.
228, 4 Ibid., 7.1.1.1–2.
228, 12 Ibid., 7.1.1.5.
228, 20 Ibid., 7.4.2.16.
229, 2 *Ṛgveda*, 2.23.1.
229, 10 Ibid., 10.12.8.
229, 14 Ibid., 3.27.8.
229, 29 *Śatapatha Brāhmaṇa*, 6.8.2.1.
229, 31 Ibid., 6.8.2.3.
229, 36 Ibid.
230, 19 Ibid., 11.2.7.32.
230, 23 Ingeborg Bachmann, *Malina*, Suhrkamp, Frankfurt a. M., 1971, p. 96 (quotes Gustave Flaubert's letter to Louise Colet of July 5–6, 1852, in *Correspondance*, edited by J. Bruneau, Gallimard, Paris, 1980, vol. II, p. 128).
230, 36 *Śatapatha Brāhmaṇa*, 1.7.3.19.
231, 36 Willem Caland and Victor Henry, *L'Agniṣṭoma,* Leroux, Paris, 1906, vol. I, p. x.
232, 21 *Śatapatha Brāhmaṇa*, 12.3.3.1–2.
232, 28 Minard, *Trois Énigmes sur les Cent Chemins,* vol. I, cit., p. 102.
232, 34 Ibid., p. 73.
233, 7 *Śatapatha Brāhmaṇa*, 12.3.3.5.
233, 21 Ibid., 12.3.3.12.
233, 29 Ibid., 4.6.4.2.
233, 36 Epistle to the Hebrews 9:12.
234, 21 *Śatapatha Brāhmaṇa*, 1.2.5.19.
234, 23 J. C. Heesterman, "Veda and Dharma," in *The Concept of Duty in South Asia*, edited by W. Doniger and J.D.M. Derrett, Vikas, New Delhi, 1978, p. 87.
234, 27 *Śatapatha Brāhmaṇa*, 1.1.2.22.

235, 1 Ibid.
235, 2 Ibid.
235, 12 Ibid., 12.9.2.7.
235, 29 Ibid., 1.1.1.4.
236, 8 *Āpastamba Śrauta Sūtra*, 14.20.4.
237, 3 *Śatapatha Brāhmaṇa*, 1.5.2.2.
237, 16 Louis Renou, "Védique 'Nirṛti' " (1955), in *L'Inde fondamentale*, cit., p. 127.
237, 20 *Atharvaveda*, 6.84.1.
237, 24 *Śatapatha Brāhmaṇa*, 5.2.3.3.
238, 18 Ibid., 4.4.4.5.
238, 19 Ibid., 4.4.4.9.
238, 29 Ibid., 4.4.4.11.
238, 31 Ibid.
239, 4 *Taittirīya Saṃhitā*, 7.3.10.3–4.
239, 10 *Śatapatha Brāhmaṇa*, 12.1.3.23.
239, 19 Ibid.
239, 28 Ibid., 12.1.4.1.
239, 31 Ibid.
239, 31 Ibid., 12.1.4.3.
239, 35 Ibid., 12.2.1.1.
240, 10 Ibid., 12.2.1.3.
240, 22 Ibid., 12.2.1.9.

XVI. THE SACRIFICIAL VISION

244, 14 Valerio Valeri, *Kingship and Sacrifice*, University of Chicago Press, Chicago, 1985, p. 64.
245, 2 Staal, *Jouer avec le feu*, cit., p. 40.
245, 15 *Taittirīya Saṃhitā*, 3.3.8.3–4.
246, 8 John Cowper Powys, *The Religion of a Skeptic*, Dodd, Mead and Company, New York, 1925, p. 30.
246, 26 Charles Malamoud, *Cuire le monde*, La Découverte, Paris, 1989, p. 214.
246, 30 *Śatapatha Brāhmaṇa*, 3.7.4.11.
247, 7 Malamoud, "Tenir parole, retenir sa voix," cit., p. 220.
247, 10 *Śatapatha Brāhmaṇa*, 1.7.3.28.
247, 16 Ibid.
247, 24 Ibid., 3.1.4.3.
248, 21 Léon Bloy, *Belluaires et porchers* (1905), Stock, Paris, 1946, p. 10.
248, 26 *Śatapatha Brāhmaṇa*, 1.2.5.24.
248, 29 Ibid.
248, 31 Ibid.
248, 34 Ibid., 1.2.5.26.
249, 31 Ibid., 9.2.3.44.
250, 2 Ibid.
250, 7 Ibid., 10.4.3.23.
250, 17 Ibid., 14.2.2.24.
250, 30 Lévi, *La Doctrine du sacrifice dans les Brâhmaṇas*, cit., p. 133.

250, 35 *Kātyāyana Śrauta Sūtra*, 22.6.1.
251, 4 *Lāṭyāyaṇa Śrauta Sūtra*, 8.8.40.
251, 10 *Śatapatha Brāhmaṇa*, 10.2.6.7.

XVII. AFTER THE FLOOD

255, 15 Genesis 8:20.
255, 19 Ibid.
255, 24 *Epic of Gilgamesh*, tablet XI, 163 (trans. A. R. George).
255, 26 Genesis 8:21.
256, 1 Ibid.
256, 5 Ibid., 9:2.
256, 12 Ibid., 9:3.
256, 13 Ibid., 9:4.
256, 20 Ibid., 9:6.
256, 24 Ibid., 8:21.
256, 28 Ibid., 9:9.
257, 22 Ibid., 4:3.
257, 23 Ibid.
257, 24 Ibid., 4:4.
257, 26 Ibid., 8:20.
257, 27 Ibid., 4:3.
258, 12 Numbers 15:30.
258, 14 Ibid.
258, 15 Ibid., 15:27.
258, 37 Ibid., 15:32–36.
259, 14 Ibid., 15:38.
259, 30 Epistle to the Hebrews 13:13.
260, 11 Roland de Vaux, *Studies in Old Testament Sacrifice*, University of Wales Press, 1964, p. 92.
260, 20 Leviticus 17:11.
261, 1 Exodus 13:8.

XVIII. TIKI

266, 3 Marcel Mauss, "La Polarité religieuse et la division du macrocosme" (1933), in *Œuvres*, cit., vol. II, 1969, p. 144.
266, 9 Ibid.
266, 15 Ibid., p. 146.
266, 25 Ibid.
266, 36 Ibid., p. 144.
267, 10 Ibid., p. 145.
267, 12 Marcel Mauss, "Rapports entre aspects religieux et sociologique des rites" (1934), in *Œuvres*, cit., vol. I, 1968, p. 557.
267, 27 Marcel Mauss, "Débat sur les visions du monde primitif et moderne" (1937), in *Œuvres*, cit., vol. II, 1969, p. 156.

268, 12 Ibid., pp. 156–57.
268, 35 Mauss, "La Polarité religieuse et la division du macrocosme," cit., p. 146.
269, 10 Charles Baudelaire, *Correspondances,* v. 8, in *Les Fleurs du Mal*, in *Œuvres complètes*, edited by C. Pichois, Gallimard, Paris, vol. I, 1975, p. 11.
269, 16 Marcel Mauss, "Conceptions qui ont précédé la notion de matière" (1939), in *Œuvres*, cit., vol. II, 1969, p. 161.
269, 27 Marcel Mauss, "Mentalité primitive et participation" (1923), in *Œuvres*, cit., vol. II, 1969, pp. 127–28.
270, 7 Marcel Mauss, "Résumé d'un exposé sur le dieu Tiki maori, image du macrocosme" (1937), in *Œuvres*, cit., vol. II, 1969, p. 161.
270, 27 Mauss, "Conceptions qui ont précédé la notion de matière," cit., p. 161.
270, 36 Mauss, "Mentalité primitive et participation," cit., pp. 125–26.
271, 10 Ibid., p. 130.
271, 32 Ibid., pp. 130–31.
272, 20 Ibid., p. 131.
272, 25 Marcel Mauss, "Extrait de la 'Leçon d'ouverture' à l'enseignement d'ethnologie à l'École des Hautes Études" (1902), in *Œuvres*, cit., 1969, vol. II, p. 229.
272, 31 Marcel Mauss, "Leçon sur l'emploi de la notion de 'primitif' en sociologie" (1932–1933), in *Œuvres*, cit., 1969, vol. II, p. 233.
273, 7 Émile Durkheim, *Préface*, in *L'Année Sociologique* II, 1899, p. iv.
273, 14 Weil, *Cahiers*, cit., vol. III, 1956, p. 194.
273, 20 Marcel Mauss, "Leçons sur la cosmologie polynésienne" (1934–1935), in *Œuvres*, cit., 1969, vol. II, p. 189.
273, 24 Ibid.
273, 28 Ibid.
274, 2 Ibid.
274, 25 Marcel Mauss, "Catégories collectives et catégories pures" (1934), in *Œuvres*, cit., 1969, vol. II, p. 150.
274, 28 Mauss, "Introduction aux mythes," cit., p. 269.
274, 37 Ibid., p. 270.
275, 15 Mauss, "Leçons sur les rapports entre certains jeux et cosmologies archaïques" (1937–1938), in *Œuvres*, cit., 1969, vol. II, p. 267.
275, 20 Ibid., p. 266.

XIX. THE ACT OF KILLING

280, 6 *Aitareya Brāhmaṇa*, 7.1.
280, 15 *Śatapatha Brāhmaṇa*, 10.3.1.1.
280, 19 *Aitareya Brāhmaṇa*, 7.1.
281, 9 *Bṛhadāraṇyaka Upaniṣad*, 5.1.1.
281, 11 *Ṛgveda*, 10.90.16.
281, 24 Ibid., 10.121.1–9.
281, 26 Ibid., 10.90.16.
281, 32 Geldner, *Der Rig-Veda aus dem Sanskrit ins Deutsche übersetzt*, cit., vol. III, p. 289.
281, 34 *Hymnes spéculatifs du Véda*, ed. Louis Renou, Gallimard, Paris, 1956, p. 100.

281, 37 Ibid., p. 248.
282, 7 *Ṛgveda*, 10.130.6.
282, 11 Ibid., 10.90.15.
282, 13 Ibid., 10.90.11.
282, 16 *Śatapatha Brāhmaṇa*, 11.1.6.2.
283, 16 Ibid., 13.2.4.1–4.
284, 33 Ibid., 1.5.2.6.
284, 35 Sāyaṇa on the *Śatapatha Brāhmaṇa*, 1.5.2.7.
285, 10 *Śatapatha Brāhmaṇa*, 3.2.1.38.
285, 18 Ibid., 1.2.3.6.
285, 31 Ibid., 11.1.2.1.
285, 32 Hermann Oldenberg, *Die Lehre der Upanishaden und die Anfänge des Buddhismus*, Vandenhoeck & Ruprecht, Göttingen, 1915, p. 15.
286, 36 *Śatapatha Brāhmaṇa*, 3.8.1.10.
287, 22 Ibid., 3.8.1.15.
287, 28 Ibid., 13.2.8.2.
287, 33 *Oracle no. 537* in H. W. Parke and D.E.W. Wormell, *The Delphic Oracle*, Blackwell, Oxford, 1956, vol. II, p. 214.
287, 37 *Śatapatha Brāhmaṇa*, 3.8.2.4.
288, 7 Ibid.
288, 9 Ibid.
288, 26 *Śatapatha Brāhmaṇa*, 3.8.5.11.
288, 33 Ibid., 3.8.3.28.
289, 6 Ibid., 3.8.5.10.
289, 23 H. Hubert and M. Mauss, "Essai sur la nature et la fonction du sacrifice," cit., p. 253.
290, 3 *Śatapatha Brāhmaṇa*, 4.1.4.8–9.
291, 1 Ibid., 3.1.3.18.
291, 5 Ibid., 3.1.3.25.
292, 2 *Bṛhadāraṇyaka Upaniṣad*, 4.2.2.
292, 16 *Śatapatha Brāhmaṇa*, 6.1.2.12.
292, 18 Ibid., 10.4.2.2.
293, 8 Ibid., 14.2.2.24.

XX. THE FLIGHT OF THE BLACK ANTELOPE

297, 10 *Manusmṛti*, 2.22.
297, 11 Ibid., 2.23.
297, 15 *Śatapatha Brāhmaṇa*, 6.4.1.6; 6.4.1.9; 6.7.1.6; 9.3.4.10; 12.8.3.3.
297, 24 Ibid., 1.1.4.1.
297, 27 Ibid.
298, 5 Ibid., 6.4.2.6.
298, 12 Ibid., 3.2.1.2.
298, 26 Ibid., 1.1.4.2.
298, 35 Lévi, *La Doctrine du sacrifice dans les Brâhmaṇas*, cit., p. 141.
299, 5 *Maitrāyaṇī Saṃhitā*, 1.11.5.
299, 15 *Śatapatha Brāhmaṇa*, 1.1.4.1.

299, 20 Ibid., 6.4.1.6.
299, 21 Charles Malamoud, *La Danse des pierres*, Seuil, Paris, 2005, p. 153.
299, 24 *Manusmṛti*, 2.23.
299, 25 *Yājñavalkyasmṛti*, 1.2.
300, 3 Malamoud, *La Danse des pierres*, cit., p. 146.
300, 21 *Śatapatha Brāhmaṇa*, 1.1.1.13.
301, 15 Knud Rasmussen, *Report of the Fifth Thule Expedition 1921–24*, vol. VII, 1: *Intellectual Culture of Iglulik Eskimos*, Gyldendalske Boghandel, Copenhagen, 1929, p. 56.

XXI. KING SOMA
308, 1 *Ṛgveda*, 10.119.8.
308, 4 Ibid., 10.119.1–13.
308, 6 Ibid., 10.119.9.
308, 7 Ibid., 10.119.10.
308, 33 Alfred Hillebrandt, *Vedische Mythologie*, Koebner, Breslau, 1891, vol. I, p. 125.
309, 6 Herman Lommel, *König Soma* (1955), in *Kleine Schriften*, edited by K. L. Janert, Steiner, Wiesbaden, 1978, p. 315.
309, 16 *Vāyu Purāṇa*, 90.2.
310, 4 *Atharvaveda*, 5.17.8.
310, 11 *Ṛgveda*, 1.190.7.
310, 15 *Brahmāṇḍa Purāṇa*, 2.65.38.
310, 32 *Śatapatha Brāhmaṇa*, 5.3.3.12.
310, 36 Epistle to the Ephesians 6:12.
311, 5 *Bṛhadāraṇyaka Upaniṣad*, 1.4.11.
311, 11 Ibid., p. 146.
311, 13 Ibid., 3.3.2.9.
311, 24 *Taittirīya Saṃhitā*, 3.2.5.2.
311, 27 Ibid., 3.2.5.3.
311, 32 Ibid., 2.3.2.6.
311, 33 Ibid.
311, 36 *Śatapatha Brāhmaṇa*, 12.7.1.10.
312, 2 *Ṛgveda*, 8.48.5.
312, 4 Ibid.
312, 12 Ibid., 10.124.1.
312, 15 Ibid., 10.124.6.
312, 22 *Śatapatha Brāhmaṇa*, 3.4.3.13.
312, 31 Abel Bergaigne, *La Religion védique d'après les hymnes du Rig-Veda* (1878), Librairie Honoré Champion, Paris, 1963, vol. I, p. 168.
313, 3 *Ṛgveda*, 1.80.2; 8.95.3; 9.87.6.
313, 6 Ibid., 1.93.6.
314, 2 *Śatapatha Brāhmaṇa*, 3.2.4.1–7.
315, 3 Ibid., 3.2.4.7.
315, 17 Ibid., 3.2.4.1.
316, 6 Ibid., 4.6.2.4 (Kāṇva recension).

316, 15 *Śatapatha Brāhmaṇa*, 3.6.2.2–11.
316, 19 Ibid., 3.6.2.5.
316, 37 Ibid., 3.6.2.16.
317, 23 Ibid.
317, 30 Ibid., 1.1.2.19 (trans. Charles Malamoud).
317, 35 Émile Benveniste, *Le Vocabulaire des institutions indo-européennes*, Minuit, Paris, 1969, vol. I, p. 171.
318, 13 Malamoud, *Cuire le monde*, cit., p. 124.
318, 26 *Śatapatha Brāhmaṇa*, 3.2.4.8.
319, 15 Ibid., 3.3.2.9.
319, 32 Ibid., 3.3.2.2.
320, 7 Ibid., 3.3.3.1.
320, 11 Ibid., 3.3.3.14; 3.3.4.13; 3.4.1.2.
320, 17 Ibid., 3.3.3.11 (Kāṇva recension).
320, 26 Ibid., 4.3.4.7.
320, 29 Ibid., 4.3.4.22.
321, 8 Ibid., 4.3.4.23.
321, 16 Ibid., 4.5.1.16.
322, 6 Ibid., 3.6.2.17–19.
322, 28 Ibid., 3.3.1.1.
323, 21 Ibid., 3.3.1.11.
323, 24 Ibid., 3.3.1.12.
323, 32 Ibid., 3.3.3.10.
323, 33 Ibid., 3.4.1.5.
323, 36 Ibid., 3.4.1.2.
324, 2 Ibid., 3.4.1.7.
324, 3 Ibid., 3.3.4.7.
324, 12 Ibid., 3.3.2.6.
324, 24 Ibid., 3.9.3.7.
324, 30 Ibid.
324, 34 Ibid., 3.9.3.14.
324, 37 Ibid., 3.9.4.2.
325, 2 Ibid.
326, 5 *Ṛgveda*, 1.164.45.
326, 31 *Śatapatha Brāhmaṇa*, 1.1.3.10.
327, 4 Ibid., 1.1.3.2.
327, 20 Ibid., 9.5.1.2.
327, 23 Ibid., 9.5.1.8.
327, 29 Ibid., 9.5.1.10.
328, 3 Ibid., 3.9.4.17.
328, 8 Ibid.
328, 19 Ibid., 4.4.5.1; 4.4.5.15; 4.4.5.20.
328, 28 Ibid., 4.4.5.16.
328, 37 Ibid., 4.4.5.23.
329, 30 Ibid., 1.7.1.1.
330, 8 *Ṛgveda*, 10.65.13.
330, 32 Ibid., 7.104.12.
331, 5 Euripides, *The Bacchae*, 69–70.

331, 8 *Ṛgveda*, 8.48.3.
331, 12 Ibid., 9.85.2.
331, 17 Ibid., 1.4.2.

ANTECEDENTS AND CONSEQUENTS

335, 16 *Śatapatha Brāhmaṇa*, 1.1.1.4.
340, 24 Paolo Zellini, *Numero e logos*, Adelphi, Milan, 2010, p. 28.
342, 8 Paul Mus, "La Stance de la plénitude," in *Bulletin de l'École Française d'Extrême-Orient* XLIV, 2, 1954, p. 603.
342, 35 *Śatapatha Brāhmaṇa*, 10.5.3.1.
344, 8 Ibid., 1.7.1.5.
344, 30 Abdellah Hammoudi, *A Season in Mecca: Narrative of a Pilgrimage*, Farrar, Straus and Giroux, New York, 2006, p. 119.
345, 11 Ibid., pp. 222–24.
352, 4 Livy, VIII, 10, 10.
352, 20 Ibid., VIII, 10, 11–12.
352, 23 Ibid., VIII, 10, 12.
352, 32 Ibid., VIII, 8, 2.
352, 34 Ibid., VIII, 6, 15.
353, 16 Ibid., VIII, 6, 9–11.
354, 8 Émile Durkheim, *The Elementary Forms of the Religious Life*, trans. Joseph Ward Swain, London, George Allen and Unwin, 1915, p. 223.
354, 13 Ibid., p. 226.
354, 17 Ibid., p. 227.
354, 20 Ibid., p. 225.
354, 28 Ibid., p. 227.
354, 35 Ibid., p. 226.
355, 10 Ibid., p. 228.
355, 22 Ibid., p. 347.
355, 24 Ibid., p. 348.
355, 31 Ibid.
355, 37 Ibid., p. 442.
356, 4 Ibid., p. 330.
357, 7 *Zuo zhuan*, VIII, Year XIII, para. 2 (trans. James Legge).
357, 9 Ibid., VI, Year II, para. 6.
357, 14 Plato, *Laws*, 716d.
358, 33 Martin Luther, *De captivitate babylonica ecclesiae praeludium*, in *Kritische Gesammtausgabe*, Böhlau, Weimar, vol. VI, 1888, p. 512.
358, 34 Ibid., p. 513.
359, 15 Paolo Sarpi, *Istoria del Concilio Tridentino*, Einaudi, Turin, 1974, vol. II, p. 900.
359, 31 Stefan Orth, "Renaissance des Archaischen?," in *Herder Korrespondenz*, LV, 4, 2001, p. 199.
359, 37 Matthew, 26:26–27.
360, 2 Saint Augustine, *De civitate Dei*, 10:20.
360, 20 Epistle to the Hebrews 13:13.
361, 17 Louis-Ferdinand Céline, *Lettres*, edited by H. Godard and J.-P. Louis, Gallimard, Paris, 2009, p. 431.

NOTE ON SANSKRIT PRONUNCIATION

The *a* is closed and is similar to the *u* in *but*; the vowels *ā*, *ī*, and *ū* are long: for example, *ī* is pronounced like *ee* in *feet*, not like the *i* in *fit*; *ṛ* is a vowel and is pronounced by resting it on a barely discernible *i* or *u*. The *e* is closed as in *better*; the *o* is closed as in *bother*.

The *g* is always hard: for example *gītā* is pronounced *geeta*; the *c* is always soft: for example, *cakra* is pronounced *chakra*. *S* is always like the *s* in *sound*; *ś* and *ṣ* are more or less like *sh* in *shun*. *Ṛṣi* is therefore pronounced *rishi*. The retroflexed *ṭ*, *ḍ*, and *ṇ* are pronounced by bending the tongue back to touch the palate, as in *utter*, *udder*, or *runner*. The aspirate occlusives *kh*, *gh*, *ch*, *jh*, *th*, *dh*, *th*, *ph*, and *bh* are single phonemes, and are pronounced with an aspiration after the consonant: for example, *ph* is pronounced as in *top hat*, not as in *telephone*, and *th* is pronounced as in *dirt heap*, not as in *think* or *father*.

Ñ is like the *n* in *country*; *h* is a sounded aspiration as in *inherent*.

The accent falls on the last long vowel (for example: *Prajāpati* is pronounced *Prajápati*). The vowels *e* and *o* are also long. Furthermore, all vowels are long when positioned before consonant groups. If there are no long vowels, the accent is placed on the third or fourth to last syllable (if this is a root syllable). For example: *Gáruda*, *Gótama*, *śrámaṇa*.

A few words that are typically Vedic are stressed with a musical tone called *udātta*, which required the pitch of the voice to be raised, but this has disappeared in Classical Sanskrit.

ACKNOWLEDGMENTS

This book has had the good fortune to encounter some most congenial people along its way: Federica Ragni, who has followed and digitalized every transformation from the manuscript to the printed page; Paolo Rossetti, who has taken care of all typographical matters; Michela Acquati, who has given her expertise during the final stages of the work; Francesca Coppola and Valeria Perrucci, who have given their help in numerous tasks; and Maddalena Buri, the Athenic eye within the text. Roberto Donatoni compensated the author's linguistic doubts with the abundance of his knowledge and rechecked the quotations from the Sanskrit texts and those translations for which the author is responsible. Finally, Lila Azam Zanganeh went through the English translation, making some valuable remarks. That this book is dedicated to Claudio Rugafiori is just an indication of how much the book itself owes to him. My gratitude to everyone.

LIST OF ILLUSTRATIONS

ILLUSTRATION CREDITS

INDEX